Crime and Culpability

A Theory of Criminal Law

This book presents a comprehensive overview of what the criminal law would look like if organized around the principle that those who deserve punishment should receive punishment commensurate with, but no greater than, that which they deserve. Larry Alexander and Kimberly Kessler Ferzan argue that desert is a function of the actor's culpability and that culpability is a function of the risks of harm to protected interests that the actor believes he is imposing and his reasons for acting in the face of those risks. The authors deny that resultant harms, as well as unperceived risks, affect the actor's desert. They thus reject punishment for inadvertent negligence as well as for intentions or preparatory acts that are not risky. Alexander and Ferzan discuss the reasons for imposing risks that negate or mitigate culpability, the individuation of crimes, and omissions. They conclude with a discussion of rules versus standards in criminal law and offer a description of the shape of criminal law in the event that the authors' conceptualization is put into practice.

Larry Alexander is the Warren Distinguished Professor of Law at the University of San Diego. He has authored and coauthored, in addition to several anthologies and 170 articles, essays, and book chapters, five books, most recently *Is There a Right to Freedom of Expression?* and, with Emily Sherwin, *Demystifying Legal Reasoning*. He is also past president of AMINTAPHIL, a founding coeditor of the journal *Legal Theory*, and codirector of the Institute for Law and Philosophy at the University of San Diego.

Kimberly Kessler Ferzan is Associate Dean for Academic Affairs and Professor of Law at Rutgers University School of Law, Camden, and is Associate Graduate Faculty in the Philosophy Department, Rutgers University, New Brunswick. The author of numerous articles, essays, and book chapters on criminal law theory, she is cofounder and codirector of the Rutgers-Camden Institute for Law and Philosophy.

Cambridge Introductions to Philosophy and Law

Editors

William A. Edmundson, *Georgia State University*

Brian Bix, *University of Minnesota*

This introductory series of books provides concise studies of the philosophical foundations of law, of perennial topics in the philosophy of law, and of important and opposing schools of thought. The series is aimed principally at students in philosophy, law, and political science.

Other Books in the Series

An Introduction to Rights, by William A. Edmundson

Objectivity and the Rule of Law, by Matthew H. Kramer

Demystifying Legal Reasoning, by Larry Alexander and Emily Sherwin

Crime and Culpability
A Theory of Criminal Law

LARRY ALEXANDER
University of San Diego School of Law

KIMBERLY KESSLER FERZAN
Rutgers University School of Law, Camden

With contributions by

STEPHEN J. MORSE
University of Pennsylvania Law School

CAMBRIDGE
UNIVERSITY PRESS

CAMBRIDGE UNIVERSITY PRESS
Cambridge, New York, Melbourne, Madrid, Cape Town,
Singapore, São Paulo, Delhi, Tokyo, Mexico City

Cambridge University Press
32 Avenue of the Americas, New York, NY 10013-2473, USA

www.cambridge.org
Information on this title: www.cambridge.org/9780521739610

First published 2009
Reprinted 2011

A catalog record for this publication is available from the British Library.

Library of Congress Cataloging in Publication Data
Alexander, Larry, 1943–
Crime and culpability : a theory of criminal law / by Larry
Alexander and Kimberly Kessler Ferzan with contributions by Stephen J. Morse.
p. cm. – (Cambridge introductions to philosophy and law)
ISBN 978-0-521-51877-2 (hardback) – ISBN 978-0-521-73961-0 (pbk.)
1. Punishment – Philosophy. 2. Criminal law – Philosophy.
3. Criminal law – United States – Philosophy. I. Ferzan, Kimberly Kessler,
1971– II. Morse, Stephen J. III. Title.
K5103.A44 2008
345´.001–dc22   2008030731

ISBN 978-0-521-51877-2 Hardback
ISBN 978-0-521-73961-0 Paperback

For Elaine, the best criminal lawyer I know,
L. A.

For Griffin,
K. K. F.

Contents

PART FOUR **A Proposed Code**

Acknowledgments

This book is the culmination of a long collaboration. It is also the product of not only our efforts but also those of countless others who have discussed and criticized it both in various colloquia and in private conversation. These include the participants at the San Diego Roundtable on Blame and Retribution, the 2007 Analytic Philosophy Conference, the Boston University School of Law faculty workshop, the Southwestern Law School faculty workshop, the Culpability in Criminal Law seminar at Rutgers-Camden Law School, and the University of North Carolina, Greensboro, Symposium on Ethical Perspectives on Risk. Among those we wish to mention by name as having made valuable criticisms and suggestions are Mitch Berman, Jeffrey Brand-Ballard, Michael Dorff, Heidi Hurd, Doug Husak, Michael Moore, Ken Simons, Peter Westen, Gideon Yaffe, and Leo Zaibert.

In addition, we were ably assisted in preparing the manuscript by our research assistants, Robert Fitzpatrick, Derek Hecht, Shana Mattson, and Meghan Powers, and the heroic efforts of our secretaries, Alessandria Driussi and Fran Brigandi. Thanks also to our indexer, Ken Hassman, and our production editor, Brian MacDonald. We would like to thank our institutions and their deans, Kevin Cole and Ray Solomon, for their support, financial and otherwise. And finally, we'd like to thank Elaine Alexander and Marc Ferzan for their love and support while we drafted this manuscript. This was truly a team effort.

PART ONE

Introduction

Retributivism and the Criminal Law

I

Criminal Law, Punishment, and Desert

Ultimately, what underlies the criminal law is a concern with harms that people suffer and other people cause – harms such as loss of life, bodily injury, loss of autonomy, and harm to or loss of property. The criminal law's goal is not to compensate, to rehabilitate, or to inculcate virtue. Rather, the criminal law aims at preventing harm.

This admission may seem puzzling, given that the authors of this book have argued in previous writings, and will continue to argue here, that whether a criminal defendant actually causes harm is immaterial to whether he should be deemed to have violated the criminal law and is likewise immaterial to the amount of punishment he should receive. But these claims do not entail that the criminal law is not ultimately concerned with harm causing. Quite the contrary.

I. The Criminal Law and Preventing Harm

To explain how we can admit that the criminal law's primary concern is the prevention of harm yet still maintain that the actual occurrence of that harm is immaterial, we will begin by exploring ways that harm might be prevented. One way to prevent the harms with which the criminal law is ultimately concerned is to make the causing of harms to others more difficult. There are three strategies for doing this. One strategy is to *increase the difficulty* of causing harm by increasing the effort or natural risk required to cause harm. We put money into safes that are difficult to crack. We put our castle behind a deep moat, perhaps filled with alligators, and build high walls. We put our high-security establishment behind an electrified fence. In all sorts of ways, we try to make harming us difficult by making it impossible, costly, or risky.[1]

The second strategy for making harming more difficult is to impose penalties on those who attempt or succeed in harming us. Penalties are meant to raise the expected cost of the harming act (amount of penalty times likelihood of detection, conviction, and so forth). In this respect, penalties are quite similar to the first strategy. If I trespass by jumping into your moat, the alligators might scarf me, or I might drown. Trespassing, therefore, looks less appealing. The fine – a penalty – that I might have to pay similarly makes trespassing look costlier and thus less appealing. Here, the strategy is one of *deterrence through prospective penalization*.

Notice that these two strategies bear no relation to the would-be harmer's desert. Take prevention. If the trespasser drowns or is killed by the alligators, we do not consider his death as what he "deserved" for trespassing. We may place limits on prevention strategies, particularly because they do not distinguish between the culpable and the innocent (alligators might find both equally tasty). Indeed, prevention seems to require both a wrongful act and notice of the consequences risked – especially if they exceed the wrongdoer's desert. On the other hand, these limitations do *not* include the requirement that the prevention

---

[1] *See* Larry Alexander, "The Doomsday Machine: Proportionality, Prevention, and Punishment," 63 *Monist* 199, 210 (1980).

strategy be proportional to the wrongdoer's desert.[2] Although we would say that in some sense, by risking death through an act he had no right to undertake, an actor brought his death on himself, we would not say that a tulip thief *deserved* to be eaten by alligators.

Just as the enterprise of prevention may be disproportionate in terms of the harms risked by the wrongdoer relative to his desert, so too may penalties premised on deterrence. For example, if possession of marijuana is a crime that many people are tempted to commit, under a deterrence theory the state may be justified in imposing a significant jail term to prevent the possession of even the smallest amount of marijuana. As is frequently pointed out, when we impose harsh treatment solely to deter, there is no necessary connection between the penalty we impose and the offender's desert. Indeed, because any penalty we impose will have failed to deter at least the offender we are imposing it on, deterrence would have warranted a higher penalty. Indeed, from a pure deterrence standpoint, the ideal penalty is one so draconian that it achieves 100 percent deterrence and therefore never has to be imposed.

There is actually a third strategy for preventing harm-causing conduct, and that is the strategy of *incapacitating those who we predict are likely to cause harm* if they are not incapacitated. Again, preventively detaining those predicted to be harmful bears no relation to the desert of those detained. One can be dangerous without being deserving of bad treatment. Assume, for example, that we can predict with some reasonable degree of certainty that if a four-year-old boy enjoys torturing puppies, he will later harm his fellow human beings.[3] If we lock him away now, we are locking him away not for what he has done (to human beings) but for what he might do. He is dangerous for what he *is*. He can *deserve* harsh treatment, however, only for his chosen acts (or, in some cases, his chosen omissions). Although preventive detention may likewise be subject to limitations, desert is not among them.

The alternative to these three strategies for preventing harmful acts, all of which attempt to make harmful acts physically difficult,

---

[2] *Id.* at 213.

[3] *Cf.* Jim Stevenson and Robert Goodman, "Association between Behavior at age 3 Years and Adult Criminality," 179 *British J. of Psychiatry* 197, 200 (2001) (finding that "[e]xternalising behaviours such as temper tantrums and management difficulties [e.g., non-compliance] were associated with adult convictions, in particular with violent offences").

impossible, or risky, is to inculcate norms that are meant to guide people's choices. The norms inform people of the reasons that should govern their choices, *and the inculcation of such norms involves as its corollary the inculcation of reactive attitudes toward those who comply with and those who violate the norms.*[4] The negative reactive attitudes, to be directed at those who choose to violate the norms, include both blame and the sense that punishment is fitting. When we say that, by choosing as the norms forbid, the chooser deserves punishment, we are invoking the reactive attitude that punishment of a certain amount is a fitting response to the choice. Thus, the criminal law both creates and reflects value by announcing which conduct is sufficiently wrong to deserve blame and punishment.

Such a view presupposes that people act for reasons and that the law can influence those reasons. Moreover, it considers an actor *deserving* of punishment when he violates these norms that forbid the unjusti-fied harming of, or risking harm to, others – that is, failing to give oth-ers' interests their proper weight. This approach to preventing harm, although setting forth the types of harms and risks that are forbidden, focuses on the actor's reasons and thus derives its ability to prevent such harms from the capacity and opportunity that agents have to act or abstain from acting for reasons.

It is this last alternative that we believe the criminal law should, and to some (imperfect) extent does, adopt. What we intend to do in this book is to explore what the doctrines of the criminal law would look like if they were structured (primarily) by the concern that criminal defendants receive the punishment they deserve, and particularly that they receive no more punishment than they deserve. We argue that the elements of crimes and defenses thereto should pick out those factors bearing on the defendant's negative desert, either to establish it or to defeat it. In our view, it is the defendant's decision to violate society's norms regarding the proper concern due to the interests of others that

---

[4] The essentially constitutive relation between "Don't do that because it's wrong" addressed to a responsible moral agent and the reactive attitudes implied thereby is frequently noted. For a recent example, *see* John Tasioulas, "Punishment and Repentance," 81 *Phil.* 279, 294–301 (2006); James Lenman, "Compatibilism and Contractualism: The Possibility of Moral Responsibility," 117 *Ethics* 7, 11–12 (2006).

establishes the negative desert that in turn can both justify and limit the imposition of punishment.

II. Questions about Retributivism

Hence, what we elaborate can be called a retributive theory of the criminal law because the structure of the criminal law that we propose is dictated by a retributive theory of criminal punishment. However, our argument in the remaining chapters deals solely with the culpable choices that give rise to retributive desert and does not focus on the retributive theory in which they are embedded. We do not more fully defend retributivism against competing theories than we just have, although our arguments about what makes an individual culpable and worthy of punishment no doubt implicitly reflect our position. We also recognize that there are a number of outstanding issues regarding retributivism and hence a retributive theory of criminal law. We touch on these issues, although our theory does not depend upon their full resolution.

A. WEAK, MODERATE, OR STRONG RETRIBUTIVISM?

First, even for those, like us, who believe that desert is a necessary condition for punishment, there remain questions about the exact relationship between desert and punishment. There are three possible positions. The first is that negative desert is merely necessary but not sufficient for punishment (weak retributivism – or perhaps, more accurately, desert-free consequentialism side-constrained by negative desert). The second is that negative desert is necessary and sufficient for punishment but that desert does not mandate punishment (moderate retributivism). The final position is that desert is necessary and sufficient for punishment and mandates punishment (strong, Kantian retributivism).

In our view, the middle, moderate position seems most preferable. We believe that weak retributivism is too weak to guide the criminal law substantially; so long as no criminal receives *more* punishment than he deserves, the criminal law could be structured completely by consequentialist considerations. In such cases, unless some additional good were served, individuals who deserve punishment would be beyond the reach of the criminal law. To us, however, deserving punishment seems to be a weighty enough reason to punish someone.[5]

On the other hand, strong retributivism is too strong. We could spend all available resources and risk all sorts of terrible harms – for example, accidentally convicting the innocent, taking resources from health and safety, and so forth – trying to ensure that all of the negatively deserving receive their due. Surely government should not be monomaniacally concerned with punishing the guilty at the expense of all other interests.[6]

Thus, only moderate retributivism looks eligible for our purposes. In contrast to strong retributivism, moderate retributivism entails that some of the guilty will not receive their negative due. In contrast to weak retributivism, however, it entails that sometimes punishment will serve no purpose other than to see that the guilty get what they deserve.

Notice that moderate retributivism has the following notable features. First, the moderate retributivist position has both a deontological and consequentialist aspect. The moderate retributivist position is deontological in placing a side constraint on punishment, namely, that no one should be (knowingly) punished more than that person deserves. (What *risk* of undeserved punishment we may subject people to is taken up later in this chapter and then again in Chapter 8, in which we also raise further questions about the implications of the deontological side constraint.) The position is consequentialist in that it rejects a deontological duty to see that all the guilty receive the punishment they deserve. Instead, it counts just punishment as one good among

---

[5] *See generally* Leo Zaibert, *Punishment and Retribution* 214 (2006) ("[D]eserved punishment is an intrinsic good"); Mitchell N. Berman, "Punishment and Justification," esp. note 59 at 32 (working paper, December 15, 2006), available at SSRN: http://ssrn.com/abstract=956610. Berman distinguishes the justification for the criminal's suffering punishment from the justification for inflicting it, pointing out that one might concede that criminals deserve to suffer while at the same time arguing that inflicting such suffering is a violation of their rights. He goes on, however, to deny that any such right against infliction of deserved suffering exists. *See id.* at 42–48. *See also* John Martin Fischer, "Punishment and Desert: A Reply to Dolinko," 117 *Ethics* 109 (2006).

[6] *See* Zaibert, *supra* note 5, at 153–155; Mark C. Murphy, *Natural Law in Jurisprudence and Politics* 144–146 (2006).

many, and one that can be outweighed by other goods that punishing the deserving puts at risk.[7] Not only does the side constraint of not punishing more than is deserved prevent maximizing the number of punishments of the deserving – otherwise, it would be permissible to punish an innocent person or to punish a culpable person more than he deserves in order to maximize the number of just punishments – but it countenances less than monomaniacal pursuit of deserved punishment within the bounds of that deontological constraint. Deserved punishment is a positive value, but it is not the only positive value. Seeing that people receive their negative desert may be an aim of criminal punishment for the moderate retributivist as it is for the strong retributivist; but for the moderate but not the strong retributivist, other values define the circumstances in which pursuit of that goal is properly undertaken.[8] On the other hand, for the moderate retributivist as for all retributivists, undeserved punishment, if administered with knowledge that it is undeserved, is always a trumping *dis*value.

Beyond this asymmetry between the positive and negative aspects of deserved punishment, a further feature of moderate retributivism is that it covers a wide range of positions on just how weighty a positive value deserved punishment is. One might deem deserved punishment to be a very weighty value, justifying huge social costs in its pursuit. On the other hand, one might deem it to be of much less weight, justifying very little expenditure of resources or risk to other values. Moderate retributivism occupies a large territory between weak and strong retributivism, with weak and strong retributivism serving as the limiting cases of the weight of the positive value of deserved punishment. (Weak retributivism represents zero weight relative to the strength of the side constraint forbidding giving anyone more punishment than is deserved, *even in order to achieve a greater number of just punishments*; strong retributivism represents infinite weight relative to other values.)

---

[7] For a discussion of how the law currently trades off retributive desert against other values, *see* Paul H. Robinson and Michael T. Cahill, *Law without Justice: Why Criminal Law Doesn't Give People What They Deserve* (2006).

[8] Murphy regards these other values as the sine qua non conditions of retributive punishment, not its aim. *See* Murphy, *supra* note 6, at 146. We believe that punishment can be called retributive if it is both constrained by negative desert and regards inflicting deserved punishment as a positive value rather than its sole aim.

The moderate retributivist must at the end of the day come up with a theory for how the value of retributive justice trades off against the values of societal welfare, distributive justice, and corrective justice. We endorse moderate retributivism, but we take no position on the weight of deserved punishment relative to other values. For our purposes here, it is unnecessary that we do so. It is enough that the weight of deserved punishment be sufficient to make desert a central focus of criminal law.

B. MEASURING DESERT

A corollary to our rejection of strong retributivism is the potential for comparative and noncomparative injustices, and this effect introduces a second conundrum for retributivism – the question of how retributive desert is measured. We must first ask whether desert is comparative or noncomparative. In other words, is the punishment an offender deserves a function solely of how much similar offenders are punished, or is there a specific amount of punishment that each offender deserves irrespective of how much others are punished? A system of punishment that required only comparative justice would be satisfied if all bank robbers received one-day imprisonment. In contrast, in a system that viewed desert from a noncomparative ("cosmic") perspective, if a bank robber A received ten years (the "cosmic" amount) but bank robber B received one day, then from the standpoint of retributive justice, this system could be criticized only insofar as B did not get his "just" deserts but not because of the seemingly unfair discrepancy between A and B. In our view, desert is itself noncomparative, but there are additional constraints on the imposition of punishment that speak to fairness, including that similarly situated defendants be treated similarly. If defendants A and B are cosmically – noncomparatively – deserving of equal punishment, but only A, who is black, receives his just deserts, whereas B, who is white, receives a lesser punishment, A's complaint is not that *his* punishment is inappropriate but is, instead, that an illegitimate norm – "whites should be treated better than blacks" – is at work and has led to B's being treated better than he deserves. The remedy may (or may not) be to reduce A's punishment if B's punishment for some reason cannot be increased. But A can have no complaint against *his* punishment.

This leads to a second measurement question: how does negative retributive desert, with which the criminal law is concerned, mesh with positive retributive desert (reward) and with distributive desert? Desert appears to be a single positive or negative unit of measurement. The currencies we employ in rewarding positive and negative desert – for example, pleasure and pain, liberty or its loss, or money or its loss – are fungible across any positive-negative desert divide. If a person serving ten years in prison performs a heroic act, he might be rewarded by getting special privileges in prison, or by having his term of imprisonment shortened, or both. Is it meaningful to ask whether his negative desert and hence his punishment were decreased, or whether instead his positive desert and reward were increased?

If one believed that everything – benefits as well as harms – should be distributed according to desert, positive as well as negative, then retributive punishment would just be an aspect of a more general scheme of distribution according to desert. This leads to yet another set of questions. If A and B commit the same crime, but A is happy and wealthy and B is unhappy and poor, do they receive differential amounts of punishment so that they are similarly situated once the punishment is imposed? Moreover, does it matter who does the distributing? What if C leaves a bank robbery and her criminal conduct warrants an "alpha" level of punishment, but as she flees the scene, she is hit by lightning and suffers an "alpha" amount of pain? Should the state still inflict the same degree of harm? In practice, a court may inflict a "shaming" punishment,[9] wherein a defendant is subject to public disapproval for his conduct; but if the defendant's loss of public respect is not the product of a judicially imposed sanction but just the product of the defendant's conviction, courts may ignore this "fall from grace" as irrelevant to what further sanction should be imposed.[10]

---

[9] This example is for illustrative purposes only. We are not taking a position on whether shaming is an appropriate form of punishment.

[10] *See, e.g.*, Gertrude Ezorsky, "The Ethics of Punishment," *in Philosophical Perspectives on Punishment* xi (Gertrude Ezorsky, ed., 1972); Jeffrey Moriarity, "Ross on Desert and Punishment," 87 *Pac. Phil. Q.* 231, 232–236 (2006); United States v. Bergman, 416 F. Supp. 496 (S.D.N.Y. 1976). *But see* Douglas N. Husak, "Already Punished Enough," 19 *Phil. Topics* 79 (1990) (arguing that public disapproval can reduce the amount of deserved punishment).

Indeed, one could ask whether the deserved punishment should take account of the defendant's "whole life." Should it matter whether before the crime he has fared better or worse than he deserved because of good fortune – in terms of wealth, fame, friendship, love, and so on? Must retributive desert for a discrete culpable act turn on the defendant's entire life history?[11]

Finally, there is the overarching problem of how to translate culpability into units of suffering. Just how much suffering does a particular culpable choice – say, setting off dynamite in a crowded neighborhood – merit? If we reject, as we do, the literal lex talionis, how do we commensurate various culpable choices with levels of punishment? This is a problem that we need not solve in this book, but ultimately it is a problem all retributivists face.[12]

C. THE STRENGTH OF THE RETRIBUTIVIST SIDE CONSTRAINT

A third problem for retributivism is that imperfect human systems of punishment will ultimately fail to perfectly mirror justice, thus resulting in too much and too little punishment. Criminal law doctrines will ultimately entail decisions as to how the balance should be struck. The burden of proof placed on the state to prove the defendant's guilt and the statutory formulations of crimes and defenses will affect how many innocent people will be punished more than they deserve. If the state must prove only a low level of culpability – or no culpability whatsoever – for the crime as a whole or for particular elements thereof, then the less culpable or the totally innocent will predictably be punished as much as the more culpable.

For those who take the victimization by criminals and punishment greater than desert to be instances of *undeserved harm*, the goal of minimizing undeserved harm might require punishing more than is deserved in some cases. Obviously, this form of retributivism is

---

[11] *See* J. Feinberg, *Doing and Deserving: Essays in the Theory of Responsibility* (1970), 116–117; Alexander, *supra* note 1, at 205; Ezorsky, *supra* note 10, at xxiv–xxvi; Berman, *supra* note 5, at 27–29 n. 47.

[12] For a comprehensive – and pessimistic – analysis of this problem, *see* Russ Shafer-Landau, "Retributivism and Desert," 81 *Pac. Phil. Q.* 189 (2000). *But see* Murphy, *supra* note 6, at 147–152.

more consonant with a consequentialism that takes desert as a basis of distribution than it is with any moral view that takes desert to be a deontological side constraint – the view that we endorse here.[13]

The issue for us is how great a risk of punishing the innocent – or punishing the culpable more than they deserve – may we impose through our criminal justice system. We impose those risks through the way we define crimes and defenses – substantive doctrines – and through the way we prove them. In the latter category are such items as burdens of persuasion, presumptions, investigatory resources, trial procedures, the law of evidence, and the quality of legal representation. We take up some of these matters in Chapter 8. For now, we merely flag them as considerations that bear on the risk of overpunishment (punishment in excess of retributive desert).

D. THE FREEWILL-DETERMINISM DEBATE

Another issue for retributivists is the freewill-determinism debate.[14] If our choices – including character-forming choices – are caused by our unchosen character, and our unchosen character is caused by our genes and our environment, is moral responsibility and hence negative desert undermined? To the extent that determinism is seen as threatening notions of responsibility and desert, it threatens to undermine retributive justifications for punishment.

There are three main types of responses to the challenge to responsibility that determinism is thought to present. The first, "hard determinism," claims that responsibility and determinism are incompatible and that determinism is true. Therefore, genuine or ultimate responsibility

---

[13] *See* Cass R. Sunstein and Adrian Vermeule, "Is Capital Punishment Morally Required? The Relevance of Life-Life Tradeoffs," 58 *Stan. L. Rev.* 847 (2005), for a discussion of desert as a side constraint versus as a distributive goal. Sunstein and Vermeule argue that only individuals, and not the state, are subject to the side constraint forbidding undeserved punishments. For them, the state may maximize with respect to just deserts, even if to do so it must occasionally punish more than is deserved. We disagree with Sunstein and Vermeule on this point. The state is subject to the same deontological side constraints as are all of us. Indeed, the state just is us. *See also* Berman, *supra* note 5.

[14] This section draws from Stephen J. Morse, "Reasons, Results, and Criminal Responsibility," 2004 *U. Ill. L. Rev.* 363.

is impossible.[15] Hard determinism cannot explain those responsibility theories and practices of the criminal law – or, indeed, most moral responsibility theories – that are retrospectively evaluative.[16] Rather, hard determinism provides an external critique of criminal law and other moral practices that obliterates moral responsibility and the reactive attitudes that are its corollary.

The second response, "metaphysical libertarianism," agrees that responsibility and determinism are incompatible, but it also claims that the choices of human beings – or, at least, normal adults – are not determined. On this view, we have a capacity for a freedom that permits us to act not entirely encumbered by the causal processes of the universe.[17] This type of freedom is sometimes called "contracausal freedom," "agent origination," and other terms such as "prime mover unmoved," meant to convey the flavor of this godlike power. For the metaphysical libertarian, the buck stops with us. Libertarianism is regarded by most as consistent with the criminal law's responsibility practices and doctrines. After all, if the causal influences of endowment luck, character luck, and all the other preact influences can be overridden by contracausally free action, then there is clearly a distinction between responsibility for action and responsibility for the luck that precedes and follows one's action. For many, however, the cost of adopting this apparently elegant solution is that it requires one to adopt a panicky and exceptionally implausible metaphysics in a material universe.[18] Quite simply, for them, libertarianism is too metaphysically insecure to ground blame and punishment.

The third response, "compatibilism" or "soft determinism," is willing to concede that determinism is probably true, but it holds that responsibility is possible in a determined universe.[19] Compatibilists

---

[15] See, e.g., Derk Pereboom, *Living without Free Will* 127–157 (2001); Janet Radcliffe-Richards, *Human Nature after Darwin: A Philosophical Introduction* 135–147 (2000); Saul Smilansky, *Free Will and Illusion* 40–73 (2000). See generally Galen Strawson, *The Impossibility of Moral Responsibility* 5 (1994).

[16] See, e.g., R. Jay Wallace, *Responsibility and the Moral Sentiments* 54–61 (1994).

[17] See, e.g., Robert Kane, *The Significance of Free Will* 3–22 (2002).

[18] See, e.g., Hilary Bok, *Freedom and Responsibility* 1–51 (1998) (arguing that libertarianism is conceptually incoherent); Pereboom, *supra* note 15, at 1–88 (arguing that libertarianism is conceptually coherent but scientifically implausible); Peter Strawson, "Freedom and Resentment," in *Free Will* 59, 80 (Gary Watson, ed., 1982) (using the term "panicky").

[19] See, e.g., Bok, *supra* note 18, at 6–29; Wallace, *supra* note 16, at 58–62; John Martin Fischer, "Recent Work on Moral Responsibility," 110 *Ethics* 93 (1999).

claim that normal adult human beings possess the type of general capacities sufficient to ground ordinary responsibility, such as the capacity to grasp and be guided by reason.[20] They also claim that just as indeterminism does not explain responsibility, determinism does not explain the excuses. Many compatibilists also couple their compatibilism with an internalist view of moral norms and the rejection of an external, mind-independent source of moral authority.[21] Compatibilism, which is probably the dominant response among philosophers, thus furnishes for many people the most metaphysically plausible internal justification of responsibility in law and morals.

We need take no stand on the freewill-determinism issue. Two of us – Ferzan and Morse – are persuaded by the arguments for compatibilism. One of us – Alexander – is not. His view is that compatibilism provides only a hollow form of moral responsibility, not the full-blooded form that our reactive attitudes assume. In particular, it seems unresponsive to the worry that what appears to an actor to be a reason, or a reason with a particular positive or negative weight, seems to be beyond the actor's proximate control. On the other hand, he also believes that libertarianism cannot deliver a form of moral responsibility worth wanting because, just like determinism, its foil, libertarianism takes control out of the agent's hands and relinquishes it to chance – or else just makes it utterly mysterious. Alexander believes, as a metaphilosophical position, that the freewill-determinism puzzle is one of those antinomies of thought that we are incapable of resolving, along with the mind-body and infinity puzzles. For him, the freewill-determinism puzzle will always dog practices of holding people morally responsible, practices that we nevertheless cannot imagine dispensing with. Because we cannot dispense with such practices, a retributivist regarding criminal punishment need not resolve or even take sides on the freewill issue.[22]

---

[20] *See* Daniel Clement Dennett, *Freedom Evolves* 9–13 (2003) (providing a naturalized, evolutionary account of these capacities without using the term "compatibilism").

[21] *See, e.g.,* Wallace, *supra* note 16, at 87–95. *See also* Victor Tadros, *Criminal Responsibility* 67–70 (2005).

[22] Alexander's position is thus that neither determinism nor indeterminism can provide a satisfactory account of moral responsibility, and together they appear to exhaust the possibilities. We cannot, therefore, comprehend the bases of moral responsibility. On the other hand, we cannot comprehend the possibility that we are *not* morally responsible. Reflecting on ourselves choosing what to do, we find that the reasons for the chosen

E. CHOICE OR CHARACTER?

A final query for retributivists is whether the ultimate desert basis is one's *choices* or whether it is one's *character* as revealed in one's choices.[23] If the basis is character, and only derivatively culpable choice, then chosen acts are only evidentiary, not constitutive of desert, and choice may be sufficient, but it is not necessary, for assessing desert.

In our view, we should not punish because of someone's character, nor should we exculpate someone because his action is somehow "out" of his character. One is not to blame for one's character because – even assuming that one could provide a precise definition of character – it is clear that one's character per se does not cause harm to others and that much of one's character is beyond rational control; and none of one's character is within one's control at the moment one acts. Only actions cause harm to others, and only actions are potentially fully guidable by reason.

Conversely, one should not be excused because his conduct was "out of character." Such an approach gets things exactly backward – action must be conceptually prior to character. Actions can be judged morally without knowing anything about the agent's character; character can be judged morally only in light of the agent's actions. Moreover, whatever action an agent performs is in a real sense "in character" for the agent. After all, the agent did it, and presumably others with apparently similar characters placed in similar circumstances would not do it. Even if the action was statistically unlikely for the agent and was not the type of thing this type of agent seems predisposed to do by her character, or even if the agent was subject to unusually stressful or tempting

---

actions present themselves as on the one hand correct but on the other hand somehow "up to us." *See also* Smilansky, *supra* note 15; Pereboom, *supra* note 15; David Hodgson, "Responsibility and Good Reasons," 2 *Ohio St. J. Crim. L.* 471 (2005).

We should note that William Edmundson has put forward an argument that the existence of moral responsibility is not necessary to either the existence of moral norms or their teachability. He refers to these as the "naming" and "shaming" aspects of moral practice, which he believes are independent of the "blaming" aspect, which *does* depend on the existence of moral responsibility. *See* William Edmundson, "Morality without Responsibility" (2007) (manuscript on submission) (on file with authors). We are concerned here with the "blaming" aspect and thus do assume moral responsibility. We express no verdict on whether the teachability or "shaming" aspect assumes moral responsibility, *contra* Edmundson.

[23] This section draws from Morse, *supra* note 14.

circumstances, it is still the case that every agent is capable of statistically unlikely behavior that she is not usually disposed to do, and not everyone subject to unusual stresses or temptations responds by offending. The criminal law fairly expects all rational agents to act properly even in the face of unusual circumstances for which the agent bears no responsibility. In summary, to punish for character would be unjust; and to fail to punish merely because a wrongdoer otherwise has good character would be to neglect the positive value of retributive desert.[24]

There is one final way in which a choice theory can incorporate "character," and that is in the law's presumptions about the minimum prerequisites for moral and legal agency. The criminal law presupposes that actors are rational actors who are capable of using reasons to guide their conduct. It also assumes that actors have the capacity for self-reflection. We are also somewhat sympathetic to the view that some level of affective capacity is likewise required. For norms to have meaning, the actor must be able to appreciate the prohibition. Thus, it appears to us that there is a plausible argument for the claim that actors must have substantial capacity to empathize with other human beings and affectively to comprehend the consequences that their actions will have on others before they can rightly be said to violate a moral or legal norm – an argument that may have implications for punishment of psychopaths.

III. Conclusion

The criminal law's purpose is the prevention of harm in the sense that the norms of conduct the criminal law embodies exist for that purpose. Although harm prevention may be accomplished by making it more difficult to commit a crime or by increasing the punishment for the crime, these methods do not require any measure of proportionality

---

[24] *But see* Tadros, *supra* note 21, at 31–53, for a defense of punishment on the basis of character. Tadros claims the evaluation necessary for punishment is of the *actor*, not the act, which may or may not reveal the actor's character. Given our conception of the grounds of culpability, it is not clear how much ultimately turns on the distinction between act-based and character-based judgments. But we do maintain that the actor's reasons are relevant, even if in most circumstances the actor gives less weight to those reasons than on the occasion in question.

between the harm sought to be prevented and the "punishment" that is meted out. We believe that the criminal law does and should reflect retributive principles. It does and should punish people according to desert. The criminal law prevents harm by inculcating and reinforcing norms about how to treat others and operates in accordance with norms about deserved and appropriate punishment for the violation of those norms.

Our subjectivist – "choice" – theory of criminal law is embedded within this moderate retributive theory. General questions about retributivism, including how desert is measured, how great a positive value is retributive desert, and how strong the retributivist side constraint is, are as applicable to our theory as they are to retributivism generally. Throughout the rest of this book, however, our focus is on culpable choices that give rise to retributive desert and not on the retributive theory within which they are embedded. We believe that, both as a side constraint on punishment and as a positive value to be realized through punishment, retributive desert is of sufficient importance to be the major organizing principle of the criminal law. In other words, the criminal law should be primarily structured to ensure to a considerable degree that actors are not punished in the criminal law more than they deserve but are punished to the extent that they deserve. What does and does not contribute to retributive desert is thus our primary focus throughout the rest of this book.

In Part 2, beginning with the next chapter, we argue that the culpability upon which retributive desert turns is a function of the risks to others' legally protected interests that the actor believes he is imposing and the reasons he has for imposing those risks. Then, in Chapter 3, we argue that unperceived risks do not affect the actor's culpability – that is, that negligence is not a basis of culpability. In Chapter 4 we examine the justifications and excuses that may nullify or reduce the culpability of what might otherwise be culpable acts.

In Part 3, Chapters 5 through 7, we turn from culpability to culpable *acts*. In Chapter 5 we argue that the results of culpable acts do not add to or detract from the actor's culpability and hence his retributive desert. Attempts and successes merit the same amount of punishment.

In Chapter 6 we consider which forms of inchoate criminality – incomplete attempts, solicitation, conspiracy, and complicity – constitute culpable acts, and we argue that inchoate criminality should be radically reconceptualized to conform to the analysis of culpability in Chapter 2. Simply put, an actor has not committed a culpable act until he engages in conduct that he believes unleashes a risk of harm over which he no longer has complete control.

In Chapter 7 we take up the locus of culpability as well as omissions to act, including crimes of possession and the individuation of crimes. The locus of culpability, we argue, is the willed bodily movement. Omissions, with a few exceptions, are not generally culpable for purposes of retributive desert because they do not impose risks to others' legally protected interests. They may evince a morally inappropriate lack of concern but not a lack of the concern that can be demanded on pain of punishment.

With respect to act individuation, we argue that, on our approach, acts may pose risks to several interests simultaneously and may do so for varying amounts of time. Culpability is determined holistically as a function of the degree and types of all such risks and their duration. This approach neatly solves what otherwise are quite nettlesome problems of double jeopardy and multiple punishment that currently bedevil criminal law doctrine.

Finally, in Part 4 – Chapter 8 – we sketch what a criminal law code would look like if structured around culpability and thus retributive desert as we have analyzed it. Its most radical effect would be to eliminate the so-called special part of the criminal law – the list of specific criminal offenses – in favor of a list of legally protected interests that should not be put at risk without adequate reasons.

The Culpable Choice

II

The Essence of Culpability

Acts Manifesting Insufficient Concern for the Legally Protected Interests of Others

The Model Penal Code revolutionized *mens rea* by reducing mental-state terminology to four concepts: purpose, knowledge, recklessness, and negligence.[1] As defined by the Model Penal Code, purpose requires that the forbidden result be one's conscious object or that one is aware – or hopes or believes – that a forbidden circumstance (e.g., that the property one is receiving is stolen) exists. Knowledge with respect to results (e.g., death, injury, destruction) requires that one be practically certain that one's conduct will bring about such results. Knowledge with respect to circumstances requires that one be aware that such circumstances exist. Recklessness entails the conscious disregard of a substantial and unjustifiable risk that a forbidden result may occur or that relevant circumstances exist. Negligence requires that one is unreasonably unaware of a substantial and unjustifiable risk that the forbidden

---

[1] Model Penal Code (Official Draft and Revised Comments) § 2.02 (1985).

result may occur or that the relevant circumstances exist. This hierarchy presupposes that purpose is more culpable than knowledge, knowledge is more culpable than recklessness, and recklessness is more culpable than negligence.[2]

Although we believe that the Model Penal Code brought much greater clarity than the myriad concepts employed by the common law, we still believe that more progress can be made. In this chapter, we reconceptualize culpability. We begin with an analysis of recklessness and argue that the substantiality prong is not independent of the justifiability prong. We also argue that recklessness must be understood subjectively, not objectively. With recklessness thus reformulated, we turn our attention to purpose and knowledge and conclude that when properly analyzed and elaborated, purpose and knowledge are merely forms of recklessness, the culpability of which lies in the insufficient concern the actor displays for the legally protected interests of others. Recklessness is plotted on two axes: (1) the degree of risk the actor believes he is imposing on others' interests and (2) his reasons for doing so. Knowledge represents the extreme on axis (1), and purpose is close to the extreme on axis (2). Our argument as to why negligence is not culpable will wait until Chapter 3.

With this new uniform conception of culpability, we turn to the details. First, we address possible objections to our approach, and we also distinguish our view from that of "indifference" proponents. Second, we turn to how "risks" should be understood for purposes of balancing, and we argue that risks should be assessed holistically. Next, looking to the actor's reasons that may justify his action, we argue that the actor must be aware of the reasons, but he need not be motivated by them. Finally, we turn to the nature of the action to be assessed, arguing that actions are assessed individually and not holistically, and that it is actions, and not beliefs, that are the proper subject of inquiry.

---

[2] *But see* Douglas Husak, "The Sequential Principle of Relative Culpability," 1 *Legal Theory* 493–518 (1995); Kenneth W. Simons, "Rethinking Mental States," 72 *B.U.L. Rev.* 463 (1992).

I. Unpacking Recklessness

Because an understanding of recklessness is central to our argument, this is where we begin our analysis.[3] The Model Penal Code defines "recklessly" as follows:

> A person acts recklessly with respect to a material element of an offense when he consciously disregards a substantial and unjustifiable risk that the material element exists or will result from his conduct. The risk must be of such a nature and degree that, considering the nature and the purpose of the actor's conduct and the circumstances known to him, its disregard involves a gross deviation from the standard of conduct that a law-abiding citizen would observe in the actor's situation.[4]

This formulation is substantially the same as the formulations of recklessness in federal and state criminal codes and judicial decisions.[5]

This formulation of recklessness makes it appear that an actor, to be deemed reckless, must consciously disregard a risk that satisfies two independent criteria: the risk must be "substantial"; and the risk must be "unjustifiable." We believe that this appearance is mistaken with respect both to the purpose behind the formulation and to a normatively attractive conception of the culpability displayed through recklessness. In our view, the "substantiality" prong of the definition should be eliminated.[6]

Consider the following hypotheticals:

1. Driver is accompanied by Passenger, who suddenly displays the symptoms of a severe heart attack. Driver speeds down city streets in order to get Passenger to a hospital in time to save his life. In doing

---

[3] This section draws from Larry Alexander, "Insufficient Concern: A Unified Conception of Criminal Culpability," 88 *Cal. L. Rev.* 931 (2000).

[4] Model Penal Code § 2.02(2)(c) (1985).

[5] *See* U.S. Sentencing Guidelines Manual § 2A1.4 cmt. 1 (1998); Ariz. Rev. Stat. Ann. § 13–105(9)(c) (West 1998); Cal. Penal Code § 450(f) (West 1999); N.Y. Penal Law § 15.05(3) (McKinney 1999); *In re Steven S.*, 31 Cal. Rptr. 644, 652 (1994); Joshua Dressler, *Understanding Criminal Law* 144 (4th ed., 2006).

[6] Ultimately, we do advocate retaining the portion of the Model Penal Code's recklessness definition that requires that the risk be a "gross deviation" from a risk that a law-abiding actor would take. *See infra* III.B. We believe, however, that one may impose what may be viewed as an "insubstantial" risk, but that risk may be so unjustified that its imposition is still a "gross deviation" from the risk a law-abiding person would take.

so, Driver creates risks to bystanders' lives, limbs, and property of magnitude R.

2. Daniel loves to set off dynamite on city streets just for the thrill of watching the dynamite explode. In doing so, he creates risks to bystanders' lives, limbs, and property of magnitude R/100.[7]

3. Deborah likes to take Sunday drives. Although she is a very careful driver, in taking Sunday drives she creates risks to bystanders' lives, limbs, and property of magnitude R/10,000.

4. Demented likes to expose others to risk. He has concocted his own version of Russian roulette in which, when he pulls a switch, he creates a risk of magnitude R/100,000 that an innocent person will die or be severely injured.

Now if the substantiality criterion is truly independent of the justifiability criterion, then there must be some level of risk imposition below which the actor cannot be reckless. Suppose that level is just above R/100. In case 1, Driver does satisfy the substantiality criterion but may escape the judgment of recklessness by failing to satisfy the (lack of) justification criterion. In other words, Driver may have justifiably imposed risk R on bystanders because his purpose in doing so was to save the life of Passenger. Deborah, the Sunday driver in case 3, also escapes the judgment of recklessness, in this case because R/10,000 is below the risk threshold, or so we are assuming.

The problem with the independent criteria approach, however, surfaces with cases 2 and 4. Both Daniel and Demented have imposed risks that by hypothesis fail the substantiality criterion, yet the intuition is virtually unshakable that they are acting culpably recklessly toward bystanders. This is perhaps clearer in the case of Demented, who subjects others to risk simply because he enjoys it. Imposing (unconsented to) Russian roulette on others, no matter how high the ratio of empty to loaded chambers, seems a clear case of culpable conduct. What is doing all the work here is, of course, the justifiability criterion, which also explains the intuition about Daniel, namely, that the mere thrill of

---

7 Our usage of "R" or "R/100" alludes to the actor's subjective assessment of the relative frequency that the harm will occur. Our view of risk is discussed later in this section.

a dynamite blast does not justify imposing more than a *de minimis* risk on others.

What emerges from consideration of these cases is the proposition that the level of risk that one may permissibly impose on others is dependent on the reasons one has for imposing that risk. The reason Driver has for imposing risks on bystanders is a weightier one than the reason Deborah, the Sunday driver, has for doing so. Thus, we deem it permissible for Driver to impose a higher risk on bystanders than Deborah may impose. Daniel's reason – the thrill of explosions – may justify even less risk imposition than Deborah is permitted. And Demented's reason – imposing risks on others for its own sake – cannot justify even the slightest increase in risk.

The conclusion that one should draw from these examples is that recklessness consists of imposing unjustifiable risks on others. The level of risk imposed will bear on its justifiability but is not itself an independent criterion of recklessness. Even very tiny risk impositions can be culpable if imposed for insufficient or misanthropic reasons, just as very large risk impositions can be nonculpable if supported by weighty reasons. It certainly may be the case that there is a level at which the risk becomes so minute that it may not be worth devoting precious resources to criminalizing the conduct or prosecuting the actor; but this practical argument does not undermine our conceptual claim that an actor's culpability hinges entirely on the unjustifiability of the risk. Imposing unjustifiable risks to others' legally protected interests is culpable behavior because it displays insufficient concern for others' interests.

A second question about recklessness is whether "risk" should be assessed subjectively or objectively. Consider the following case: David wants to get home in time to watch the Lakers game on television. He accelerates until his speedometer reads ninety miles per hour, a speed that he believes creates a very substantial risk of death, serious bodily injury, or property damage to other drivers, passengers, and pedestrians. In fact, his speedometer is broken, and he is going only fifty-five miles per hour, a reasonable speed given the road and traffic conditions. Is David acting recklessly?

There are two approaches one might take to this case. Under an "objective" approach, we could distinguish between the "risk imposed" and the "risk the actor believes that he is imposing." The risk imposed serves as an *actus reus,* whereas the risk the actor believes he is imposing speaks to his culpability.[8] Under this view, David would not be reckless because the actual risk imposed is not of a magnitude that would render one negligent if imposed inadvertently. Or to put the point another way, were David to be aware of the actual risk he is imposing, he would be neither negligent nor reckless, because that level of risk is justifiable. Notably, David would still be culpable in that he would be attempting to act recklessly; but he would not in fact be reckless.

In contrast, we might take a "subjective" approach: an actor is reckless if he believes he is imposing a level of risk that would be unjustifiable (given his reasons) regardless of the actual risk he is imposing. On this approach, David is driving recklessly at fifty-five miles per hour because he believes he is driving ninety miles per hour.

As we discuss in Chapter 5, we believe that attempts and successes should be regarded as equally culpable and, because they are equally culpable, equally deserving of punishment. It therefore ultimately matters little whether the objective or the subjective approach to recklessness is chosen. On either approach, David is equally culpable and therefore equally blameworthy and punishable.

Still, as a conceptual matter, we reject distinguishing attempted recklessness from recklessness. We believe the correct approach is the subjective one because it avoids the troubling notion of an objective risk on which the objective view depends. Risk is an essentially epistemic concept. Risk is always relative to someone's perspective, a perspective that is defined by possession of certain information but not other information. In law, when we say that there is a "risk" of x's occurrence, we are using "risk" in the sense of relative frequency. That is, any given reference class will yield a relative frequency for an event's occurrence. However, one may formulate the reference class widely or narrowly, thus changing the relative frequency. To ask what the risk is that John will be hit by lightning, we can give accurate answers if we say that there is a one in a billion chance that a person gets hit by lightning, a one in a

---

[8] *See, e.g.,* Paul H. Robinson, "Prohibited Risks and Culpable Disregard or Inattentiveness: Challenge and Confusion in the Formulation of Risk-Creation Offenses," 4 *Theoretical Inquiries in Law* 367 (2002); George P. Fletcher, *The Grammar of Criminal Law: American, Comparative, and International,* vol. 1: *Foundations* 8.4.2 (2007).

million chance that a person gets hit by lightning in the area in which John lives, a one in a thousand chance that a person gets hit by lightning on a golf course in the area where John lives, a one in one hundred chance that a person gets hit by lightning on a golf course during a rain storm in the area where John lives, and a one in one chance that John got hit by lightning on a golf course during a rain storm this Tuesday in the area where John lives. All of these probability assessments are correct within their given reference classes. In contrast, with full information, there is no need to resort to a probability. For God – who possesses complete information about everything – risk does not exist. For God, all events have a probability of either one or zero (leaving aside quantum events).[9] So even though Albert was playing golf with John – and thus all the relative frequency accounts (except the last one) applied – in actuality Albert did not get hit by lighting, and thus, though he was "risked" to different degrees depending upon the reference class, there was no harm at all.[10]

Thus, the "objective" approach creates the following quandary. We must be able to assign a risk to an activity that is different from both whatever risk the actor perceives and the risk God perceives (one or zero). Thus, this approach requires that we construct an artificial perspective containing some but not all information. There is obviously an indefinite number of such possible perspectives, each one generating a different risk. Depending on how narrowly or widely one defines the reference class, the relative frequency will change. But there is simply no nonarbitrary way for us to select among reference classes. Nor does it make any sense to us why the culpability of an actor should hinge not upon what the actor knows, or what God would know, but upon what some other individual's perspective might be. One who drops a bowling ball from the top of a building to measure the force of gravity for himself, and who believes there are people below whom he is

---

9 *See* Robert E. Goodin and Frank Jackson, "Freedom From Fear," 35 *Phil. & Pub. Aff.* 249, 256 (2007). We use the discussion of "God" as a shorthand method for illustrating that with complete information, risks disappear. There are only harms and misses. Thus, our discussion should not be read as entailing any sort of position on determinism and the like.

10 For further argument as to why risks are not themselves harms, *see* Stephen R. Perry, "Risk, Harm, and Responsibility," in *Philosophical Foundations of Tort Law* (David G. Owen, ed., 1995).

putting in extreme danger, is reckless. This is true despite the fact that his companion believes the risk is greater than he does; the building's doorman would have estimated the risk to be slightly lower; and a window washer, with a better view below, knows that there are very few people below so that dropping the ball is unlikely to injure anyone. It simply makes no sense to allow the actor's liability to hinge not upon what he knows, or God knows, but upon the arbitrary selection among the friend, doorman, and window washer for the correct perspective for assessing "objective risk."

Or, to take a different example, suppose A and B are each driving cars on a two-lane highway and are approaching a blind curve. They both believe that if they stay on their side of the highway, the probability of causing injury or death when they go around the curve is very small. Likewise, they both believe that if they veer over into the left lane when rounding the curve, the probability of causing injury or death (by striking an oncoming vehicle) is quite high. Moreover, actuarial tables support their beliefs – very often an oncoming car will be entering the curve from the opposite direction, but rarely will there be a stalled vehicle or pedestrian in the right hand lane. Nonetheless, C, a bystander situated at a good vantage point, can see that this time there are *no* vehicles approaching from the opposite direction, but there *is* a small child just around the curve in the right lane. Thus, C estimates the risk of injury or death of veering into the left lane to be zero but the risk of remaining in the right lane to be virtually one. If A were to remain in the right lane, we would not deem him culpable. On the other hand, if B were to veer into the left lane, we *would* deem him reckless – not attempting to be reckless, but reckless full stop. Yet, from C's perspective, A would be creating a huge risk, and B none. If any risk is "objective" then, it is the risk C assesses. Yet C's assessment, like God's, should be immaterial.[11]

---

[11] There are other examples to illustrate our view that risk is a perspectival, relative-to-information-possessed, epistemic notion, not an ontic one (if we leave quantum physics, which is irrelevant to our concerns, aside). Consider a lottery that sells 1 million tickets for $1 each and pays out $1 million to the holder of the winning ticket. It should not matter whether the lottery officials have drawn the winning number before the lottery tickets are sold or draw it afterward, so long as they keep the number secret and do not trade on their knowledge if they draw it before the tickets are sold. So suppose they do draw the winning number before selling the tickets, and the winner will be the buyer of ticket 1436. The buyer of 1436 will, at the time of the purchase, assess the value of the ticket to be $1,

There is no gap between the actor's subjective estimate of the risk and the "true" or "objective" risk because the latter is either illusory (other than as a referent to the one or zero "probability" of whether harm occurs) or arbitrary (as there is no principled way to select among relative frequency accounts). For the very same reasons, as we discuss in the next chapter, we believe that negligence is not an appropriate basis of criminal responsibility.

In summary, properly understood, recklessness is a subjective concept that tracks the defendant's assessment of the risk. Moreover, the evaluation of whether an action is reckless hinges upon its justifiability. We further examine the nature of this assessment later in this chapter. But next we turn to why knowledge and purpose are mere species of recklessness.

II. Folding Knowledge and Purpose into Recklessness

In this section we argue that knowledge and purpose are forms of recklessness.[12] We begin by showing how knowledge is merely a limiting case of recklessness along the axis of degree of perceived risk of harm. We argue that once knowledge is properly understood, it becomes clear why some instances of recklessness are more culpable than some instances of knowledge and why treating instances of willful blindness as instances of knowledge is erroneous. Next, we turn to purpose, arguing that such cases are instances of recklessness where the actor's reasons are presumptively unjustifying. We argue, however, that just as recklessness contemplates that risk impositions can be justified by certain reasons, an actor's purposeful conduct can also be justified by certain reasons. Because purposeful conduct is not always unjustified, we argue that it is

---

the price he pays, for he will assess his chances of winning $1 million as 1 in 1 million. But the officials will assess his chances as 1, and everyone else's chances as 0. Their God's-eye perspective provides them with an information base and epistemic position different from that of the ticket buyers.

The same point can be illustrated by a coin flip. If one of us flips a coin, the others will estimate the chance that it lands heads as 50 percent, and they will do so even if the coin flipper already knows the results of the flip but has not revealed it. From the flipper's perspective, if the coin landed heads, the "chance" of its doing so is 1. If not, its "chance" is 0.

[12] This section draws from Alexander, *supra* note 3.

not necessarily more culpable than knowledge or recklessness. Finally, we address how our conception resolves questions about how one can act purposefully as to an attendant circumstance.

A. KNOWLEDGE

A person acts with criminal "knowledge" with respect to an element of a crime when he believes to a practical certainty that his conduct is of a particular nature, that an attendant circumstance exists, or that his conduct will bring about a particular result.[13] Unlike recklessness, which focuses on both the risk imposed and the actor's justification for imposing it, at first glance knowledge appears to focus only on risk – of forbidden conduct, resulting harm, or circumstance – and the actor must be practically certain it will result.

One might think from a superficial comparison between the formulation of knowledge and the formulation of recklessness that when an actor is practically certain that his act will be harmful to others, he is forbidden from undertaking it regardless of his reasons for doing so, whereas if he believes the risk is less than that of practical certainty, he may act if his reasons are sufficiently weighty. But it is not the case that knowingly imposing harm is always unjustified. For example, one may justifiably impose a practically certain harm on another to defend oneself or others or, in some cases, where worse harm to another or a similar harm to many others can only be averted thereby.[14]

"Knowledge" – acting with the belief that it is practically certain that one's act will be harmful to others or turn out to be of a forbidden nature – is merely a limiting case of recklessness along the axis of degree of perceived risk of harm. The other recklessness axis, the axis of the actor's reasons, remains fully operative. The only real distinction between knowledge and recklessness in the criminal law is that at some point as the risk of harm (or forbidden conduct) approaches a practical certainty, the burden of proof (or production) on the issue of whether the defendant-actor's reasons for acting justified the risk of harm he created shifts from the prosecution to the defendant-actor. That shift in

---

[13] Model Penal Code § 2.02(2)(b) (1985).
[14] Id. §§ 3.02–3.05.

the burden of proof (or production) makes sense in terms of both the probability that the act is or is not justified and the relative access to the justifying circumstances, if any. But the difference in the allocation of burdens does not reflect any substantive distinction between knowledge and recklessness.[15] Moreover, in our view, the Model Penal Code is correct in its assessment that lack of justification is something the prosecutor must prove beyond a reasonable doubt, though this burden may be aided by a permissive presumption placing the burden of production on the defendant.

Seeing knowledge as just a species of recklessness enables us to avoid two errors. First, it allows us to avoid the error of deeming all cases of knowledge to be more culpable than all cases of recklessness, even where the harm risked is the same. For example, someone who imposes a very high risk of harm on another – a risk just short of practical certainty – for a very frivolous reason, such as a thrill, is surely more culpable than one who imposes a practically certain harm for a quite weighty, but ultimately insufficient, reason. For example, if Albert knowingly inflicts severe bodily injury on another to prevent him from accidentally destroying Albert's entire life's work, Albert may be culpable; but he is surely less culpable than if he imposes a slightly lower risk of the same harm on another just to satisfy his urge to drive like a madman. In short, instances of what we now call extreme indifference to human life may not only be equal to but also more culpable than some cases of knowledge.

The second error averted by seeing knowledge as just a species of recklessness is the misclassification of cases of willful blindness. A typical case of willful blindness is one where the actor is asked by someone at an airport in a drug-producing country to carry a package on the plane and give it to a specific person when he arrives in the United States. Where the applicable statute punishes only "knowing" drug smuggling, courts have struggled to find the actor – whom they rightly regard as culpable – guilty by deeming his willful blindness to be tantamount to knowledge.[16] Yet willful blindness is not knowledge; it is an attempt to

---

[15] The Model Penal Code regards (the absence of) justification as part of the prosecutor's burden of proof. *See* Model Penal Code § 1.12(2) (1985). It is constitutional, however, to place this burden on the defendant. *See, e.g.,* Martin v. Ohio, 480 U.S. 228 (1987).

[16] *See, e.g.,* Mattingly v. United States, 924 F.2d 785, 792 (8th Cir. 1991) ("[T]he element of knowledge may be inferred from deliberate acts amounting to willful blindness....");

avoid knowledge, and this hiding of one's head in the sand frequently achieves that goal in that actors who display willful blindness do not in fact believe to a practical certainty that their conduct is harmful.

The prototypical willfully blind actor is, of course, reckless. The risk he is taking – of, say, smuggling drugs – is an unjustifiable one. The unjustifiability of the risk cannot, however, convert his recklessness into knowledge without absurd results. For example, suppose a drug smuggler employs 100 "mules" to do his smuggling.[17] His modus operandi is to give each mule a suitcase to carry into the target country. He tells the mules that in ninety-nine of the suitcases he places only innocent items, such as clothes, and in one he places drugs. The mules are not told which suitcase holds the drugs, and they do not open the suitcases. In such a situation, it would be absurd to deem the mule with the drugs to have "knowingly" smuggled them. What he has done is take a one in a hundred chance of smuggling drugs for no legally sufficient reason. If a similar risk imposition would not be deemed "knowing" if undertaken for good reasons – say, for example, you are visiting a foreign country and a person whom you greatly admire asks you to carry a gift to a friend in the United States, and you entertain the thought that there is a tiny but real chance that the person you admire is a drug smuggler – then it is misguided to deem the risk imposition "knowing" merely because one disapproves of the reasons for undertaking it.

In some sense, all risk imposition is willful blindness in that the actor could always seek more information about the risk before acting, although the act thereafter undertaken would be different temporally and circumstantially from the act undertaken without gathering more information. Moreover, in ordinary recklessness cases, when we assess the actor's reasons for imposing the risk, we are also implicitly assessing his reasons for not investigating the danger further. Viewing recklessness as the all-encompassing conception of criminal culpability, rather than as different from and less culpable than knowledge, allows us to

---

State v. LaFreniere, 481 N.W.2d 412 (Neb. 1992); *see also* United States v. Whittington, 26 F.3d 456 (4th Cir. 1994); United States v. Mancuso, 42 F.3d 836 (4th Cir. 1994); United States v. Jewell, 532 F.2d 697 (9th Cir. 1976); United States v. Incorporated Village of Island Park, 888 F. Supp. 419 (E.D.N.Y. 1995).

[17] *See* Douglas N. Husak and Craig A. Callender, "Willful Ignorance, Knowledge, and the 'Equal Culpability' Thesis: A Study of the Deeper Significance of the Principle of Legality," 1994 *Wis. L. Rev.* 29, 37 (1994).

evaluate correctly the willful blindness cases and does not tempt us to distort them into cases of knowledge.[18]

B. PURPOSE

A person acts with criminal purpose with respect to the conduct or result elements of an offense if "it is his conscious object to engage in conduct of [the required] ... nature or to cause [the required] ... result."[19] Unlike knowledge, which at first glance appears to focus only on the actor's assessment of the risk of harm, purpose at first glance appears to focus only on the actor's desires regarding the possibility that his conduct will prove harmful, while ignoring his beliefs about this possibility. But as with knowledge, this initial appearance proves to be misleading.

The crucial point is that in order to act with criminal purpose, the actor must believe that his conduct increases the risk of harm, even if the increase is very slight. Consider the Jackal, who fires a shot at de Gaulle from the Eiffel Tower believing his chance of success to be one in a million. If he does succeed, he will have shot de Gaulle "purposely," given that it is his "conscious object" in shooting that de Gaulle be killed (that is how he collects his assassin's reward). But characterizing this act as purposeful assumes that the Jackal believes that, although firing the gun produces only a one in a million chance of killing de Gaulle, firing the gun does increase the probability of de Gaulle's being killed over the probability of de Gaulle's being killed if the Jackal refrains from firing the gun. If the Jackal does not believe his firing the gun increases the probability of killing de Gaulle – if he believes de Gaulle has no worse chance of surviving if he fires the gun than if he does not – then were the shot to kill de Gaulle, it would not be a purposeful killing. For in such a case, the Jackal would not have fired the gun for the purpose of killing, given that he did not believe firing the gun produced any increased chance of killing de Gaulle.

---

[18] Recklessness, because it is sensitive to both risks and reasons, allows us to distinguish between those whom David Luban calls ostriches, who merely do not want to know, and those whom he calls foxes, who contrive deniability. *See* David Luban, "Contrived Ignorance," 87 *Geo. L.J.* 957, 968–975 (1999). Ostriches and foxes may take the same risks, but they have different reasons for doing so. Both may be culpably reckless, but foxes are more culpable than ostriches given the same level of risk and the same harm.

[19] Model Penal Code § 2.02(2)(a) (1985).

Now, there are outlier cases where, even though the actor believes that his action has some chance of success, he may also believe that he is *decreasing* the overall chance of harm to the victim. Imagine that David wants to kill the president but knows that he is a terrible shot.[20] He also knows that a hired hit man (a far better shot) intends to kill the president later in the day. David also believes that if he takes his shot and misses, then security will be improved and it will decrease the chances that the later hit man will be successful. Thus, David may come to believe that his taking the shot will actually decrease the chance of the president's being killed. If David proceeds to shoot at the president and, against all odds, the shot finds its mark, is it correct to characterize David's act of homicide as "purposeful"?

In our view, David has purposefully killed the president. To do something on purpose requires the actor to understand that his action can have some effect in the world – some chance of success. Indeed, it would be irrational for David to proceed if he believed that he could not kill the president. Thus, it may be said that David is acting purposefully even if he knows that if *he fails* he will then decrease the probability of the president's being killed, and to a greater extent than his shooting by itself increases that probability.[21]

Some may argue that, as a conceptual matter, our claim that purpose entails both a reason to cause the harm and a belief that one may succeed runs counter to the standard position within the philosophy of mind and

---

[20] Private correspondence of David Dolinko, Professor of Law, UCLA School of Law, and Larry Alexander.

[21] This hypothetical also raises a second question about the relevance of David's knowledge that his action might actually decrease the overall probability that the president will be killed. This belief may have the effect of justifying David's action. The question is complex, as it requires us to ascertain whether David must be motivated by, or simply aware of, the justifying circumstances *and* whether David may avail himself of a lesser-evils defense when he chooses the lesser, but perhaps not the least, evil. We attend to all of these questions in Chapter 4. The important point for now is that purpose does require both that the actor act on his desire to cause a harm and that he believe that his action has a chance of success.

Another point that the hypothetical raises, again relevant to the question of justification, is whether imposing a risk of dying *sooner* can be justified by averting a greater risk of dying *later*. Obviously, we believe it can be, which is why we consent to risky surgery to prevent a later but riskier disease. But because we are mortal and will die no matter what precautions we take, not every present risk can be justified by averting a later and greater risk.

to a common view that the degree of risk is irrelevant to the culpability of purposeful actions. Let us discuss each of these objections.

First, consider the objection that an intention to A does not entail a belief that one will A.[22] To use an example of Michael Bratman's, if Alex discovers a log blocking his driveway, he may form the intention to move it, but not form the belief that he will move it. Then, there is nothing irrational about Alex's (1) forming the intention to move the log, and (2) forming the intention to call a tree company if or when he fails.[23] As a conceptual matter, it appears that actors can form intentions to p and yet not believe that they will p.

At the outset, we do not argue that acting purposefully requires that one believes one *will succeed*. Rather, our claim is far more limited – it is that acting purposefully requires a belief that one has *some* chance whatsoever of success. When Alex tries to lift the log, he may not believe that he will lift it, but he surely does not believe it to be absolutely certain that he will fail.

Second, it seems just as natural to say that what Alex intends is "to try to lift the log." When we are cognizant of the likelihood of our failure, we sometimes cast our intentions not in terms of results but in terms of "tryings." Of course, once one does not believe that one will succeed, but only that one will "try," one is not committed to any degree of success. But now one can see just how fine (or nonexistent) the line is between purpose and recklessness. Purposeful riskings – like Russian roulette – are commonly seen as instances of recklessness. If Cowardly Jackal is paid $1,000 to kill de Gaulle, and, afraid of being caught, fires from a distance from which he estimates his likelihood of success at 1/1,000, he imposes the same risks for the same reasons as Risky Jackal, who is paid $1,000 to create a 1/1,000 chance of de Gaulle's death.

Also, although we may speculate about the activities that we can engage in without believing that we can succeed, this objection hardly hits the mark when it comes to criminal activity. An actor who purposefully engages in conduct to cause harm to another does so in order to succeed (or at least to try to succeed). Indeed, instances of pure factual impossibility (voodoo and the like) are cases in which the defendant

[22] *See* Michael Bratman, *Intentions, Plans, and Practical Reason* 37–41 (1987).
[23] *Id.* at 39.

irrationally believes in the likelihood that she will succeed despite all science and common sense to the contrary. If there exists an actor who intends to harm another through a particular act but does so without a belief in *any* likelihood of that act's success, we will concede that such an actor is not culpable for that act.

Finally, even if one does not agree with our claim that one may conceptually reduce purpose to recklessness, we still believe that *normatively* we can. That is, in instances of both purpose and recklessness, the actor's culpability ultimately turns on *both* his reasons for acting and his belief as to the likelihood of success.

This last normative claim brings us to the second possible objection – that the culpability of a purposeful actor does not turn on his estimate of the likelihood of his success. As between two actors, each of whom has the same harm as his purpose and acts for the same reasons, is the one who believes the risk he is imposing is higher more culpable than the other? In other words, if we hold reasons constant, and among those reasons is the purpose to harm, do variances on the "perceived risk" axis affect culpability?[24]

We are inclined to say that culpability does vary with the actor's estimate of the probability. Our culpability assessment evaluates the defendant's choice to impose *this* risk for *these* reasons. Even if the actor would have imposed a greater risk – something we can presumably assume because he acts purposefully[25] – this is not the choice he made.[26] Moreover, even though the actor wants the harm to occur, he may be unwilling to impose a greater risk. The Cowardly Jackal who wants to kill de Gaulle but by imposing only a 1/1,000 risk is less culpable than the Brave Jackal who holds a gun to de Gaulle's temple and then pulls

---

[24] For a discussion of this issue, *see* Itzhak Kugler, *Direct and Oblique Intention in the Criminal Law* 90–102 (2002). We return to this issue in Chapter 8.

[25] As suggested by Kugler, *id.*

[26] Alan Michaels suggests something akin to this argument in "Acceptance: The Missing Mental State," 71 *S. Cal. L. Rev.* 953 (1998). Michaels's argument is that some actors who believe their conduct only risks harm feel the same degree of indifference as actors who believe their conduct will certainly cause harm, and because both types of actors "accept" (i.e., psychologically resign themselves to) the harm, both are equally culpable irrespective of their different estimates of the probability of the harm's occurrence. Although we believe that this equal level of indifference shows both actors to have *bad characters*, still, only one was presented with the opportunity to impose a practically certain harm. Thus, they are not equally *bad actors*.

the trigger. The risk the Cowardly Jackal has decided to impose – the extent to which he has decided to threaten de Gaulle's life – is simply smaller, and therefore less culpable. Of course, it may be the case that where the actors' reasons are highly unjustified, variances in belief as to probability will only slightly reduce or increase the actor's culpability.

Because purpose, too, is a comparison of risks and reasons, it is also just a special case of recklessness. There is an axis for the actor's belief about risk and an axis for the actor's reasons for imposing it, the latter in the case of purpose being the actor's desire to bring about the prohibited result or conduct. As with knowledge, the possibility of justification is not eliminated, but rather the burden of proof (or production) is shifted to the actor to justify his purpose by citing some reason that would justify his purpose. In other words, just as knowledge can be viewed as a special case of recklessness, in which the actor's belief regarding risk (that it is very high) creates a presumption of sorts that his reasons are inadequate to justify his conduct, so too can purpose be viewed as a special case of recklessness, one in which the actor's reason is presumptively (but not necessarily) unjustifying.

We say that the conscious object to engage in harmful conduct or produce harmful results is only presumptively unjustifying because there are cases in which purposeful criminal conduct can be justified. Having harm to others as one's conscious object is not the same thing as having that harm be one's ultimate object. Nor is it the same thing as appropriating others' bodies, talents, or labor, something some deontologists might claim can never be justified. Thus, for example, it might be the actor's conscious object to wound a homicidal maniac who otherwise will kill an innocent party. The actor's wounding him sufficiently to foil his attack will be a purposeful battery. Nonetheless, he may be acting justifiably in defending others against his attack.

Or consider the case of the trapped spelunkers.[27] Suppose that they kill one of their party because they calculate that his continued breathing will deprive the rest of the oxygen they need to survive until the rescue party can reach them. Whether or not they are ultimately deemed to have been justified in killing the one member, they have not "appropriated" him to benefit themselves. Rather, they have merely prevented him from harming

---

[27] *See* Lon L. Fuller, "The Case of the Speluncean Explorers," 62 *Harv. L. Rev.* 616 (1949).

them. But they surely harmed him "purposely"; it was their conscious object to do so, even if doing so was not their ultimate purpose.

If purposeful criminal conduct is not always unjustified, neither is it always more culpable than knowledge or recklessness. One may well believe that the spelunkers lack a justification for homicide without believing they are more culpable than those who impose high risks of death on others for the mere thrill of it but who do not have others' deaths as their conscious object. One may also conclude that a purposeful criminal actor who imposes a very tiny risk – for example, our hypothetical Jackal – is less culpable than a nonpurposeful actor who imposes huge risks for weak reasons. Thus, as we saw for knowledge, a unified conception of criminal culpability may actually avoid the potential problems that arise within the existing category of purpose.

Finally, our unified conception also resolves questions about how one can act purposefully as to an attendant circumstance.[28] According to the Model Penal Code, an actor acts purposefully as to an attendant circumstance when he is aware, believes, or hopes that the circumstances exist.[29] We believe that this formulation blurs important culpability distinctions. Compare one rapist who engages in sexual intercourse and knows that the woman is not consenting, with another who not only knows she is not consenting but is also motivated by the victim's lack of consent. The latter certainly seems more culpable than the former, yet the Model Penal Code does not distinguish between them. Moreover, the Model Penal Code does not capture the root of the actor's culpability, for it is misleading to characterize the actor's attitude toward the victim's not consenting as "hope." Rather, the very reason the actor has engaged in his conduct is because he believes the victim is not consenting.

In addition, even when an actor is motivated by an attendant circumstance, there are shades of gray here as well. Suppose the actor purposely takes X's computer. "Purposely" here might mean it was the

---

[28] Bentham thought this was not possible. Jeremy Bentham, *Introduction to the Principles of Morals and Legislation* 88 (1781; 1988) We disagree for the reasons we give below. *See also* Michael S. Moore, *Act and Crime: The Philosophy of Action and Its Implications for Criminal Law* 203–205 (1993).

[29] Model Penal Code § 2.02(2)(a) (1985).

actor's purpose *to take the computer*, which he believed to be X's. Or it could mean it was the actor's purpose *to take X's computer* (he would not have taken it were it abandoned by X and free for the taking). The latter purpose seems worse than the former. Combine this insight with the facts that (1) the risk the actor estimates of successfully accomplishing his purpose can vary from just > 0 to 100 percent, and (2) the actor's ulterior purposes (the further purposes his purpose to harm serves) can vary in their positive or negative weight, and it seems almost beyond cavil that some cases of culpable purpose are less culpable than some cases of recklessness.[30]

III. A Unified Conception of Criminal Culpability

Criminal culpability is always a function of what the actor believes regarding the nature and consequences of his conduct (and the various probabilities thereof) and what the actor's reasons are for acting as he does in light of those beliefs. Recklessness, minus its substantiality of risk requirement, perfectly expresses these two dimensions of culpability. In the last part of this chapter, we turn to more specific questions about this culpability calculation.

A. UNDERSTANDING INSUFFICIENT CONCERN

As defended in the preceding sections, we believe that, as a conceptual matter, purpose and knowledge are simply species of recklessness. Culpability, at bottom, is just about risks and reasons. Because of the novelty of our view, we wish to respond to some potential (and not so potential) objections.

---

[30] The folding of purpose into recklessness also helps with certain "lit fuse" situations. Suppose, for example, D lights a fuse with the purpose of burning down V's business. D is obviously reckless the instant he lights it, as there is some chance he will not be able to snuff it out even if he has a change of heart. He has imposed this risk – which increases as time passes – for no good reason, in this case a purpose to destroy. Now suppose D does have a change of heart in time to snuff out the fuse, but he has an epileptic seizure before he can do so, and V's business burns down. Did D burn it down purposefully, because he lit the fuse with that purpose, or only recklessly, because he had a change of heart? Both answers have their temptations. On our theory, there is no need to decide.

1. How Many Categories Do We Need?

The first concern is that our view "flattens" culpability.[31] Rather than recognizing four distinct mental states, we reduce it all to one. How in the world can all the shades of culpability fit within one mental state? Our response – that we actually recognize finer gradations – seems to throw us into Charybdis, as other critics may worry about unfettered discretion in the hands of juries and prosecutors.[32] These objections are quite different, but both certainly cannot be right.

The first question, we believe, should be the conceptual one. How many different mental states are there *really*? If purpose and knowledge require that we look to both risks and reasons, then they function in exactly the same way as does recklessness. Although acting with purpose or knowledge regarding forbidden conduct, results, or circumstances appears *presumptively* unjustified, nevertheless, as we argue earlier, justifications may be available in such cases.

Moreover, despite the fact that our view appears to reduce all culpability to one level, it does quite the opposite. We can recognize shades of gray that current legal formulations cannot. Our view explains why some instances of extreme indifference to human life are just as culpable as some purposeful and knowing killings. In addition, our view can accommodate the intuition that harming someone purposefully can be a very bad reason for acting. That is, we may think that a person is more culpable for trying to harm someone than she is if she merely foresees and tolerates it. On the other hand, there seem to be many other reasons that may be just as bad as aiming at the evil. If an actor blows up an airplane and kills the pilot, we might think him no more culpable for killing the pilot to marry the pilot's wife (purpose) than for blowing up the plane for insurance money and killing the pilot as a side effect (knowledge). Identifying with and aiming at evil are extremely culpable, but so, too, is the indifference manifested in acting for weak reasons while risking atrocious harm.

As noted previously, our ability to accommodate these nuances comes at a price; it may afford greater discretion to courts and juries.

---

[31] Joshua Dressler, "Does One Size Fit All? Thoughts on Alexander's Unified Conception of Criminal Culpability," 88 *Cal. L. Rev.* 955 (2000).

[32] Alexander, *supra* note 3, at 953 n.62.

This may be true, but we doubt this objection is all that forceful. In terms of legitimate error, there may be more errors under our scheme, but they will likely be smaller than when juries are forced to place the actor's mental state into one of four (supposedly hierarchical) categories. Moreover, because all subjective mental states are notoriously difficult to prove, and all rely on inferences made by juries, we think there is little reason to believe that juries will misuse our unified conception in ways that they cannot already misuse current mental state categories.

Finally, we contend that the law should continue to require that the imbalance of risks and reasons represents a gross deviation from the standard of care that a law-abiding citizen would observe in the actor's situation.[33] The criminal law should not be concerned with those actors who, although they impose risks that are not justified by their reasons, are only minimally culpable (because their reasons *almost* justify the risks they perceive). Moreover, by requiring a gross deviation, the risk of juror error is reduced.

2. Indifference Compared

Some criminal law theorists argue that we should add indifference as a distinct type of culpable mental state.[34] To us, such proposals turn on what one means by "indifference."[35] Consider the following example. Danielle decides to play Russian roulette with Andrew. Danielle does not particularly care for Andrew and is wholly equivocal as to whether Andrew is killed. Danielle pulls the trigger, and Andrew dies.

Contrast Darla who plays Russian roulette with Abe. Darla is very fond of Abe; indeed, the two are dating. Yet, Darla and Abe enjoy the rush that comes from playing Russian roulette. Darla pulls the trigger, and Abe dies.

In the first example, Danielle can be said to be indifferent in two different respects. First, her desire state about Andrew's fate is one of

---

[33] As suggested by Dressler, *supra* note 31.

[34] *See, e.g.*, Simons, *supra* note 2; Kenneth W. Simons, "Culpability and Retributive Theory: The Problem of Criminal Negligence," 5 *J. Contemp. Legal Issues* 365, 371 (1994); R. A. Duff, *Intention, Agency, and Criminal Liability: Philosophy of Action and the Criminal Law* 162–163 (1990).

[35] This section draws from Kimberly Kessler Ferzan, "Opaque Recklessness," 91 *J. Crim. L. & Criminology* 597 (2001) and Kimberly Kessler Ferzan, "Don't Abandon the Model Penal Code Yet! Thinking Through Simons's *Rethinking*," 6 *Buff. Crim. L. Rev.* 185 (2002).

indifference. She cares not whether he lives or dies. Second, she may be said to be indifferent because, although faced with imposing the risk of death, she chooses to pull the trigger.

Darla, on the other hand, is indifferent only in the latter sense. That is, Darla does care, indeed she cares deeply, about Abe. She is not indifferent toward his death. Nevertheless, we may still say that her choice, to play Russian roulette, manifests culpable indifference to human life.

The first meaning of indifference reflects attitudes that the actor has irrespective of how she chooses. The latter sense represents a normative evaluation of the actor's choice. For the normative sense of indifference, we do not care about how the actor feels when we label her indifferent. Rather, no matter what she may wish, hope, or desire, we may decide that she does not care enough.

We are not opposed to the term "indifference" in the latter sense. Whether we employ the term "recklessness," "indifference," or "insufficient concern," all three seem to encompass the disrespect for others that makes reckless conduct culpable. To us, culpable indifference is exhibited by the choice to engage in reckless conduct, the willingness to risk the bad side effects of one's action for insufficient reasons. It is the outcome of the actor's practical reasoning that is problematic. For us, all recklessness exhibits culpable indifference, and some reckless choices, because of the degree of their unjustifiability, exhibit extreme indifference.

On the other hand, we deny that indifference as an attitude is itself sufficient for culpability. First, we are opposed to this conception of indifference insofar as it might license punishment in the absence of conscious choice, as we discuss in our argument against punishment for negligence in the next chapter. But we are likewise unconvinced that this approach places responsibility on the correct aspect of the actor's practical reasoning. For example, assume David runs the red light to get to the Knicks game, and he recognizes that there is a substantial risk of harm to others. But his desire to go to the game is so great that he decides to run the light anyway. We believe that David is reckless because, although he appreciates the substantiality and unjustifiability of the risk, he chooses to disregard it. But in deciding to disregard the risk of harm to others, David's practical reasoning might go a variety of ways: David might value his desire to go the Knicks game at 100 and the potential harm to others at 10 (in terms of his desire to avoid it). Or he might value the Knicks game at 10, but the harm to others at 9. We contend that it is the choice, to pick the game over others' interests, whatever values David gives these variables, that makes David's conduct culpable.

However, we believe that an "indifference as attitude" proponent could be placing blame earlier in the calculation – to the precise amount of weight given to the interests of others. David is indifferent because he is not giving the appropriate weight to the interests of others. But let us assume that David decides not to run the light, still valuing others' interest at 9, but not being a basketball fan, weighing the interest of the game at 1. Here, although David does not run the light, his value system is still such that were he to become a fan, he would be willing to impose great risks on others to get to a Knicks game. Do these theorists wish to punish David for *stopping* at the light because he in fact gives the interests of others too little weight? Alternatively, is David indifferent if he correctly assesses the value of others' lives at 100 but grossly overvalues the Knicks game at 1,000 and thus runs the light? If so, his indifference is being manifested in his choice, not merely in the weights of others' interests that inform the choice.

3. Bizarre Metaphysical Beliefs and Culpability

In *Bad Acts and Guilty Minds*,[36] Leo Katz collects some cases from the colonial period in Africa that, rendered schematically, look like this: The actor kills someone and claims that the victim was an evil spirit or a witch, not a human being. The law proscribed knowingly killing human beings, not evil spirits or witches. But the actor's mistake is not of the ordinary factual kind. The actor, even if shown the body, the organs, the DNA, and so forth, would probably have said, "Yes, it looks like a human being, but see that mole: that mole proves that this is really a witch. Witches look like human beings in all respects, right down to their DNA, but they are not."

Assuming these actors were otherwise sane, what should we say regarding whether they acted culpably? Their mistakes were, unlike the usual mistakes that negate *mens rea* in criminal law, not factual

---

[36] Leo Katz, *Bad Acts and Guilty Minds: Conundrums of the Criminal Law* (1987).

but metaphysical. These actors believed in a richer ontology than the criminal law contemplates.

Were they nonetheless reckless under our scheme? Or do bizarre metaphysical mistakes exculpate just as do factual mistakes, no matter how bizarre? If one accepted their ontological views the way we argue one must accept actors' factual views when assessing culpability, then it would be difficult to deem them culpable. Believing one's victim is a "witch" would be no different in its exculpatory power from believing one's victim is a scarecrow, not a live human being. Of course, to the extent that the actor is aware of some risk that he may be wrong (she might not be a "witch" despite the fact that "she looks like one"),[37] the actor might still be reckless for taking the risk of killing a nonwitch. Whether he would be will depend in how he estimates the competing risks, and what dangers he believes witches present.

4. Deontological Norms and Consequentialist Justifications

In balancing risks and reasons, we must also take into account deontological constraints on when actions may be consequentially justified. This leads to the question of whether we deem an actor who violates a deontological norm in order to do good – for example, he draws blood from nonconsenting X in order to save the lives of Y and Z – to have acted with insufficient concern. We are inclined to say that appropriating another for one's own purposes, however benign, simply *is* manifesting insufficient concern toward that person. In such cases, the risks cannot be outweighed by the actor's reasons. We take up this issue much more fully in Chapter 4, and we raise it again in Chapter 8 when we look at the retributive desert of those who act in ways that are justified by a consequentialist calculus but who violate deontological side constraints.

B. ASSESSING THE RISK

1. The Holism of Risk Assessment

In determining whether the actor is reckless, risk is assessed holistically. That is, we aggregate risks. Suppose, as will ordinarily be the case,

---

[37] This is the test according to *Monty Python and the Holy Grail* (EMI Films, 1975): "How do you know she's a witch?" "Because she looks like one."

that a given act increases by varying amounts the risks to various legally protected interests. So the actor might believe that act A increases the risk to legally protected interest I_1 by R_1, increases the risk to legally protected interest I_2 by R_2, and so on. His culpability for A is a function of the sum of the risks he imposes on those interests. It is not just based on, say, the highest risk A imposes, or on the risk to the most important interest. An armed robbery increases the risk to the bank's money by a significant amount, to the physical safety of employees and customers by a different amount, to their emotional states by a still different amount, and so on. The risks created are to different interests and are of different magnitudes. Similarly, a speeding car increases risks of death, of bodily injury, and of property damage, and again the risks are of different magnitudes. Even if no one of the risks, viewed in isolation, would render the speeding reckless, the sum of them might. This is what we mean by the "holism" of risk assessment.

This raises the concern that if one were accidentally to kill in the commission of what is, under current law, a petty crime, our analysis would treat the accidental homicide as a reckless homicide so long as the commission of the petty crime entailed an ever-so-slight increase in the risk of an accidental killing (and the actor disregarded this risk). For the petty crime is unjustifiable, making every risk it imposes an unjustifiable risk, no matter how slight. We accept this result. First, as we argue in Chapter 5, results should not matter to desert and punishability. But, second, the holism of risk assessment means that committing a petty crime is reckless, not with respect to any discrete legal interest such as death but with respect to the whole array of legal interests the risks to which it increases. Because the actor believed that the increased risk of accidental death was very small, whereas the increased risk to whatever interest the petty crime is concerned with was much greater, his overall culpability for his recklessness will be pretty low, as compared with one who adverts to a high risk of death and a low risk to a petty interest.[38] One is not discretely reckless as to death, discretely

[38] This means, of course, that the recklessness involved in committing what is – again, under current law – a petty crime will vary according to the circumstances. One who attempts to kill a deer out of season will be reckless with respect to, inter alia, killing or wounding a human being. But he will be more or less reckless depending on whether he shoots at the deer in a sparsely or heavily populated area, or uses a bow and arrow or a bazooka. One would expect that the culpability for committing and attempting to commit what are

reckless as to injury, and so forth for a given act; one is just reckless, as determined by the sum of risks and interests, with the level of culpability determined by which interests are subjected to which risks (and, of course, why).

There is a second nettlesome problem lurking in this neighborhood. Consider Frankie, who is driving quite carefully to Johnny's house, intending to kill him. She is aware that even careful driving increases the risks of death, injury, property damage, and so on. And her *reason* for driving – to kill Johnny – is surely not a reason that would justify imposing even very tiny risks on anyone. So should we conclude that her *driving* – remember, it is *careful* driving – is reckless?

There are two possible solutions that we reject. One is to resurrect the substantiality prong of recklessness; the other is to measure risk by comparison to a counterfactual baseline. Ultimately, it is our view that we should accept that Frankie *is* reckless, even if she is only slightly so.

First, as we stated previously, we believe there are good reasons to reject the substantiality prong. Actors who play low-risk Russian roulette impose risks (albeit minuscule ones) for bad reasons. We believe these actors are culpable. Moreover, when an actor purposefully tries to harm another, it is immaterial how unlikely the risk of success is; if the actor believes he has even the slightest chance of success, he still acts purposefully and may, under current law, be punished quite severely despite his estimated low probability of success. We see no reason why it is normatively or conceptually desirable to view low-level risk imposition as immune from criminal liability.

The other possibility involves the baseline by which increases or decreases in risk are measured. For example, if Frankie were not driving to kill Johnny, would she be sitting at home watching TV, imposing virtually no risk to anyone of anything untoward, or would she instead be driving to the mall to shop, a route that is more heavily trafficked than the route to Johnny's house and thus entails higher risks to others from

---

crimes under current law already includes culpability for the average amount of risk such crimes and attempts create regarding interests other than the interest that is the crime's primary concern. But if the crime is committed in a way that imposes above-average risks on these other interests, the actor could justifiably be punished for the basic crime or attempt and for the additional amount of recklessness.

even careful driving? If she would be going to the mall, then her driving to Johnny's seems to be decreasing, not increasing, risks to others.[39]

One problem with a counterfactual analysis is figuring out what the actor would have been doing if she had not been doing what she did. There seems to be an endless array of possibilities, and the only thing we know about Frankie is that she chose to do what she did at that time; thus, it seems wholly speculative to predict what she would have been doing had she not made the very choice that she did make, and speculative in a way that seems immaterial to the culpability of what she did choose.

The counterfactual also presents a second problem. A counterfactual analysis takes us outside the subjective decision making of the actor

---

[39] This counterfactual analysis may well be relevant in assessing damages in tort law. *See* Ariel Porat, "Offsetting Risks" (Olin Working Paper No.316, University of Chicago Law and Economics, 2007), available at SSRN: http://ssrn.com/abstract_id=946764. We argue here only that the counterfactual analysis should not be relevant in assessing culpability and hence criminal liability.

We should point out that were Frankie on a dual purpose trip – if, for example, she were driving safely to the grocery store, but planned to stop at Johnny's house en route and kill him – then her driving would *not* be reckless. Our claim that her driving is reckless is premised on the assumption that killing Johnny is her sole reason for driving. On the other hand, the mere fact Frankie is aware that another person, one in need of groceries, could drive Frankie's precise route and manner nonculpably does *not* eliminate *her* culpability. Someone else's reasons are not hers. Nor does this point contradict the position we take in Chapter 4 that an actor can be justified in imposing risks if he is aware of the existence of justifying reasons for his precise act, even if he is not motivated by those reasons. Frankie's awareness that another person, in need of groceries, could nonculpably drive precisely as she is driving does not mean she is aware of reasons that justify *her* act. (If Frankie's trip and her route had a dual purpose – kill Johnny *and* get groceries – then her carefully driving that route would *not* be culpable.)

Finally, the Frankie and Johnny scenario is useful in illustrating why purpose should be folded into recklessness. For under current law, if Frankie were to kill Johnny in a traffic accident while en route to his house to kill him with her .45, whether her killing of Johnny could be deemed "purposeful" would turn on whether Frankie was pleased, a la the Jackal, to be increasing the risk ever so slightly of killing Johnny by driving (safely) toward his house (rather than walking or biking there) – even though she thought her chances of killing him by shooting him were much, much greater – or whether, instead, Frankie wanted to kill Johnny only by shooting him, either because she wanted to have the time en route to reconsider, or because she wanted Johnny to know that she was going to kill him and to hear her reasons. In the latter case, Frankie's accidental killing of Johnny is only reckless, in the former case it is purposeful. (Indeed, it would be purposeful through "transferred intent" even if Frankie's accident killed someone other than Johnny, just as would the Jackal's killing be purposeful if the bullet struck someone other than de Gaulle.) Yet the culpability in the two cases seems roughly the same.

and into a hypothetical objective construct. In assessing recklessness, we need to know what the actor perceived her conduct to be risking and what her reasons for imposing that risk were. Certainly, if Larry goes to a nearby shopping mall to randomly fire a machine gun for the fun of it, it would be no defense for Larry to claim that his conduct actually decreased the risk to others because had that mall been closed he would have gone to a mall three blocks farther away, where *more* people would have been present. Larry and Frankie both impose risks that they are not at liberty to impose.

Our analysis seems to commit us to the claim that because the purpose of Frankie's trip is illicit, all risks she adverts to are themselves illicit. This is exactly right. Someone who drives 100 miles per hour just to be able to see the first pitch of the game is reckless because his reasons for driving 100 miles per hour do not justify the risks he adverts to; likewise, even Frankie's low level of advertent risk imposition is unjustifiable given her reasons for action. A carefully driving would-be murderer is acting recklessly in driving to the scene of the crime. As we argue in Chapter 6, those whom the criminal law now deems guilty of "inchoate crimes" – solicitation, conspiracy, and (incomplete "substantial step") attempts – are not in fact culpable for the risks they have as yet failed to unleash. They are, however, culpable for the perceived risks they are currently unleashing en route to their ultimate criminal objective.

We suspect that the reason why Frankie's case seems so intuitively problematic is because she is *driving*. Driving has become an absolute necessity in many areas of the country – people must drive to get to work, to go grocery shopping, and so on; and yet, driving surely imposes a myriad of risks on others. We are forced to tolerate these risks to some extent, and speed limits set a presumptive level of permissible risking. We allow people to drive within this level of risk creation, even when their reasons do not justify it. Thus, even if Deborah (mentioned earlier) only slightly liked driving, so long as she is driving carefully, we do not stop to ask her reasons for action. In principle, though, we should. Simply put, we should not be driving if we do not have a good reason for imposing the risks of driving on others. Once we get outside of the driving context, Frankie no longer appears problematic. If she walks to Johnny's house with a gun strapped to her back and it misfires (a low-level risk she was conscious of), she is certainly reckless (and would have been so even had it not misfired). If she fires a rocket at Johnny that misses him and hits Joe – a risk she estimated to be low but greater than zero – she is surely reckless. The case of careful driving en route to kill Johnny is no different.

In summary, we believe that risks should be assessed holistically. All of the reasons that the actor has for acting are weighed against all of the risks of which she is aware.

2. Opaque Recklessness

Even if we assess risk holistically, it may first appear as though it is unlikely that any actor actually parses through and consciously disregards all the risks inherent in her conduct.[40] What if the actor's thought is "this is risky" without any thought of the precise magnitude of the risk or the precise interests put at risk? Such an actor is "opaquely reckless." What should we do with such cases? We believe that oftentimes the actor is just as culpable as when she is fully aware of the risk (is "transparently" reckless).

Our defense requires a brief discussion of the conscious and preconscious. Following Michael Moore, we believe that consciousness is "the kind of awareness we have as an experience."[41] Consciousness is therefore to be distinguished from (1) the "preconscious," the domain of routine actions that have become so habitual that we need not focus on them but can, when necessary, call them to mind, and (2) the "unconscious" in the Freudian sense.[42] Moore suggests that we learn many behaviors that we do not monitor consciously.[43] Thus, many of our "conscious" actions are relegated to preconscious monitoring. And Moore contends that, even when we think about complex actions, we are "dimly aware" of the more discrete bodily movements that we are undertaking.[44] Moore adds that "even when this dim awareness of the movement is absent, it is nonetheless accessible to consciousness. It is preconscious in the sense of easily called to mind if attention is focused on it, and so remains part of

---

[40] This section draws from Ferzan, "Opaque Recklessness," *supra* note 35.
[41] Moore, *supra* note 28, at 15.
[42] *Id.* at 152.
[43] *Id.* at 151–152.
[44] *Id.* at 154.

a person's mental states."[45] Moore concludes that although these bodily movements may have become so routine that they remain in our preconscious – and, in fact, may be hard to focus on in our conscious awareness – the objects of our intentions are discrete bodily movements.[46]

This account seems to be correct. With many complex movements, we do not focus on each discrete bodily movement, just on our overarching goals. Yet we are able and may choose to focus on each individual movement. It is simply the fact that these behaviors have become so routine, so easy for us, that we need not pay attention to them. Thus, when someone is driving, many of his actions are part of his preconscious. The driver no longer has to focus on how to stay in his lane, how to turn the wheel, and so forth. The intention to cause these various bodily movements exists at the preconscious level.

We believe that our understanding of the risks inherent in a given activity may also exist at the preconscious level. Consider an actor who decides to run a red light, thinking "this is dangerous." If we ask what she has consciously chosen to do, she will reply: to engage in risky or dangerous activity. If further inquiry is made, the driver can immediately rattle off the reasons why running the light is dangerous. She might say that it is dangerous because she might cause an accident or hit a pedestrian. The actor may not focus on each and every consequence of her actions; nevertheless, the reasons why her actions are risky are immediately accessible to her.

By contrast, the negligent driver, who diverts her attention from the road to change the radio station, never thinks that she will fail to look up in time to avoid running a red light (and thus killing a pedestrian). That risk does not make it into her preconscious awareness and thus is not accessible to her in any way. If the negligent driver does not advert to any risk, ex ante, nowhere in her mind is there any awareness about any risk that she is running. Surely, she may have background knowledge about why it is a bad thing to run red lights, but asking her why it is dangerous

---

[45] *Id. See also* Ken Simon's discussion of "latent knowledge" in Kenneth W. Simons, "Does Punishment for 'Culpable Indifference' Simply Punish for 'Bad Character'? Examining the Requisite Connection between Mens Rea and Actus Reus," 6 *Buff. Crim. L. Rev.* 219, 250–253 (2002).

[46] Moore, *supra* note 28, at 154.

to run the red light ex ante is no different from asking you, the reader, as you sit in your desk chair, why one should not be running red lights.

The opaquely reckless and negligent actors may also differ in reaction when a harm materializes. The opaquely reckless actor may be upset that the harm she risked actually materialized – in the same way that a transparently reckless actor might react. The negligent actor, on the other hand, is likely to be surprised by the materialization of the harm.

Descriptively, then, the "opaquely reckless" actor with whom we are concerned is someone who both consciously chooses to create a risk – to act in a way that she understands to be "risky" or "dangerous" (or some other vague description) – and preconsciously understands why that act *is* "risky" or "dangerous." Normatively, we must ask whether we should hold the opaquely reckless actor responsible for the preconscious aspects of her decision making. The answer to this question depends on whether the preconscious description informs her practical reasoning. If the preconscious aspect is part of her choice, she may fairly be held accountable for it.

In our view, opaquely reckless actors are just as reckless as purely reckless actors. To be rational, the driver, when asked, "Why is this dangerous?" must have an answer: "This action is dangerous because it risks lives, injury, and property damage." [47] Given that the actor must have a sense of what he means when he consciously thinks that an activity is "dangerous," that meaning must figure in his practical reasoning about whether to engage in the activity. He may have habitualized that the concept of "dangerousness includes risking harm to other people's lives or property"; therefore, these specific risks may not consciously enter his decision making. Nevertheless, it is still appropriate to view this underlying conception of dangerousness as part of the actor's decision making because "dangerous" must mean something to the actor. It does not exist in the actor's mind independent of its meaning. Or, to put our argument within the rubric of philosophy of mind, we are not impermissibly substituting references; we are simply looking to the actor's "sense" of her intentional object. [48]

[47] *Cf.* Michael Luntley, *Contemporary Philosophy of Thought: Truth, World, Content* 238 (1999).
[48] *See id.*

Consequently, when an actor chooses to engage in "dangerous activity," the actor chooses to do what "dangerous activity" means to her. Because this definition of dangerous activity is part of the actor's decision making, it is fair and appropriate to hold her accountable for this definition, just as if she had explicitly referenced the meaning of the dangerous activity in her conscious decision making.

Notably, the determinative factor here is that the actor's understanding of "dangerous" includes the appropriate appreciation of the underlying risk. A defendant is merely negligent if he does not realize his act is highly risky but should, or realizes that it is risky in some respect but not with respect to the harm in question. However, where the actor's sense of the risk does include, even on a preconscious level, the harm sought to be prevented, there is no reason to treat him any differently from the purely reckless actor.

Thus far, we have endeavored to describe opaque recklessness, finding that it involves partly conscious, partly preconscious decision making. We have also explored whether this kind of decision making is sufficient for culpability. To this point, however, we have focused on conduct that is monitored at the conscious level. One consciously chooses to type; the driver consciously chooses to drive; the opaquely reckless actor consciously chooses to engage in "dangerous" behavior. But what of the actor who makes a decision entirely at the preconscious level?

Here, the question is whether we should hold someone responsible for risks to which he never consciously adverts but simply dismisses while on automatic pilot. For instance, when driving, an actor makes many preconscious choices without noticing a pedestrian, another car, or a cyclist. Yet the actor may engage in conduct that imposes substantial and unjustifiable risks on these people. Should this risk taking, created without ever being a part of the actor's consciousness, be considered mere inadvertence to risk, or should it be considered culpable recklessness?

In this area, our prior discussion of the actor's "sense" of the risk, on which we relied for dealing with opaque recklessness, is of little utility. That is because the question is not whether, given one's conscious "sense" of the risk, another preconscious "sense" may be substituted for it. Rather, the question is whether choices made by the preconscious actor are the type of choices for which we may hold the actor culpable.

This turns on the importance of consciousness to culpability. As we discuss in Chapter 4, we do not hold actors culpable for actions taken while in altered states of consciousness, such as sleepwalking. Why is consciousness so fundamental to culpability?

Consider Michael Moore's answer to the question of whether one is responsible for an unconscious action, such as dreaming about killing the emperor?[49] Moore concludes that responsibility for unconscious "actions" violates the moral principle that "ought" implies "can": "Whatever else the principle of responsibility might include, it should include the power or ability to appraise the moral worth of one's proposed actions. A person has such ability only if he has moral and factual knowledge of what he is doing and is able to integrate the two to perceive the moral quality of his action. One who lacks this ability cannot fairly be blamed because, although he is acting intentionally, he does not know that what he is doing is wrong."[50] Thus, for us to deem an actor culpable, she must be able to reason through her actions and choose to do wrong. Where there is no choice, there is no responsibility.

But preconscious decision making is different from "acts" that are purely unconscious. The problem in punishing unconscious acts lies in the failure of the actor to have any control over whether she does wrong. But preconscious decision making is another matter. In the case of preconsciousness, the actor is, at some level, aware of the risk presented. Or is she? Such a question depends on two different meanings of the word "aware," as Daniel Dennett has pointed out.[51] Dennett reveals that when we use the term "aware," we may mean two different things.[52] The first sense we have of the term is introspective; the second is behavioral.[53] A man swerves to avoid a tree, and he can report to us that he was aware that a tree was in his way and that because of it, he moved. Likewise, a bee may swerve to avoid a tree, obviously aware that an obstacle is in its way. But, as Dennett asks, "[w]as the bee aware of the tree as a

---

[49] Michael S. Moore, "Responsibility and the Unconscious," 53 *S. Cal. L. Rev.* 1563, 1619 (1980) (discussing this example of Freud's).

[50] *Id.* at 1624 (footnotes omitted).

[51] D. C. Dennett, *Content and Consciousness* 116–118 (1969).

[52] *Id.* at 114–131.

[53] *Id.*

tree, or just as an obstacle?"[54] The man is aware of the tree both as an introspective reason for avoiding the tree and as a behavioral reason to avoid an obstacle. The bee, on the other hand, does not introspect and decide to avoid the tree; but behaviorally, the bee is aware of some obstacle (the tree).[55] Applying this analysis to our driver on autopilot, he is not aware in the introspective sense of the curves of the road. But he is aware of them in the behavioral sense, thus his ability to navigate them.

Which level of awareness should suffice for culpability? Well, Moore dismissed responsibility for the unconscious because it violates "ought" implies "can." Does the preconscious fall victim to the same problem? It does. As Dennett notes, animals can be aware only on the behavioral level, not on the introspective level, because they lack the propositional attitudes that people have.[56] That is, the introspective sense of awareness can be defined as: "A is [introspectively aware] that p if and only if p is the content of the input state of A's speech center at time t," whereas, behavioral awareness is defined as: "A is [behaviorally aware] that p at time t if and only if p is the content of an internal event in A at time t that is effective in directing current behavior."[57]

Thus, when we act from the preconscious, we are only behaviorally aware of obstacles. To be introspectively aware, we must trigger our speech center and recognize these obstacles as what they are: curves in the road, pedestrians, or other drivers. Without triggering our speech centers, we are not reasoning through our actions and are not appraising their moral worth. To hold us responsible in such cases would be to violate "ought" implies "can."[58]

---

[54] *Id.*

[55] *Id.*

[56] *Id.* at 120 ("People are [behaviorally aware] of things, but also are [introspectively aware] of things, a possibility ruled out in the case of dumb animals").

[57] *Id.* at 118.

[58] Of course, we may be responsible for "delegating" our decision making to our preconscious. This would then be an instance of genetic recklessness, which we discuss in the next section. In contrast to the genetic recklessness position, Samuel Pillsbury has argued that our reliance on awareness is misplaced because it rests on the assumption that perception is passive. Samuel H. Pillsbury, "Crimes of Indifference," 49 *Rutgers L. Rev.* 105 (1996). He contends that "[r]ecognizing that perception represents a learned activity brings it closer to our conception of choice." *Id.* at 143. Thus, because we choose how much attention to devote to any given subject, we may properly be faulted for our perception deficits when we lack a good reason for our failure to recognize obvious risks. *Id.* at 152. Consequently, when we "choose" not to pay attention because we are "indifferent" rather

THE ESSENCE OF CULPABILITY

We have now considered whether preconscious decision making is itself sufficient for culpability. We have concluded that consciousness plays a critical role, realizing that placing moral responsibility on the preconscious violates "ought" implies "can."[59]

than because we have a good reason for our attention failure, Pillsbury argues this indifference, even without advertence to the risk, should be sufficient for both manslaughter and depraved heart murder. *Id.* at 206–213.

Why may we be faulted for our failures of perception? Pillsbury argues that responsibility is appropriate without regard to whether (1) the decision whether to pay attention is made at the time of the act, (2) our "perception priorities" were determined in the past, or (3) our "perception priorities" are unchosen products of our environment and the like. *Id.* at 144–153. Considering these possibilities in turn, each has its own failings. First, examine Pillsbury's argument that the actor is responsible for not paying attention because "he chooses" not to pay attention. Well, who is the "he" here? Is it the actor's conscious decision or is it a preconscious decision? If we make many choices on the preconscious or unconscious level, the question still remains whether these choices are the kinds of choices upon which to rest moral responsibility. When we "choose" not to pay attention, are *we* doing the choosing in a morally significant way?

Even if this choice were properly attributable to the actor, it falls victim to the same problem as Pillsbury's second argument. If we make self-conscious choices about our "perception priorities," we still must find the requisite degree of culpability. When an actor learns to be selfish, to what extent does he appreciate that he might cause future harm? Perhaps we could accept Pillsbury's claim if it were limited to distinguishing between types of negligent actors – selfish inadvertence may be worse than clumsy inadvertence. But Pillsbury is willing to replace recklessness with negligence plus indifference. Under Pillsbury's regime, an actor who embarks on a path of selfishness, never recognizing that this selfishness might result in death to others, may find herself guilty of manslaughter.

Finally, Pillsbury anticipates our next complaint – that indifference, or the roots thereof, may be an unchosen character trait. Untroubled by the steepness of this slippery slope, Pillsbury accepts that "perception priorities may be neither consciously nor freely chosen." *Id.* at 151. He views this determinism as no different than punishing people for their motivations, for which he believes we are responsible. *Id.* at 150–151. We, however, would dispute this view of responsibility. So long as we are rational and not compelled, we have the ability to evaluate our choices and decide whether to violate the law's commands. That one is lazy or poor or greedy may make his choice somewhat harder than it is for others, but this choice is still completely within one's control. However, to blame people for why they have not seen risks – their perception priorities – when these priorities may themselves be unchosen, conflicts with any conception of free will worth having.

Pillsbury, we believe, would argue that we have placed far too great an emphasis on the conscious-preconscious distinction. Drawing on Dennett and others, he shows us that "[t]he line between aware and unaware mental activity appears very much a matter of degree." *Id.* at 147. But this difference in degree is where responsibility rests. We are not responsible for our heartbeats, even if our body and mind control them, nor are we responsible for our dreams, despite our unconscious control over them. What we are responsible for are those actions that we can do something about – where we can decide whether to act. And to have this sort of control, we must be aware, in the introspective sense, of what we are doing.

59 We have also explored alternative means for holding the preconscious actor responsible – looking to prior culpable choices and to failures in perception priorities. We have

However, nothing in this section undermines the fact that the opaquely reckless actor should be considered reckless whenever the actor recognizes on a conscious level that her behavior is "risky" and is aware on a preconscious level why her conduct is "risky."

Thus, we believe that where the actor consciously recognized that her conduct was "dangerous" and, at the preconscious level, appreciated the reasons why her conduct was dangerous, she may be said to be "conscious" of those risks. Whether she is reckless turns on whether her reasons for acting outweigh the degree of risk that she recognizes (even preconsciously).

3. *Genetic Recklessness*

Sometimes the actor's act at T_1 creates an unjustifiable risk that the actor himself will engage in nonculpable but highly risky behavior at T_2. Suppose, for example, that the actor gets highly intoxicated at T_1, so intoxicated that he cannot be deemed a responsible actor at T_2. He might, at T_2, drive a car dangerously and kill someone, or brandish a weapon and do so. He might cause lesser harms. Or he might luckily avoid injuring anyone. The same goes for an actor who deliberately fails to take his antipsychotic medication, or for the actor who deliberately fails to take his antiseizure medication before driving a car.

The Model Penal Code approach is to wait until T_2 to assess the actor's culpability. If he harms someone through risky behavior that he would have realized was too risky had he been sober or on his medications, then the Model Penal Code deems him guilty of recklessly causing the harm.[60] If he does not cause harm or engage in conduct that itself would be the crime of reckless endangerment,[61] he is not guilty of any crime.

The proper analysis is to view the actor's act at T_2 as the result of his reckless act at T_1. If results do not affect culpability, as we argue in Chapter 5, what the actor does or does not do at T_2 should be immaterial. If the actor's act at T_1 created, for insufficient reasons, what the

---

concluded that any prior choice likely lacks the requisite degree of culpability, and that the "choice" of perception priorities is elusive.

[60] Model Penal Code § 2.08(2) (1985).

[61] As we have shown, the notion of conduct itself being objectively reckless despite not causing harm requires the incoherent notion of "objective risk."

actor perceives as a risk of harmful conduct at T_2, then the actor acted recklessly at T_1 and should be punished for his act at T_1 *irrespective of what occurs thereafter.*[62]

C. REASONS AND JUSTIFICATION

Although we defend our view of justification in Chapter 4, at this point it is necessary to discuss how justification figures in the recklessness calculus. First, we should note that frequently – usually? – the actor's beliefs about justifying facts are, like his beliefs about risks, probabilistic. Thus, Driver might believe not that his passenger will certainly die unless rushed to the hospital but only that there is a probability P that he might die. If P is low enough, or R is high enough with respect to others' injury or death, then Driver's rushing the passenger to the hospital might indeed be reckless.

However, unlike risk, justification is objective. In general, the actor's mistaken belief that his reason X justifies his act's risk R is immaterial to his culpability. That is, once we know that David is rushing home to get to the Knicks game, and he believes his speeding is increasing the risk of harm to persons, property, and the like, then the balance of perceived risks versus reasons for imposing risks is itself a question of law. David is reckless even if he sincerely believes that watching the Knicks game *is* more important than human lives. On the other hand, if Darren is speeding to get a passenger to the hospital but is mistaken about how sick his passenger is – and Darren's reason (sick passenger), if Darren's beliefs were correct (the passenger *is* ill), *would* justify the risk – then Darren is not reckless. But if his mistake is not about the facts giving rise to the reason but about the *weight* of the reason and whether

[62] Many cases of inadvertent negligence – which, as we argue in Chapter 3, is itself nonculpable – may be the result of earlier reckless and therefore culpable acts. The parents of William Tabafunda might have decided to skip out on the parenting class on "How to Spot Dangerous Medical Conditions in Your Children," realizing that by doing so they were creating some (probably small) risk to William, but wanting to watch Fear Factor on television. *Cf.* State v. Williams, 484 P.2d 1167 (Wash. Ct. App. 1971). If so, they may have been reckless, albeit only slightly so. But that act, not their subsequent failure to recognize William's life-threatening condition, should have been the focus of their prosecution. *See* Larry Alexander, "Reconsidering the Relationship among Voluntary Acts, Strict Liability, and Negligence in Criminal Law," 7 *Soc. Phil. & Pol'y* 84 (1990).

it justifies the risk, such a mistake is in most instances immaterial to his culpability.

At the theoretical level, our approach eliminates the problem of *inculpatory legal mistakes*. As an illustration, consider an actor who believes that reason X does *not* justify the risk R he is imposing *when in fact it does*. Thus, consider Doug, who believes that it is legally impermissible to drive eighty-five miles per hour to get his sick passenger to the hospital but does so anyway. In fact, his reasons for action do justify his speed. If Doug's legal analysis about what reasons justify what risks cannot exculpate him, can it inculpate him?

We think not. In Doug's case, he has essentially done two calculations. First, he has judged that, *from his perspective*, it is so important to get his passenger to the hospital that it is worth the risks to others. If he did not think so, he would not speed to the hospital. After all, he has already assessed that his friend is sick, and that this is a sufficient reason to drive fast. Second, Doug believes that *the law* forbids this speeding. Yet, despite Doug's belief that his act is legally unjustified, he has not shown insufficient concern for others. Rather, his concern for others *actually mirrors* the calculation the law makes.[63]

In looking at whether the actor's reasons justify the risk he believes himself to be taking, we must also ask which reasons count. Must the reasons that either justify or fail to justify the actor's imposition of risks be the reasons that actually motivate the actor, or can they be merely reasons of which the actor is aware but that do not actually motivate him? (Given that risks are either one or zero, the actor obviously has to be at least aware of justifying reasons; otherwise, any putatively reckless act that failed to cause harm would be nonreckless *because there were reasons of which the actor was unaware that did in fact justify the act, given that it was harmless*.) But is it sufficient that the actor is aware of reasons that *would* justify his risk imposition even if he is motivated by reasons that do not justify the risk imposition?

For example, suppose the driver with the passenger who needs urgent medical care would not race him to hospital were that not a risky

---

[63] We take up some complications when we consider proxy crimes, crimes that are defined to capture stock examples of insufficient concern but that include some case of sufficient concern within their scope. If an actor shows sufficient concern but believes he is violating a proxy crime when he is not, has he acted culpably?

thing to do. (He is motivated by the thrill of imposing risks on others and unmotivated by saving his passenger's life.) But he also knows that saving his passenger's life is a reason that is sufficiently important to justify his risk imposition. In our view, if he then races at high speed to the hospital, he should *not* be deemed reckless. (One might imagine an ambulance driver who simply loves the thrill of running red lights, or an executioner who enjoys killing people.) The law seeks to guide an individual to act or to forbear. We do not care why an actor avoids committing a crime so long as he does. That is, the actor may not be motivated by the law's prohibition but may still have other reasons not to commit a crime. For example, an actor may decide not to take possession of something she believes to be stolen property, not because the law forbids such an action (a prohibition of which she is aware), but because she does not care for the property. So long as the actor's practical reasoning is informed by justifying reasons, it should not matter that the actor is not motivated by those reasons.

Now it is certainly the case that our nonreceiver of stolen property (or our thrill-seeking rescuer or misanthropic executioner) is not an admirable person. He does not act for the reasons for which we would like him to act. Nevertheless, although he *has* insufficient concern for the interests of others, his actions do not *display* insufficient concern. He is perhaps a bad person but not a bad actor.[64]

It is worth explicating the implications of our position for the permissibility of actions by third parties. If a third party is aware of the justifying reasons, he may permissibly aid an actor who is undertaking an act the actor believes to be risky irrespective of the actor's awareness of the justifying reasons or the actor's culpability. That is, a third party may permissibly lend his car to the thrill-seeking rescuer to drive

---

[64] This distinction between bad actor and bad person may explain some of the experimental findings identified by Knobe and Doris. *See* Joshua Knobe and John M. Doris, "Strawsonian Variations: Folk Morality and the Search for a Unified Theory," in *The Oxford Handbook of Moral Psychology* (J. M. Doris et al., eds., forthcoming).

In Chapter 4 we make a concession, prompted by Mitch Berman, that in some situations, it is possible that an actor who is aware of reasons that would justify his risk imposition is still not justified in imposing the risk if those reasons are not his reasons for acting – that is, they do not motivate his action. Even then the actor himself may have difficulty determining whether he would have acted in the absence of either the justifying reasons or the motivating ones.

the passenger to the hospital so long as the third party believes that the passenger is ill and speeding is therefore necessary. Even if the actor himself is not motivated by these reasons – and even if he does not know these reasons exist and is himself acting culpably in speeding – the third-party car owner's act of lending the car is still justified. The actor may be acting recklessly (as he would be were he unaware of the passenger's illness), but the third party is not. Indeed, in some cases, a third party may *encourage* the actor's culpable act, which is reckless from the actor's perspective but quite salutary from the third party's.

If someone perceives reasons that justify a risky act, he may undertake that act or encourage another to undertake it, even if the one encouraged would be culpable (because he is unaware of the justifying reasons), and even if the one who perceives the justifying reasons is not motivated by them. If Strategic Bomber would be justified in bombing the munitions factory despite the civilians he will kill, Terror Bomber will be justified in bombing it *and will be nonculpable if he is aware of, though not motivated by, the supporting strategic reasons.* Moreover, even if Terror Bomber is unaware of the justification and thus culpable in bombing, if Strategic Bomber would be justified in bombing, one who *is* aware of the justifying reasons may encourage Terror Bomber to bomb.

Again, as we earlier noted, but it is important to bear in mind, the actor's beliefs about justifying facts, like his beliefs about risks, are probabilistic. The driver may believe not that it is certain his passenger will die unless rushed to the hospital but only that there is a certain probability P that he might die. Whether the actor is reckless will then turn on the relative magnitude of P with respect to outcomes for the passenger and R with respect to outcomes for those at risk from the actor's driving. The higher the probability of a really bad outcome for the passenger and the lower the risk of bad outcomes for those at risk from the actor's driving, the more we are compelled to the conclusion that the actor is not culpable or is culpable only to a slight degree. Conversely, the lower the probability of bad outcomes for the passenger and the higher the risk of bad outcomes for those at risk from the actor's driving, the more we are compelled to the opposite conclusion. The same holds for third-party interveners: *their* culpability for aiding (or resisting) the actor's act turns not on the *actor's* culpability but on *their* estimate of the probability of justifying facts – good outcomes – and the risks of bad outcomes. What is crucial to keep in mind is first, that justifying reasons are, like risks of bad outcomes, probabilistic and must be discounted by the probabilities the actor assigns to them and, second, that it is each actor's subjective *beliefs* about the probabilities of outcomes, good and bad, that determines *his* culpability.

D. SINCERE, UNREASONABLE, AND RECKLESS BELIEFS AND THE CULPABILITY DETERMINATION

In Chapters 5, 6, and 7, we discuss what sort of *act* suffices for a culpable act. (We argue there that the actor must believe he has unleashed an unjustifiable risk, even if he has not, but that *any* act that the actor believes unleashes such a risk suffices for culpability.) Here, we want to address further how the actor's beliefs affect the culpability of his actions. First, we believe the focus of the culpability judgment is the actor's actual beliefs about the effects of his acts – and not the reasonableness or unreasonableness of those beliefs. That is, suppose the actor believes that fact F exists, and that F supports reason X, which in turn justifies risk R. And suppose that F does indeed support X, which does indeed justify R. But suppose the actor is mistaken about F's existence. As we have argued at length, if, taking the facts as the actor believes them to be, his action is justified, then his action is not culpable. This means that the question of whether the actor's beliefs were reasonable simply drops out of the calculation. In other words, even if the actor's assessment of the situation is unreasonable (from some external point of view), this alone is not sufficient to render the actor culpable. Our analysis is based on two claims: first, that negligence is not itself culpable; and, second, that there is no such thing as a reckless belief.

In Chapter 3 we are going to argue that negligence – "unreasonable" underestimation of risk or overestimation of the benefits the risky action will produce – is not culpable. That means the actor's mistake about R – given that true risks are either one or zero, *all* beliefs about R, where R is greater than zero but less than one, are mistaken – is never itself culpable just for being "unreasonable." The same should be true of the actor's "unreasonable" mistake about F, the facts that would, if present, give rise to the justifying reasons. Negligence regarding the justifying facts should not be deemed culpable.

But what if the actor's unreasonable belief in R or F were "reckless?"[65] That is, what if the actor has a reckless belief about his act's riskiness, or a reckless belief in facts that, were they present, would justify the risks he believes his act imposes? But note the oddity of the notion of a *reckless belief*, as opposed to a *reckless act* based on a belief. It seems to us that the notion of a reckless belief is incoherent. With respect to R, the actor's belief regarding R's magnitude necessarily includes his belief about the magnitude of 1 − R. And with respect to F, the notion of a reckless belief posits a belief that F is true, coupled with a belief that it is so likely F is untrue that it is unjustifiable to believe F is true. In believing F with probability P, the actor has already taken account of the likelihood (1 − P) that F does not exist. If the actor's believing F at probability P does justify his imposing risk R, then his believing not-F with likelihood 1 − P cannot render his act unjustified − for it is only the logical corollary of his justifying belief.

Because we need not focus on negligence (because it is nonculpable), and because "reckless beliefs" are an incoherent concept, all we need to determine insofar as recklessness is concerned is what did the actor sincerely believe about the risks he was imposing and about the facts supporting justifying reasons for imposing those risks. We need not determine whether his factual beliefs were "reasonable." We need address only the actor's actions as he perceived them.

E. RECKLESSNESS AND ACT AGGREGATION

A final clarification about how the actor's actions are assessed: the recklessness analysis applies to discrete acts and not to aggregations of acts. Suppose the actor performs A believing it poses a 0.01 risk of death or serious injury. And suppose his reasons justify that level of risk. But suppose, as well, that the actor intends to repeat A day after day, with the same risks and reasons each time − for example, he's building a tunnel, and A is careful dynamiting. With enough repetitions, the risk of death or injury over time will rise to a high level. Nonetheless, the recklessness analysis should be focused on each discrete risky act. (We take up how to individuate acts in Chapter 7.)

---

[65] This formulation is suggested by the Model Penal Code § 3.09(2) (1985).

There are some further implications that we should mention. First, our folding knowledge (and purpose) into recklessness means that we do not have to concern ourselves with whether those like the tunnel builder who repeatedly engage in acts, each of which carries a low probability of harm, but which with enough repetitions raise the probability that one of them will cause to harm to almost a certainty, "knowingly" cause the harm if and when it occurs. They may believe to a practical certainty that if they repeat these acts a sufficient number of times, they will eventually cause harm. However, whether they do so "knowingly" is beside the point. All that matters is what risk the actor believes is entailed by each particular act, and whether that risk is justified by reasons the actor is cognizant of when acting (and the probability the actor assigns to their existence). If the risks of tunnel building – say, to bystanders who have not consented to their imposition – are justifiable given the benefits of tunnels, then even if the risk is very high that, say, seven people will be killed in the process, tunnel building is not a culpable activity. Nor is any component act thereof culpable if it is not too risky in itself given the costs of less risky alternatives. This is merely the corollary of the point made earlier: Even a very minimally risky act *is* reckless if undertaken for frivolous or malicious reasons (and no weightier reasons exist of which the actor is aware).

(We leave aside the interesting moral question of whether it matters that most repetitive activities that are risky to bystanders, such as tunnel building, automobile and air travel, blasting, and so on, impose their risks on "statistical" rather than on identifiable persons. Suppose, for example, that the risks of tunnel building were concentrated on one known individual – Sam. Sam lives near the construction site, has a rare medical condition such that repetitive jack-hammering will eventually cause him to die, and cannot be moved. If tunnel building's benefits justify the loss of several statistical lives, does it likewise justify the killing of Sam?[66] It is possible that some acts are justifiable only if, from our ungodlike epistemic vantage point, the risks of an act are borne by many individuals rather than concentrated on one – even if God knows the one on whom the harm will actually fall, and whose risk is therefore one.)

[66] *See* Guido Calabresi and Phillip Bobbitt, *Tragic Choices* (1978).

IV. Proxy Crimes

Some crimes may usefully be distinguished as "proxy crimes." [67] As Richard McAdams explains, a proxy crime refers to prohibited behavior that, "while not inherently risking harm, stands in for behavior that does risk harm." [68] McAdams points out that "frequently the origin of a proxy crime is a modification of a pre-existing offense where the conduct did inherently risk harm. The legislature decides, however, that it is difficult for the prosecutor to prove all the elements of the standard crime, so [it removes] ... certain hard-to-prove elements, including ones that produced a necessary risk of harm. The result is a prophylactic crime, that bars conduct that neither causes nor risks harm but is correlated with conduct that is harmful or risky." [69]

If we substitute for the ultimate harms we wish to prevent the conduct proscribed by the proxy crime, then just as we can have culpable risking of ultimate harms, we can have culpable riskings of that conduct, or so it might seem. The actor may believe that what he is doing creates the risk R that he will engage or is engaging in the proxy conduct. If the actor's reasons are insufficient to justify risk R, the actor appears to be culpable.

But is he? Suppose the actor believes he is creating risk R_P of the proxy conduct but only a much lower risk R_H of the ultimate harm. And suppose his reasons justify taking risk R_H. Then no matter how high R_P, one could argue that the actor is justified in taking that risk. In other words, if the actor is justified in risking the ultimate harm, he cannot be *unjustified* in risking the proxy conduct.

It is perhaps for this reason that McAdams says that retributivists will reject proxy crimes and that only consequentialists regarding

---

[67] Richard H. McAdams, "A Tempting State: The Political Economy of Entrapment," 43 (Working Paper No. 33, Illinois Law and Economics, 2005). The first use of the term "proxy crime" that we are aware of appears in Moore, *supra* note 28.

[68] McAdams, *supra* note 67, at 44.

[69] *Id.* We should note that proxy crimes may be created not merely to relieve the prosecutor of the need to prove hard-to-prove matters but also to relieve actors of difficulties in estimating whether particular conduct is unduly risky. *See, e.g.,* R. A. Duff, "Criminalizing Endangerment," 65 *La. L. Rev.* 941, 960–961 (2005).

punishment can justify them.[70] For the moment, however, we accept proxy crimes into our repertoire and advert to their possibility from time to time in the following chapters. In Chapter 8, however, when we take up how our theory might be operationalized in a criminal code, and particularly whether the components of culpability may be rebuttably or conclusively presumed from proof of certain conduct,[71] we return to proxy crimes and their legitimacy at much greater length.

We should also point out that a problem structurally identical to that raised by "proxy crimes" for culpability-based punishment is raised by formal legal exclusion of specific justificatory reasons because of slippery-slope, consequentialist fears. Suppose, for example, that some cases of voluntary euthanasia – indeed, some cases of nonvoluntary euthanasia as well (mercy killings) – are in fact justifiable. Suppose also, however, that there is a real risk that if a euthanasia justification is legally countenanced, many more cases of unjustified killings will occur. People in good faith will believe they are in circumstances that justify killing when they are not. And others in bad faith will kill unjustifiably believing that they will escape punishment by convincing a court that their killing was justified, whether or not they in fact do escape punishment. Society may decide that net fewer unjustified killings and forgoings of justified killings will take place if euthanasia is forbidden even in cases where it would otherwise be justifiable. In that event, an actor who commits otherwise justifiable euthanasia, aware of the justifying facts, will still be punished. But is such an actor culpable, and if not, is his punishment justifiable?[72] We take this issue up again in Chapter 8 when we take up "proxy crimes."

In this chapter, we have sought to clarify insufficient concern, which we take to be the essence of culpability. Insufficient concern entails choosing

---

[70] McAdams, *supra* note 67, at 44. *See also* Douglas Husak, "Crimes outside the Core," 39 *Tulsa L. Rev.* 755 (2004).

[71] For an excellent analysis of this question, though not from a retributivist perspective, *see* Frederick Schauer and Richard Zeckhauser, "Regulation by Generalization," (AEI-Brookings Joint Center for Regulatory Studies, Working Paper No. 05-16, 2005), available at http://ksgnotes1.harvard.edu/Research/wpaper.nsf/rwp/RWP05-048.

[72] *See* Larry Alexander and Emily Sherwin, *The Rule of Rules: Morality, Rules and the Dilemmas of Law* 92 (2001).

to take risks to others' legally protected interests for insufficient reasons. We have argued that a modified version of recklessness embodies insufficient concern, as a comparison of risks and reasons, and that purpose and knowledge may be normatively and conceptually folded into this evaluation. We have also addressed particular questions about how risks and reasons are identified and balanced. In the next chapter, we argue that negligence does not manifest insufficient concern and is not an appropriate target of the criminal law.

III

Negligence

Unlike purpose and knowledge, negligence cannot be collapsed into recklessness. To be negligent, one does not advert to (in the sense of "be aware of") the unreasonable risk that one is creating with respect either to the proscribed result or to the proscribed nature of one's conduct. It is adverting to such risks that converts one's negligent conduct into recklessness. True negligence is inadvertent creation of unreasonable risks. What distinguishes negligence from strict liability is that the negligent actor's unawareness of the risk is a failure to meet the objective "reasonable person" standard.

The Model Penal Code's definition of negligence is representative:

> *Negligently.* A person acts negligently with respect to a material element of an offense when he should be aware of a substantial and unjustifiable risk that the material element exists or will result from his conduct. The risk must be of such a nature and degree that the actor's failure to perceive it, considering the nature and purpose of his conduct and

the circumstances known to him, involves a gross deviation from the standard of care that a reasonable person would observe in the actor's situation.[1]

I. Why Negligence Is Not Culpable

Essentially, those who deem negligence to be culpable argue that failure to advert to a risk that one had a fair chance to perceive (had one tried) is culpable, even though it does not entail a conscious choice to produce or to unreasonably risk harm.[2]

We disagree.[3] The world is full of risks to which we are oblivious. Or, more accurately, because risk is an epistemic, not ontic, notion, we frequently believe we are creating a certain level of risk when someone in an epistemically superior position to ours would assess the risk to be higher or lower than we have estimated. Sometimes the epistemically superior position is the product of better information: for example, the doctor knows that what we believe is just a mole is in fact a life-threatening melanoma. At other times, we have failed to notice something that another might have noticed, or we have forgotten something that another might have remembered. Once in a while, our lack of information, failure to notice, failure to make proper inferences from what information we do have, or forgetfulness results in our underestimating the riskiness of our conduct and causing harm.[4]

---

[1] Model Penal Code § 2.02(2)(d) (1985).

[2] Michael D. Bayles, *Principles of Law: A Normative Analysis* 295–300 (1987); H. L. A. Hart, *Punishment and Responsibility: Essays in the Philosophy of Law* 132–140 (1968); James Brady, "Punishment for Negligence: A Reply to Professor Hall," 22 *Buff. L. Rev.* 107, 107–122 (1972); George Fletcher, "The Theory of Criminal Negligence: A Comparative Analysis," 119 *U. Pa. L. Rev.* 401 (1971); Jerome Hall, "Negligent Behavior Should Be Excluded from Penal Liability," 63 *Colum. L. Rev.* 632 (1963); Richard A. Wasserstrom, "H. L. A. Hart and the Doctrines of Mens Rea and Criminal Responsibility," 35 *U. Chi. L. Rev.* 92 (1967).

[3] This section draws from Larry Alexander, "Reconsidering the Relationship among Voluntary Acts, Strict Liability, and Negligence in Criminal Law," 7 *Soc. Phil. & Pol'y* 84 (1990).

[4] It should be borne in mind that the negligent actor is negligent irrespective of whether his act actually causes harm. He may estimate the risk from his act as lower than the non-negligent, "reasonable" actor would have estimated, and it may turn out that his estimate is actually closer to the true risk – zero – than his nonnegligent counterpart.

We are not morally culpable for taking risks of which we are unaware.[5] At any point in time we are failing to notice a great many things, we have forgotten a great many things, and we are misinformed or uninformed about many things. An injunction to notice, remember, and be fully informed about anything that bears on risks to others is an injunction no human being can comply with, so violating this injunction reflects no moral defect. Even those most concerned with the well-being of others will violate this injunction constantly.[6]

II. Attempts at Narrowing the Reach of Negligence Liability

Indeed, because people can make momentary mistakes, and because acts of clumsiness and stupidity hardly seem to be the sort of things for which we wish to hold people criminally liable, even those theorists in favor of punishing for negligence often seek to restrict its reach. That is, even for these theorists, the failure to live up to the "reasonable person" test is not alone sufficient for criminal liability. The challenge for those who wish to punish for negligence, then, is to find a principled way to distinguish those people whose substandard conduct renders them criminally liable from those who do not.

A. SIMONS'S CULPABLE INDIFFERENCE

Ken Simons argues that it is appropriate to hold a negligent actor accountable when she is culpably indifferent. Assume Alice and Betty both fail to appreciate a particular risk while they are driving. Alice fails to do so

---

5 To be fair, the proponent of negligence liability requires that the risk be unjustifiable. Our view, that one is not culpable for taking risks of which we are unaware, perforce, extends to the subset of unjustified risks.

6 It also does not help to say the actor should have gotten more information before he acted. Sometimes, when there is time to wait, the actor will be *reckless* for acting rather than waiting and inquiring further. He will be aware that even though he now perceives the risks of his acting to be low, waiting will reveal whether his perception of the risk is warranted. If his reasons for not waiting are insufficient to justify acting even in the face of the low risk that he perceives, his taking the low risk is unjustifiable. But again, all that shows is that the actor was reckless. It is not a case of negligence.

because she is distracted by a call that a friend is in the hospital. Betty fails to do so because she is putting on lipstick using her rear-view mirror. Whom should the criminal law punish? In an early article, Simons argued that the determination should be made using a counterfactual test: if the person had been aware of the risk, would she have proceeded anyway?[7]

Unfortunately, this test raises new difficulties because it conflicts with our conception of free will (or, perhaps more aptly, our view that actors should be treated as capable of responding to the right reasons at the critical moment of action).[8] It punishes an actor not for what she has done, but for the choice she *might* have made had she been presented with the choice. Under Simons's theory, we should punish Betty if she has the sort of character on the basis of which we would *predict* that she would choose to take this risk had she adverted to it. Yet, many actors in a given set of circumstances might resort to crime, but we should not punish them until they have actually made that choice and acted on it. Responsibility should not turn on the prediction of future choices. Nor should it turn on assessments of the types of people we are.

Indeed, Simons recognized that his theory of culpable indifference creates a "significance in action" problem.[9] That is, feelings about causing harm are passive, so how does one tie culpable indifference to an act? Simons argued that perhaps this desire (or lack thereof) must figure as a factor in the actor's practical reasoning in performing the action.[10] Such an approach, however, looks as if it collapses culpable indifference into our conception of recklessness. The actor is making a choice that involves consciously disregarding the interests of others and is indifferent to these interests in that sense.

Alternatively, Simons asserted that the relationship between indifference and the actor's choice need only be causal.[11] If by causal Simons meant that the indifference figured causally in the actor's deliberations without figuring consciously in them, then, as Michael

---

[7] Kenneth W. Simons, "Culpability and Retributive Theory: The Problem of Criminal Negligence," 5 J. *Contemp. Legal Issues* 365 (1994).

[8] This section draws from Kimberly Kessler Ferzan, "Opaque Recklessness," 91 J. *Crim. L. & Criminology* 597 (2001) and Kimberly Kessler Ferzan, "Don't Abandon the Model Penal Code Yet! Thinking Through Simons's *Rethinking*," 6 *Buff. Crim. L. Rev.* 185 (2002).

[9] Simons, *supra* 7, at 391–394.

[10] *Id.* at 392.

[11] *Id.*

Moore has noted, there are problems with relying on that type of causal approach. For example, when a man forgets his appointment with his girlfriend, "this failure to arrive at the appointed time shows that he does not care, not that he adopted this behavior as a means to show the woman that he no longer cares. His emotion, or lack of it, explains his behavior, but does not mean that he chose, even unconsciously, that specific behavior as the means of achieving some particular desire."[12]

A causal account, moreover, is inherently problematic, as it opens the floodgates to problems associated with determinism. If everything is caused, are we then morally responsible for everything caused through our agency? Or are we responsible for nothing?

In his most recent work on the subject, Simons adopts a six-factor test to resolve the "significance in action" problem.[13] Among the factors that he proposes is the "deflationary" requirement: "The basis of this prediction [that the actor would have acted in the face of a greater risk] is that when the actor is initially prepared to take the action, he possess the 'higher' mental state of knowledge, but by the time he acts, his mental state has 'deflated' to recklessness."[14] In contrast, Simons rejects punishing "inflated" mental states, where we predict the actor would have continued in the face of a greater risk because of "the principle of respecting the actor's autonomy."[15] This restriction is important. However, for us, it does not go far enough, whereas for negligence proponents it may go too far. For the latter, Simons's test fails to punish negligent Betty because that would require "inflating" her culpability. On the other hand, we fail to see why Simons's reasoning that "the actor should be free to change his mind, even if at one point in time he firmly intends to commit a serious crime" does not apply as well to "deflationary cases" in which the actor *does not act* in the face of a greater risk but simply the lesser one that he now perceives.[16] In a deflationary case,

---

[12] Michael S. Moore, "Responsibility and the Unconscious," 53 *S. Cal. L. Rev.* 1563, 1631 (1980).

[13] Kenneth W. Simons, "Does Punishment for 'Culpable Indifference' Simply Punish for 'Bad Character'? Examining the Requisite Connection between Mens Rea and Actus Reus," 6 *Buff. Crim. L. Rev.* 219 (2002).

[14] *Id.* at 275.

[15] *Id.* at 280.

[16] Simons views his account to be an extension of Alan Michaels's acceptance theory. *See* Alan Michaels, "Acceptance: The Missing Mental State," 71 *S. Cal. L. Rev.* 953 (1998). In our

we may have better evidence about what an actor would have otherwise done, but punishment in such a case is still punishment for a choice the actor did not make but (very well) might have made under different circumstances. From either perspective, Simons takes an untenable middle position.

B. TADROS'S CHARACTER APPROACH

Victor Tadros has also sought to narrow negligence.[17] He claims, first, that as agents, what we believe reflects on our character. We are therefore responsible for those things we believe and do not believe if those beliefs are attributable to our virtues and vices. Second, of those beliefs (or lack thereof) for which we are responsible, we should be held criminally responsible for those beliefs that manifest insufficient concern for others' interests.

We have our doubts about both parts of this test.[18] First, consider Tadros's argument that we are responsible for the way that we form beliefs. According to Tadros, our belief formation reflects our character, and we are responsible for those actions that reflect our character. He further claims that the "character" for which we are responsible is evidenced by our desires, including not only those desires with which we identify but also those desires that are alien to us if we make no attempt to change them.

But there is a significant gap between our omitting to get rid of a desire and our actually causing harm to another. First, we might ask at what point the actor becomes aware of this vicious trait. Sometimes we learn about our values only when we act. (Nor would hours of navel gazing or therapy usefully help us to divine some of our own values.) If we do not know we have a desire, how can we be said to accept it? Second, the very character trait that leads to insensitivity to others may prevent

---

view, Michaels's account is quite different as it seeks to track an actual psychological state of the actor – not to punish the actor for a mental state she would have otherwise had. *See* Kimberly Kessler Ferzan, "Holistic Culpability," 28 *Cardozo L. Rev.* 2523, 2531–2532 (2007). Indeed, Michaels himself does not seek to extend acceptance beyond those cases in which the actor is already aware of the risk. Michaels, *supra* note 16, at 962 n.26.

[17] Victor Tadros, *Criminal Responsibility* ch. 9 (2005).

[18] This section draws from Kimberly Kessler Ferzan, "Act, Agency, and Indifference: The Foundations of *Criminal Responsibility*," 10 *New Crim. L. Rev.* 441 (2007).

the actor from recognizing her own character flaws. Finally, even if we know we have a particular desire, is it fair to say that we know what its implications are? How often will an actor recognize that her flaws could result in harm to other people?

As for the second part of the test, we are uncertain as to how an act can manifest insufficient concern for others in the absence of some sort of culpable choice by the actor. The driver who believes that she can put on mascara while driving may have a flawed character, but how exactly is it that her action *manifests* her insufficient concern? Tadros has the very same "significance in action" problem that we saw with Simons's approach.

C. GARVEY'S DOXASTIC SELF-CONTROL THEORY

Stephen Garvey has recently produced a sophisticated argument for why *some* cases of inadvertence to risk are culpable.[19] To the question of how retributive punishment of those who inadvertently create lethal risks can be warranted, Garvey gives this reply:

> The answer I propose is this: An actor who creates a risk of causing death but who was unaware of that risk is fairly subject to retributive punishment if he was either *nonwillfully ignorant* or *self-deceived* with respect to the existence of the risk, and if such ignorance or self-deception was due to the causal influence of a desire he should have controlled. The culpability of such an actor does not consist in any choice to do wrong, but rather in the culpable failure to exercise *doxastic self-control*, i.e., control over desires that influence the formation and awareness of one's beliefs. An actor who is nonwillfully ignorant allows desire to preclude him from forming the belief that he is imposing a risk of death when the evidence available to him supports the formation of that belief, while an actor who is self-deceived forms that belief but allows desire to prevent him from becoming aware of it. In either case the actor could and should have controlled the wayward desire, thereby allowing the relevant belief to form and surface into awareness.[20]

19 Stephen P. Garvey, "What's Wrong with Involuntary Manslaughter?" 85 *Tex. L. Rev.* 333 (2006).
20 *Id.* at 337–338.

Garvey goes on to argue that not just any desire that prevents one from becoming consciously aware of a risk that one either does subconsciously recognize or possesses the information required for recognizing suffices for culpability. He contrasts the case of Walter and Bernice Williams, whose desire not to have their son Walter taken from them by the welfare authorities perhaps prevented them from perceiving Walter's urgent need for medical care and the risk of death he faced, with the fictitious Sam and Tiffany, whose desire to further social climbing by putting on "the party of the decade" caused them to fail to recognize a similar risk to their child.[21] For Garvey, the less admirable desire of Sam and Tiffany, given its causal role in their not adverting to the risk to their son, renders them culpable for their inadvertence, while the *Williams* case is a much closer call.

Garvey makes it clear that no one deserves punishment merely for possessing base or nonadmirable desires.[22] It is only when the desire interferes with the actor's perception of risk that culpability ensues. The actor in that case is culpable because he does not resist the desire that blocks his formation of the belief about risk that he otherwise would form. The actor has failed to exercise "doxastic self-control."[23]

But what puts the actor on notice that he should exercise such doxastic self-control? For Garvey, it is the awareness that his act is somewhat (but not unduly and hence culpably) risky.[24]

All of our acts are potentially risky, however. Suppose Sam and Tiffany recognize that there is *some* risk their son needs prompt medical attention. They would not be any different from any parent who rightfully does not rush her child to the pediatrician at the drop of a symptom. (Any common complaint – a headache, a sore throat, an upset stomach – *can* be the sign of an emergency, although it usually is not; and we do not deem the average parent, who surmises "it's just a cold," reckless for not seeking immediate medical attention.) So why then would Sam and Tiffany be culpable for continuing with their party planning?

---

[21] State v. Williams, 484 P.2d 1167 (Wash. Ct. App. 1971); Garvey, *supra* note 19, at 333–337.
[22] *See* Garvey, *supra* note 19, at 362–363.
[23] *Id*. at 365.
[24] *Id*. at 368–369.

Garvey's argument is fatally circular. One only has a reason to control the desires that might interfere with one's perception of risks if those desires are preventing you from perceiving risks. But if one cannot perceive the risks, one has no (internal) reason to control the desires. The desires may blind the actor to the risks he is imposing. But if they do, they likewise blind him to the reasons he has to control them.

Or, to put the point another way, Garvey's self-deception view conflates a notion of agency that focuses on one's conscious decision-making abilities with a notion of agency that includes conscious and unconscious desires. Blameworthiness, as Garvey concedes, rests on the first notion of agency, but the inappropriate desires are found within the second, broader agency account. Therefore, Garvey cannot maintain (as he does) that the actor is to blame for not controlling his self-deceiving desires, the very existence of which blind him (in the narrow agency sense) to both the desires' existence and the reasons to act otherwise.

III. The Strongest Counterexample to Our Position

Despite our dissatisfaction with current theoretical defenses of liability for negligence, we realize that both the current criminal law and most people's intuitions run against us on the issue of whether inadvertent negligence is culpable, so we would like to construct what we believe is the strongest example on the side of majority opinion. Sam and Ruth are a self-absorbed yuppie couple with a small child. They are throwing a dinner party for some socially prominent people who can help both of their careers and social standing, and Sam and Ruth are quite obsessed with making sure the party is a success. They put their child in the bathtub and begin drawing bathwater, but just then the first guests begin to arrive. Sam and Ruth both go downstairs to greet the guests, both realizing that the child would be in grave danger if they failed to return and turn off the water, but both believing correctly that at the rate the tub is filling, they will have plenty of time to return to the child after they have welcomed the guests. Of course, when they greet their guests they become so absorbed with making the right impression that both forget about the child, with tragic consequences.

If there is ever a case of culpable negligence, this is it.[25] Sam and
Ruth are not morally attractive people. And their moral shortcomings
have played a role in their child's death. Still, we would argue, they did
not act culpably.[26] When they went downstairs they did not believe
they were taking any substantial risk with their child, perhaps no more
substantial a risk than we believe we are taking (for the sake of our
careers) when we attend a workshop and leave our children with a sitter.
Of course, once Sam and Ruth became engaged with their guests, the
child's situation slipped out of their minds. And once the thought was
out of their minds, they had no power to retrieve it. They were at the
mercy of its popping back into their minds, which it did not.

Some may worry that by not punishing Sam and Ruth, we are breed-
ing selfish actors, who are then likely to engage in conduct without car-
ing sufficiently about others to advert to risks they are creating. Such
actors seem to be rewarded for training themselves to be negligent. This
objection can actually be divided into two different concerns. The first
is that the law, as formulated, may encourage this behavior. We may
be telling people that it is okay for them to act incautiously rather than
for them to parse through the risks they are presenting. What should
be noted about this concern is its consequentialist nature. Rather than
being concerned with punishing culpable action, this objection fears
that we are promoting unwelcome behavior. Our project, however,
should first be to determine who the culpable actors are. If actors with
bad characters such as Sam and Ruth do not warrant punishment, we
simply cannot punish them. The criminal law serves to prohibit bad
conduct; it is not a device to make citizens more virtuous.

The second approach to take toward actors who manifest bad character traits by failing to advert to risks is to say that such failure to advert
is culpable. But character traits are not under actors' direct control. We
do not choose our characters, nor can we change our characters at will,

---

[25] Of course, if they adverted to even the minuscule risk that they would forget about their
    child in the bath, and their reasons for taking this risk did not justify it, they would have
    acted recklessly in going downstairs, not negligently. *Cf.* Andrew Halpin, *Definition in the
    Criminal Law* 133 n.236 (2004). But it should be noted that we often expose our children to
    trivial risks for fairly unimportant reasons.

[26] *Contra* Kyron Huigens, "Is Strict Liability Rape Defensible?" in *Defining Crimes: Essays
    on the Special Part of the Criminal Law* 196, 202–204 (R. A. Duff and Stuart P. Green, eds.,
    2005).

at least not at any given moment in time. The hallmark of criminal responsibility is culpable choice, and negligent actors have not chosen to risk or to cause harm.[27] As we argued in response to Tadros's position, the way in which we understand our own characters and our own failings is limited. We may not know our true character. Our weak character traits may be the very traits that keep us from being aware of our failings. We may not understand how our vices might result in harm to others. Even when we become aware of our flaws, we have limited ability to change our characters. Therapists rarely offer one-time solutions; rather, they offer weekly visits and years of introspection.

As Gideon Rosen, Michael Zimmerman, and Ishtijaque Haji have written, one is culpable only for acts over which one has control.[28] If one is unaware that, say, someone has replaced the sugar on the table with poison, then one is not culpable for placing that poison in another's coffee and thereby killing her. For although one is in control of the conduct of placing the white substance in the coffee, the mistaken belief that it is sugar deprives one of the kind of control necessary for culpability. What holds true for conduct taken in ignorance of its nature or likely consequences also holds true for the ignorance itself. One is not culpable for one's ignorance unless one is in control of it. And one can be in control of one's ignorance only indirectly, say, by deliberately refraining from learning something while being aware that one is running an unjustifiable risk of dangerous ignorance.

---

[27] Even some who believe we are morally evaluable on the basis of our attitudes, beliefs, and perceptions do not deem us blameworthy or punishable for such attitudes because of our lack of direct control over them. *See, e.g.,* Angela M. Smith, "Responsibility for Attitudes: Activity and Passivity in Mental Life," 115 *Ethics* 236, 266–267 (2005). *But see* George Sher, "Out of Control," 116 *Ethics* 285 (2006) (arguing for a more capacious notion of control).

Stephen Garvey concurs, arguing that even racists who honestly perceive as a threat something that they would not have perceived as threatening had they not held racist beliefs cannot be deemed culpable for their mistakes. The mistake was a product of their racism, but they can neither be punished for being racists nor be blamed for having their beliefs affected by their racism. Stephen P. Garvey, "Self-Defense and the Mistaken Racist," 11 *New Crim. L. Rev.* 119 (2008). We agree.

[28] *See* Gideon Rosen, "Skepticism about Moral Responsibility," in *Philosophical Perspectives* 18, *Ethics* (2004), 295–313; Ishtiyaque Haji, "An Epistemic Dimension of Blameworthiness," 57 *Phil. & Phenomenological Res.* 523 (1997); Michael J. Zimmerman, "Moral Responsibility and Ignorance," 107 *Ethics* 410 (1997). For an attempt to rebut Zimmerman, *see* James Montmarquet, "Zimmerman on Culpable Ignorance," 109 *Ethics* 842 (1999). *See also* Peter B. M. Vranas, "I Ought, Therefore I Can," 136 *Phil. Stud.* 167 (2007).

Because the purpose of the criminal law is to prevent harm by giving us reasons to act and to refrain from acting, the criminal law does not reach the negligent actor *at the time he undertakes the negligent act*. At that time, the negligent actor is not aware that her action unjustifiably risks causing harm, and thus cannot be guided to avoid creating that risk by the injunction to avoid creating unjustifiable risks.[29]

Now, there may be times when an actor has made a culpable choice that results in her later inadvertence. These cases are not instances of negligence. They are instances of recklessness. Consider the well-known case of *People v. Decina*.[30] Assume that the actor, knowing he is prone to epilepsy, consciously disregards the risk that he might suffer a seizure and kill four people, but decides to drive anyway. At the moment of the seizure, there is no voluntary act. However, if when Decina got into the car, he consciously disregarded the later risk that he might suffer from a seizure, then this choice – the choice to drive anyway – is a culpable choice. It is upon this culpable action that criminal responsibility can rest.

Of course, looking for prior culpable choices is not without its practical problems. When we look back from a negligent act, there may be a prior culpable choice, but there may not be.[31]

Consider someone who, as he is returning from work and driving into his driveway, notices that his brakes are soft. He realizes that it would be reckless to drive with the brakes in that condition, so he resolves to have them fixed before driving. He also knows that he is likely to forget this by the next morning, so he resolves to write a reminder note to himself when he gets inside his house.

Suppose he does not do so. Then he may be reckless for deciding not to write the note, even if the next morning he remembers to get the brakes fixed, or drives without incident. For he consciously ran an unjustifiable risk of forgetting the brakes, then driving, and then causing an accident.

On the other hand, if his failure to write the reminder note was due to being greeted upon entering the house with the news that his father

---

[29] Of course, punishment for negligence may deter the *reckless* actor who would otherwise believe that his recklessness could not be proved at trial. But it does so at the cost of punishing some who are known or believed to be nonculpable.

[30] 138 N.E.2d 799 (N.Y. 1956).

[31] *Cf.* Simons, *supra* note 7, at 380–386.

was deathly ill, or that his daughter had been severely injured in a soccer collision – news that completely occupies his attention and crowds out his resolution to write himself a reminder about the brakes – then his failure to write the note will not be reckless, again irrespective of what it leads to the next day. The cost of averting one's attention from, say, news of a family crisis in order to write a reminder note about one's car is high relative to the risks (of forgetting to write the note, then forgetting about the brakes, then driving, and then having an accident). Forgetting is itself involuntary. Failing to act to avert forgetting is voluntary and may be culpable depending on the reasons for failing to act. But very often, those reasons will be good reasons and will not display insufficient concern for others' welfare. And frequently, we just forget important matters in situations where taking prior precautions against forgetting would be rightfully viewed as obsessive.

Parenthetically, this discussion of the costs of adverting illustrates why Judge Learned Hand's Carroll Towing formula for negligence is really a formula for recklessness instead.[32] For the cost-benefit formula that Hand puts forward assumes an actor is adverting to all the elements in the formula – the possible harms, the risks thereof, and the alternative courses of action and their costs and risks – whereas the negligent actor is not adverting to those elements. For the formula to represent negligence, it would have to add in the costs of getting the actor to advert – costs that might be quite substantial.

IV. The Arbitrariness of the Reasonable-Person Test

There is also a second significant problem with punishing negligence, and that is that there is no principled and rationally defensible way to define the "reasonable person in the actor's situation" (the RPAS). There is no moral difference between punishing for inadvertent negligence and punishing on the basis of strict liability, and the lack of a moral difference evidences itself in the inability to draw a distinction between strict liability and negligence on any basis other than arbitrary stipulation.

[32] *See* United States v. Carroll Towing Co., 159 F.2d. 169 (2d Cir. 1947).

There are two clear boundary lines for the RPAS. First, the RPAS could be a person apprised of all the facts about the world that bear on a correct moral decision. At the other possible conceptual boundary, the RPAS could be someone with all the beliefs that the actor actually held. Put somewhat differently, where action falls below the standard of reck- lessness – the *conscious* disregarding of an unjustifiable risk – the action will appear reasonable to the actor and thus to the RPAS if the RPAS has exactly the same beliefs as the actor.

The two possible boundaries that provide the frame for character- izing the RPAS present us with this dilemma. If the RPAS knows all the facts, the RPAS always chooses the action that averts the harm (in the absence of justification, of course). But if this is the standard of the RPAS, then every case of strict liability will be a case of negligence as defined by the RPAS standard. It will never be reasonable not to know. (Notice, as well, that because risk is epistemic, the omniscient actor deals only in certainties: for her, the "risk" of a particular harm entailed by any act is either one or zero. On this construct, then, not only is there liability for every avoidable and regrettable – unjustifiable – harm, but there is also no negligence where harm does not occur.)

On the other hand, if the RPAS knows only what the actor knows, there is never any negligence either, only recklessness. The RPAS will always act as the actor acted where the actor is not conscious of the level of risk, and will act differently only where the actor is conscious of the level of risk, that is, is reckless.

At either conceptual boundary, therefore, RPAS collapses negligence into either strict liability or recklessness. The question, then, is where between those boundaries the RPAS is to be located.

The answer is that any location between these two boundaries will be morally arbitrary. Between the boundaries, any RPAS will be a construct that will include some beliefs of the actual actor together with beliefs that the constructor inserts. Which beliefs are inserted other than the ones the actor actually had will determine whether the RPAS would act as the actor acted. But there is no standard that tells us which of the beliefs of the actual actor should be left intact and which should be replaced by other (correct) beliefs. The RPAS standard, cut loose from the alternative moorings of the actor's actual beliefs or of the world as it really was at the time the actor acted, is completely adrift in a sea of alternative constructions, none of which is more compelling than others.

Some commentators at this point assert the possibility that the RPAS is like the actual actor in all material aspects but claim that the RPAS "would have" adverted to and properly assessed the risks because the actual actor "could have" adverted to and properly assessed them.[33] But there is an equivocation here in the reference to what the actor "could have" adverted to and assessed in the actor's situation. If we take the actor at the time of the "negligent" choice, with what he is conscious of and adverting to, his background beliefs, and so forth, then it is simply false that the actor "could have" chosen differently in any sense that has normative bite. For although it may be true that the actor "could have" chosen differently in a sense relevant to the freewill-determinism issue, it is false that in that situation the actor had any internal reason to choose differently from the way he chose.

To have such a reason, an actor will have to advert to that to which he is not adverting. But one has no control at such moments over what one is adverting to or is conscious of: try thinking of what you are not thinking of, but should be! The "could have adverted to the risk" position is directly at odds with the voluntary act principle as a reflection of the value of restricting punishment to choices over which the actor has fair control.

To put the point another way, an actor may fail to form a belief (or a correct belief) if he (1) lacks the requisite background beliefs, (2) lacks the intellectual ability, or (3) lacks the motivation to form the belief.[34] With respect to (1), we do not see how it can be fair to say that an actor "could have" believed *a* if only he had believed *b* without articulating how it was within the actor's control to believe *b*. One would then have to show why it was, at the time belief *b* was available to him, a *culpable decision* not to form that belief.

In addition, as to (2), we do not see how we can blame an actor who either intrinsically (because of limited intelligence) or extrinsically (because of momentary distraction) fails to be able to form belief *a* at

[33] Hart, *supra* note 2, at 148; Brenda M. Baker, "Mens Rea, Negligence, and Criminal Law Reform," 6 *L. & Phil.* 53, 83–85 (1987); Fletcher, *supra* note 2, at 401, 417.
[34] *See* Garvey, *supra* note 19, at 351–352.

the appropriate moment. An agent lacks the requisite control over her ability to form the correct belief at the appropriate time.

Finally, with regard to (3), there may be two reasons why an agent is not motivated to form a belief. First, an agent may simply not see any reason to gather additional information. Suppose someone more epistemically favored than the actor – an epistemically favored observer (EFO), who we shall assume is the equivalent of a RPAS – would estimate the risk that the actor is imposing on others to be higher than the risk the actor actually estimates. The EFO we shall assume would be culpable for acting as the actor acts. The problem for the actor, however, is that for him to become an EFO would require the expenditure of resources – time, energy, and perhaps material resources, plus the cost of forgoing the act in question at the time in question – and given his appraisal of the situation, that expenditure of resources appears unreasonable. After all, the actor does not know what risk the EFO estimates. The risk of harm could be higher than the actor estimates, but it could as well be lower, or the same. (If the EFO is God, then the risk *will* be higher or lower; it will be one or zero.) Nothing that the actor is aware of indicates to the actor that he should spend the resources to become an EFO.[35]

Second, she may be a bad person. However, we fail to see how someone who has no internal reason to form a belief is culpable for not doing so when, for whatever characterological reason, she does not recognize that such a belief should be formed. And if the negligence proponent wants to hold us responsible for our characters, he will have to offer some evidence that we have control over them.

In this last respect, consider the recent attempt by Peter Westen to construct the RPAS.[36] Westen argues that we can construct the RPAS with all of the actual defendant's beliefs, desires, education, intelligence, and so forth, but the jury must then ask the question whether an actor who truly had sufficient concern for others would have come to form

---

[35] *See* John Conlisk, "Why Bounded Rationality," 34 *J. Econ. Literature* 669 (1996); Philippe Mongin, "Does Optimization Imply Rationality," 124 *Synthese* 73 (2000). *See also* Larry Alexander, "Foreword: Coleman and Corrective Justice," 15 *Harv. J. L. & Pub. Pol'y.* 621 (1992).

[36] Peter Westen, "Individualizing the Reasonable Person in Criminal Law," 2 *Crim. L. & Phil.* 137 (2008).

the belief that the defendant did not form. So, Westen argues, the proper question in *Williams* is whether otherwise identical parents with sufficient concern would have recognized the life-threatening nature of the risk that the defendants did not recognize.

This inquiry takes us out of the individuation frying pan and back to the character fire. Here, we have the same concerns that we voiced with Tadros's view – can we fairly hold people responsible for faulty characters of which they may or may not be aware, and which they may or may not be able to change? On the other hand, and consistent with our views about genetic recklessness, we are somewhat sympathetic to the claim that when a defendant becomes aware of a potentially dangerous trait, he may then have a duty to correct it. A man who discovers that he has a short temper that has caused him to lose control and hit his child does have a duty to take some affirmative steps to control his temper. He will be culpable for failing to do so (irrespective of whether he again loses control of his temper) if the risk of harm to others outweighs the burden of trying to get his temper under control (discounted by the likelihood of success).[37]

A culpability-based criminal law will not include liability for negligence. Culpability entails control, and the negligent actor does not have this requisite control. Any control a negligent actor has over her character can only partially and indirectly affect whether the actor will fail to advert to a risk at the requisite time. Moreover, because none of us is perfect, even those with relatively "good" characters will constantly fail to advert to risks that they should have chosen to avoid had they adverted to them.

Moreover, even if we could control these failings, there is simply no nonarbitrary way to determine the standard against which we should be judged. The reasonable person is neither the actual actor nor the omniscient god, but some construct that lies in between. Because there is no principled way to determine the composition of this construct, punishment for negligence is morally arbitrary.

---

[37] We also wonder how far this duty extends. For instance, if one discovers that because of his racist beliefs, he is more likely to misinterpret an act by a black man as an attack, does he have a duty to attempt to rid himself of these beliefs? Or must a liberal society tolerate this sort of potentially dangerous character? For the claim that a liberal society must tolerate the chosen retention of illiberal character traits, *see* Garvey, *supra* note 27.

IV

Defeaters of Culpability

As we have established, primarily in Chapter 2 and by exclusion of inadvertent negligence in Chapter 3, an actor's culpability is the product of the risk(s) to others' protected interest(s)[1] that he believes he has unleashed[2]

---

[1] As we point out in Chapters 2 and 8, sometimes the law will deem certain conduct to be an illegitimate risking of others' interests even when not every token of that conduct creates significant risks of that type. In such cases, the actor may believe that he is taking what would be an otherwise unjustifiable risk of engaging in that conduct – or may have the purpose to so engage in it – but also believe that he is taking only a negligible risk of the primary interest(s) that the prohibition of that conduct is supposed to safeguard. He may, for example, be risking exceeding the speed limit or intending to exceed it in circumstances where he perceives little or no risk to others' persons or property. How to assess his culpability in such cases is a topic we take up in Chapter 8.

[2] And as we elaborate in Chapter 5, because risk is an epistemic, not an ontic notion, and because the relevant risk for culpability is the risk the actor believes exists, there are no objective components to culpability. Whether we are interested in *results* – harms to others' interests – or in result-threatening *conduct* (such as speeding), what we care about for culpability-desert-punishment are solely the risks that the actor perceived himself to be unleashing beyond his control through an act of his will. If he perceives himself to be firing

by a temporally fixed[3] act of his will and the reason(s) he had for so willing. We believe that the criminal law should intervene at the point at which the imbalance of risks and reasons represents a gross deviation from the standard of care that a law-abiding citizen would observe in the actor's situation.

This formulation – encompassing both a comparison of risks to reasons and a comparison of the actor to the law-abiding person – contains within it much of the current doctrines of justification and excuse.[4] That is, whenever the actor's reasons are sufficient to justify the risk, the actor is justified. Even if the actor's actions were not justified, if she has lived up to all that we can fairly expect of her, then she is excused. Despite the fact that much of what currently constitute defenses are subsumed within our culpability calculation in Chapter 2, we offer our thoughts here on those special reasons that justify risks often thought to be "justifications," and we offer our view on how excusing conditions should be construed.

We begin with agent-neutral justifications. First, we discuss the lesser-evils defense, the paradigmatic consequentialist justification. We also explore deontological side constraints on the consequentialist calculus. Second, we turn to defense against culpable aggressors and address myriad issues that bear on when an individual may act defensively.

a bullet at someone, it does not matter that he is actually a brain-in-a-vat and that his willing to move his finger was unsuccessful, much less that his finger moved but the trigger was stuck, the trigger moved but the gun was unloaded, the gun was loaded but the bullet missed, and so on. Similarly, if the actor believes he is depressing the accelerator in a manner that will result in the car's speeding instantaneously and thus with no further action or omission on his part, it does not matter that the car is actually in neutral, or that the actor is unbeknownst to him in a car simulator rather than a car, or that his foot is paralyzed and will not depress in response to his will, or that he is a brain-in-a-vat. Indeed, in some cases it may not matter that the speed that he is trying to achieve is not prohibited at this location if he believes that it is and is unaware of the facts that make it safe to go that speed at that location.

3 Another topic that we address in Chapters 6 and 7 concerns risks that are inappropriately created at T_1 but that the actor can reduce through subsequent action at T_2. When the actor drives very fast, he may be aware that he is risking others' persons and property unjustifiably as long as he continues to drive at that speed. But he may then slow down. Or when the actor lights a fuse to burn down another's home, he may realize there is a small risk that even if he has a change of heart in the next moment, he will for some reason fail to snuff it out. So he has created an unjustifiable though small risk, though one that becomes larger as time goes by and his ability to effectuate any change of heart declines.

4 *Cf.* George P. Fletcher, *The Grammar of the Criminal Law: American, Comparative, and International* § 8.4.2 (2007) (Model Penal Code definitions of recklessness and negligence embody within them questions of justification and excuse).

Next, we turn to excuses. We begin with duress and discuss how this "excuse may actually encompass a personal justification. That is, an actor may have an agent-relative justification – a moral permission – when she defends herself or her loved ones. After discussing duress, we turn to instances of mistake. Although the determination of whether an actor is culpable is based upon her epistemic perspective – so that mistakes regarding either harms or reasons are ordinarily exculpatory – we also consider whether the actor is entitled to an ignorance-of-the-law excuse when she is unaware of the existence of a proxy crime.

Finally, we address the sorts of rationality impairments that may exempt an individual from liability; excuse his conduct on a given occasion; or, at the very least, mitigate his culpability. Among the candidates for excuse are infancy, insanity, and altered states of consciousness. Sometimes, of course, these facts defeat culpability without regard to demonstrating defective reasoning, as when they explain why the actor did not perceive substantial risks from his conduct or believed that certain justifying facts were present. Because ignorance regarding risks and reasons straightforwardly negates culpability, and because infancy, insanity, and altered consciousness explain ignorance, there is nothing special about using the latter to negate culpability.

Sometimes, however, the actor is aware of the risks and does not perceive any facts that would justify imposing such risks but nonetheless is deemed not culpable for acting in the face of such risks and the absence of justifying reasons. The explanations for deeming such actors nonculpable are varied and controversial. Lack of sufficient maturity or sanity to grasp fully the import of otherwise culpable acts and lack of the ability to access fully all of one's reasons for not acting are oft-cited though not fully explained. Are the young, the insane, the hypnotized, the somnambulant, or those acting in the grip of "automatism" different in kind or only in degree from the impulsive, the habitual, the daydreamer, and so on? We cannot answer these questions fully here. What we can do is identify them and show where they fit into our schema.

I. Justifications and Excuses: Reorienting the Debate

Our view leads to a somewhat radical revision of the current understanding of criminal law defenses. Criminal law defenses are typically divided into the broad categories of justifications and excuses. In addition to these defenses, there are also nonexculpatory defenses, such as diplomatic immunity.[5] One final area of so-called defenses entails "exemptions," those cases in which the actor lacks sufficient rationality to be deemed a moral agent.[6] Although we briefly address exemptions, our focus in this chapter is on justifications and excuses, as these are the defenses that must be understood to assess whether the actor is culpable and therefore worthy of blame and punishment.

There is considerable controversy over how best to understand justifications and excuses. Some argue that justifications are actions that are "right"; others claim justifications entail "permissible" actions.[7] There are questions as to whether justifications are ultimately based on a consequentialist balancing of evils, or whether there is room for deontological considerations.[8] Some think that justifications cannot conflict and that an actor's being justified has implications for what third parties may and may not do.[9] Others think that justifications simply announce that an act is either permissible for the actor or simply not punishable, with no implications for how other parties may behave.[10]

Whereas justifications are thought to focus on the wrongfulness of the *act*, excuses center on the blameworthiness of the *actor*. Theories

---

[5] *See* Paul H. Robinson, *Structure and Function in Criminal Law* 71–78 (1997); R. A. Duff, "'I Might Be Guilty, But You Can't Try Me': Estoppel and Other Bars to Trial," 1 *Ohio St. J. Crim. L.* 245 (2003).

[6] *See* Michael S. Moore, *Law and Psychiatry: Rethinking the Relationship* 64–65 (1984); Victor Tadros, *Criminal Responsibility* 55–57 (2005).

[7] *See, e.g.,* Joshua Dressler, "Justifications and Excuses: A Brief Review of the Concepts and the Literature," 33 *Wayne L. Rev.* 1155, 1161 n.22 (1987) (noting that self-defense may be permissible as opposed to "right"); Claire O. Finkelstein, "Self-Defense as Rational Excuse," 57 *U. Pitt. L. Rev.* 621, 624 (1996) ("In the criminal law, to call a violation of a prohibitory norm justified is to say not only that it is permissible, but that it is encouraged."); George P. Fletcher, "Should Intolerable Prison Conditions Generate a Justification or an Excuse for Escape?" 26 *UCLA L. Rev.* 1355, 1359 (1979) (rejecting permissibility definition in favor of a view of justification as right action); Hibi Pendleton, "A Critique of Rational Excuse Defense: A Reply to Finkelstein," 57 *U. Pitt. L. Rev.* 651, 665 (1996) (critiquing Finkelstein's narrow definition of justification).

[8] *See* Douglas N. Husak, "Justifications and the Criminal Liability of Accessories," 80 *J. Crim. L. & Criminology* 491, 505–506 (1989).

[9] *See* George P. Fletcher, *Rethinking Criminal Law* 761–762 (1978); Heidi M. Hurd, "Justification and Excuse, Wrongdoing and Culpability," 74 *Notre Dame L. Rev.* 1551, 1553 (1999).

[10] *See* Mitchell N. Berman, "Justification and Excuse, Law and Morality," 53 *Duke L.J.* 1, 62–64 (2003).

of excuse also run the gamut. As we discussed in Chapter 1, character theorists argue that an actor is excused if her action is not a reflection of her settled character.[11] Choice theorists, on the other hand, argue that an actor is excused if she lacked the capacity and fair opportunity to conform her conduct to law.[12] Still other theorists argue that excuses depend on one's role or on the dispositions the law wishes to encourage.[13]

Because our approach, at least at an idealized level, eliminates the formal distinctions between offenses and defenses, the terms of the debate shift. That is, those who argue that justifications are parallel to negating offense elements, but excuses are equivalent to negating culpability,[14] will find that these neat categories have completely disappeared within our framework. Nevertheless, we believe that much of the current understanding and debate about justifications and excuses can be accommodated within our model.

Our model requires an analysis of the justifiability of the actor's act. As we note, culpability is about weighing risks and reasons. An action is not culpable if the actor's reasons for acting outweigh the risks he foresees. Thus, we need some theory of when reasons do outweigh risks. Such an analysis is simply another way of understanding justifications – an act is justified when, all things considered, it is permissible to engage in what would otherwise be wrongful risk imposition.

Our conception of culpability also encompasses excuses. As we have argued previously, by acting recklessly, unjustifiably privileging one's reasons over others' legally protected interests, one manifests insufficient concern for the interests of others. That is, our subjective approach to determining culpability describes the moral vice of insufficient concern.[15] Excuses, in turn, serve to negate our inference of (or indignation toward) this moral vice.[16]

---

[11] See Fletcher, supra note 9, at § 10.3.1.

[12] See Michael S. Moore, Placing Blame: A General Theory of Criminal Law 548 (1997).

[13] See, e.g., John Gardner, "The Gist of Excuses," 1 Buff. Crim. L. Rev. 575 (1998); Claire O. Finkelstein, "Excuses and Dispositions in Criminal Law," 6 Buff. Crim. L. Rev. 317 (2002).

[14] See, e.g., Hurd, supra note 9.

[15] See also Kimberly Kessler Ferzan, "Don't Abandon the Model Penal Code Yet! Thinking Through Simons's Rethinking," 6 Buff. Crim. L. Rev. 185, 212–215 (2002); Kimberly Kessler Ferzan, "Holistic Culpability," 28 Cardozo L. Rev. 2523 (2007).

[16] See Peter Westen, "An Attitudinal Theory of Excuse," 25 Law and Phil. 289 (2006).

Excuses get a doctrinal foothold in our theory in two ways. First, by judging the actor's conduct to be a gross deviation from what a reasonable person would do, our theory already encompasses the realm of reasonable actions that are excused, such as those taken because of duress. Second, the question of whether the actor has consciously disregarded a risk for unjustifiable reasons should take into account the quality of the actor's deliberations. To the extent that the actor's rationality is partially or fully impaired, he is entitled to mitigation or a complete excuse.

We devote the vast majority of this chapter to explicating how justifications and excuses fit within our model. We explore the normative questions raised by many of these doctrines. Although we do not answer all of the questions we raise, we show how they fit within our schema.

At this point, however, we wish to address some preliminary questions. There is significant debate over the nature of justification and excuse, and over the way these doctrines can and should operate. Because our view radically revises the terrain, we begin by discussing the anticipated objections to our remodeling.

A. EVISCERATING THE OFFENSE-DEFENSE DISTINCTION

Some will argue that our model collapses important moral distinctions. For example, George Fletcher argues that the distinction between offenses and defenses is substantive, not formal. The prima facie norm tells people, "Do not kill," and then a defense allows people "to kill only when threatened with deadly force by another." Collapsing these two, Fletcher contends, is equivalent to treating the unlawful aggressor like a "fly" because we eliminate the prima facie norm against killing other people.[17]

We disagree. It is difficult to see why an offense definition cannot embody both a prima facie norm and its negation. Offenses are more complex than prima facie norms. Many require *mens rea* terms that, at least according to some theorists, are not part of the norm itself but part of the grounds for attributing the offense to the actor. Offenses can also require that the actor's conduct be, or the actor believes his conduct to be, justified. Indeed, a significant number of laws are risk-creation

---

[17] *See* George P. Fletcher, "The Nature of Justification," in *Action and Value in Criminal Law* (Stephen Shute et al., eds., 1993).

offenses, in which we tell people that it is permissible to risk harm for certain reasons but not for others. If, ultimately, the message to citizens is that it is permissible to kill culpable attackers, there is no reason why this message, rather than requiring a separate defense, cannot be embodied within the definition of the offense.

B. ELIMINATING THE WRONGDOING-CULPABILITY DISTINCTION

A similar distinction that our formulation eliminates is that between wrongdoing and culpability. In our view, the focus of the criminal law should be on whether the actor has committed a *culpable act.* We do not believe that the criminal law should concern itself with nonculpable harmings, such as when an actor, unaware of the risk of death he is imposing, kills another human being.

Those who believe that justifications must be understood to be the mirror image of wrongdoing, and excuses the mirror image of culpability, may object that our model conflates justification and excuse.[18] Justifications, they claim, are mind independent; excuses, on the other hand, look to the mental states of the actor.

Our theory, however, is perfectly consistent with various understandings of justifications and excuses. Our justification formula is about whether the reasons for acts outweigh risks those acts impose. We excuse those who are substantially rationally or volitionally impaired. As we discuss later in this chapter, we are also quite sympathetic to the view that justifications are objectively defined. However, because on our view the criminal law's concern should be *culpability,* whether the actor's conduct is justified because of the facts that actually exist or alternatively because of his beliefs about such facts will not matter because his culpability is not affected by any mistaken beliefs. Whether these alternative theories of justification matter in terms of their implications for third parties is a matter we discuss later in the context of self-defense.

Additionally, we doubt that all justifications can be understood independently of the subjective mental states of the actor. Consider Ken who decides to kill Leo. After Ken shoots Leo, we learn that Leo was

---

[18] *See* Hurd, *supra* note 9; Westen, *supra* note 16.

about to shoot Ken. This problem raises the question of whether Ken must have justificatory intent. We believe that a proper understanding of self-defense requires that Ken believe that Leo was about to kill him.[19] Otherwise, all we have is two bad guys who tried to kill each other, one of whom succeeded.

C. SUMMARY

We believe that culpable action is the proper target of the criminal law. Although theorists may believe that our formulation elides important distinctions, it does so by bringing to the forefront the most critical question for the criminal law. If a more perspicuous formulation of culpability leads to a rethinking of other current categorizations, we are willing to accept this result.

II. Socially Justifying Reasons

A. IN GENERAL: THE LESSER-EVILS PARADIGM

As stated previously, because we consider an actor's culpability to consist in his imposing a risk to others' legally protected interests for reasons that do not legally justify imposing that level of risk, the question of whether the actor's reasons justify imposing the risk (as he assesses the risk) is built into every assessment of culpability. In our schema, justifications for risk imposition are central in every case, not extraordinary items of only occasional concern to the criminal law. For example, a careful drive to the grocery store for a bottle of wine increases risks to others' lives, limbs, and property but is almost never culpable. Nonetheless, there will be occasions when the risks the actor perceives himself to be imposing are so high and the others' interests so important that, in the absence of some extraordinary justifying reason, the act would surely be culpable. In the typical case of using deadly force in self-defense, the actor typically believes he is imposing a high

---

[19] *See* Larry Alexander, "Unknowingly Justified Actors and the Attempt/Success Distinction," 39 *Tulsa L. Rev.* 851 (2004); Kimberly Kessler Ferzan, "Justifying Self-Defense," 24 *Law & Phil.* 711 (2005).

risk of death or severe bodily injury on someone whom he perceives to be aggressing against him. In the famous Trolley hypothetical, the actor believes, when he switches the trolley to a siding on which a worker is trapped or asleep, that he is imposing a high risk of death or serious bodily injury. Although imposing what one perceives to be a high risk of death or serious bodily injury is almost always culpable, sometimes it is not. Our focus here will be on such extraordinary situations. However, it should always be borne in mind that the considerations that go into justifying risk impositions apply in every case.

1. The General Consequentialist Structure of Lesser-Evil Choices

Let us suppose that our actor, now a criminal defendant (D), imposed what she perceived at the time to be a high risk of death on victim (V). She redirected an out-of-control trolley to a siding on which V appeared to be trapped. As we argue in Chapter 5, it is immaterial to D's culpability whether anything untoward actually happened to V. All that matters is that D believed at the time that her redirecting the trolley imposed a very high risk of death or injury on V. Normally, D would be culpable – highly so – for such an act.

Suppose, however, that D argues that she is not culpable because she believed that by imposing the risk on V she was bringing about other consequences that were so beneficial that they justified the risk imposition. For example, D believed that unless she redirected the out-of-control Trolley, it would strike and kill five trapped workers on the main track. (Again, it does not matter whether the five workers were actually in danger; it matters, at least for D's culpability, only that D *believed* they were.) If saving five workers' lives at the price of one (different) worker's life is a consequentialist-justified act, then D is not culpable for her risk imposition. She is a morally and legally correct reasoner, and her act displayed proper concern for others' interests. Moreover, if third parties (TP) assessed the situation as D did – if they, too, saw it as a choice between five deaths (almost certainly) and one death (almost certainly), they would have been justified in encouraging and assisting D. And if V saw the situation the same way, V would not have been *socially* justified in resisting D and TP – say, by shooting them – although, as we shall see, V might have been *personally* justified or excused in doing so.

Most risk impositions are or are not justified by their expected consequences, discounted by the probabilities of those consequences. Even nonconsequentialists recognize that most of the domain of potentially harmful interactions of actors can be governed only by norms that are consequentialist. Because in acting we are always subjecting others to risks, deontological norms can play only a limited role in constraining those acts.

We proffer no general consequentialist theory here. For our purposes, we do not need to take sides on whether the proper consequentialist calculus for justifying risk imposition is *welfarist* or *nonwelfarist*; whether, if welfarist, welfare is based on an *objective list* of goods, on *satisfaction of preferences*, or on *hedonic states*;[20] whether, if preference based in whole or in part, the preferences are *raw*, or *corrected for misinformation*, and/or *laundered* of malicious, envious, and other antisocial content, and/or *restricted to self-regarding preferences* as opposed to other-regarding or impersonal ones, and so on; whether all consequences are commensurable, so that the results of comparing consequences, discounted by their probabilities, are determinate;[21] whether, when harms to human beings are being weighed, all harms of the same magnitude should be deemed equal, or whether instead the bearers of those harms should be compared in terms of their age, their social contributions and other deeds and misdeeds, their character, and so on;[22] and whether the consequentialist calculus in assessing risk impositions is sensitive to distributional considerations, and if so, which ones.

---

[20] For an interesting attack on welfarism, one that disputes that moral evaluations track the transitive rankings of states of affair that welfarism and the Pareto principle posit, *see* Leo Katz, "Choice, Consent, and Cycling: The Hidden Limitations of Consent," 104 *Mich. L. Rev.* 627 (2006). And there is abundant literature on whether and how harms to different people should be aggregated, and on whether enough lesser harms to some can outweigh greater harms to fewer others. On this latter point, *see, e.g.,* Alastair Norcross, "Contractualism and Aggregation," 28 *Soc. Theory & Prac.* 303 (2002); Thomas Scanlon, "Replies," 28 *Soc. Theory & Prac.* 337, 354–357 (2002). An excellent article that discusses these problems in the context of asking which risks to others are justifiably imposed is Kenneth W. Simons, "Tort Negligence, Cost-Benefit Analysis and Tradeoffs: A Closer Look at the Controversy," *Loyola of Los Angeles L. Rev.* (forthcoming).

[21] *See* Larry Alexander, "Lesser Evils: A Closer Look at the Paradigmatic Justification," 24 *Law & Phil.* 611 (2005).

[22] We take up an aspect of this when we discuss culpable aggressors and other culpable actors in self-defense scenarios.

2. Deontological Constraints on the Consequentialist Calculus

For our purposes, some consequentialist theory determines whether D
has properly employed the consequentialist calculus in deciding that the
risk imposition on V is justified by untoward consequences so averted,
discounted by their probability. Having said that, however, we acknowledge that deontological norms can bear on whether the actor's risk imposition is justifiable and thus nonculpable. For suppose it is justifiable for
D to switch the trolley from the main track on which five workers are
trapped to the siding on which one worker is trapped (Trolley). Would
it also be justifiable for D to kill a healthy person in order to harvest his
organs and thereby save five people from imminent death (Surgeon)?
Almost everyone would say that the cases are different and that D would
not be justified in Surgeon, even though, as in Trolley, a net four lives
are saved. Indeed, most would say that the risk imposition in Surgeon is
unjustifiable, even if far more lives will likely be saved than in Trolley.

There is no consensus as to why Surgeon differs from Trolley; the
only consensus is that it does. In our opinion, the difference between
Surgeon and Trolley is that in Surgeon, but not in Trolley, D violates a
deontological norm that constrains D's pursuit of what otherwise would
be justifiable on the consequentialist calculus.[23]

One group of theories regarding the content of that deontological norm makes D's *intentions* central to its violation. The so-called
Doctrine of Double Effect is one – but only one – of such intent-based
theories of the content of the constraining norm.

On the intent-based theories, D's risk imposition in Surgeon is
unjustifiable because D intends the victim's death; in Trolley, by contrast, D does not intend the one worker's death, however certain D is
that the worker will be killed. (D would, after all, presumably be happy
if the worker survived.) Similarly, in another pair of contrasting cases
frequently used to illustrate the same point, Strategic Bomber – who
bombs a munitions factory in order to reduce the enemy's arsenal and
thereby assure its defeat – may be acting justifiably despite his knowledge
that many innocent civilians living next to the factory will be killed,
whereas Terror Bomber – who bombs the same factory in order to kill

---

[23] *See* Alexander, *supra* note 21, at 615–616.

the nearby civilians, and thereby terrorize the enemy's population, and thereby bring about its surrender – has acted unjustifiably. For Terror Bomber intends the civilian deaths, whereas Strategic Bomber foresees their deaths but does not intend them.

We are skeptical that such intent-based theories can provide the proper moral boundary. First, intentions, when understood as those things which motivate us,[24] can be so narrowly described as to render the prohibition meaningless. D in Surgeon need not intend the death of the healthy patient. D wants the organs, not the death, and would be overjoyed if the now organless patient survived in the pink of health. And Terror Bomber will be satisfied if the civilians are not killed but only appear to be to the rest of the enemy's population. And there are other difficult theoretical problems with making a major normative distinction turn on distinguishing what D "intends" from what D merely "foresees".

Furthermore, the intent-based theories produce perverse results. Suppose, for example, that D will switch the trolley to the siding only to kill the one worker, whom she hates. Other witnesses, who only want to save as many lives as possible, will want D to switch it. Suppose they point out to D – who has no legal obligation to throw the switch (she has no legal obligation to act to save others) – that if she throws the switch, she will save (net) four lives. D is, however, unmoved by this. D *can* be moved by an intent to kill the one worker, however. D is an unsavory, misanthropic person, to be sure. But we should want her to switch the trolley. If her intent will render her culpable for doing so and hence punishable, she may be deterred from doing what we desperately want her to do. Therefore, we should not deem her culpable for engaging in the very same act token that others, with exactly her understanding of the situation, but with more benevolent intentions, would be completely justified in taking.[25] Nor should third parties who likewise

---

[24] For the argument that what an actor intends is broader than what is motivationally significant to the actor, *see* Kimberly Kessler Ferzan, "Beyond Intention," 29 *Cardozo L. Rev.* 1147 (2008). For an argument to that effect that relies on the notion of "closeness" and that we believe is less successful, *see* Neil Francis Delaney, "Two Cheers for 'Closeness': Terror, Targeting and Double Effect," 137 *Phil. Stud.* 335 (2008).

[25] *See, e.g.*, F. M. Kamm, "Terrorism and Several Moral Distinctions," 12 *Legal Theory* 19, 31 (2006); F. M. Kamm, "Failures of Just War Theory: Terror, Harm, and Justice," 114 *Ethics*

98

see the situation as consequentialist justified be deemed culpable for encouraging D to throw the switch, even if they cite the one worker's death as the incentive for D to do so.[26]

Likewise, suppose the bombing run has been programmed by Strategic Bomber, who is now ill and unable to fly the plane. The only available pilot is Terror Bomber; and although he knows that the bombing is justified by the destruction of the munitions factory despite the deaths of innocent civilians, he will fly the route only to further his intention to kill the civilians and terrorize the population. If we regard him as culpable for the bombing, he will not fly the route. (He may wish to terrorize, but he may also wish to comply with his moral obligations.) Because when he flies, he will be doing exactly what Strategic Bomber would have done – dropping the same bombs at the same location – his act should be deemed justifiable and hence nonculpable. We want him to fly the route despite his intent. His intent reveals an unsavory character, but it does not convert his otherwise justifiable act into an unjustifiable one.[27]

650, 658 (2004); David Enoch, "Ends, Means, Side-Effects, and Beyond: A Comment on the Justification of the Use of Force," 7 *Theoretical Inquiries in Law* 43, 50–51 (2005). For a criticism of shifting the focus to the actor's *desires* rather than his intentions, in an effort to avoid the criticisms of the latter focus, *see* Uwe Steinhoff, "Yet Another Revised DDE? A Note on David K. Chan's DDED," 9 *Ethical Theory & Moral Practice* 231 (2006).

[26] *See* Alec Walen, "Permissibly Encouraging the Impermissible," 38 *J. Value Inq.* 341 (2004).

[27] Consider, as well, the situation in which the only person who will volunteer to carry out a lawful execution is one who does so solely to fulfill an intention to kill the condemned man. *Compare* Alexander, *supra* note 21, at 620, *with* Mitchell N. Berman, "Lesser Evils and Justification: A Less Close Look," 24 *Law and Phil.* 681 (2005). We question whether such behavior necessarily reveals an unsavory character. If an actor enjoys hitting, running red lights, or killing people, and thereby chooses to box, to drive an ambulance, or to perform executions as a lawful way of acting on his otherwise illicit intentions, one might think he acts commendably, not viciously.

It should be added that even if the bombing has two effects that help shorten the war – the destruction of the munitions factory and the terrorizing of the citizenry from the collateral civilian deaths – but only the former is what justifies the civilian deaths, this does not mean that Strategic Bomber acts wrongly in deliberately targeting, say, a civilian establishment *if picking that target is the best way to ensure that the bombs actually hit the munitions factory* (which may be difficult to pick out). And if Strategic Bomber may deliberately target that civilian establishment, so may Terror Bomber, even if he does so only to kill civilians and terrorize others, again so long as he knows he is doing what Strategic Bomber would do.

Of course, Terror Bomber must be aware of reasons that justify the precise conduct in which he is engaging. He is not justified in imposing risks that others, *for reasons specific to them*, could justifiably impose. That is why Frankie, in Chapter 2, is not justified in

In our view, the deontological constraint on achieving the best consequences is means focused rather than intent focused. That is, what makes an act that is otherwise consequentialist justified deontologically wrong is that the justifying consequences are produced by using a non-consenting person's body, labor, or talents – "appropriating" them for others' benefits. In Surgeon, D does not have to intend that the victim die, or suffer pain, or be handicapped in any way. What makes D's act violative of deontological constraints is that the justifying consequences that he plans to bring about – the saving of the five ill people's lives – require him to use the victim's body. In Surgeon, if the victim and his organs were not present, the five ill people would be out of luck. Not so in Trolley with respect to the worker trapped on the siding. The plan to save the five workers on the main track would succeed if no one were on the siding. And with respect to Terror Bomber, the presence of civilians in harm's way is not required to produce the consequences that justify the bombing, even if their presence provides *him* with his motivation.[28]

---

imposing the risks of careful driving while she is en route past the grocery store to kill Johnny, even if someone else who, unlike Frankie, needs groceries could justifiably drive the same route in the same manner.

We concede the possibility of situations where an actor may have some permission to impose risks on others that depend not only on his belief that justifying facts exist but also on his acting *because* of those justifying facts. We do not think that Trolley is such a case. Nor do we think that ambulance drivers who like to speed, boxers who like to hit people, or surgeons who like to cut them are such cases. Moreover, even when the actor has a bad reason for acting but also is aware of justifying reasons, it will be difficult for the actor himself, not to mention third parties, to determine whether the justifying reasons would themselves be sufficient to motivate him to act, necessary to motivate him to act, or completely inert motivationally.

The same point holds with respect to duress, which we deem to be a personal as opposed to social justification, and which we discuss later in this chapter. If the actor would be personally justified in committing a crime if ordered by another to commit it on pain of being killed if he did not, that personal justification should not be withdrawn upon finding that the actor had decided to commit the crime prior to being threatened. The actor's bad reasons will have been preempted by the good reason of avoiding the threat. For the actor can no longer reconsider, as he might have done in the absence of the threat.

Thus, although there may be some moral permissions to impose risks that turn on the reasons that motivate the actor rather than the reasons of which he is aware, we believe that in most cases, an actor is not culpable for imposing a risk if he believes that reasons that would justify the act exist, even if his motivation derives from other reasons. We thank Mitch Berman for pressing us on this point. *See also* Enoch, *supra* note 25.

28 We should add that the proscription on using others as means rules out calculating as a beneficial consequence satisfaction of any preferences directed at others' sufferings or endangerings. So, even if Deborah gets a huge thrill from imposing risks on others, that

This idea of appropriating others – using their bodies, labors, and talents without their consent as the means of producing the beneficial consequences that would otherwise justify the bad consequences – accounts better than any other theory for our deontological intuitions about the limits on pursuit of the best consequences.[29] Thus, in Fat Man, where the five trapped workers can be saved, not by diverting the trolley to a siding, but by pushing a large person into its path, the "no appropriation" theory assimilates the case to Surgeon and distinguishes it from Trolley, corresponding to almost universal intuitive responses to those scenarios.[30]

thrill should not be capable of tipping the consequentialist balance in favor of her risk impositions.

[29] Our account of the deontological constraint in pursuing the best consequences is very similar to, but slightly different from, those of several others. *See, e.g.,* T. A. Cavanaugh, *Double-Effect Reasoning: Doing Good and Avoiding Evil* (2006); Delaney, *supra* note 24; Neil Francis Delaney, "A Note on Intention and the Doctrine of Double Effect," 134 *Phil. Stud.* 103 (2007); William J. Fitzpatrick, "The Intend/Foresee Distinction and the Problem of 'Closeness,'" 128 *Phil. Stud.* 585 (2006); Joseph Shaw, "Intention in Ethics," 36 *Canad. J. Phil.* 187 (2006); Joseph Shaw, "Intentions and Trolleys," 56 *Phil. Q.* 63 (2006); Alec Walen, "The Doctrine of Illicit Intentions," 34 *Phil. & Pub. Aff.* 39 (2006); Warren Quinn, "Actions, Intentions, and Consequences: The Doctrine of Double Effect," in *Morality and Action* 175–193 (W. Quinn and P. Foot, eds., 1994); Kamm, "Failures of Just War Theory: Terror, Harm, and Justice," *supra* note 25; F. M. Kamm, "The Doctrine of Triple Effect," 74 *Aris. Soc.* 21, 21–39 (2000); Kamm, "Terrorism and Several Moral Distinctions," *supra* note 25. For a recent argument rejecting such a deontological constraint, *see* Cecile Fabre, *Whose Body Is it Anyway?: Justice and the Integrity of the Person* 1–9 (2006).

[30] *See, e.g.,* John Mikhail, "Aspects of the Theory of Moral Cognition: Investigating Intuitive Knowledge of the Prohibition of Intentional Battery and the Principle of Double Effect" (Georgetown Public Law Research Paper, Paper No. 762385; Georgetown Law and Economics Research Paper, Paper No. 762385, 2002), available at http://ssrn.com/abstract=762385. The most difficult cases are those like Loop, where the trolley tracks divide and form a loop. No matter which track the trolley goes down, it will eventually hit the five workers if unimpeded. Suppose the switch is set so that the trolley will go down the left track, and there is a single large worker trapped on the right track. Redirecting the trolley will result in the death of the single worker and will also stop the trolley from looping around and killing the five. It might seem that on our theory, one may switch the trolley only if one would have done so in the single worker's absence – say, to give the five workers a second or two more to live (perhaps they were slightly on the left side of the loop). On the other hand, one might argue that, on our theory, it will also be okay to switch the trolley if one would have done so in the presence of the single worker but in the absence of the five – say, to give the single worker a few seconds to live (because he, too, is on the left side of the loop, behind the five workers but still closer to the trolley if it goes left but not if it is switched to the right). After all, if the trolley is currently routed so that it will hit the five workers, whose bodies will stop it, the single worker is benefiting from the presence of the five.

A couple final points about this "no appropriation," means-focused theory of deontological constraint. It explains why scenarios in which defendant (D) or D's family is threatened with death or severe injury unless D commits a crime that does not involve death or severe injury are usually governed by the *excuse* of duress rather than the *justification* of lesser evils.[31] After all, in such scenarios the evil that D is threatened with *is* a greater evil than the evil he inflicts or risks inflicting, so that it might appear natural to regard D's otherwise criminal act as justified by the consequences. But note that typically in such scenarios, D is using the victim (V) – or, perhaps more controversially, V's property that V created – as a *means* of producing the otherwise justifying consequences (saving D or his family from harm). V is under no obligation to rescue D from the threatened harm and has not consented to do so. Rather, V is being appropriated by D to produce the good consequences. D is therefore violating a deontological constraint and cannot claim a lesser-evils justification. The excuse of duress is the only available way to negate D's culpability for the risk imposition on V.

Second, deontological constraints on the pursuit of the best consequences – no matter what theory of deontological constraints one adopts – produce the following puzzle: the actor may have acted wrongly in violating those constraints, but if he really was acting to produce net

---

One further point. Kamm argues, and we concur, that where using V as a means brings about better consequences than harming him permissibly – *and using him as a means does not result in his being harmed sooner or differently from how he would be permissibly harmed* – then he may permissibly be used as a means. Thus, if deliberately targeting a smaller number of the same civilians who will be killed (justifiably) by Strategic Bomber will, by inducing terror, cause the war to end sooner with less loss of life, then they may permissibly be targeted – so long as the citizenry would have been equally terrorized by the deaths caused by Strategic Bomber. *See* Kamm, "Terrorism and Several Moral Distinctions," *supra* note 25, at 58; Kamm, "Failures of Just War Theory: Terror, Harm, and Justice," *supra* note 25, at 659–660. Likewise, it would seem to be an implication of Kamm's, to us, plausible qualification of the proscription of the use of persons as means that if one kills B at T_1 in order to avert A's killing B and C at T_2, one has wronged B – even if the interval between T_1 and T_2 is very short. Killings are, after all, only shortenings of life; and we see no way in principle to draw a bright line between longer and shorter life-shortenings. (On the other hand, A might be justified, even in the absence of B's consent, in imposing a slight risk of early death on B to avert a greater risk of B's death – after all, this is what risky surgery does – although in the ordinary case, we might assume that B would consent to the risk imposition and demand further that his consent be obtained if that is feasible.)

[31] *See* Model Penal Code § 2.08(1) (1985).

beneficial consequences, it is questionable how blameworthy he really is. From one perspective, violating a deontological constraint is the epitome of insufficient concern, as these constraints forbid using, and thus disrespecting, persons. On the other hand, does an actor really engage our negative reactive attitudes if, as in Surgeon, he has saved (net) four lives, especially if he was not only aware of the good consequences but motivated by them? If the act of saving (net) four lives would be praiseworthy but for its violating a deontological constraint, is D's "culpability" the same as it would be had he killed the patient for reasons that could not consequentially justify the killing, such as for D's personal gain or to settle a grudge? And suppose the appropriation that violates the deontological constraint is minor – D only has to touch nonconsenting V's brow, or borrow V's rowboat, to save some lives. How does its deontological wrongness translate into retributive desert? Is it possible that deontologically wrong acts that have good consequences that D is aware of and motivated by produce conflicting reactive attitudes – both blame and praise? We offer no solution to this problem but only raise it as one that deontologist-retributivists must solve.[32]

In summary, what justifies a risk imposition is its beneficial consequences, discounted by their probability and constrained by the means through which they are brought about.[33] What renders a risk imposition that threatens legally protected interests nonculpable is the actor's *belief* that certain (good) consequences will be achieved thereby, discounted by his assessment of the probabilities of their occurring. He need not be imposing the risk *in order* to achieve the good consequences so long as he believes in a sufficient likelihood of their occurring to offset the risk (of bad consequences) he perceives himself to be imposing. In other words, his *motivating reasons* are immaterial to his culpability (though not to his character) so long as he believes *justifying reasons* exist (or

---

[32] *See also* Kamm, "Terrorism and Several Moral Distinctions," *supra* note 25, at 58–59.

[33] Again, we are bracketing questions of how consequences are evaluated, compared, and distributed. And, although we have offered a theory of deontological constraints on pursuit of good consequences, our basic schema depends neither on the correctness of that theory nor even on the existence of deontological constraints beyond the constraint of not knowingly (or recklessly) punishing actors in excess of their retributive desert. Nonetheless, although our arguments against intent-based and in favor of an appropriation-based account of deontological constraints are detachable from our principal account of justification, we believe they are persuasive.

exist with sufficient likelihood). (Obviously, if he does not believe justifying reasons exist, or are sufficiently likely to exist, he is culpable even if his reason for acting is not itself malicious but is merely insufficiently weighty in the consequentialist calculus.)

3. Second- and Third-Party Implications

Because the justification of lesser evils entails a balancing of good and bad consequences, the justifiability of the actor's action has implications for what the victim and third parties may do. That is, if justifications turn on the facts that actually obtain when the actor acts – the objective view of justifications – then if the actor's action is justified, it necessarily follows that a third party will also be justified in assisting the actor and that the victim will *not* be *socially* justified in resisting the actor (although the victim might be *personally* justified or excused).

However, what is crucial for us is culpability, not justification per se. Because an actor's culpability is determined by his *perception* of the facts, a third party's culpability may depart from the actor's. Suppose defendant (D) is attempting to turn a valve that will divert a river and flood the victim's (V's) farm. If D believes that if the valve is not turned, the river will destructively flood much more valuable property further downstream, he will not be culpable for flooding V's farm, even if it turns out that he was mistaken about the situation (the forecast of a flood that D heard on the radio was in error). If a third party (TP) aids D by shouting instructions for turning the valve, TP may be culpable if *he* is unaware of the flood and believes D is just up to mischief, mischief TP would like to assist. On the other hand, if TP but not D has heard about the threatened flood – D *is* up to mischief – D will be culpable for turning the valve but TP will not be culpable for assisting D. Indeed, and somewhat more controversial, TP will not be culpable for encouraging D to turn the valve *culpably* – say, by stressing that it is V's farm, reminding D how much he hates V, and not mentioning the saving of the downstream property (for D may be a misanthrope regarding those downstream as well).[34] (And, again, as we discuss in Chapter 5, nothing

---

[34] *See* Walen, *supra* note 26. *See also* R. A. Duff, "Rethinking Justifications," 39 *Tulsa L. Rev.* 829, 845 (2004).

turns on whether turning the valve actually does flood V's farm, or not
turning it actually does result in downstream flooding.)

The justifiability of D's action also has implications for V. If V has
heard and believes the forecast of a flood, then V realizes that the flooding of his farm is justified, even if D (and/or TP) is culpable in doing
so. If the flooding is justified, then V will not be justified in resisting.
(The same would be true of the single worker in Trolley: he would not
be justified in shooting D to prevent D's switching the trolley if he knew
that five workers were trapped on the other track.) V might be *excused*
(or personally justified) for resisting, and as excused (or personally justified), nonculpable by a route different from justification, a point we
discuss later in this chapter. But even if V is excused, his not being justified means that TP may aid only D, not V, at least if TP understands the
situation as V does. (Obviously, if V does not know about the flood but
instead believes D is acting unjustifiably, V's resistance is nonculpable,
even if the facts are such that D's act *was* justified.)

4. The Special Case of Lesser versus Least Evil

Thus far, we have endorsed a consequentialist "lesser evils" approach
to justification. We have further explored a limitation on this justification – deontological constraints that prevent an actor's justifying the
appropriation of others. There is another potential qualification of the
"lesser evils" approach that we should explore, namely, the question of
the lesser versus the least evil.

Let us return to Trolley. We concluded that D would be nonculpable
for switching the trolley to the siding even if she believed V, the one
trapped worker, would likely be killed, so long as D believed that if not
switched, the trolley would likely kill the five trapped workers on the

---

Likewise, in the example in which A is driving on the correct side of the highway
approaching a blind curve, B is attempting to pass on the blind curve, and C, a bystander
at the bend of the curve, sees that there are no cars coming in the opposite direction that
B will endanger but that there is a child in the right-hand lane, A will not be culpable for
endangering the child whose presence he is unaware of, and B will be culpable for passing
because he cannot see that there are no oncoming cars. Nonetheless, C acts nonculpably
if he gestures to A to change lanes, even if A would be culpable for doing so. Likewise, if
C shouts encouragement to B to pass, he does not share in B's culpability for doing so. In
both cases, C is acting justifiably in light of the risk that he, but not A or B, perceives.

main track. (D need not, however, be motivated by saving the five lives so long as she believes she is likely doing so. So long as D believes she is saving the five, she is a nonculpable, though morally flawed, actor if she switches the trolley solely to kill V.)

Suppose now that there is not one siding but two. On one siding is a single trapped worker (V_1), whereas on the other siding are two trapped workers (V_2 and V_3). And let us suppose that imposing a high risk of death on V_2 and V_3 is nonculpable if D believes that by doing so she is averting a high risk of five deaths. Finally, let us suppose D is aware of the five trapped workers, of V_1, and of V_2 and V_3. This time, however, D is a friend of V_1 but hates V_2 and V_3. She therefore wishes to switch the trolley to the siding occupied by V_2 and V_3. If she does so, she will have chosen what from her perspective is a *lesser evil* but not the *least evil*. Would that choice be culpable (as opposed to regrettable)?

On the one hand, D has no (enforceable) obligation to save anyone. She can let the trolley proceed unimpeded and kill the five. And she will not save anyone if to do so she must save V_2 and V_3 rather than V_1 – if she will be deemed culpable and hence punishable for saving V_1 and imposing the risk on V_2 and V_3. In the absence of the siding with V_1, she would have been nonculpable in switching the trolley to the siding with V_2 and V_3 regardless of her motivating reasons. And we would prefer that the trolley be switched to some siding rather than left on the main track.

On the other hand, D cannot say, as she could in the original Trolley, that her misanthropic intention produces no social harm. After all, were it not for her animus toward V_2 and V_3, she might have saved the five at the cost of only one death (V_1's). In some sense, she chose the greater evil (two deaths) over a lesser one (one death).

The case for finding D culpable for not choosing the least evil is strongest when D's path to the lesser but not least evil requires a sequence of choices – first, the choice to avert the greatest evil; then second, the choice of the greater of the lesser evils. For example, suppose there is a single spur track off the main track, which then divides into two spurs. From her position at the switch, D can first redirect the trolley to the spur and then, by further manipulating the switch, direct the trolley to either of the spur's branches. On one of the spur's branches are the two workers D hates. On the other is the one worker. As before, there are five workers on the main track.

Now suppose if D switches the trolley from the main track but then does not manipulate the switch further, the trolley will take the branch on which the two hated workers are trapped. This case is surely a strong case in favor of deeming D to be justified. After all, we do want D to switch the trolley. And although we would prefer that D then switch it again to the track with one worker, D has no affirmative obligation to act here any more than she had an affirmative obligation to switch the trolley from the main track.

Suppose, however, that when D switches the trolley from the main track but then refrains from further manipulation of the switch, the trolley will take the branch of the spur on which there is the one worker. Now suppose that D will switch the trolley from the main track to the spur only if it is permissible for her then to switch it to the branch with the two workers. Will it in fact be permissible for her thus to switch it and thereby choose the greater of the lesser evils? Her choice to switch the trolley from the less occupied to the more occupied spur, viewed in isolation, looks like a paradigmatic culpable choice. After all, again viewed in isolation, it is a choice of a greater, not a lesser, evil. On the other hand, if D's two choices are viewed as a single course of action – directing the trolley from the five workers to the two, D's second preferred course of action being doing nothing to save the five – it looks more like a permissible action. (Imagine a surgeon telling a patient, "You desperately need my services to save your life, services that I may permissibly withhold; but I will provide them only if you will let me carve my initials in your chest.")

Does the fact that D has no enforceable obligation to save the five and can be motivated to do so only if she is permitted to redirect the trolley toward V_2 and V_3 force us to conclude that so redirecting it is nonculpable? Perhaps. The case is really on all fours with cases of rescue in which D has no obligation to rescue V and will do so only if she may exploit V, or carry out the rescue in a way more dangerous (to V) than necessary. In these cases, there is a course of action open to D that is optimal – a nonexploitive rescue, or a safe rescue – but one that D is not motivated to choose. Telling D that she will be culpable and punishable if she chooses a rescue other than the optimal one (of which she is aware) may lead her to choose the least desirable course of action (doing nothing). On the other hand, perhaps most Ds, if not every D, will choose the optimal rescue over doing nothing if suboptimal rescues are forbidden.[35]

Of course, in many cases of suboptimal rescues, the suboptimal act – say, the dangerous way in which the rescue is carried out – occurs simultaneously with the rescue itself. In other cases, however, and in our case of the branching spur, the suboptimal act – the directing the trolley to the spur with two workers – occurs after the rescuing act. Even if the rescuer undertook the rescuing act only on the assurance that he could then choose the suboptimal act, it is still possible – and we think correct – to conclude that he acts wrongly in so choosing. After all, one cannot justify a murder at T_2 by having rescued, with no duty to do so, two people at T_1. And that it is wrong to choose the suboptimal act after having rescued others may be true even if such a verdict reduces the number of rescues and would therefore be rejected ex ante by those who might require rescue.

We raise the issue of the choice between a lesser evil and the least evil not in order to resolve it here but to flag it as one worthy of further consideration. We are confident that D's motivating reasons play no role in her culpability in the ordinary binary choice cases. Whenever D is aware of a third option or more, however, her reasons for not choosing the least evil, even though as in the binary case they motivate her to bring about a lesser evil, also motivate her to forgo averting a harm, a factor not present in the binary case. In the nonbinary cases D is always doing more than she is *morally obligated* to do (in the strong, legally enforceable sense of morally obligated) but less than she *morally ought* to do.[36]

One thing seems clear where D chooses a lesser but not the least evil. Even if D is in some sense acting justifiably and nonculpably in choosing a lesser but not the least evil, a third party – or the victims of the lesser-evil choice – may justifiably prevent D from choosing the lesser but not least evil if *they* intend, by so preventing D, to bring about the least evil. Thus, where D switches the trolley from the main track to a

35 For an interesting discussion of suboptimal rescues and the ability of the rescued to give effective consent to them, *see* Katz, *supra* note 20, at 653 et seq. Perhaps any moral theory that creates moral space for permissions will encounter problems with suboptimal but better-than-permitted acts.

36 *See also* Carolina Sartorio, "Moral Inertia," 140 *Phil. Stud.* 117, 128–130 (2008); Alastair Norcross, "Harming in Context," 123 *Phil. Stud.* 149, 163–168 (2005).

siding with, say, three workers, whom he hates, instead of to the siding with only one worker, D's friend, the three threatened workers, or some third party should be privileged to stop D, even at the cost of D's life, if they in turn intend to switch the trolley to the one-worker siding. D is not culpable for his intended choice of the lesser but not the least evil. But the loss of his life and the life of the worker on the siding represent a lesser evil than the loss of the three workers' lives.

B. SELF-DEFENSE, CULPABLE AGGRESSORS, AND OTHER CULPABLE ACTORS

How does the culpability of the victim of the actor's risk imposition bear on whether the actor's act is socially justified? Put differently, assume the actor's risk imposition would otherwise fail to be socially justified because the harms to victims, discounted by their probability, outweigh the social benefits, discounted by their probability. The question we are asking is whether that risk imposition can nevertheless be socially justified (and hence nonculpable) if the potential victims, or some of them, are culpable actors?

This question raises the issue of the justification of self-defense and its limits. Entire books, as well as a mountain of journal articles, have been devoted to the justification and limits of self-defense. We do not intend to produce a theory of self-defense here. Rather, what we intend is to show how self-defense and cognate matters fit into our schema and to raise the questions about self-defense that our schema requires be answered.

This categorization of these cases as "self-defense" is somewhat misleading, however, because the topic we address here is both narrower and broader than that of self-defense. It is narrower because we focus here only on *culpable aggressors* and not on innocent threats, innocent shields, or innocent bystanders, much less on the variety of innocent threats (the duped, the mistaken, the insane, the immature, and the nonacting). We take up innocent threats, shields, and bystanders later in the chapter when we consider the excuse of duress. Our topic is also broader than self-defense because we take up all types of culpable victims (of the actor's risk imposition), not just culpable aggressors.

1. Rights-Based Justifications

A preliminary question about self-defense is whether it is simply a species of the lesser-evils justification, or whether it has a separate justifying rationale. There is reason to believe that self-defense against a culpable aggressor need not be consequentially justified. Rather, one may be justified in killing in self-defense even if, all things considered, one brings about more harm than good.

Consider a defender who defends against an imminent culpable attack. Now, from a God's-eye perspective, it may be the case that, although the attack is imminent, the attacker will change her mind. From a purely consequentialist perspective, a live culpable aggressor is still better than a dead one, and thus, defending against the attack is unjustified. Nevertheless, because defenders can never wait until the attack is over, their actions will always be preemptive and must therefore be based upon some fair apportionment of the risks *they* perceive. (For God, there are no risks, only certainties.)

In this instance, it would not ultimately matter on our theory whether the defensive force is actually justified because the defender is not culpable in any event. That is, even if his action is not justified because the aggressor would not have killed him, the defender still *believes* that he is acting against a fatal attack, and that if his belief were correct, he would have a sufficient reason for killing his attacker.

A defender who is aware of a risk of an attack, however, will also be aware of the risk that the attack may not come to fruition. Indeed, as we discuss in this chapter, we must ask what level of perceived risk justifies the defender's response. Certainly, if the defender estimates the risk to be 100 percent likely – a risk that only God should estimate – he may defend. But it also seems permissible to defend against an (unconsented to) game of Russian roulette with a 20 percent chance of success, and even a game where the chances are much lower. Given that it seems permissible for a putative victim to defend against even small risks, we believe that this reveals that the justification for self-defense may be rights based and not consequentially justified – at least if we leave aside the possibility that the attacker's interests in the consequentialist balance are steeply discounted because of his culpability.[37]

Of course, this leaves a number of unanswered questions. When is the right triggered? Against whom may the defender act? Does the culpable aggressor *forfeit* his right to life (or against bodily harm), or is his right so *specified* that it is not implicated when the aggressor culpably attacks another?[38] Or, is this a case in which a defender may justifiably *infringe* another's right?[39] We cannot answer these questions here. We only suggest that, in responding to culpable aggressors, imposing some risks may be justified, even if they are not consequentially justified (at least in the absence of a steep discount of the aggressors' interests).

2. Third-Party Focus

The question of whether self-defense may be justified, but not consequentially justified, leads to a further complication – the implications for third parties. If a self-defender is justified under both rights-based and consequentialist theories, then it is clear why third parties may intervene to aid the defender or to hinder the aggressor. On the other hand, what are the implications for third parties if the defender's action is justified in the sense of being nonculpable but is not consequentially justified?

This conflict may rarely arise. Under our theory, defenders may defend whenever they believe there is a culpable attack (as discussed later), and third parties may intervene whenever *they* believe there is a culpable attack. And even if these two viewpoints differ, the *culpability* of each party is determined by his own perspective.

Nevertheless, there will be rare cases where the third party is *epistemically privileged* in comparison to the defender. In these cases, the third party may know the gun is unloaded, or the aggressor is not

---

[37] For additional arguments that self-defense is not simply an instantiation of the lesser-evils calculus, *see* David Rodin, *War and Self-Defense* 51–55 (2002); Sanford H. Kadish, "Respect for Life and Regard for Rights in the Criminal Law," 64 *Cal. L. Rev.* 871, 882–883 (1976).

[38] *See* Judith Jarvis Thomson, "Self-Defense and Rights," Lindley Lecture at the University of Kansas (April 5, 1976), reprinted in Judith Jarvis Thomson, *Rights, Restitution, and Risk: Essays in Moral Theory* 33 (William Parent, ed., 1986).

[39] *See* Judith Jarvis Thomson, "Some Ruminations on Rights," 19 *Ariz. L. Rev.* 45 (1977).

culpable, or the trolley track shifts and will not hit the workmen. In these instances, the law must give guidance to third parties regarding whether they may permissibly help or hinder the actor. That is, should a third party stop an actor who falsely believes that he must switch the trolley and kill the one workman in order to save the five if the third party knows that the trolley will, as currently directed, actually kill no one? May a third party stop a self-defender, if this intervener (correctly) believes that the culpable aggressor will either stop or fail in his imminent attack? In the former case, because the lesser-evils justification that would justify the trolley switcher if his beliefs were correct does not actually justify the trolley switcher, his action is not justified, and third parties can and should intervene to stop these nonculpable but mistaken actors. On the other hand, if culpable attacks themselves justify defensive responses under a rights-based theory, it is less clear to us what the implications are for third parties. After all, if the only way that a third party may intervene is by killing the mistaken but nonculpable self-defender, it seems the third party should not so act. What one might say here is that a third party, although he should not aid a mistaken self-defender, should also not harm the mistaken self-defender. The culpable aggressor's behavior has led to a lesser-evils trade-off, and the culpable party's life should be sacrificed before the defender's.[40]

Ultimately, we believe the moral territory is far richer and more complex than we can synthesize here. Because there is no reason for the law to make the fine-grained distinction between an action's being right and an action's being permissible, if we deem both the right and the permissible "justified," then justifications do not conceptually entail any implications for third parties. That is, if an action is right, then third parties may aid and attackers may not defend; but if an action is only permissible, then it is possible to have conflicting justifications. This problem arises simply because we are attempting to place complex moral questions within blunt legal categories.

As we have said, for our purposes, these questions of taxonomy have very few implications because every actor's liability is determined by his own perceptions of the risks and reasons. Because we are at present interested in justifications for the actors' risk impositions, not excuses,

---

[40] *See* Jeff McMahan, "Self-Defense and Culpability," 24 *Law & Phil.* 751, 772 (2005).

we examine these questions through the least controversial case where our actor is a third-party intervener who is trying to protect someone else from a risk imposition by the victim. We argue later that many cases of self-defense that are nonculpable are best viewed as instances of excuse or agent-relative (personal) justification, not as conduct that is impersonally justified; but we concede the complexity of these questions. Although putative victims will always be entitled to defend where a third party would be, the converse is not necessarily the case. Third parties cannot claim the *excuse* of self-protection that those under attack can claim. If third parties impose risks in order to protect others from having risks imposed on them, the third parties are culpable unless their acts are socially justified given their perception of the facts.

3. *Justified Responses to Culpable Aggressors*

In our view, self-defense is not justified against any and all threats. An actor may perceive the need to defend himself against a *culpable aggressor* (CA), an *innocent aggressor* (the mistaken, insane, or immature), or an *innocent threat* (a body hurled down at him). Alternatively, an actor, in striking out against her attacker, might know that she risks killing an *innocent shield* or nearby *bystander*. Out of all these possible cases of self-defensive risk imposition, it seems to us that self-defense is *justified* (from a social, impersonal perspective) only against culpable aggressors. When an actor decides to harm an innocent attacker, innocent threat, innocent shield, or innocent bystander, his action, if nonculpable, is so because it is either personally justified or excused, not because it is socially justified. We discuss the use of defensive force in such situations of personal justification and excuse later in this chapter.

Under either a consequentialist or rights-based rationale, we fail to see how self-defense can be justified (in an agent-neutral sense) other than when it is used against culpable aggressors. When we are dealing with innocent attackers, threats, and shields or bystanders, on a purely consequentialist balance, the numbers on either side of that balance are even – or, if there are more innocent attackers, threats, or shields or bystanders than there are defenders, the numbers come out in favor of the attackers, threats, and so forth. Moreover, under a rights-based approach, it seems to us that the innocent attackers, and a fortiori the innocent threats and shields or bystanders, have done nothing wrongful that would render them liable to attack. For these reasons, our discussion of self-defense focuses on culpable aggressors, or CAs.

The critical question then is what makes a CA a culpable aggressor. We argue in Chapter 6 that the standard culpable aggressor *is* culpable, but not for the risk he intends but has yet to impose. We believe that he is culpable for creating a risk that others will fear an attack, and for creating *that* risk for no good reason – indeed, for the bad reason of intending the attack that is feared.[41]

To flag an issue that we treat more fully in Chapter 6, the ordinary culpable aggressor is not culpable merely by virtue of intending harm. Nor is he yet culpable for imposing the risk of harm he intends to impose in the future. (If he has not yet imposed the risk of harm, then he cannot be culpable for imposing it, no matter how soon he intends to impose it.) If he has already imposed the risk, then those imposing a risk on him cannot be *defending* against that risk imposition but must either be *retaliating* – which is quite distinct from defending – or defending against some feared future risk imposition.

So the standard culpable aggressor is culpable, though his culpability is not the same as it would be were he to unleash the risk he now intends to unleash only in the future. For were he to unleash the risk, he would be more culpable, but he would at the same time no longer be a threat and the legitimate target of *defensive* risk imposition. Thus, what authorizes the defender to respond is the *fear of attack* and not the attack itself.

Now, this fear of attack must be culpably created by the aggressor. CAs need not be *intending* to harm their victims (Vs). Rather, CAs are culpable when they intend to impose a risk on Vs for unjustifiable reasons. If Deborah intends not to kill Vance but to play involuntary Russian roulette on him, Deborah is a CA.[42] Moreover, if Dana intends to speed to impress Edgar and, by doing so, knows she will be risking death to Vickie, Vickie, too, may defend against Dana's action. Anyone

---

[41] Of course, a CA may be culpable imposing a risk of harm other than merely the fear of an attack. For example, the CA may have a loaded gun that could accidentally discharge. And that risk is a culpable one to impose, given that the CA's reason for carrying the loaded gun is to attack someone with it. Or, like Frankie in Chapter 2, the CA may be driving to a location where she intends to impose an unjustified risk and thus be imposing an unjustified risk by driving.

[42] *See* Ferzan, *supra* note 19, at 711–728.

whose planned (or culpably risked) future act would be culpable under the analysis of culpability we set forth in Chapter 2 will be a CA.

Finally, we should understand that what links the aggressor's culpability to the defender's fear of attack is the very fact that the culpable aggressor *has aggressed*. That is, the CA has performed some action that creates apprehension of an impending culpable risk imposition. In our view, this requirement is currently subsumed within the doctrinal requirement that the threat be imminent. The imminence requirement not only assures that the defender will not act before it is necessary to do so but also effectively requires that the aggressor have acted. It serves as the *actus reus* for aggression.[43] Although displaying that one is an imminent threat is a more threatening act than we would require, we would dispense with the imminence requirement only while at the same time recognizing that *some culpable act* on the part of the aggressor is required. (We address later the treatment of anticipated culpable aggressors [ACAs] who have yet to attack.)

With the rough notion of a CA in hand, let us pick Dina as our stand-in for all CAs. Dina, who loves the sights, sounds, and smells associated with setting off dynamite, intends to set off several sticks of it next to a school in session. She is aware of the school and the children in it, and aware that she is subjecting them to a basket of decent-sized risks – of death, bodily injury, psychological trauma, property destruction, and disruption of education. She does not have as her purpose the production of any of those harms. Her purpose is solely her enjoyment of blasting.

Tipper is our third-party defender. Tipper sees Dina put the dynamite near the school, attach the fuse, and take out a match. Tipper is too far way to put out the fuse herself, but she does have a rifle and may be able to prevent the anticipated blast by shooting Dina. Tipper realizes that shooting Dina will impose a high risk of death or serious injury on Dina. Would Tipper's imposing such a risk on Dina, our CA, be justifiable or be culpable?

Under traditional self-defense doctrine, Tipper's risk imposition would be justified only if Dina's threat were *imminent*; if Tipper's

---

[43] *See* Kimberly Kessler Ferzan, "Defending Imminence: From Battered Women to Iraq," 46 *Ariz. L. Rev.* 213, 259–260 (2004).

response to the threat were *necessary* and *proportionate*; and if Tipper cannot effect a safe *retreat* for Dina's potential victims. We discuss each of these requirements in turn.

a. The Temporal Dimension: The criminal law traditionally required that the use of defensive force be restricted to situations where the feared harm was *imminent*. Most commentators argue that the imminence requirement serves as a proxy for necessity – that the actor must need to act – and thus, if action is necessary before it becomes imminent, the defensive act should be justified.[44] We believe the imminence requirement should be dropped as well, but we believe that the imminence requirement has more normative and conceptual purchase than merely standing in as a proxy for necessity. As discussed earlier, we believe that the imminence requirement also serves as the *actus reus* for aggression, the requirement that the aggressor act in a way that culpably creates a fear of harm.

To the extent that imminence serves as a proxy for necessity (or, more aptly, serves as a rule that instantiates the necessity standard), we believe that the Model Penal Code approach that the use of the defensive force be *immediately necessary* is a salutary change.[45] For example, suppose Dina's fuse is many minutes long, but Tipper still cannot disable it or warn the school. It would be odd to say that Tipper cannot use defensive force in such a situation. Her defensive action *is* immediately necessary to prevent the blast, even if the blast itself and its feared harmful consequences are not imminent.

Moreover, if, as we believe, the temporal aspect serves only an evidentiary function with respect to how likely the feared harm is to occur, then the Model Penal Code's revision should be given an interpretation consistent with that function. Suppose, for example, that if Tipper shoots at Dina the moment Dina takes out a match, the feared blast is less likely to occur than if Dina waits until Tipper strikes the match. And suppose the blast is even less likely to occur if Tipper shoots Dina while Dina is laying the fuse.

---

[44] *See* 2 Paul H. Robinson, *Criminal Law Defenses* § 131(b)(3) (1984); Stephen J. Schulhofer, "The Gender Question in Criminal Law," 7 *Soc. Phil. & Pol'y* 105, 117 (1990).

[45] *See* Model Penal Code § 3.04 (1985).

It seems to us that the key issue here is not the temporal interval between Tipper's defensive action and the harm that Tipper is attempting to avert. The key issue is the degree of likelihood that the harm will occur. If there is a threshold degree of likelihood of the harm's occurrence that suffices to justify Tipper's defensive action, then once that threshold is reached, Tipper should be justified in taking that action. If waiting longer will raise the likelihood of the harm's occurrence, then Tipper need not wait. Time affects the probabilities of harm and nothing else.

Of course, time affects the probabilities of harm because it affects not only the likelihood of Dina's setting off the dynamite but also Tipper's alternatives. With enough time, Tipper may be able to warn the school and get the children out of harm's way, or warn the police so that they can stop Dina. These alternatives, however, may be less effective than Tipper's shooting Dina. That is, their likelihood of averting the danger may not be high enough to reduce the risk below the threshold at which Tipper's shooting Dina is justified. Moreover, those alternatives themselves involve costs to Tipper (the effort involved in warning versus the lesser effort involved in shooting), and costs to others (the loss of part of the school day, the diversion of police resources, and so on). So these costs of alternatives to Tipper's shooting Dina must be weighed against the cost to Dina, a CA, of Tipper's shooting at her. It is to this issue we turn next.

b. Proportional Response: Necessity, Proportionality, and Retreat: Another traditional tenet of Anglo-American criminal law is that defensive force must be *proportional* to the threat it is meant to avert. Still another traditional requirement is that defensive force, even if proportional, must be *necessary* for averting the threat. And a third tenet, at least with respect to deadly defensive force, is that such force is not justifiable if the defender can avoid the threat by *retreat*.

These three tenets are actually only one tenet, what we call the *proportional response* tenet. To see this, let us return to Dina and Tipper. Suppose that, considered in isolation, Tipper's shooting Dina is considered a proportional and therefore justifiable response to the basket of risks Dina is about to unleash. But suppose also that Tipper, with a little more effort, can just as effectively avert the threatened harms by running to a nearby house and calling the school. So shooting Dina is not necessary for averting the threat to the school and its children. It *is* necessary, however, for averting a different harm. That is the harm Tipper suffers as a result of running to the nearby house, which requires substantial effort, instead of shooting Dina, which is relatively easy. And Tipper, we shall assume, in general has a right not to be forced to make such an effort.

The necessity question is really just a component of the proportionality question. For suppose that, although shooting Dina is a proportional response to the threat of death and injury (from the blast), it is not a proportional response to the harm of expending the effort required to phone the school. If Tipper may not shoot Dina to avoid the latter harm, then she must not shoot Dina if she can just as effectively avoid the threat by running to the nearby house and phoning the school.

It should now be apparent why the retreat doctrine is also merely a component of proportional response. Retreating forces a defender to sacrifice his interest in remaining where he is and avoiding the effort, other costs, and risks of retreating. If, however, the interests sacrificed by retreating are of insufficient weight to justify the harm inflicted defensively, then defensive force cannot be justifiably employed if retreat is an option.[46]

Proportional response and its corollaries of necessity and retreat raise many daunting issues. One issue is, of course, whether morality demands proportionality in dealing with CAs. Why should anyone

---

[46] In an earlier article, one of us raised the following questions about the retreat requirement: if retreat is required, when is the requirement triggered? Suppose the Marshal knows that the man he sent away to prison has just gotten off the train and is aiming to settle the score in a gun fight. It is a fifteen-minute walk from the station to Main Street, where the Marshal presently is waiting. Assume the Marshal should retreat rather than kill in self-defense (forget his law enforcement status). *When* must he do so? He has the greatest chance of retreating safely now, but if he does so, he sacrifices several minutes on Main Street. Moreover, the chances are greater now than they will be later that, even if he waits, no gun fight will ever occur. The attacker may have a change of heart, become scared, get waylaid, fall and injure himself, and so on. On the other hand, if the Marshal waits too long, he may be unable to retreat safely and will then have to shoot to protect himself. And if he waits until the very last moment before he believes a gun fight will be virtually inescapable, something may happen – he may trip and fall, for example – that will force the gunfight in any event, and perhaps on less favorable terms to the Marshal. *See* Larry Alexander, "A Unified Excuse of Preemptive Self-Protection," 74 *Notre Dame L. Rev.* 1475, 1480 (1999).

have to sacrifice a legitimate interest to avoid risking harm to CAs, who by hypothesis have no sufficient reason to act as they are acting? And suppose the defender predicts that the CA will respond to proportional defensive acts by escalating her attack to one that is more dangerous to the defender, at which point the defender, even if now permitted a more dangerous (to the CA) defensive response, will be in much greater danger. May the defender skip the proportional response and go straight to the more effective and, at present, less risky, more dangerous (to the CA) response? Indeed, what if the defender both predicts the escalation and its greater risks for him and knows that his proportional response would be quite ineffective? (The CA, who is much larger than the defender, intends to hold the defender down but not seriously injure him; the defender's proportional force will be ineffective because of his size disadvantage, but it will provoke the CA to become murderous. May the defender use proportional force and then use his gun when the CA's attack turns deadly? If so, may he skip the proportional force and go straight to the gun if provoking the response would be riskier? Or must he give the CA the benefit of the doubt and assume the CA will not be provoked to a murderous response by a proportional – but ineffective – resistance?)

Another issue raised by proportional response and its corollaries is whether proportionality, if it is a moral requirement, rules out such defensive measures as protecting relatively minor interests by means that make it dangerous for CAs to infringe those interests. Suppose Martha is not morally permitted to use deadly force to prevent apple thieves from picking apples off her tree. May she surround the apple tree with a moat filled with alligators or a deadly electrified fence? (Assume she posts clear warnings that attempting to pick her apples will confront CAs with these deadly dangers.) And may she rig her apple tree with a device that will set off a deadly bomb in her house, with the result that she can now treat apple picking as a deadly attack, one entitling her to shoot potential apple thieves? Is rigging the tree with a bomb and then shooting to prevent the blast morally different from the moat or electrified fence? Are the latter morally different from placing one's apple tree on a dangerous-to-climb ledge, or one's apples in a safe that it is dangerous (to life) to blast open?[47]

---

[47] *See* Larry Alexander, "The Doomsday Machine: Proportionality, Prevention and Punishment," 63 *Monist* 199 (1980); Larry Alexander, "Consent, Punishment, and Proportionality," 15 *Phil. & Pub. Aff.* 178 (1986).

We doubt, however, that there *should* be a proportionality requirement when responding to culpable aggressors. (We qualify this strong position slightly at the end of this section.) The problem arises when we note that a defender is never acting against just one risk but rather a basket of risks, all of which have different probability levels.

Assume that Tipper will be justified in shooting Dina only if shooting is a proportional response given the interests threatened. Those interests may be quite varied, and each interest may be threatened to a different degree (i.e., subject to a different level of risk). We listed the interests that Dina's intended blasting will threaten: death, bodily injury, psychological trauma, disruption of education, and property damage. Moreover, the risks to each of these interests may differ, with each risk located at a different point between zero and one. The risk of death may be relatively low, the risk of bodily injury higher, and the risk of education disruption higher still.

The level of risk for each interest at stake is a function of Tipper's assessment of such matters as the potency of dynamite, whether this dynamite is at normal potency, whether the fuse is good or defective, and whether Dina's match will light, as well as the location of the school children, the condition of their health, the construction of the school buildings, and myriad other matters. (In the ordinary case of defensive force against a murderous attack with a gun, the probability that, unless repelled, the attack will result in the defender's death is a function of the likelihood that the gun is loaded, the bullets functional, the trigger not stuck, the attacker's aim good and hand steady, the defender's body vulnerable, and so on. A low probability for any of these will result in a low risk of death.)

Moreover, where CAs are concerned, there is one more, and quite important, probability that bears on the overall set of risks. That is the probability that the CA will have a change of heart and desist from the planned culpable act. Defensive force against CAs is always preemptive. It always occurs before the CA has unleashed the risk. Therefore, it is always possible for the CA to call off the attack; and that possibility reduces the overall risk of harm if the defender refrains from defensive action. We do assign probabilities to free choices by human beings, so there is nothing unusual about assigning a probability to whether the CA will or will not desist if her attack is not preempted by defensive action. Still, one may feel somewhat uneasy about predictions of choices that are not only free but culpable, which is why many feel uneasy about other measures to preempt predicted criminality, such as preventive detention of "the dangerous," bans on firearms, and restraining orders, just to mention a few.

Of how great a magnitude and to what interests must a risk be to warrant imposition of a serious risk of death as a defensive matter? Suppose Tipper is confronted not with Dina and her threat to the school-children from blasting but Deborah, who is about to play involuntary Russian roulette on Vance. Tipper believes Deborah is a CA. Tipper also believes Deborah has placed one live round in a six-chamber gun, that she is aiming the gun at Vance's head, that her hand is steady, that Vance is wearing no bulletproof headgear, and so on. Tipper also esti-mates the chance that Deborah will desist from this plan if not stopped to be virtually nonexistent. Tipper therefore concludes that unless she shoots Deborah now, Vance faces a one-in-six chance that he will be shot and, if so, that he will almost certainly be killed or suffer severe brain damage.

Would a one-in-six chance of Vance's death or serious injury justify Tipper's shooting and likely killing Deborah? If so, then what if Tipper believed Deborah's gun held one live bullet but had eight chambers? Twenty chambers? One hundred chambers? One thousand chambers? If Tipper believes Deborah and Dina are CAs, what is the threshold level of risk of death or serious injury that CAs appear to pose above which Tipper would be justified in subjecting Deborah and Dina to severe risks in defense?[48] To us, at least, the answer seems to be that if Tipper believes there is *any risk*, she should be justified in imposing severe risks on CAs in defense. Moreover, this is true no matter how numerous the CAs; even one thousand Deborahs playing involuntary Russian roulette with a thousand-chambered gun on one Vance should be permissible targets of Tipper's deadly defensive force.

Abandoning a proportionality constraint places significant pres-sure on the question of when an individual is a CA. Notice that we can assess CAs Deborah and Dina along two dimensions. We can ask

---

[48] Put differently, if defensive risk imposition that would otherwise be deemed unjustifiable is justifiable if the risks are imposed on a CA, just how culpable must a CA be to fall into this more vulnerable category? *See, e.g.,* McMahan, *supra* note 40, at 760–765.

about the magnitudes of the risks they appear to be about to impose –
to which interests of others, and with what probability. But we can also
ask about their culpability. A CA imposing a high risk to an important interest such as life and limb may nonetheless be only margin-
ally culpable. A CA may be driving dangerously to get a sick friend
to the hospital, which reason may fall short, but only barely so, of justifying the serious risks he is imposing on others. Or Deborah may
believe she has placed only one live round in her gun, whereas she actually placed more live rounds in it. Or Sam, who intends, culpably, to
slap Sandra's face, does not realize that Sandra is in an extraordinary
"egg shell skull" condition and may die from a mere slap. And CAs
like Deborah and Dina, whose purpose is not to bring about harm but
only to risk it, may be quite culpable, even if the risks they are about to
impose are quite small. Deborah, with the one-thousand chambered
gun, may be much more culpable when she pulls the trigger than the
typical reckless driver, who imposes higher risks but for better, albeit
insufficient, reasons.

CAs may also impose different risks with varying levels of culpability. Because risks come in bundles – a reckless driver may impose
W risk of death, X risk of serious injury, Y risk of minor injury, Z risk
of property damage, and so on – and because almost any culpable act
may increase others' risks of serious injury or death by a finite if slight
amount, it is difficult to know what would count as a proportional
response, which is one reason to reject a proportionality constraint
on defensive risk impositions. (And because the necessity and retreat
requirements are corollaries of the proportionality requirement, they
fall if proportionality falls.) What *would* be a proportional response to
Deborah's Russian roulette? What *would* be a proportional response
to a reckless driver? To a CA who intends to pinch you, raising your
chances of dying by .0001 percent?

In summary, the requirements of necessity, proportionality, and
retreat are all one requirement – the requirement of a proportional
response. If V can retreat, shooting is not necessary. If shooting is not
necessary, then it certainly is not proportionate to the threat. Apart
from the conceptual relationship of these requirements, there remains
the question of whether it is normatively attractive to have a proportionality requirement. We do not believe so, as any given threshold ignores

the fact that the V is always defending against a multitude of risks with varying degrees of probability and that, as between a CA and a V, it is difficult to understand why it is the V who should bear the risk of harm. We recognize that our position places significant pressure on the definition of CAs, but we believe that the question of what makes an actor culpable and therefore liable to defensive force is the appropriate place for analysis.[49]

Does this mean that there are no limits on the risks V or TP can impose on a CA to defend V? May V run over a CA who is culpably blocking V's driveway rather than avoid him and waste an extra second or two or injure his lawn? We qualify our rejection of a proportionality

---

[49] We usually consider the use of defensive force as at most permissible but surely not mandatory. (We leave aside those special situations where the defender is obligated to defend another regardless of the other's wishes, such as when a parent defends a child, or more generally, when a guardian defends a ward.) Suppose, however, that although CA Deborah, who is playing involuntary Russian roulette on Vance, would otherwise be a legitimate target of risk imposition by TP Tipper, Vance holds religious or moral beliefs that lead him to forswear imposing serious risks on others, even in his own defense. So if Tipper were out of the picture, Vance would not shoot Deborah to stop her from playing Russian roulette on him. If Tipper is aware of Vance's beliefs, would she be justified in shooting Deborah to protect Vance? How do Vance's moral and religious preferences affect the consequentialist balance for Tipper? *See* David Mellow, "Iraq: A Morally Justified Resort to War," 23 *J. Applied Phil.* 293, 297 (2006) (asserting that the personal convictions of victims of immoral acts do not undermine the justifiability of third-party interventions on their behalf).

Or, to complicate matters further, suppose Vance's beliefs would lead him to forswear violence against everyone except Deborah, whom he hates for reasons unconnected to Deborah's current assault – bad reasons, we shall assume. If Vance's preference for nonviolence would otherwise cause Tipper's risk imposition on Deborah to be deemed unjustified, can Vance's hateful exception with respect to Deborah change the outcome?

Of course, unless Tipper has special knowledge about Vance, she will undoubtedly believe that Vance, like most people in his situation, will welcome defensive risk imposition on those about to culpably impose risks on him. If, however, Tipper knows of Vance's more idiosyncratic wishes, how should that knowledge affect what Tipper would otherwise be justified in doing?

If we are right, and a greater-than-proportional response to a CA is morally permissible – along with the logical implications that neither retreat nor strict necessity is required of the defender – then if defense by those like Tipper is rights based, the right is one against any culpable imposition of risk. When faced with the choice between allowing a culpably imposed risk to any irreparable and substantial interest and a defensive risk imposition on a CA, the latter can be preferred. This is not due to the CA's negative desert – the defensive risk imposition may be more severe than the CA would deserve as punishment if he unleashes his intended risk. The defensive harm, in other words, may exceed the CA's retributive desert were he to act as he intends. Rather, by becoming a CA, the CA completely forfeits his moral immunity from defensive risks and harms.

constraint to this extent: if the alternative and more proportional defensive measure does not entail any increased risk of irreparable (and perhaps severe) harm, then V or TP must choose that measure rather than the more severe one. On the other hand, if the less severe measure entails an increased risk of irreparable (and perhaps severe) harm, then the more severe measure may be chosen. An increased risk of such harm is in principle no different from the risk imposed by Deborah, the involuntary Russian roulette player, a risk against which V and TP may surely defend with lethal force.

4. *The Risk That a Possible Culpable Aggressor Is Not One*

We have been discussing CAs as if Tipper can know with certainty that Dina is one. But because our ultimate concern is Tipper's culpability, if any, for imposing various risks on Dina, it is crucial to keep in mind that defenders like Tipper can never know for certain that someone who appears to be a CA *is* a CA. Dina may have something innocent that only appears to be dynamite. Or Dina may have been informed that a dynamite blast was needed immediately to avert some dire consequence. Or Dina might be sufficiently mentally ill to be nonculpable. (If, on the other hand, Dina is playing a practical joke with fake dynamite, she may be a CA for creating apprehension, if we assume her desire to play a practical joke does not justify the apprehension she expects to cause.)

If one takes the position that defensive risk impositions on CAs are *justifiable* – as opposed to *excused* – *even if the same risk impositions on the nonculpable would not be*, then that must be because the CAs are CAs. But any person on whom a risk is imposed defensively *might* or *might not* be a CA.

Notice that so long as Tipper believes that Dina is or is not a CA, then whether she is right or wrong, it is easy to assess her culpability. If Tipper correctly assesses Dina to be a CA, then she is not culpable for using defensive force. And if Tipper incorrectly assesses Dina to be a CA, then, although she is not justified, she is still not *culpable* for using defensive force – with the consequence that Dina or a third-party defender of Dina, if aware of Tipper's false belief that Dina is a CA, may not treat Tipper as a CA but must treat her as a nonculpable risk imposer (on Dina). (And if Tipper does not believe Dina to be a CA, then Tipper may be objectively justified but culpable or objectively unjustified and culpable, but culpable either way.)

The problem arises when Tipper's evaluation is not one of flat-out belief but, as it should be, one of probability. For example, imagine that Dina is always an evil malefactor, but Dina's twin Donna is unfortunately quite mentally ill. Tipper again sees Dina – or Donna – about to use the dynamite, but Tipper, who knows both Dina and Donna, cannot ascertain whether the actor is Dina or Donna.

Consider the implications if the person whom Tipper sees is Donna. Because killing Donna is a lesser evil than allowing the schoolchildren to die, it would be permissible for Tipper to kill Donna in order to defend the children. (And if, in light of our earlier discussion of lesser versus least evils, Tipper is not required to select the least evil, then she may permissibly kill Donna rather than use lesser force.)

However, what if Dina/Donna threatens only one person? Here, Tipper may not intervene if it is Donna because the balance of evils is not positive. On the other hand, if it is Dina, then Tipper may intervene, and in fact, we want her to do so.

If the culpability of the target of a risk imposition makes a difference to the justifiability of that risk imposition, then how confident must the risk imposer be that the target is relevantly culpable? One position would be bivalent – once a threshold level of probability is reached, Tipper may treat Dina/Donna as a CA. But then we have to determine where to set the threshold. One possible position to take is that the risk imposer – Tipper – must be as certain that the target – Dina – is culpable as a jury should be to impose punishment on the basis of Dina's culpability. If a jury would have to believe in Dina's culpability beyond a reasonable doubt, then so must Tipper.

Another possible position is that Tipper's degree of confidence that Dina is culpable just discounts the effect of Dina's culpability in the consequentialist calculus that determines the justifiability of Tipper's act. If the balance of consequences, discounted by their probabilities, justifies Tipper's act if Dina *is* a CA – because the consequences of the risk imposition on Dina are discounted by her culpability – then the question for Tipper is whether the balance still tips in favor of imposing the risk if Tipper believes there is, say, a 60 percent probability of Dina's being a CA (or a 30 percent probability, and so on).

Of course, if we drop the proportionality constraint on imposing risks on CAs, the effect of that is to treat Dina's being a CA as a total elimination of her side of the consequentialist balance. Essentially, her being a CA would produce a 100 percent discount of the bad consequences of Tipper's defensive action. But what if Tipper is not 100 percent certain that Dina is a CA? Do the bad consequences for Dina now count, albeit at less than face value? Is it possible that if Tipper is only, say, 95 percent sure that Deborah, with her thousand-chambered gun, is a CA, that even a 95 percent discount of the serious risks Tipper is defensively imposing on Deborah will still result in those risks outweighing the risks Deborah (if she *is* a CA) is about to impose on Vance?

On the other hand, we can start from the default position that Tipper should assume that she sees Donna, not Dina.[50] Then, in these cases, Tipper should treat the problem as one of lesser-evils balancing, similar to when it is clear that the actor is an innocent aggressor. However, because Tipper believes that Donna might be Dina – say, she believes it to be equally likely that it is one or the other – she may discount Dina/Donna's relative weight in the consequentialist balance commensurate with the probability that Tipper assigns to the likelihood that Dina/Donna is culpable. That is, if Tipper sees Dina/Donna attacking one person, Tipper may intervene because she should treat Dina/Donna as counting for .5 of a person, and thus the consequentialist balance comes out in favor of the victim, not Dina/Donna.

Interestingly, this problem draws a sharp distinction between self-defense and defense of others. From the potential victim's perspective, it may not matter whether the attacker is a CA or an innocent aggressor, because either way she will not be culpable if she is personally justified (excused) in acting to defend herself. That is, even if the victim believes there is some chance that she is attacking an innocent person, she will still be excused whenever a person of reasonable firmness would defend herself thusly rather than use lesser force or retreat. On the other hand, Tipper, because as a nonthreatened third party she has

---

[50] *Cf.* Jeff McMahan, *The Ethics of Killing in War: The Oxford Uehiro Lectures* (forthcoming) (arguing that most unjust combatants can be supposed to be innocent [excused] actors, and that the rules as to when a just combatant may kill an unjust combatant should assume as much).

no personal justification or excuse, needs a rule that tells her how to act under conditions of uncertainty. This is because even after she assesses the probabilities (no matter how complex they are), the law still must make a determination as to what level of confidence Tipper must have to intervene. We do not believe there is any easy answer to this question.

5. Culpable Aggressors versus Culpable Aggressors

Consider another complication. Suppose Tipper confronts a situation in which Deborah appears to be playing involuntary Russian roulette on Vance and is thus (apparently) a CA. But suppose that Vance also appears to Tipper to be playing involuntary Russian roulette on Deborah. As Tipper perceives matters, both Deborah and Vance are CAs. May Tipper intervene and defensively impose a risk on one of the two, and if so, on whom? Is the situation analogous to Trolley with one worker on each track? Suppose Deborah's gun has more chambers than Vance's or vice versa? Suppose Deborah appears less likely than Vance to go through with the game and pull the trigger (or vice versa)?

There are two options here. One is to say that both actors are acting wrongly; and because protecting one would be aiding the other, Tipper should not intervene at all because she may not aid unjustified conduct. The other approach is to say that this conflict has created a lesser-evils choice. The question would then be how to determine who should live and who should die.

6. The Provoked Culpable Aggressor

Suppose that Tipper, wanting to eliminate the menace of Dina, tells Dina that setting off dynamite near a school would be especially thrilling and dares Dina to do it. Tipper plans to wait until Dina is about to light the fuse, at which point Tipper plans to shoot Dina. If Tipper may otherwise shoot Dina in such a circumstance, may she do so if she has instigated Dina's culpable aggression in this way? (Readers will, of course, be reminded of Charles Bronson's provocative vigilante walks through Central Park in *Death Wish*.) Dina is no less a CA for having been egged on by Tipper. And Tipper's motive is a public-spirited one. (She may believe that Dina will commit many more such dangerous culpable acts if not caught in the act.) So how should we regard Tipper's risk imposition on Dina?[51]

One thing seems clear. Once Dina decides to set off the dynamite and thereby becomes a CA, Tipper is *not* culpable for then imposing a defensive risk on Dina. If Tipper does not do so, Dina, a CA, will impose a risk on the children. So Tipper is justified in defensively imposing a risk on Dina despite being implicated in Dina's plan.

If Tipper is culpable, it is for egging Dina on, not for acting defensively once Dina acts to set off the dynamite. No one whose act is otherwise justifiable should lose her justification merely by virtue of having culpably created the circumstances that give rise to the justification. The question is whether Tipper should be deemed culpable for acting in a way that would provoke or entice Dina to become a CA and expose herself to Tipper's defensive risk imposition. Tipper did, by so acting, increase that risk to Dina. On the other hand, Tipper's reasons were laudable. And presumably Dina is always free to reject temptations to act culpably.

If Tipper *is* culpable for egging on or provoking Dina into becoming a CA, her culpability will mandate that she act to prevent Dina from setting off the blast. Normally, Tipper will be permitted but not required to impose a defensive risk on Dina. But if Tipper is culpable for provoking Dina and thereby endangering her (from defensive risk impositions),

---

[51] Ironically, as Leo Katz has pointed out to one of us in private correspondence, one is not required to turn over one's wallet to a mugger who demands "your money or your life," even if one expects a deadly attack to follow and intends to respond with lethal force. In other words, one may *assume* the mugger will act rightfully and not launch the threatened attack. That permissible assumption then entitles one to use deadly force, ultimately in defense of one's wallet. If one generalizes this permission to stand one's ground (keep one's wallet), the retreat requirement dissolves. *See* e-mail from Leo Katz, Frank Carano Professor of Law, University of Pennsylvania Law School, to Larry Alexander, Warren Distinguished Professor of Law, University of San Diego School of Law (January 3, 1999) (on file with author).

If Tipper may egg Dina on and then impose a risk on her once Dina becomes a CA, may Tipper provoke Dina through some culpable act – say, by punching her – if Tipper does so in order, say, to kill Dina in response to an anticipated culpable retaliatory response by her? If Charles Bronson justifiably provoked his assailants by walking through Central Park, would his deadly response have been nonculpable had he provoked them to a culpable, murderous response through some minor but culpable act, say, by grabbing their property or slapping them? Or would his culpability be limited to the minor level of the provoking act?

Tipper's culpability will be *increased* if she then refuses to endanger culpable Dina and thereby leaves the innocent schoolchildren at risk. Put differently, Tipper's initial act of provoking Dina, if culpable, created either an unjustifiable risk to culpable Dina or an unjustifiable risk to innocent schoolchildren, depending upon whether Tipper now acts to stop Dina. (If she does not, then she converts the alternative risks into a single – and more culpable – risk to the schoolchildren.)

Moreover, if Tipper is culpable for endangering Dina, then even if a nonculpable Tipper could respond disproportionately to Dina, culpable Tipper might be required to use the least force necessary to stop Dina. For even if nonculpable Tipper could choose shooting Dina over the equally effective but more burdensome (to Tipper) means of phoning the school or the police, culpable Tipper may have to sacrifice her interests and undertake the more burdensome but less dangerous (to Dina) means of stopping Dina so long as those means are, Tipper believes, as effective as the more dangerous ones (to Dina). So even if Dina, as a CA, may be stopped with disproportionate force – because innocent people acting to prevent risk impositions need not sacrifice *any* interests to avoid imposing greater risks on CAs – defenders who are CAs may have to impose the least risk necessary, up to risks that are proportionate to that threatened, even at great sacrifice.

7. The Range of Culpable Actors

We have been discussing how a CA's act of culpable aggression may render him liable to others' use of defensive force. But culpability potentially enters the justification calculus in forms in addition to that of the culpable aggressor. The person on whom the actor is now imposing a risk may have committed a past culpable act for which he has not been punished. He may have culpably imposed a risk on the actor or on others.

Culpable aggressors (CAs) can be distinguished from what we shall call culpable persons (CPs). With respect to CPs – who include CAs but also those who are not CAs – there are two principal issues: First, may CPs have their interests discounted in the consequentialist calculus that determines whether the actor's risk imposition is justifiable or is culpable? Does the fact that those at risk are CPs mean that the actor, holding his reasons for acting constant, may impose a greater risk of harm than he otherwise may? And does it mean that, holding the degree of risk constant, the actor may act for less weighty reasons than he otherwise may?

Suppose, for example, that the interests of CPs may be discounted in the consequentialist calculus that determines the justifiability of risk impositions. And suppose that in Trolley, instead of five workers trapped on the main track, there is only one worker; but as before, there is one worker trapped on the siding. Leaving aside other factors that might be relevant to a justifiable risk imposition – the relative ages of the trapped workers, consent, the relative likelihood of escape, and so on – switching the trolley would not be choosing the lesser evil. Suppose, however, that the trapped worker on the siding is a CP. For example, suppose his recklessness is what caused the trolley to go out of control. Would it now be justifiable to impose the risk on him rather than allow the risk to the worker on the main track to persist? Similarly, would it be *un*justifiable to switch the trolley in the original Trolley scenario if the five trapped workers were CPs and the one trapped worker a saint? (Suppose the five workers knew they were not suppose to work on the main track because of the danger of a runaway trolley but did so anyway, thereby knowingly risking a forced choice between their lives and that of the one worker on the siding. Or suppose the five workers were on work furlough from the penitentiary, where they were serving life terms for a series of brutal murders.) Or, where a bystander is innocently preventing one who is being fired at by an attacker from having a clear shot at the attacker, may the defender shoot the bystander if the bystander is a CP?[52]

---

[52] *See* McMahan, *supra* note 40, at 762–763. Suppose, for example, that two attackers, A and B, culpably shoot at V, intending V's death. A's gun is now empty, and he finds himself stuck in V's window. B is still firing at V but is shielded from V's return fire by A. Because A is a CP, may V deliberately kill him in order to defend himself from B? *See also* Jeff McMahan, "The Basis of Moral Liability to Defensive Killing," 15 *Phil. Iss.* 386, 392–393 (2005) (making the case that CAs who are no longer CAs but are now CPs may be killed in defense against other CAs).

Or suppose A has swallowed V's pacemaker, and V will die if A is not killed and cut open. Or suppose terrorist T has swallowed the map with the location of the "ticking bomb" that T's confederates planted. T does not know its location without consulting the map, and thousands will die unless T is killed and cut open. May A and T be defensively killed because they are CPs even if not at present CAs? For affirmative answers, *see* Uwe Steinhoff, "Torture – The Case for Dirty Harry and against Alan Dershowitz," 23 J. *Applied Phil.* 337, 341 (2006); Phillip Montague, "The Morality of Self-Defense: A Reply to Wasserman," 18 *Phil. & Pub. Aff.* 81 (1989).

Second, may CPs be "used" in ways that would otherwise violate the deontological constraint against using persons' bodies, labor, and talent as means to what are otherwise on-balance justified consequences?[53] Suppose, for example, the patient in Surgeon whose organs are harvested to save five lives is an unpunished ax-murderer. Does that change the verdict on the justifiability of Surgeon's act?[54]

Perhaps the permissibility of appropriating a CP may turn on whether the CP created the very risk that led to the lesser-evils predicament. In Surgeon, would it be justifiable to harvest the one patient's organs – to use his body as a means of saving others – if the one patient culpably caused the illnesses of the five who now require his organs to survive? Or suppose Fat Man, standing on the bridge over the trolley tracks, who can be pushed onto the tracks to save the five trapped workers, is the one who culpably started the trolley on its deadly course.

It might seem that any discounting of the CP's interests in the consequentialist calculus must be consistent with the deontological constraint against punishing more than one retributively deserves. That might not be true, however, where imposing a risk on the CP is meant to prevent harm from a risk that the CP has himself unleashed but which has not yet culminated in harm. Intuitions can go either way in such a case. On the one hand, the predicament is the CP's fault, so that he might be viewed as having forfeited any right not to be "used" to prevent the harm. On the other hand, the CP has already acted, and, although he deserves retributive harm, his retributive desert may be far less than the harm to him necessary to prevent the harm he has risked to others.

---

[53] Jeff McMahan appears to be sympathetic to the position that CPs may be targeted for defensive purposes or even be "used" for others' benefit. *See* Jeff McMahan, "The Ethics of Killing in War," 114 *Ethics* 693, 721–722 (2004); McMahan, *supra* note 52, at 392–393. *See also* Richard J. Arneson, "Just Warfare Theory and Noncombatant Immunity," 39 *Cornell Int'l L.J.* 663 (2006) (deeming CPs to be legitimate targets even if they are not currently aggressing or otherwise contributing to a threat). But in earlier works he definitely rejected that position. *See, e.g.*, Jeff McMahan, "Self-Defense and the Problem of the Innocent Attacker," 104 *Ethics* 252, 260 (1994). For another denial that CPs may be "used," *see* Yitzhak Benbaji, "Culpable Bystanders, Innocent Threats and the Ethics of Self-Defense," 35 *Canad. J. Phil.* 585, 600–611 (2005). F. M. Kamm, on the other hand, explicitly endorses "using" CPs. *See* Kamm, "Failures of Just War Theory: Terror, Harm, and Justice," *supra* note 25, at 656–659.

[54] *See* F. M. Kamm, "Terror and Collateral Damage," 9 *J. Ethics* 381, 392 (2005).

If CPs' interests may be discounted in the consequentialist balance that determines whether imposing risks on them is justifiable, or if CPs may be appropriated despite deontological constraints that protect the interests of non-CPs, we then must confront the epistemic question that arose in our discussion of CAs: How likely must the defender believe that the CP *is* a CP to warrant the defender's discounting the CP's interests? Should the defender discount the CP discount by the likelihood that the apparent CP is *not* a CP? Or is there a threshold likelihood, beyond which the apparent CP may be treated as if he were a CP, and short of which he must be treated as if he were not one?

Beyond CPs and its subclass CAs, there is another interesting category that we shall call anticipated culpable aggressors (ACAs). What are ACAs? Consider the following scenario of defensive action. Al has been sleeping with his colleague Sam's wife. In our first version of the scenario, in the hall outside Sam's office, Sam tells Dana – our third-party actor – that he has found out about Al and intends to kill him as soon as he gets his gun, which is in his office. Sam's office has a back door that opens into another hallway directly across from Al's office. Al, who is in his office, has broken his leg and is unable to move quickly. Dana, who carries a gun, believes that unless she shoots Sam as he is entering his office, he will go out the other door and immediately kill Al. So Dana shoots Sam as he is entering his office. In this first version, Sam is a CA.

In the second version, Dana knows from a conversation with Al that Sam's wife has left Sam a message on his office voicemail confessing the affair with Al. Sam this time tells Dana, "My wife has been having an affair with someone, and whoever he is, I intend to kill him. Right now I'm going into my office to play my voicemail." Again, Dana knows Sam keeps a gun in his office, and she believes that once Sam plays his voicemail, he will immediately get his gun, leave his office by the back door, and kill Al. So she shoots Sam as he is entering his office.

Is Sam a CA in this version? Well, he intends to kill someone – or so he says. On the other hand, Sam does not yet know at the moment Dana acts who his victim will be. Should that matter, if, as we have assumed, in the first version, Dana is justified in using force against Sam to protect Al?

Now for the third version. In this version, Sam is unaware of his wife's affair, much less that it is with Al. Sam cheerfully informs Dana that he is going into his office to play his voicemail. Dana knows what's on the voicemail, knows that Sam keeps a gun, and knows that Sam is a murderously jealous individual. (He has told Dana many times that if his wife cheated on him, he would kill whoever was involved.) Dana estimates the likelihood that if she fails to stop Sam now, he will kill Al, as exactly the same as it was in the first two scenarios. So she shoots Sam.

Is Sam a CA in *this* scenario? In the first two scenarios, Sam realized that he was creating a risk that others – Dana – would fear that Sam would attempt to kill someone. And Sam created this risk for a reason – his intention to kill his wife's lover – that presumably did not justify the risk. So in the first two scenarios, Sam is arguably a CA. Remember that a CA has not yet imposed a risk of harm on his intended victim(s). He has, however, imposed a risk that others will fear a future attack by him, and he has imposed *that* risk for an insufficient reason. That is why the CA is culpable.

In our third version of the Sam, Al, and Dana scenario, however, Sam may not have adverted to that risk. Or, if one wishes to argue that his past statements to Dana about his murderous jealousy were themselves culpable risk impositions with respect to fear of an attack, assume Dana infers Sam's murderous jealousy, not from any statement by Sam or any other act of his that he would realize would express that trait, but solely from involuntary behavior by him. In such a case, we could not attribute any culpability to Sam with respect to any act committed before the time Dana shoots him. We can, however, as Dana does, *predict* a future culpable act by Sam. Sam is not a CA but is only an ACA.[55]

If CAs are special cases in terms of the consequentialist balance that determines when risk impositions are justified, are ACAs similarly situated? Many sex offenders, for example, are predicted to offend again and thus, with respect to preempting their future sex offenses, are

[55] Or consider a case where a dictator has ordered the firing of a nuclear missile at another country. A soldier in the dictator's army is approaching the hardened missile silo to begin his shift. He currently has no intention to fire the missile; but he is disposed to follow orders, and the order to fire awaits him once inside the hardened silo. Special forces of the targeted country lie in wait outside the silo, having been sent there after the dictator's intention to attack was discovered by spies. Their only way to avert the attack – if we assume the soldier will form the intent to fire the missile once he reads the order inside the silo – is to kill the soldier now, before he enters the silo, but also before he has formed the lethal intent. If we assume the soldier would be a CA once he forms the intent to fire, he is now only an ACA.

ACAs, not CAs. And depending on the likelihood and severity of harm that justify preemptive (preventive or defensive) risk impositions, many more people than sex offenders might be ACAs.

It would take us too far afield to address fully the justification of preventive detention or restraint of the dangerous but not yet culpable. ACAs such as Sam in our third version of the Sam, Al, and Dana scenario are dangerous but not culpable. For they have not yet chosen to act culpably. Preventive restraint of ACAs may be justifiable in some circumstances, but it does not fall within the present topic of justified risk impositions on the culpable.

C. SOCIALLY JUSTIFYING REASONS: SOME CONCLUDING REMARKS

We have argued that in general, what justifies risk impositions is the balance of consequences. We have offered no general theory of how such a consequentialist balance should be constructed, whether it should be welfarist or based on a list of objective goods; if welfarist, whether it should be based on preference satisfaction or on some other measure of welfare; and if preference based, whether preferences should be taken raw or laundered to eliminate those which are misanthropic, misinformed, other-directed, and so on.

We have also argued that the most plausible such balance of consequences would be subject to deontological side constraints, and we have argued as well that a means-focused deontological side constraint looks more plausible than intent-focused ones. For purposes of our general schema for determining culpability, however, nothing turns on whether our deontological theory is correct, or even on whether deontological constraints are ultimately tenable as a matter of the best moral theory. For even if they are not, although the outcome of some cases might be affected, the general schema will not be. In the absence of deontological constraints, Surgeon might be no different from Trolley in terms of justification and culpability.

Moreover, we have raised but surely not resolved the issue of how the culpability of one on whom the actor imposes a risk affects the consequentialist balance or otherwise justifies a defender's action. Indeed, as we have attempted to demonstrate, that issue is really a complex web of a multitude of issues involving the various ways and degrees by which the culpable victim can be culpable, the actor's perceptions of both the risk from and the culpability of the victim, the actor's alternatives for avoiding the risk, and the actor's implication in the victim's culpability. To resolve these issues would require a separate book. For our purposes here, raising them suffices.

Finally, in Chapter 8 we ask whether these various factors that bear on the actor's culpability are best dealt with by making fine-grained, case-by-case determinations of culpability or are instead best dealt with by blunt, coarse-grained rules. The latter will, of course, treat some truly nonculpable actors as culpable and thereby deserving of punishment for the purpose of securing a better match of verdicts of culpability to actual culpability over the long run of cases. Whether *that* is itself a "using" (of the nonculpable) and violative of a deontological constraint is a serious question. On the other hand, the fine-grained approach tells citizens nothing more than that they may not impose "unjustified" risks. It is surely possible that such a vague standard of behavior will produce more unjustified risk imposition among the well-meaning but epistemically limited – and among those who are not well meaning but who believe, rightly or wrongly, that they can convince a trier that they are – than will coarse-grained but much more determinate rules. We return to this issue when, at the end of the book, we ask what an ideal culpability-based criminal law would look like.

III. Excuses

Even when an actor's conduct is not justified, because of a peculiarity of the actor or the situation in which she finds herself, she may be nonculpable. Under current law, duress and insanity offer the actor an excuse in certain instances where the actor lacks the capacity or fair opportunity to know the nature and quality of her act, to know that it is wrong, or to conform her conduct to the requirements of law.[56]

We believe, however, that the current law should be modified in a number of ways. First, we believe that the doctrine of duress should be expanded so that it excuses not only actions that currently are criminal

---

[56] *See* Model Penal Code §§ 2.09, 4.01 (1985).

but also actions that the law incorrectly deems to be justified. We believe that actors should be entitled to an excuse in any situation in which a "person of reasonable firmness" would impose the risk that the actor believed he was imposing. Within our discussion of duress, we also consider the question of whether most instances of duress are best viewed as instances of personal justification.

We next discuss mistakes. There is typically nothing special about mistakes, as the actor's culpability is determined by his own perceptions, whether or not mistaken. However, when we turn to cases of "proxy crimes," in which the actor's conduct comes within the definition of the crime but does not itself create the risk that the crime was designed to prevent, we argue that the actor should have an ignorance of the law defense if he is unaware of the existence of the proxy crime itself.

Finally, we suggest that the criminal law should offer a broader account of rationality impairments. Simply put, diminished rationality diminishes culpability. Depending upon the degree of impairment, the actor is entitled to either a full excuse or, at the very least, mitigation of his punishment.

These proposals, like those for justification, work within the framework that we have already set forth in Chapter 2. Because we believe that an individual is culpable when her balance of risks and reasons deviates from what a reasonable person in the actor's situation would do, this section serves to elucidate that reasonable-person standard. If a reasonable person would act as did the actor in the situation, then the actor is not culpable even if her action is unjustified from an agent-neutral perspective. Moreover, because our theory of culpability focuses on the actor's *choice* to privilege her reasons over the risks she imposes on others, degradations of her capacity to choose may also undermine her culpability.

A. PERSONAL JUSTIFICATIONS AND HARD CHOICES

We believe that an actor should have a defense to any crime that the actor committed to avoid harm to himself, his property, or others, if a "person of reasonable firmness" in the actor's situation would have committed the crime. We believe that these situations include much of what currently constitutes the excuse of duress and much of what currently is deemed justified self-defense. It would include, for example, self-defense against innocent aggressors – the young, the insane, the mistaken or duped, and even those who themselves are excused under the excuse proposed here.[57]

In this section, we begin with the reasons why this excuse can and should capture many cases currently deemed to be instances of justifiable self-defense. In so doing, we confront what we take to be hybrids of justification and excuse – instances of personal justification. Next, we turn to how and why we expand the law beyond the current boundaries of duress. Finally, we address some of the implications of this standard.

1. Personal Justifications

We believe many instances of self-defense are not properly deemed to be justified. As we discussed previously, there are two reasons why we might think that an actor is justified in acting in self-defense. The first consequentialist reason is that the net consequentialist balance is positive when an innocent victim is threatened by a culpable aggressor. A second theory is one that is rights based. Even if we do not want to say that the CA's life is worth less than an innocent's, it may be fair to say that the aggressor has forfeited his rights or that his rights were specified such that he has no right against defensive harm when he culpably threatens another. Under either approach, it seems to us that the actor is justified in acting in an agent-neutral sense of justification.

There are other circumstances in which the actor – D – is not justified in imposing the risk in an agent-neutral sense but is nonetheless personally justified in imposing it. That is, D has an agent-relative justification. One paradigm instant would be one in which D faces a deadly attack from an aggressor who is not a CA – because the aggressor either

---

[57] The one worker on the trolley siding, for example, would not be *justified* in shooting someone attempting to switch the trolley to save the five, but he could easily be *excused* under the excuse proposed here; that would mean in turn that the one throwing the switch would be excused under the same excuse in using force against the worker to protect himself, though he would also be justified because of the five lives he is trying to save.

Likewise, if the trolley is heading toward the one worker, one would not be *justified* switching it to head toward the five, but one might be *excused* for doing so if the solitary worker were one's child.

has made a mistake (e.g., he erroneously believes D is a CA), is insane, is a child, or is not acting at all (he is an "innocent sword," accidentally falling toward the actor). In these cases, the consequentialist balance does not dictate that the innocent "aggressor" should die. The risk to the aggressor is no less a negative consequence than the risk to D it is designed to avert; and there may be several innocent aggressors who outnumber D and therefore count more in the consequentialist balance, or who face defensive risks from D greater than the risks they are imposing on D. Because innocent aggressors are not culpable, there is no reason why their rights should be forfeited or dispreferred vis-à-vis those of the defender. For these reasons, an uninvolved third party, if the consequentialist balance tips in favor of the innocent aggressor, will be justified in going to the aggressor's defense and imposing a risk on D.

In these instances, D is not justified in a social, agent-neutral sense in imposing a defensive risk on innocent aggressors – and, if necessary, on innocent shields and bystanders.[58] (Shields and bystanders differ only in their morally irrelevant physical location relative to the target of the risk imposition.) On the other hand, he may nonetheless be nonculpable for doing so because the reasons *he* has for so acting – defending himself or his family (and perhaps others closely tied to him) against serious harm – outweigh (for him) the reasons against imposing the risk on innocent persons. He may be *personally* justified in imposing the risk even if he is not *socially* justified and cannot permissibly be aided by a fully informed third party.

Personal justifications are hybrids between agent-neutral justifications and excuses. They function like excuses in many respects: First, as we have just indicated, parties whose own or whose families' interests are not in jeopardy, who believe that D is facing a risk imposition from a nonculpable person or person(s), and who believe that the consequentialist balance of reasons prohibits imposing a risk on the latter, may not impose risks on the innocent in order to defend D. Second, although D herself is not a culpable aggressor toward those who are innocently aggressing against D, once D begins to launch a defensive risk on the

---

[58] *See* Ferzan, *supra* note 19, at 734; McMahan, "The Ethics of Killing in War," *supra* note 53, at 720; Noam J. Zohar, "Innocence and Complex Threats: Upholding the War Effort and the Condemnation of Terrorism," 114 *Ethics* 734, 742–744, 748–751 (2004).

innocent aggressors, the innocent aggressors, if they outnumber D and cannot otherwise escape the risk D is about to impose, may *justifiably* impose a defensive risk on D. When the numbers are even, personal justifications can even conflict.

On the other hand, we recognize that personal justifications and excuses are not quite equivalent. To describe an action as an instance of personal justification involves allowing and endorsing the actor's giving her interests more weight in the balance than the interests of others and deeming her action "right" or "permissible" at least in some sense. Indeed, it creates a narrow conduct rule for the actor that tells her that it is permissible for her to act in this way. Excuses, on the other hand, are cases in which the actor has not acted correctly according to any perspective. Excuses are cases in which we regret the actor acted as she did and would not want others to act similarly.

We believe that there may be situations where, given the increased weight an actor may permissibly give to his own interests, he may have an agent-relative justification rather than an excuse. We are agnostic as to how to treat such cases. One approach would be to argue that personal justifications modify the weighing of risks and reasons, thus leading to a different balance from what would otherwise obtain. Alternatively, one could argue that the weighing of risks and reasons must be justified agent-neutrally, but that actors are entitled to an excuse if their conduct did not deviate from how a reasonable person would act under those circumstances. There should not be any practical implications for which approach we choose. What is important is that even if the law tells actors that they may permissibly value their own interests *more* than those of others, they will understand that this permission has no application when their own interests are not implicated.[59]

We believe that much of the debate over whether duress is a justification or an excuse can be better understood by recognizing that duress captures within it instances of personal justification. The Model Penal Code's rendition of duress is illustrative:

> It is an affirmative defense that the actor engaged in the conduct charged to constitute the offense because he was coerced to do so by

---

[59] *See* Husak, *supra* note 8, at 518–519.

the use of, or a threat to use, unlawful force against his person or the person of another, which a person of reasonable firmness in his situation would have been unable to resist.[60]

Under the Model Penal Code, duress functions as an excuse in that the actor may not be aided by informed third parties and may be resisted by the victims of his offense, neither of which would be the case if the actor's act were consequentialist justified agent-neutrally. The excuse of duress is not redundant of the justification of lesser evils.

Some believe that we excuse those who commit crimes in circumstances of duress because they face "hard choices." That is, the choice to forgo committing the crime and thereby fall victim to the threatened harm is one so difficult for ordinary people to make that we excuse from criminal liability those who do not forgo it. We do not regard them as culpable for imposing risks of harm on their victims.

Others believe that duress is an excuse because those who commit crimes under duress do not display the viciousness of character that ordinary criminals display. As we said in Chapter 1, we believe that it is one's choices to which culpability attaches, not one's character. Nonetheless, we doubt that the "hard choice" theorists and the "character" theorists of duress will come to different verdicts about the specific cases in which the excuse of duress should be granted.

Underlying the "hard choice" conception of duress is probably a view of the relation of moral reasons to reasons more generally. One such view would be that moral reasons are not always overriding *qua* reasons. D's reasons for avoiding the threat and therefore committing the crime – her or her family's safety – may trump the moral reasons that would otherwise render her act culpable.

Another view of reasons that supports the excuse would be one that holds not that personal reasons such as D's override moral reasons but that they are incommensurate with moral reasons. D has (moral) reasons to refrain from committing the crime and so acts reasonably in refraining. But D has (personal) reasons to commit the crime and so also acts reasonably in committing it. Up to a point, D's personal reasons are fully accounted for and subordinate to moral reasons. When, however,

---

[60] Model Penal Code § 2.09(1) (1985).

the threat to D or those in close relation to D becomes sufficiently grave, D's personal reasons and moral reasons no longer stand in that relation. Either choice D makes is reasonable.[61]

In looking at these two theories, one sees that, as it is currently formulated, the excuse may conflate two different types of cases. First, as we have been discussing, there may be cases in which an actor is personally justified. Second, it may be possible for an actor not to be personally justified but still to be excused. When duress excuses because the actor's "will is overborne," the argument is that the actor was volitionally impaired, not that the actor was personally justified.

Moreover, we might wonder whether there is even a third type of case that should be covered by duress. As we have discussed previously, there are times when an actor performs a consequentialist-justified act but does so by violating a deontological side constraint. Sometimes one violates a deontological side constraint for personal reasons. For instance, D "uses" a victim to prevent harm to herself or to someone she loves. (Many of the quotidian duress cases are of this type: they would pass the lesser-evils justification test but for the fact that they involve appropriating another to avert the threatened harm.) But might not D have an excuse, even if she is not attached to the persons threatened? If Surgeon could save 100 people unrelated to him by cutting up 1, might we say that a person of reasonable firmness might be swayed by the desire to prevent such harm? What if we could appropriate 1 person to save 1,000 strangers? Even if one does not believe that there is a threshold at which deontological constraints yield,[62] we certainly may want to excuse an actor faced with such a terrible choice.

In any event, we need not adjudicate the underlying theory of the duress excuse. Our purpose here is to illustrate it as one way D's prima facie culpability can be rebutted, a way that differs from the

---

[61] Douglas Portmore argues that this shows that moral reasons are not always *morally* overriding, much less rationally overriding. Douglas Portmore, "Are Moral Reasons Morally Overriding?" 11 *Ethical Theory & Moral Prac.* 369 (2008). *See also* Paul E. Hurley, "Does Consequentialism Make Too Many Demands, or None at All?" 116 *Ethics* 680 (2006) (arguing that consequentialist *moral standards* fail to provide agents with *decisive reasons* to act in accord therewith).

[62] *See, e.g.*, Larry Alexander, "Deontology at the Threshold," 37 *San Diego L. Rev.* 893 (2000). If an actor can be personally justified in violating a deontological constraint by the prospect of a grave loss, can he likewise be personally justified by the prospect of a large gain?

agent-neutral, lesser-evil form of justification that extends to all persons who view the situation similarly.

2. *Expanding Duress*

The excuse of duress must and should be expanded beyond its typical doctrinal formulation illustrated by the Model Penal Code. First, it should cover the kind of threat posed by innocent aggressors, swords, shields, and bystanders. As we said, in a large number of cases of this kind, D's defensive risk imposition cannot be deemed justified. D nonetheless should not be deemed culpable if the risk she or loved ones face is sufficiently grave and good alternatives to defensive risk imposition are unavailable. And D should be excused and deemed nonculpable for the same reason that we excuse those who commit crimes because they are threatened with serious harm. In both cases, there is a threat of serious harm that can be averted only by imposing a risk on an innocent party or parties. In the case of the innocent aggressor, the innocent party on whom the defensive risk is imposed is the aggressor herself. In duress, it is one who is not any sort of a threat. But both, along with swords, shields, and bystanders, are innocent victims of the bad situation in which D finds herself.

So the duress excuse should be reformulated to handle innocent threats. Moreover, there is no reason why the threat that causes D to impose a risk on V be "unlawful." It is true that in the paradigm case of duress, T's threat to D is unlawful. But that does not bear on *why* D gets the excuse. D's choice is no less a hard one, and D's personal reasons are no less compelling, where D is "threatened" *lawfully* with a grave harm. (Suppose D is "threatened" with lawful execution and beats up the executioner in an attempt to escape.)[63] After all, in the paradigm case of duress, we excuse D for externalizing the unlawful threat to her onto the lawfully acting V. There is no moral difference between D's imposing a defensive risk on "lawful" V and D's imposing it on "lawful" T. Any threat that if

---

[63] Would it matter if D were not the condemned but a close family member? Not necessarily, although it might be easier for the "person of reasonable firmness" to refrain from killing the law executioner of a family member than to refrain from killing an innocent aggressor against the family member, and easier to refrain than it would be for the condemned himself. *See* Alexander, *supra* note 46, at 1490–1491.

unlawful would support an excuse of duress should support that excuse when the threat is lawful. The one trolley worker on the siding would not be justified in shooting to stop the "switcher" if aware that five workers will die if he succeeds; but he should be arguably excused for the same reason he would be in shooting five innocent aggressors. Arguably, so also should the one worker's spouse be excused in shooting the switcher even though the spouse would not be socially justified in doing so.

For similar reasons, duress should not be limited to avoidance of human threats. Suppose D is threatened by passenger T that if D does not keep driving and run over the three babies who have been left on the highway, T will shoot D and kill her. If D gets the defense of duress for running over the babies, then she should get it if she is faced with death from a landslide if she does not run over the babies. The fact that one threat has a human source and is illegal, whereas the other threat is from a natural source, is completely immaterial for purposes of D's culpability. D's reasons for imposing the risk on the babies – to save her life – is the same in both cases and should be all that matters.[64] (Consider whether it would be sensible to distinguish these three reasons D has for running over the babies: (1) T has threatened to start a deadly landslide if D does not run over the babies; (2) T has started the landslide, which will prove deadly to D if D does not run over the babies; (3) the landslide has started because of natural causes, and it will prove deadly to D if she does not run over the babies.) An upshot of this is that in Surgeon, although Surgeon is not *justified* in carving up the patient to save the five who are dying, the latter might be *excused* for coercing Surgeon to do so (or Surgeon might be excused if the five were his children).

---

[64] Occasionally it is suggested that the limitation of duress to unlawful threats is premised on the idea that there should be someone to hold liable if D imposes an unlawful risk on someone. If D is not to blame because of duress, at least we can convict D's coercer. *See* Model Penal Code § 2.09 cmt.3 (1985).

This suggestion is just plain silly. Sometimes, tragically, bad things happen for which no one is to blame. Ada mistakenly concludes that Sam is about to kill her and kills him in self-defense. Neither Ada nor Sam is blameworthy, and Ada should not be deemed criminally liable.

Likewise, in the case of duress, it should not matter whether it is T, the threatener, or a landslide that threatens D. And if it is T, it should not matter whether T acted culpably. T himself might be laboring under a misapprehension that defeats ascribing culpability to him for threatening D. Or T might be insane. And so on. Sometimes there just is no one to blame for tragic situations.

The excuse of duress should also be reformulated to cover cases where D defensively imposes the risk on T, the threatener, rather than on V. Imagine that T threatens D with death unless D kills V. D kills T instead. T was not in the ordinary sense "coercing" D to kill T. And it was not necessary for D to kill T in order to avoid a likely death, for D could have killed V instead. Moreover, T may not have been a CA (he may have been insane or an innocent dupe). Surely, however, if D would be excused for killing V, she should be excused for killing T.[65]

Finally, the excuse of duress should be reformulated so that the triggering threat need not be one of inflicting death or bodily injury on D or D's family. These will typically be the kinds of threats that will induce the person of reasonable firmness to commit crimes – the kind of threats that will personally but not socially justify his doing so. Consider, however, a threat to withhold life-saving medication, or even a threat to destroy an artistic masterpiece that someone devoted her entire life to creating. Neither threat is a threat to inflict death or bodily injury. The first is a threat of death, but not a threat to *inflict* it. The second is not a physical threat of any type. Yet surely they are capable of personally, if not socially, justifying otherwise criminal acts. The person of reasonable firmness would likely fear death through withholding medication as much as death by other means and so should be excused for, say, shooting an insane person who is absconding with D's life-saving medications, or for stealing from an innocent person in response to T's threat to otherwise destroy the medication; and she might fear loss of her lifetime creation more than death itself.[66]

In sum, D should be excused for imposing a risk on V that is not consequentially justified or that violates a deontological constraint if, on the basis of the gravity of the risk that D otherwise faced, discounted by its likelihood, and taking into account the feasibility, costs, and risks of any alternatives, D had sufficient personal reason so to act.[67] Obviously,

---

[65] *Cf.* Joshua Dressler, "Battered Women Who Kill Their Sleeping Tormentors: Reflections on Maintaining Respect for Human Life While Killing Moral Monsters," in *Criminal Law Theory: Doctrines of the General Part* 259 (Stephen Shute and A. P. Simester, eds., 2002) (advocating a duress defense when battered women kill their abusers in nonconfrontational settings).

[66] *See* Alexander, *supra* note 46, at 1492.

[67] If D takes an unjustified risk of landing in a situation where he is likely to be coerced into committing crimes – say, by joining a criminal gang – he should not lose the defense of

the excuse will turn not only on the severity and likelihood of the threat to D but on the gravity of the risk D must impose on others to avert the risk. The threshold for the person of reasonable firmness to impose a risk of death should be much higher than the threshold for imposing, say, a risk of property loss.

The excuse we conceptualize extends beyond the current excuse of duress and current justification of self-protection in various ways indicated by our criticisms of these doctrines. It extends to attacks on innocent shields and bystanders. It extends to crimes committed in response to lawful as well as unlawful threats. It extends to crimes committed in response to threats to injure other than by force. And it would extend to cases of situational duress, that is, cases where the crime is committed to escape a nonhuman threat. In these cases (situational duress), the actor's act would not be preemptive in the sense of anticipating a human choice, though it would, of course, rest on a prediction about future events and be preemptive in that sense. Finally, like the current defense of duress, the proposed excuse extends beyond protection of the actor himself to include protection of immediate family members and any other persons (and perhaps, in some cases, animals or even possessions) whom a "person of reasonable firmness" would commit a crime in order to protect.

3. Duress, Preemptive Action, and Proportionality

Like the lesser-evil justification and its corollary defense against culpable aggressors, the excuse of duress involves preemptive action to avert a threatened harm. D imposes a risk on V to avert a threatened harm from the threatener T. Duress therefore requires the same calculations that these other preemptive risk impositions involve: D must decide how likely the threatened harm is if she refrains from imposing a risk on V. Is T bluffing? Did T forget to load the gun? Is the gun jammed? Is T a good shot? What are the risks of waiting? Is there an alternative

duress if so coerced. At that point, he may lack culpability for what he does. Rather, he should be deemed culpable for the initial act of placing himself in the risky situation – just as we would hold someone culpable for unjustifiably risking a situation where a lesser-evils choice is warranted – but not culpable for the lesser-evils choice itself. We thus disagree with the Model Penal Code's treatment of such recklessness in the context of duress. *See* Model Penal Code § 2.09(2) (1985).

to imposing a risk on V that will avert the threat, and if so, what are its chances of success, and how risky or difficult is it? (Whatever is the correct position on proportional response, retreat, and necessity with respect to defense against CAs, surely D has a duty to undergo some degree of sacrifice to avoid harming innocent aggressors, shields, swords, and bystanders. The excuse or personal justification of duress is premised on D's facing a sufficiently hard choice. If D invites the hard choice by not availing herself of less difficult opportunities to avoid the threat, D herself becomes a CA against the innocent aggressors, et al.)[68] How D answers these questions affects her culpability if she chooses to impose the risk on V.

4. Implications

a. Formulation: Standard versus Rules: The first issue regarding the proposed excuse concerns its formulation. We have essentially taken a "person of reasonable firmness" standard from the Model Penal Code's defense of duress and made it the standard governing a much broader

---

[68] *See, e.g.,* Benbaji, *supra* note 53, at 598–599 n.20.

Outside of criminal gangs, it is not clear what the law envisions as culpably placing oneself in a position where duress is likely. But one possible scenario is intriguing. Suppose there is a particularly rough section of town – or some rough establishment, say a pool hall – and outsiders who venture in are frequently threatened with violence unless they commit crimes as directed by the threateners. Suppose further that an actor ventures into this area aware of the risk and is indeed threatened with death unless he mugs someone, which he does. Would the actor be one whose ability to raise duress has been lost or diminished?

Despite the law's reference to recklessly or negligently placing oneself in situations of duress, the average reader is likely to balk at attaching this consequence to merely going where one has a legal right to go. Even if visiting a particular pool hall carries a high risk of being threatened, and not visiting it represents only a very minor setback of interests, wrongdoers should not be able to limit liberty in this way, or so one might believe.

Notice, however, that reading the law of duress to preclude the defense in such a situation is quite consistent with the requirement of retreat in the law of self-defense. That requirement entails that I must give up my liberty, on pain of forfeiting the right to employ deadly force to defend myself, rather than remain where I have a right to be. By logical extension it entails that I may not go where I otherwise have a right to go, again on pain of forfeiting the right to use deadly force in self-defense, if I am aware that in so going I am likely to be attacked. Thus, if I must retreat from the 7-Eleven to my house to avoid a deadly attack by a knife-wielding lunatic, even if in doing so I must forgo getting a Mars Bar, then likewise I should not be able to venture from my house to the store to get the Mars Bar, prepared to shoot my .45 to protect myself, if I am aware that the lunatic is there. If that is what the retreat doctrine requires regarding self-defense, the same requirement should hold for duress.

domain of self-protection. And the standard is quite abstract and
informal, giving very uncertain guidance both to actors before the fact
and to judges and juries after the fact. Why have we not proposed determinate rules instead?

If the cases of self-protection we are interested in are truly cases of
excuse, then a standard rather than guidance-providing rules is appropriate. We are not telling actors when it is all right for them to succumb
to their self-protective desires. We are asking whether they constrained
those desires in order to avoid harming others to the extent we expect
ordinary persons to do so. We are not asking whether they did the right
thing: they did not. We are asking whether their having done wrong is
excusable given their situation. For an excuse – whether one believes
that excuses rest on assessments of the difficulty in choosing correctly or
on the character reflected in the choices – a standard rather than rules
seems appropriate. The situations actors will confront will be impossible to anticipate and to cabin in general rules.

On the other hand, although we have deemed our proposed defense
an excuse, we are in fact equivocal regarding whether in some situations
it is better seen as a personal justification. A personal justification would
be a justification reflecting the moral permissibility of an actor's giving
more weight in the moral calculus to his and his family's interests than
those interests would be given from an impersonal perspective. In other
words, the defense could reflect the fact that morally speaking, an actor
may treat his life as more important than, say, the lives of five innocent
aggressors, even though from society's perspective their five lives morally outweigh his.

If our proposed defense is a personal justification rather than an
excuse, then perhaps it could and should be "rulified."[69] If we can cali-
brate the extra moral weight that we can assign to our own interests in
the moral calculus, then we could perhaps decide, say, that one may kill
two but not more than two innocent aggressors to save one's own life,
and so forth.[70]

---

[69] In Chapter 8, when we take up the translation of our theory into criminal law doctrine, we
return to the question of how much of our theory can be "rulified," how that can be done,
and whether it is desirable to do so.

[70] The personal nature of the justification would still render it excuselike – that is, unjustified – insofar as third-party interveners and the targets of the actor's risk imposition are

We here assume that the defense is, like duress, a pure excuse and thus avoid any speculation about how the defense might be reduced to rules. If that is the proper approach, then a "person of reasonable firmness" is the proper standard for assessing the actor's self-protective crimes.

b. The Objectivity of the "Person of Reasonable Firmness" Standard: One of the perennial problems in criminal law is the question of whether the reasonable person should be altered to include the particular characteristics of the actor. Indeed, one of our primary complaints about liability for negligence is that there is no principled and rationally defensible way to determine with which features of the actor to endow the "reasonable person." One objection to our proposal is that our "person of reasonable firmness" standard resurrects this problem. It does not. Let us explain why.

The "person of reasonable firmness" standard is wholly objective. It asks a normative question, that is, whether the actor has lived up to what society can reasonably expect of him.[71] This standard does not change subject to the peculiarities of the actor.

Notice, however, that the characteristics of the actor will be part of the culpability calculation itself. For that calculation involves asking what *risks* did the actor perceive, and what *reasons* for the action was the actor aware of. Both of these questions are entirely subjective in their focus: the actor's perceptions inform the risks of which she is aware, and her perceptions and motivations inform the reasons that she believes justify her behavior. It is only after both of these subjective features are placed on each side of the scale that an objective moral weighing is appropriate. Thus, the fact that a petite woman will feel threatened when a large man will not is captured by the risks and reasons that each individual actor will perceive and possess.

Moreover, although the question is whether the actor has shown the fortitude necessary to deem him nonculpable, there is some room for individualizing and thus subjectivizing in assessing the difficulty of his choice. Extreme phobias, philias, manias, addictions, and temptations

---

concerned. (Third parties might have to intervene on the side of the two innocent aggressors rather than the one personally justified defender.)

[71] *Cf.* Fletcher, *supra* note 4, at § 8.4.1 (discussing the German concept *zumutbarkeit* – what can fairly be expected of offenders); Peter Westen, "Individualizing the Reasonable Person in Criminal Law," 2 *Crim. L. & Phil.* 137 (2008).

may render the consequentially preferred or deontologically demanded choice quite dysphoric for the actor. And because culpability is scalar rather than binary, such dysphoria could render the actor's choice less culpable than it otherwise would have been or even completely nonculpable. We believe, however, that these impairments are better viewed as offering an independent excuse or mitigation for diminished rationality. We note, though, that it is possible that an actor will experience a "hard choice" because of his diminished rationality, leading to the conjunction of two different theories of excuse or mitigation. We leave this possibility open.

c. Probabilities, Retreat, and Proportionality: Our proposed defense of preemptive self-protection, with its single standard of a "person of reasonable firmness," handles, in one fell swoop, the vexing problems of what probability of attack is necessary to trigger preemptive force, when the defender must retreat rather than use preemptive force, and whether the defender may use disproportionate force to prevent an attack. With respect to the first question, the actor is excused for using preemptive force whenever he estimates that the likelihood of attack on him is at a level at which a "person of reasonable firmness would use force self-protectively rather than wait for the probability of attack to increase. And, with respect to the interrelated doctrines of retreat and proportionality, viewing self-protection as an excuse rather than a justification helps support their presence in the law. The choice between killing an attacker and safely retreating is not a hard choice, nor is the choice between killing to protect one's apples and losing one's apples if proportionate force will not succeed. A "person of reasonable firmness" would safely retreat rather than kill and would lose his apples rather than kill. Or, put differently, it takes no extraordinary courage or resolve to forgo killing and suffer the minor losses of retreating or employing lesser force.[72]

d. Mistakes: Because the proposed defense of preemptive self-protection is an excuse, not a justification, it is immaterial whether the actor's

---

[72] We leave to the side whether the retreat or proportional force or necessity requirement applies when the actor believes the attacker is a CA or CP.

assessments of the probability of attack, the likely consequences of attack, the time left to retreat, the safety of the retreat, the force necessary to resist, and so forth are correct or mistaken. The question is whether, given the actor's beliefs on these matters, he acted as would a "person of reasonable firmness" in the situation as the actor assessed it. And if the actor's beliefs were mistaken in a way such that a "person of reasonable firmness," apprised of the mistake, would have acted differently from the actor and not committed the crime, the actor still may invoke the defense.

e. Third-Party Intervention: Because the proposed defense is an excuse or a personal justification, it is limited to the actor. Third parties who are not themselves threatened cannot stand in the actor's shoes and invoke his excuse or personal justification to justify or excuse their conduct. Thus, if two innocent aggressors are attacking one innocent defender, the latter may be excused for using deadly force against the former. Third parties, however, if they may intervene at all, may not intervene with deadly force on the *defender's* side of the struggle.[73] Because the actor is only excused and not justified, and because the third parties are

---

[73] At least they may not do so as a matter of justification. If the actor were, say, a close family member, the third parties might themselves be able to invoke duress to excuse their aiding the defender rather than his attackers.

Jeff McMahan has argued that at least some of those whom we deem to be innocent aggressors can be justifiably harmed (in a social, not personal, sense of justifiability), even if they are more numerous than those they threaten. *See* McMahan, "The Basis of Moral Liability to Defensive Killing," *supra* note 52, at 393–394. He gives as an example a driver whose car goes out of control nonculpably and threatens a pedestrian, who can save himself only by killing the driver. He contends that the pedestrian would be justified in the social sense were he to kill the driver. Presumably, as well, a third party could assist the pedestrian in killing the driver.

We disagree. McMahan assumes that the driver is threatening the pedestrian in a way that the pedestrian is not threatening the driver – that is, that this is a case of nonreciprocal risk imposition – and that this is what justifies the pedestrian and third-party aiders in killing the nonculpable driver. But this is incorrect. A pedestrian who is armed and prepared to kill nonculpable drivers who lose control is as much a threat to drivers as the drivers are to pedestrians. We think the driver's lack of culpability is sufficient to make this a case of excuse or personal justification.

McMahan also claims that some victims of socially justified risk impositions are socially justified in resisting the socially justified risk imposers. *Id.* at 399. Again, we disagree. The one worker on the trolley siding is not justified in shooting the actor to prevent the actor from killing him but saving the five. Nor, contrary to what McMahan claims, may the victims of Strategic Bomber justifiably (as opposed to excusedly) attempt to shoot him down.

not in danger themselves, the third parties would be neither excused nor justified.

Moreover, a friend who assists the mother who is acting under duress is not a counterexample to this position. Rather, one reason why a friend might be entitled to assist the mother would be the friendship relationship. Thus, the friend may be personally justified in giving more weight to her friend's interests, or the friend, too, may be excused because the emotional bonds of friendship bear on what a "person of reasonable firmness" would do.

5. A Possible Extension? Preemptive Collective Protection and Preventive Detention

The excuse of preemptive self-protection, except for cases of situational duress, deals with commission of crimes on the basis of predictions of future human choices. Whether the actor is reacting to one who appears to be about to attack him or to one who has threatened him with a future attack, what gives rise to the excuse is the actor's prediction that if he does not commit the crime, another will choose to aggress against him.

Actions that are preemptive in that way are troubling. We generally condemn preemptive restraints on liberty on the basis of predictions of future dangerous choices. There are exceptions, of course. We countenance not only self-defense but also restraining orders, peace bonds, gun restrictions, and restrictions on information that is dangerous in the wrong hands, and we do allow the preventive detention of those who, because of mental defects, will not be morally responsible for their predicted dangerous acts.

We draw the line, however, with preventive detention of those who are predicted to commit future crimes but who are fully responsible actors. We associate such preventive detention with totalitarian regimes, which paradigmatically act preemptively.

If, however, actors are excusable for acting preemptively in self-defense and duress situations, then is it possible that society as a whole could be excused for preventively detaining the sane but dangerous? The idea of a society's being "excused" rather than justified may seem strange, but a society is nothing but those individuals who compose it. If those individuals, acting as "persons of reasonable firmness," would preemptively restrain the sane, but dangerous, rather than wait for the latter to choose to commit crimes, then it is possible that collectively they may *excusably* impose preventive restraints. Of course, because excuses serve as ex post evaluations of an actor's action, and not as ex ante rules of conduct prescribing what an actor may permissibly do, excusing such preemptive actions does not constitute an endorsement of such actions. In any event, it is worth exploring whether looking at preemptive restraints through the prism of excuse is more enlightening than working out the contours of when preemptive action is justified.[74]

B. EXCULPATORY MISTAKES

Do the actor's mistaken beliefs defeat her culpability and, if so, how? Let us first take up the actor's mistaken beliefs about the risk she is imposing.

As we have pointed out, risk is itself an epistemic notion. The "true" risks to others' interests that the actor's acts unleash are either one or zero – the interest is either set back or not. Therefore, if the actor estimated those risks at greater than zero but less than one, she will always be mistaken. Because culpability depends upon her estimate of the risks and the reasons she has for imposing them, such mistakes cannot defeat her culpability. If, given her estimate of the risks and her reasons for acting in the face of those risks, she should not have so acted, she is culpable whether or not the risk turns out to be zero, and thus lower than she estimated, or one, and thus higher. Similarly, if she acted appropriately in the face of the risks she estimated, the fact that the risks

---

[74] For an excellent discussion of preventive detention of the dangerous but nonculpable, including whether compensation would make such detention permissible, *see* Richard L. Lippke, "No Easy Way Out: Dangerous Offenders and Preventive Detention," 27 *Law & Phil.* 383, 406–414 (2008). Another matter for speculation along these lines concerns social schemes that appropriate others in order to avoid great losses. Such schemes include conscription for the military. But they might also include mandatory organ pooling. Because they are appropriative, they cannot be *justified*, at least for libertarian liberals. But, as with duress, which often involves appropriation, such schemes might be deemed "excused." Likewise, as we said previously, the surgeon who cuts up a healthy patient for organs to save five dying ones might be "excused" for such an appropriative act if the five patients were, say, his children.

turned out to be one, and others' interests were set back, should not matter any more than had they turned out to be zero. (The same holds for her erroneous but sincere beliefs about the likelihood that justifying reasons exist. If those beliefs would justify her choice were they correct, then they render the choice nonculpable no matter how fanatical those beliefs appear.)

Moreover, because we deny that negligence – inadvertence to risks that the so-called reasonable person would have adverted to – is culpable, all that matters to the actor's culpability is what risks to others' interests the actor *believes* she is imposing and why she is imposing those risks. It does not matter that the actor underestimates the risks due to ignorance about brute facts (e.g., this material is combustible) or about the legal characterization of such facts (e.g., because of the rules of property law, this paneling that the actor is destroying belongs to the landlord and not to the actor).[75]

The same analysis applies to the actor's beliefs regarding the facts that ground her reasons for imposing the risks. If she is driving fast and thereby imposing high risks on others because she believes her passenger is seriously ill and needs urgent medical attention, or if she is diverting a river and flooding someone's farm because she believes doing so is necessary to avert catastrophic flooding of a downstream town, the fact that she is mistaken about the illness of her passenger or the necessity of the diversion of the river is immaterial to her culpability. If the risk that she perceived to her passenger or to the town justified the risk she believed she was imposing by acting as she did, then she is no more culpable for being mistaken about the former risk than she is for being mistaken about the latter. Again, negligence is not culpable.

Suppose, however, that the actor is mistaken about whether the risks she perceives herself to be imposing on others' interests are *justified* by her reasons for doing so. Suppose she drives ninety miles per hour in traffic, aware that she is imposing a high risk to others of death, injury, and property loss, in order to get home in time to see the beginning of her favorite TV soap opera. And suppose she sincerely believes she is justified in doing so, although she is not. Does this latter mistake negate her culpability?

[75] Regina v. Smith (David), (1974) 2 Q.B. 354.

In general, the answer is no. A choice that reflects insufficient concern for others' interests is the paradigmatic culpable choice. The fact that the actor believes her lack of concern is justifiable cannot make it so. Callousness, cruelty, self-centeredness, avarice, and other vices that are revealed in unjustified risk impositions explain culpability rather than negate it.[76]

This point underpins the criminal law's reluctance to excuse ignorance of the criminal law. At least with respect to crimes that are *mala in se*, ignorance that the conduct they proscribe is legally prohibited does not undermine the culpability and negative desert of those who commit such crimes.

One can imagine the existence of someone from a culture so alien that ignorance regarding what reasons justify imposing what risks

---

[76] Of course, our perceptions of the strength of reasons, just like our beliefs about matters of fact, including facts that bear on risks, come on us "unbidden." If the actor perceives her reason for speeding – catching her favorite soap opera – to outweigh the interests of others she is putting at risk, she can claim that that is just how she saw things at the time she acted. If a claim of that succeeds with respect to her beliefs regarding the risks she is creating, why does it not succeed with respect to her beliefs about the strength of justifying reasons?

Pamela Hieronymi accepts that our beliefs, including our evaluative ones, are nonvoluntary, but she argues that we are responsible for them nonetheless. They constitute one's moral personality and are the proper targets of our reactive attitudes. Pamela Hieronymi, "Responsibility for Believing," 161 *Synthese* 357 (2008).

On the other hand, Gideon Rosen derives from the nonvoluntary character of beliefs a powerful skeptical argument. Gideon Rosen, "Skepticism about Moral Responsibility," in *Philosophical Perspectives* 18, *Ethics* (2004), 295–313. He begins by accepting the position we put forward in Chapter 3, namely, that ignorance of the risks one's act imposes is not culpable (although it may be evidence of some earlier culpable act, one in which the actor takes a risk of his future ignorance for no sufficient reason). *Id.* at 300–304. Rosen then argues that *normative* ignorance – ignorance regarding whether the reasons one has for imposing the risk one perceives are sufficiently weighty to justify so doing – can also be (and usually is) nonculpable for the same reason ignorance of the risk is nonculpable, namely, its being acquired nonculpably. Rosen concludes that all truly culpable acts will be akratic, that is, undertaken despite the actor's knowing they are unjustified – a position that, of course, has its roots in the Platonic notion that all evil reflects ignorance. *Id.* at 304–308.

The questions of responsibility and culpability for normative beliefs is a deep one, and one with obvious ties to the freewill–determinism–moral responsibility debates. A satisfactory answer will depend ultimately on a satisfactory resolution of that debate. Here we can do no more than merely assert our belief, one that most of our practices of blaming and punishing presuppose, that one is morally culpable for "mistakes" of justificatory strength but not for mistaken beliefs about factual matters, including facts that bear on legal characterizations. (Or perhaps akratic choices, choices that the actor realizes are against the balance of reasons, are much more common than Rosen believes.)

might negate culpability. (Consider "It is a matter of honor to stone to death an unchaste daughter.") Sometimes mistakes regarding justifications reveal culpability-negating insanity rather than culpability. And psychopathy reflects a certain type of ignorance regarding justification – emotional rather than cognitive – although whether psychopathy negates culpability is, of course, controversial.[77]

But what if the actor imposes risks of engaging in conduct that is treated as a "proxy crime" but is unaware that such conduct is so treated? If she believes – correctly – that her conduct imposes risks of harm that are justified by her reasons for acting, but is unaware that she is risking engaging in legally proscribed proxy conduct to such a degree that her risking *that* is *not* justified by her reasons, is she culpable? Suppose, for example, that possessing a machine gun is legally proscribed because of the frequency with which such possession leads to undue risks of death or injury. And suppose the actor is (1) aware that she possesses a machine gun, (2) unaware that such possession is proscribed, (3) and correctly believes *her* possession of a machine gun is not unduly risky to others.[78] (She is well trained in machine gun use, keeps the machine gun in a highly secure place, and has very good reasons for possessing it.) Is the actor culpable for unduly risking possessing a machine gun – in this case, by actually possessing one – despite her ignorance of the law's absolute proscription of such possession?

Given our analysis of culpability and its bases, we must conclude that the actor is not culpable for possessing the machine gun. She is not culpable for the risks to others she perceives. For she estimates them to be so minimal that her reasons for possession really do justify her imposing them. Despite the fact that she is risking the proxy conduct of possessing a machine gun at a quite unjustifiable level – she believes the risk is virtually 100 percent, given that she believes to a virtual certainty that she does in fact possess a machine gun – she is unaware that possessing a machine gun is forbidden.

Ignorance of crimes of proxy conduct is therefore a defeater of culpability for risking such conduct. Such crimes may be quite appropriate components of regulatory schemes. Nonetheless, one who is not

---

[77] *See* the discussion of psychopathy *infra.*
[78] *See* R. A. Duff, "Criminalizing Endangerment," 65 *La. L. Rev.* 941, 959–961 (2005).

culpable with respect to risking the harms that these proxy crimes are designed to minimize should not be deemed culpable with respect to risking the proxy conduct when he is ignorant that risking that conduct is illegal.[79]

We return in Chapter 8 to this topic when we examine how our theory of criminal liability should be implemented in terms of doctrine. But however the theory should be implemented, ignorance of proxy crimes defeats culpability. One may be culpable for risking this ignorance for insufficient reasons. A gun collector would likely be culpable for failing to read the latest laws pertaining to gun ownership when aware that laws regulating gun ownership have been enacted. But culpability for unjustifiably running *that* risk (of ignorance of criminal regulations) will be different from the culpability attached to knowingly risking violating a known proxy crime – much as the culpability for getting intoxicated will differ from the culpability for consciously risking the specific harms one causes inadvertently because of intoxication.

C. IMPAIRED RATIONALITY EXCUSES

1. Excuses versus Exemptions

Before discussing when an individual's rationality may be sufficiently impaired to warrant either an excuse or mitigation, we should begin by distinguishing excuses from exemptions. Irrational people are exempt from the criminal law. Rationality is the cornerstone of responsible agency. If an actor cannot comprehend or respond to norms,[80] then it cannot be said that laws or morality are properly addressed to the actor.[81] Young children, and the very insane, lack the capacity to reason sufficiently about their actions and are thus exempt from criminal liability.[82]

One problem in this area is how to deal with psychopathy. The psychopath appreciates that his reasons do not *legally* justify the risk

---

[79] For an excellent discussion of ignorance of the criminal law, *see* Peter Westen, "Two Rules of Legality in Criminal Law," 26 *Law & Phil.* 229 (2007).

[80] On rationality, *see generally* Moore, *supra* note 6; Stephen J. Morse, "Rationality and Responsibility," 74 S. *Cal. L. Rev.* 251 (2000).

[81] *See* Moore, *supra* note 6, at 62.

[82] *Id.* at 64–65.

he is imposing, but his understanding of why they do not *morally* justify the risk is bereft of the affective aspect of moral understanding. In the limiting case, the psychopath understands "morally wrong" as "others will get angry if you do it." It is the understanding that small children have.[83] The psychopath lacks empathy and lacks the reactive emotions associated with moral understanding, such as indignation and guilt.[84]

The issue of psychopathy, of course, raises the general question, If failure to understand moral reasons *at all* is exculpatory, why should not every misperception of the *strength* of reasons be exculpatory? Why is failure to understand the reason against killing exculpatory, but failure to understand that that reason is weightier than, say, the countervailing reason of thrill seeking is not exculpatory? After all, we have no control over how weighty reasons appear to us any more than we have over how the facts appear to us. Even if we have the general mental capacity to understand the proper weights of various reasons, on any given occasion we may have a temporary malfunction of reason so that a bad reason appears to us as good, or a less weighty reason as weightier. This issue obviously becomes part of the general freewill–determinism–moral responsibility issue and its implications for culpability.

2. Insanity

To understand how mental illness might eliminate culpability, we must again assume an actor who otherwise meets the criteria for culpability. He acts believing he is imposing a risk of a certain magnitude for reasons that do not justify imposing a risk of that magnitude.

So one way mental illness obviously can affect culpability must be put to the side. Mental illness can affect the actor's estimate of the riskiness of his behavior, making him believe the risk to be lower than he would otherwise have estimated it. Or it may cause him to believe in the existence of facts that, if they did exist, would provide him with

---

[83] *See* Westen, *supra* note 16, at 364 (discussing why children are excused).
[84] *See* David Shoemaker, "Moral Address, Moral Responsibility, and the Boundaries of the Moral Community," 118 *Ethics* 70 (2007); Peter Arenella, "Convicting the Morally Blameless: Reassessing the Relationship between Legal and Moral Accountability," 39 *UCLA L. Rev.* 1511 (1992).

good reasons for imposing the risk that he estimates. He may believe, because of his mental illness, that switching the trolley is not risky to the worker because the worker is an inflated balloon, not a human being. Or he may believe that he is saving five workers, although the five workers are in actuality only the product of a hallucination. In these cases, the actor is not culpable, and his mental illness plays an explanatory role. However, his mental illness is not itself material to his culpability or lack thereof.

In the criminal law there have traditionally been thought to be two ways that mental illness may defeat culpability when the criteria establishing culpability – the perceived risks and the reasons for imposing it – are otherwise present. One way is by mental illness's effect on the actor's ability to appreciate the wrongness of imposing the risks for the reasons he has for doing so. The other way is by its effect on the actor's ability to refrain from acting culpably – that is, by its effect on his volitional control.

We are quite dubious about the volitional control prong of the defense of insanity, the so-called irresistible-impulse prong. We are skeptical that anyone can distinguish between an impulse that is truly irresistible – and remember, we are dealing with choices, not tropisms or reflex movements – and an impulse that is just not resisted.[85] We have no doubt that some who are mentally ill act quite impulsively. But we do not see any reason to separate the impulsive and mentally ill actors from the larger group of impulsive but not mentally ill ones. Impulsivity undoubtedly affects the clarity with which actors perceive the risks of their acts and their ability to weigh reasons for and against those acts. But impulsivity is a different malady from insanity.

With respect to the cognitive prong of the insanity defense, again we must keep in mind that we are concerned with those actors who but for their mental illness would be culpable – they have acted for reasons that are insufficient to justify the risks that they themselves have perceived. So their mental illness must somehow cause them to fail to understand

---

[85] See Stephen J. Morse, "Culpability and Control," 142 *U. Pa. L. Rev.* 1587 (1994); Stephen J. Morse, "Uncontrollable Urges and Irrational People," 88 *Va. L. Rev.* 1025 (2002). *See also* Tadros, *supra* note 6, at 341–346 (arguing that for mental illness to undermine culpability by its effect on volition, the desire must be both inconsistent with the actor's values and sufficiently strong to induce action regardless of its inconsistency).

why their reasons do not justify those risks, and to fail to understand in a way different from how culpable actors fail to understand. It must render them unable to be guided by a proper balance of reasons in a way that the culpable are not unable so to be guided.[86]

3. Degraded Decision-Making Conditions

a. Altered States of Consciousness: Sometimes D will impose a risk on V while sleepwalking, or under hypnosis, or in a dissociative state known as automatism. D will, in some sense, be conscious of the risk he is imposing. And D will be acting for reasons, reasons that are insufficient to justify the risk. Yet because of the altered state of consciousness D is in, we may hesitate to deem him culpable.

Why are those in the grip of somnambulism, hypnotism, or automatism arguably nonculpable? If those states rendered them unaware of what they were doing, or made what they were doing completely unresponsive to their beliefs and conscious reasons, then their lack of culpability would be obvious. Those in such altered states, however, are responsive to beliefs and reasons. One can carry on conversations with them. They do not stumble about, bumping into walls. They appear, rather, to be responsive to their environment.[87]

Criminal codes, however, do deem the somnambulant, the hypnotized, and those in states of automatism to be nonculpable. Although these actors meet the ordinary criteria for culpability by virtue of their awareness of the risks they are imposing and the absence of sufficiently weighty reasons for imposing that risk, their awareness of the risk and their reasons for imposing it operate at such a low level of consciousness that the law excuses their conduct.[88]

---

[86] For a sophisticated version of the view that insanity should not be excusing so long as the actor believes he is imposing a risk that would not be justified by the facts as he believes them to be, and so long as the actor can control whether he acts or not, *see* Christopher Slobogin, *Minding Justice: Laws That Deprive People with Mental Disability of Life and Liberty* 42–57 (2006).

[87] For a description of somnambulism and a survey of some of the medical and legal literature on the topic, *see* Mike Horn, Note, "A Rude Awakening: What to Do with the Sleepwalking Defense?" 46 *B. C. L. Rev.* 149 (2004).

[88] In Chapter 2, we argued that D may be held accountable for the preconscious aspects of his conscious choice. In the cases presented here, *no* part of the actor's decision making occurs at the level of consciousness.

Perhaps the leading work on altered states of consciousness as they bear on the criminal law is Robert Schopp's *Automatism, Insanity, and the Psychology of Criminal Responsibility*:

> The defense of automatism is appropriate when the offense involves behavior performed "in a state of mental unconsciousness or dissociation without full awareness, i.e., somnambulism, fugue." Normal consciousness includes the person's awareness of himself, his environment, and the relation between the two. The difficult cases in which the defense of automatism is raised are those in which some event, such as physical trauma or an epileptic seizure, has induced some degree of clouding of consciousness. When consciousness is clouded, the person experiences a state of reduced wakefulness and awareness. His ability to perceive and apprehend his environment and his situation in it is impaired, leaving him with an incomplete and inaccurate grasp of his environment and his place in it. In effect, the person is deprived of access to information regarding himself, his environment, and the relationship between the two. This condition of partial isolation from access to orienting information is directly relevant to the process by which an actor's wants and beliefs characteristically produce his actions.[89]

After describing normal practical reasoning, Schopp continues:

> A central ingredient in this account of a competent practical reasoner is access to a relatively complete array of information regarding himself, his environment, and the relationship between the two – that is, normal consciousness. A person who acts in a state of impaired consciousness is acting in a state of distorted awareness and attention such that his acts may be caused by an action-plan, but the plan is selected with access to only a small and nonrepresentative portion of his wants and beliefs. The actor's wants and beliefs do not cause his acts, therefore, in the manner characteristic of ordinary human activity. Such an actor acts on an action-plan, and thus the relation specified by the culpability level between the act-token constituting the objective elements of the offense and the action-plan can obtain. Yet, the act is not voluntary because the process by which the actor's wants and beliefs cause the

---

[89] Robert F. Schopp, *Automatism, Insanity, and the Psychology of Criminal Responsibility: A Philosophical Inquiry* 137 (1991) (footnotes omitted).

act is impaired by his state of clouded consciousness, which limits and distorts his access to his own wants and beliefs.[90]

In other words, if Schopp is correct, we have to imagine that an actor in such a state of altered consciousness is aware that he is imposing a risk for a reason that does not justify the risk imposition, but he is unaware that there is another reason that is *his* that counsels against imposing the risk and outweighs his reason for doing so. He is unaware of this reason that he normally would act upon because his condition prevents him from accessing that reason.[91]

One hallmark of the altered states of consciousness characteristic of somnambulism, hypnotism, and automatism is the actor's inability to recollect acts committed in those states. That in turn raises the question whether acts committed on "automatic pilot" might also be nonculpable.[92] We have all experienced driving on a familiar route while daydreaming or engrossed in serious thought (about matters other than our driving) and finding ourselves at our destination with no ability to recall the trip. We obviously negotiated it successfully, attentive to risks and directions; yet we have no present recollection of having done so. Were we in the "fugue state" characteristic of the hypnotized or the somnambulant? Would we have been culpable had we imposed undue risks on others?

Finally, it must be kept in mind that even if those in certain altered states of consciousness are nonculpable for unjustified risk impositions, they may be culpable for imposing unjustified risks by getting into such states – by drinking, taking drugs, failing to take medications, undergoing hypnosis, and so on. Moreover, they are, as excused rather than justified actors, innocent aggressors, and they cannot be aided by third parties who lack their excuse. Their position in this regard is identical to those acting under duress or on mistaken beliefs.

b. Habitual, Impulsive, and Compulsive Conduct: We frequently act out of habit. If we attend too closely to the mechanics of bicycle riding or the golf swing, we will usually perform these actions poorly. And sometimes when acting out of habit, we consciously impose unjustified risks.

---

90 *Id.* at 145.
91 *See also* Westen, *supra* note 16, at 368.
92 *See also* our discussion in Chapter 2.

Habitual conduct is in many respects similar to impulsive conduct. Both are characterized by lack of deliberation. With respect to the question of culpability, both habitual and impulsive actors are in some sense conscious that they are imposing a risk at a magnitude that is not justified by their reasons for doing so. But they are acting so much on automatic pilot that their consciousness of the risk is, as with altered states of consciousness, both dim and not fully accessible.[93]

The criminal law does not, however, treat habit or impulse as an excusing condition, despite the similarity of each to altered states of consciousness with respect to access to beliefs and desires. The interference with such access is, to be sure, somewhat different. In the case of habits and impulses, the interference is a function of a sort of preprogrammed response that precludes deliberation, whereas in the case of altered states there is usually some unusual causal factor – physiological or, with hypnotism, influential.

It is also the case that most habitual or impulsive conduct has a conscious aspect to it. Although an actor may type the letter "t" out of habit (or on an impulse), she is very conscious of each and every word that she is typing. Thus, to the extent that acts committed out of habit or impulsively are accompanied by a conscious mental state with respect to risk, there is no reason to excuse the actor. Moreover, causally complex actions are typically committed at the fully conscious level (with the exception, perhaps, of reckless highway driving). We do not habitually pull the trigger, break and enter, force intercourse, or sell narcotics; nor do we execute those complex acts completely impulsively.

The criminal law is also not sympathetic to claims of weakness of will or, in general, claims that the actor's desires did not conform to his values and yet overpowered his will to act in accord with those values. Compulsive desires to engage in otherwise-culpable risk imposition confront the actor with "hard choices," just as do those threats that give rise to the excuse of duress. The alcoholic may have a compulsive desire to drink himself into a state of intoxication, which he realizes unreasonably risks harms to others. But unlike the "hard choices that

---

[93] See, e.g., Tillman Vierkant, "Owning Intentions and Moral Responsibility," 8 *Ethical Theory & Moral Practice* 507 (2005) (raising doubts about occurrent responsibility for habitual conduct); Bill Pollard, "Explaining Actions with Habits," 43 *American Phil. Q.* 57 (2006) (claiming that we are responsible for habitual acts).

underlie duress, these compulsive desires are not in any way reasonable and do not justify the actor's choice to act on them, even in a personal as opposed to social sense of justify. They may or may not be in harmony with the actor's stable values; but even if they are not, it is not at all obvious that the actor is not morally responsible and culpable for acting on them.[94]

IV. Mitigating Culpability

Even when an actor's decision-making capacities are not sufficiently degraded to excuse her conduct, her culpability may be diminished by her impaired rationality. Indeed, the Supreme Court's opinion in *Atkins v. Virginia*,[95] which categorically prohibited capital punishment of people with retardation on Eighth Amendment grounds, was based precisely on the insight that individuals may be only partially morally responsible for their choices. In this section, we argue that nonculpable diminishments of rationality should mitigate the actor's punishment. We begin with a rare doctrinal-mitigating doctrine – provocation – and discuss the current attempt to synthesize provocation into either a justification or an excuse. From here, we argue that the factors at work in provocation should be expanded so that any individual who is nonculpably impaired should be entitled to mitigation. Finally, we explain how this mitigating feature can be assimilated within our culpability framework.

A. THE PERPLEXING PARTIAL EXCUSE OF PROVOCATION

The criminal law recognizes provocation as a partial defense to a charge of murder (and, in some jurisdictions, attempted murder). If successful, the defense operates to reduce the actor's crime from murder to voluntary manslaughter. Although the effect of the defense is clear, the rationale for it is anything but.[96] Some commentators argue that a provoked homicide

---

[94] Victor Tadros believes the actor is morally responsible only when the compulsive desire is in accord with his higher-order values. *See* Tadros, *supra* note 6, at 31–43, esp. 42.

[95] *See* Atkins v. Virginia, 536 U.S. 304 (2002).

[96] For an excellent survey of the conflicting theories of provocation, *see* Stephen P. Garvey, "Passion's Puzzle," 90 *Iowa L. Rev.* 1677 (2005).

is (partially) justified. Others argue that it is (partially) excused, although those in this camp divide over whether provocation excuses because the actor does not display the ordinary character traits associated with murder or because the actor's decision-making and control capacities are degraded by his understandable emotional response to the provocation.

1. Provocation as Justification

Let us begin with the view that provocation is a justification. Suppose V provokes D by taunting D, or fondling her, or, as her husband, committing adultery. D responds by pulling a gun and shooting V, killing him. One reaction to D's killing V would be that V "had it coming." V deserved his fate. In the consequentialist balance that determines justification, the proper weight assigned to V's interest in living was reduced by his culpability.

Now because we doubt that death is the deserved punishment for taunting, fondling, or cuckolding, D's killing V is not justified. On the other hand, one might argue that even if V's culpability does not justify V's being killed, it does make D's killing V less culpable than had D killed someone completely innocent of wrongdoing. And that is why D should get a reduction from murder to manslaughter, or so it is argued.[97]

The problem with this rationale is that, although it might be true that a victim's culpability reduces the culpability of those who impose risks on him, this cannot explain the contours of the provocation defense. For it would not explain why only D is (partially) justified in killing V. If provocation is a justification, then should it not be available to third parties? Yet, V's provoking D cannot be used even as a partial defense by a TP who kills V.

Now a proponent of the justification rationale might reply that provocation is a justification not because V's culpability discounts his interests in the consequentialist balance but because V assumed the risk of D's murderous response when V provoked D. Even if D's response were predictable, however, it is quite another thing to say it was justified. V

---

[97] *See, e.g.,* Andrew Ashworth, "The Doctrine of Provocation," 35 *Cambridge L.J.* 292, 307 (1976); Vera Bergelson, "Victims and Perpetrators: An Argument for Comparative Liability in Criminal Law," 8 *Buff. Crim. L. Rev.* 385 (2005).

might have been quite imprudent in addition to being culpable, just as a
woman wearing sexy clothing may be quite imprudent in walking alone
through a rough neighborhood at night. But V's imprudence does not
function as D's justification.

Finally, provocation as justification cannot explain why we require
that the actor be acting out of "heat of passion." After all, it should not
matter whether D is angry, upset, or just mildly irritated, if what D does
is justified because of what V did as opposed to its effect on D.

2. Provocation as Excuse (1): The Character Explanation

Another rationale for the provocation defense views it as an excuse
and therefore not available to third parties. On this rationale, provocation (partially) excuses because D's anger at V is quite appropriate and
represents no character defect.[98] Although D's justified anger was not
a sufficient reason for killing V, and although D should have exercised
more self-control than she did, her failure to control what was justifiable
anger was less culpable than had she killed V "in cold blood." In killing
V, D did not display the character of the ordinary killer and is therefore
less culpable than the ordinary killer.

This rationale for provocation is something of a hybrid. Its focus on
revealed character traits suggests that culpability is ultimately a matter
of character rather than choice. On the other hand, to the extent this
rationale *does* focus on D's choice, the reference to revealed character
traits seems to point to D's *reasons* for her act. And D's reasons – that
V taunted, fondled, or betrayed her – sound in justification rather than
excuse and arguably should extend to third parties.

3. Provocation as Excuse (2): The Decision-Making Explanation

Another excuse rationale for the provocation defense looks at the effect
of D's emotional response to the provocation on D's ability to weigh reasons and exercise self-control.[99] D's rage might affect her ability to delib-

---

[98] For variations on this theme, *see, e.g.*, Dan Kahan and Martha C. Nussbaum, "Two
Conceptions of Emotion in Criminal Law," 96 *Colum. L. Rev.* 269 (1996); Gardner, *supra*
note 13, at 578.

[99] *See, e.g.*, Joshua Dressler, "Why Keep the Provocation Defense?: Some Reflections on a
Difficult Subject," 86 *Minn. L. Rev.* 959 (2002).

erate about whether killing V is warranted. And, even if D concludes that it is not, her rage may overpower her self-control. She may in effect have a will too weakened by her rage to resist the impulse to kill.

This rationale faces two principal difficulties. First, if D could not deliberate rationally or control her conduct, why is she culpable at all? If she was not at the time of the killing a morally responsible actor because of the impairments of her evaluative and self-control mechanisms, why is she not *fully* excused?[100]

Second, on this rationale, why do only some provocations justify the defense?[101] If the Godfather flies into a murderous rage whenever someone fails to bow in his presence, he will not get the defense, despite the fact that his anger is as crippling to his judgment and self-control as is the anger of those who *do* get the defense. And if a recent immigrant from an "honor" culture kills his daughter upon discovering her lack of chastity, his rage will probably fail to win a provocation verdict for the same reason as the Godfather's, however understandable the origins of their emotions are. The defense is available only to those whose murderous rage was somehow justified by the provocation. Yet this evaluative component is difficult to square with a rationale that focuses on the impairment of D's deliberation and will.

One response here might be to argue that those who are murderously provoked by acts that would not so provoke people of ordinary virtue are culpable for not taking preemptive steps to avoid being provoked to murder. For example, the Godfather should have gone to anger management class. However, this response assumes that one knows one's weaknesses before encountering them in tragic form. Moreover, the culpability of the progenitor act – for example, not attending anger management class – is undoubtedly lower than the culpability of murder (just as the culpability for getting intoxicated or for failing to take one's antiseizure or antipsychotic medication is lower than the culpability for intentionally causing the greatest harm that one was consciously risking by such failures).

---

[100] *See, e.g.,* Garvey, *supra* note 96, at 1702–1705.
[101] *Id.* at 1704–1705.

B. ASSIMILATING PROVOCATION

We believe that provocation, properly understood, is but one instance of cases in which the actor's capacity for rational reflection is impaired, and he therefore is entitled to mitigation.[102] The criteria for the mitigating excuse would be, first, that the actor's capacity for rationality was substantially diminished at the time of the crime and, second, that the actor's diminished rationality substantially affected his or her criminal conduct.

Both criteria are critical. First, there must be a substantial diminution in rationality because less serious impairments are insufficient to warrant lesser blame and punishment. Imperfect creatures that we are, we never act with perfect, godlike rationality, and we are always subject to the distorting influences of temporal urgency and emotion. But, as long as the actor retains substantial capacity for rationality, it is not unfair to require the actor to exercise this capacity. In brief, there must be serious difficulty in thinking "straight" about one's behavior.

One key question is whether the diminution in rationality must be nonculpably caused. In other words, should we distinguish between the justifiably provoked and the Godfather? Let us begin by noting that in instances where the actor's rationality is impaired because he has, for example, consumed alcohol, there are two levels of culpability at work. The first question is the actor's culpability in choosing to drink. Although we are opposed to any sort of forfeiture rule, it is certainly true that many folks are on notice that when they drink they get into fights, become more hot-tempered, and so on. When they know of these risks, actors may be culpable for their choice to take them, irrespective of whether any harm occurs. Assume, then, that such an individual does drink and does get into a fight because of some minor insult that would not have angered him but for his intoxication. Here, we see no problem in deeming the actor's culpability for this act reduced because of his drinking. After all, at this later point in time, the actor's lack of rationality *does* render the choice harder for him than it would were he not intoxicated. Notice, however, that the sum of the two culpable choices (the choice to drink knowing one is hot-tempered and the choice to then

---

[102] This section draws from Stephen J. Morse, "Diminished Rationality, Diminished Responsibility," 1 *Oh. St. J. Crim. L.* 289 (2003).

injure another) is likely to add up to the same level of culpability as if we had focused only on the actor's later choice without allowing his voluntary intoxication to mitigate. We believe, however, that our approach properly captures the actor's culpability by focusing on these two different instances of decision making. We would use the same analysis for other circumstances in which the actor's anger may or may not be justified or reasonable. We believe that this reasonableness requirement operates as a forfeiture rule punishing actors for failing to control or to alter potentially dangerous character traits. As we noted in Chapter 3, we believe that actors may sometimes be accountable for these omissions. On the other hand, there may be times when an actor is not on notice that his failure to control a character trait will result in his losing control; and in such situations, he will be less culpable the first time he does so. But he should have only one bite at this apple. In any event, we would look to this element (of notice and failure to correct or otherwise control dangerous traits) directly, rather than through the operation of a reasonability requirement.

The second criterion requires that the actor's impaired rationality substantially and specifically affected his practical reason with respect to the culpable choice at issue. The relation required should not be confused with reductive, "mechanical" causation or causation simpliciter. We are not trying to smuggle back into the law the infamous "product" test for legal insanity that was adopted and then abandoned by the United States Court of Appeals for the District of Columbia. Diminished rationality does not simply function as a "but for" cause of the criminal conduct. It must also have substantially impaired the actor's ability to access and to consider reflectively the good reasons not to make the culpable choice on this occasion. This criterion is required to address the actor whose substantial rationality impairment plays only a limited role in affecting his or her specific criminal behavior, or who may be suffering from nonculpable diminished rationality that plays no role in the criminal conduct, but that simply co-occurs. For example, an actor with paranoid beliefs about certain types of people would not be entitled to mitigation if he were charged with bank robbery or fraud. If the actor attacked a victim from the group he thought was planning to "get him," however, he might be entitled to the mitigation. Perhaps, however, the human mind cannot be compartmentalized as we imply because it is impossible to say that irrationality in one behavioral domain does not subtly affect rationality in another. One cannot conclusively refute this suggestion, but it is a clinical common-place that some symptoms of mental disorder appear to operate in limited behavioral domains and do not affect functioning more generally.

C. HOW MITIGATION WORKS

In Chapter 8, we turn to our idealized criminal code. We believe that among the questions that the jury must answer is the question of whether the actor's decision making was sufficiently impaired to render him less culpable for his choice to impose risks of harm on others.

This question is a matter of degree, but so too, are all the questions about culpability that we confront. Whether such a vague standard should be rulified, or instead whether a bright line should be drawn (and where), is the practical question that we address in that chapter.

In taking into account the degree of impairment, the jury will have to focus on how impaired the actor was, given his decision to risk harm to a legally protected interest. The mitigation, it seems to us, is inversely related to the seriousness of the offense. If we assume, in general, equal degrees of impairment across actors, criminals engaged in serious crimes have more reasons weighing against offending and are therefore more culpable for failing to heed those reasons. An actor has a greater duty to overcome his impairment when greater harm is at stake. Remember, none of these cases involve instances where the actor's rationality is so impaired that he is unaware of what he is doing or that it is wrong. Those are cases of full excuse.

Because culpability turns on the actor's choice to risk others' legally protected interests for insufficient reasons, the criminal law must evaluate when reasons are sufficient and when the actor had the requisite capacity and fair opportunity to make that choice. Questions about justification and excuse are therefore subsumed within our culpability model. Although this chapter has not offered a theory of every (or even paradigmatic) justification and excuse, our aim has been to sketch out the pertinent questions and to show how they fit within our scheme.

PART THREE

The Culpable Act

V

Only Culpability, Not Resulting Harm, Affects Desert

Individuals exhibit insufficient concern through their actions. When an actor knowingly risks harm to others, she manifests her respect (or lack thereof) for others and their interests. In our view, this theory of culpability sets forth not only the necessary conditions for blameworthiness and punishment but also the sufficient conditions. We thus believe that current law is incorrect to the extent that it provides that resulting harm makes an actor more blameworthy and deserving of more punishment.

In this chapter, we argue that resulting harm is immaterial to what the actor deserves.[1] We begin by articulating our position that results do not matter to the actor's blameworthiness. Recognizing that we are fighting an uphill battle against common intuitions, we try to undermine

---

[1] This chapter draws from Larry Alexander, "Crime and Culpability," 5 *J. Contemp. L. Iss.* 1 (1994); Kimberly D. Kessler, Comment, "The Role of Luck in the Criminal Law," 142 *U. Pa. L. Rev.* 2183 (1994); and Stephen J. Morse, "Reason, Results and Criminal Responsibility," 2004 *Ill. L. Rev.* 363 (2004).

the intuitive appeal of the claim that "results matter" by introducing cases that do not support such intuitions and by offering an alternative account of why results sometimes do seem to matter. Beyond relying on intuitions, we reveal the flaws in law's dependence upon results. We also argue that a principled distinction can be drawn between this sort of luck (so-called moral luck), which we believe does not matter, and constitutive and opportunity luck, the existence of which we do not believe undermines criminal responsibility. After setting forth our argument as to the irrelevance of results, we then consider the implication of our position for voluntary intoxication and other ancestral and (potentially) culpable acts, for inchoate crimes, and for factually and legally impossible attempts.

I. The Irrelevance of Results

Consider the following thought experiment. Assume that you are watching a DVD in which an actor decides that he wishes to kill his victim. He buys the gun. He lies in wait until she arrives home. He fires the gun. *Now, press stop on the remote control.* At this point, the actor has revealed his willingness to harm the victim. He has shown that he does not respect her life. He has acted with the purpose of killing her. *Now, hit play.* The bullet hits the victim, and the victim dies.

What have these later frames told you about what the actor deserves? We submit that they tell you nothing. These later frames speak neither to the influence that law and morality can have over the actor nor to the influence that the actor can have over the harm that occurs. Choice is a desert basis. Causation is not.

Our view that choice is a desert basis is uncontroversial. Even those who wish to punish attempters less than completers still believe that attempts may be punished. That is, choice and acting on that choice (as we discuss in Chapter 6) are sufficient grounds for desert and punishment. Moreover, it is not difficult to see why acting on a decision to harm or to risk harming someone is sufficient to ground desert and punishment. The criminal law seeks to influence that very choice.

Establishing that choice is a necessary (and sufficient) desert basis does not by itself establish that causing harm does not increase the actor's desert. But we fail to see how causation gets its moral magic. First, as we have just said, causation is not necessary for negative desert. There is no question that attempters and riskers deserve punishment even if they do not cause harm. Second, causation is not sufficient. For if causation were sufficient, then even actors who exhibited sufficient concern for others and who exercised maximum care could be held criminally responsible for causing harms. In other words, we would have a strict liability regime. But strict liability runs counter to the very notion of desert because even individuals who care about others will occasionally (often?) harm them accidentally.

What is interesting about the current debate is that neither of these points is in dispute. The question is whether culpability *plus causation* has some moral magic that causation itself lacks. Quite frankly, we just do not see how causation suddenly gets this moral power.

Consider the following claim by Michael Moore: "'Causation matters' seems a pretty good candidate for a first principle of morality."[2] Really? It seems to us that "you break it, you buy it" is not a first principle of the criminal law. Rather, the first principle is "treat others with sufficient concern." Now, whatever the actor is going to *do*, the criminal law can influence the actor only by guiding the choice he makes. It is at this point that law and morality guide action, and it is through his choice that the agent controls his action and the results of his action. If the agent does not foresee harm, he is not held responsible for harm just because he caused it. In other words, causation without choice does not matter. So, if the criminal law's power and the agent's power over results occur at the point in time that the actor chooses to act, from where does the result itself derive additional moral power?

So far we have not so much made an argument as claimed that the other side should make one. But perhaps this is sufficient to shift the burden to the "results matter" folks. Indeed, we also do not have an argument for why it does not matter if one's victim has eleven toes, or the killing occurs on a Tuesday, or the shooter uses his left hand, or the reckless driver's car is red, and so forth. All we can say is that these things *do not matter* until we hear a compelling argument for why

---

[2] Michael S. Moore, *Causation and Responsibility* ch. 2 (forthcoming) (manuscript on file with authors).

they do. If one is going to punish another person, one needs an account of why that person is deserving of punishment. "Results matter" and "results do not matter" folks alike both understand the force of the choice account. Choice based on practical reasoning provides a principled basis for holding individuals responsible in a determined world. Choice is something law and morality can influence. Choice reveals when an actor does not have sufficient concern for others' interests. Thus, the arguments for choice are powerful. These arguments go to the heart of understanding the purposes of the criminal law, the nature of practical reasoning, and the root of criminal responsibility.

What are the arguments for results? Consider one argument that really goes nowhere. Results matter because the criminal law punishes people for what they *do*. An attempter does not kill. A killer does. Hence, even if the law cannot guide results as it guides actions, perhaps it serves a different function in retrospectively attributing blame to the causing of harms. But this approach ignores the fact that our actions may be redescribed in many ways, and we are not held accountable for some of those descriptions. That is, if an actor puts "sugar" in her companion's tea, but someone has switched the sugar with poison, we may say that the actor *poisoned* her companion. However, even though this may be an appropriate description of the actor's action, we do not hold her accountable for it. Once again, where choice and causation come apart choice trumps causation. So, it is not as though "doing" something that can be described as a harm causing is itself a desert basis.

The only argument on the table for punishing results more (as a matter of moral desert) is a phenomenological argument. We feel guiltier and blame others more when harm occurs. Before discounting the phenomenology (as we do in the next section), we wish to note here the contrast between the strength of the choice argument and the weakness of the results argument. The powerful and persuasive reasons that we have in favor of choice simply do not exist with respect to causation of results. Whereas the focus on the actor's choice points to understanding human action as a matter of practical reasoning, the focus on results shifts the emphasis back to our mechanistic causal universe. The very significance of human action is absent from an account that points to harm caused as independently desert enhancing. So, even though all three of us are sympathetic to arguments premised on emotion and intuition, none of us can find a compelling principle beyond these purported emotions in the case of results.

II. The Intuitive Appeal of the "Results Matter" Claim

Undoubtedly, the man on the street believes that an actor's killing of his victim is worse than an actor's attempt to kill his victim. Such intuitions have, in fact, been verified empirically.[3] Despite these intuitions, however, we must ask in what respect do results matter and, specifically, do they affect the actor's blameworthiness?

Although the reader may initially feel the intuitive pull of the "results matter to blameworthiness" claim, consider the following two hypotheticals.

1. *The Satanic Cult*: Members of the gang have kidnapped someone. They have strapped him to a chair behind a partition, with the barrel of a rifle running through a small hole in the partition and pointing at the kidnapped victim's heart. The rifle holds twenty rounds, and the gang loads it with nineteen blanks and one live shell. No one has any idea which shell is the live one. Twenty gang initiates who want to become full-fledged gang members are each required as a condition of membership to pull the rifle's trigger once. (The initiates are unknown to one another and are not in any way acting in concert.) Each initiate pulls the trigger, and at the conclusion of the rite, the victim is found to have been killed by the one live round. No one can tell which initiate fired the round that killed him, nor is there a scientific test that can determine who did so.

Should we care which one of the twenty actually fired the live bullet if each thought he might have and is thus as culpable as the others? In what respect is this one person more blameworthy? Each person knew there was a chance that he might kill an innocent victim and chose to take that risk to join the cult. Each has shown the same disrespect for the victim's life. None of the actors cared whether he actually succeeded.

---

[3] Paul H. Robinson and John M. Darley, *Justice, Liability and Blame: Community Views and the Criminal Law* 23 (1995). Importantly, the Robinson and Darley study compares *incomplete* attempts with *completed* crimes.

The one who pulled the trigger that fired the live round, whoever it was, is no more culpable than the other nineteen.[4]

2. *The Broken Window:* Suppose that two children have been told not to toss and hit baseballs into their neighbor's yard because the ball might hit the neighbor's window. And suppose, while the parents are away, each child acting alone at different times of day, tosses and hits a baseball into the neighbor's yard. At the end of the day, when the parents return, an angry neighbor appears with two baseballs – one from his yard and one from his house – and one piece of broken glass. Each child, when summoned, admits hitting a baseball into the neighbor's yard, but neither knows if his baseball hit the window.

It seems to us that no parent would spend one second trying to determine which child caused the damage, but rather, all parents would punish both children and both children equally. Indeed, if after having grounded both children for two weeks, any parent discovered an eyewitness who knew which child broke the window, we doubt that any parent would believe that he overpunished the one attempter and would therefore seek to make amends, say, by granting the child extra television time. Whether these parents seek to deter future conduct or to punish current conduct, parents will want to punish their children for violating the conduct rule, "Do not hit balls into the neighbor's yard," irrespective of which child caused the harm that justifies that rule – "because so doing might break the neighbor's window."

This second hypothetical underscores an important point. We do not claim that harm does not matter. Of course it does. If the children miss the window, the neighbor is not (as) angry, and the parents are not paying for a new pane of glass. (Alternatively, we often feel guilt for causing harm, even in the absence of culpability, such as when we break something through no fault of our own.) Our criminal laws embody and enforce norms the aims of which are to prevent the unjustified harming of other people. The criminal law is aimed at reducing harm. Harm is what the criminal law ultimately cares about.

---

4 This example illustrates the absurdity of a real-life analogue: the practice of putting a blank in one of the rifles in a firing squad so that everyone might later feel less guilt because *his* rifle *might* have had the blank.

Notably, simply because preventing the harm may justify the rule does not mean that causing the harm increases the actor's blameworthiness. In any case in which the actor consciously disregards an unjustifiable risk by engaging in reckless action, he displays insufficient concern for causing that harm. The risk of harm an actor unleashes is preventable. The actor's act, and whether it is unduly risky, may be guided by reasons. The results of his act cannot be. These results can be guided only by those same reasons and by the same choice to act.

Criminal law, therefore, is about reducing harm because the occurrence of harm itself is not irrelevant to us. In some sense, it is all that matters. No one doubts that the success of the actor has a significant effect on the victim. The difference between murder and attempted murder is quite simply the difference between death and life. We hope to keep our lives, limbs, and valuables, and to the extent that actors aim at depriving us of these items, it certainly matters whether actors succeed or fail.

Simply because results matter, however, does not mean that they matter for purposes of moral desert. We make many decisions each day, and the results of these decisions may matter to us, but the results are morally irrelevant to an actor's praiseworthiness or blameworthiness. Just as results matter for even the most simple of life's decisions, results matter for the most important actions we take. Indeed, imagine a case in which someone tries to rescue a friend from drowning. The praiseworthiness of the behavior is independent of success or failure, despite the fact that success or failure is critically important to the rescuer (and the friend). Conversely, our praise for a successful painter's beautiful work may be greater than our endorsement of an unsuccessful painter's unsightly one, but these views are not *moral* judgments about the painters.

In summary, although it may be true that individuals have unprincipled intuitions that results matter, there is reason to doubt that these intuitions are moral intuitions that the actor deserves less punishment for his offense.[5] First, the generalization that harm intuitively matters

---

[5] For some recent attempts to explain these intuitions without accepting the conclusion that results matter to moral desert, *see* Edward Royzman and Rahul Kumar, "Is Consequential Luck Morally Inconsequential? Empirical Psychology and the Reassessment of Moral Luck," 17 *Ratio* 329 (2004) (attributing the intuitions to hindsight bias); Darren Domsky,

is undermined by examples in which harm intuitively does not matter to the actor's desert. Second, the fact that results affect our lives certainly can influence our intuitions, even when the results do not bear on desert.

III. "Results Matter" Quandaries

For those readers who remain unpersuaded, we wish to turn to the problems with the "results matter" view. Anyone who believes that criminal law should take results into account must be able to offer principled answers to the following questions.

A. IF NEGATIVE RESULTS INCREASE BLAMEWORTHINESS, DO POSITIVE RESULTS DECREASE BLAMEWORTHINESS?

The first question is, If results can increase blameworthiness and punishability, can they also decrease blameworthiness? Consider the Israeli bomb thief who stole a backpack from a crowded area, brought it to a secluded area, opened up the backpack, and found a bomb.[6] Although some theorists argue that the thief's action was unjustified because he did not know of the bomb, other theorists claim that the thief, whose

---

"There Is No Door: Finally Solving the Problem of Moral Luck," 101 *J. Phil.* 445 (2004) (attributing the intuitions to hindsight bias and optimism bias). Ken Levy defends the intuitions because he asserts that the culpable make a "moral deal" – a gamble – with the "casino of morality." Unfortunately for Levy, his argument assumes the point in question, namely, that there is consequential moral luck. Ken Levy, "The Solution to the Problem of Outcome Luck: Why Harm Is Just as Punishable as the Wrongful Action That Causes It," 24 *Law & Phil.* 263, 286 (2005). Peter Westen defends the intuition by assuming that we should inflict deserved punishment only if we care enough to do so (or if some other goal, such as deterrence, is served thereby); and, he argues, sometimes we only care enough to inflict the full measure of deserved punishment if harm results. Peter Westen, "Why Criminal Harm Matters: Plato's Abiding Insight in the *Laws*," 1 *Crim. L. & Phil.* 307 (2007). Although we disagree with Westen that the choice to inflict deserved punishment should turn on how much we care about the crime's results, he agrees with us that results do not affect desert. *See also* Michael J. Zimmerman, "Moral Luck: A Partial Map," 36 *Canad. J. Phil.* 585, 596–599 (2006) (denying that either culpability or responsibility can turn on results).

[6] Paul H. Robinson, "The Bomb Thief and the Theory of Justification Defenses," 8 *Crim. L.F.* 387 (1997).

ONLY CULPABILITY AFFECTS DESERT

action resulted in the lesser evil, was justified.[7] These latter theorists would grant the thief a defense to the completed crime of theft but punish him for attempted theft.[8] To us, it seems immaterial to the actor's culpability and the amount of punishment that he deserves that his action actually resulted in less harm. Why should his punishment decrease owing to the fortuity that his theft saved lives when, like other thieves, he intentionally stole someone else's property?

Indeed, suppose that a would-be killer misses his victim and kills a terrorist who was about to kill 1,000 people. Is there a point at which the actor deserves not only less jail time but also no jail time? A ticker-tape parade? The key to the city? Can the fortuitous results of one's culpable action fully absolve the offender of any blameworthiness whatsoever?[9] Defenders of "results matter" typically deny that results matter in the absence of culpable mental states (or, in cases where praise and not blame is at issue, in the absence of an intent to bring about a good result). But if results are morally inert in the absence of the requisite mental states, what explains their moral valence in the presence of such mental states? If a person tries to help an old lady across a street, but brings about the saving of 1,000 lives, unaware that he is doing so, is his positive moral ledger enhanced by that result? In other words, defenders of the claim that "results matter" need more than a handful of intuitions; they need an account of *how* choice and causation interact.

Moreover, if such fortuities can decrease punishment, then no one's moral ledger is complete until the end of time. For if results matter, including the results of bringing about lesser evils, then what looks to be a net harmful result might prove at some distant time to be net

---

[7] The famous debate began with the exchange between George Fletcher and Paul Robinson. Paul H. Robinson, "A Theory of Justification: Societal Harm as a Prerequisite for Criminal Liability," 23 *UCLA L. Rev.* 266 (1975); George P. Fletcher, "The Right Deed for the Wrong Reason: A Reply to Mr. Robinson," 23 *UCLA L. Rev.* 293 (1975).

[8] *See* Paul H. Robinson, *Structure and Function in Criminal Law* 111 (1997); B. Sharon Byrd, "Wrongdoing and Attribution: Implications beyond the Justification-Excuse Distinction," 33 *Wayne L. Rev.* 1289 (1987) (advocating attempt liability for the unknowingly justified actor). *But see* J. C. Smith, *Justification and Excuse in the Criminal Law* 43 (1989) ("Can we sensibly say that, at one and the same time, a person is (i) justified in firing a gun at another with intent to kill him and (ii) guilty of attempted murder?").

[9] Ken Levy argues that resulting harms and resulting benefits are not symmetrical vis-à-vis the question of moral luck, but his justification – society cares more about the former than the latter – is unconvincing. *See* Levy, *supra* note 5, at 288–289.

beneficial. Perhaps the Holocaust so moved the civilized world that even worse future holocausts were averted. Would that lessen Hitler's desert?

B. CAUSAL CONUNDRUMS

The expected rejoinder to our claim that moral ledgers continue ad infinitum is that causation determines the ultimate "cutoff" point. However, the introduction of causation into the criminal law reveals the very problems inherent in a "results matter" approach.

Fortuity pervades causal questions. Causation is typically a bifurcated analysis. We first ask whether the result Y would have occurred without the act or omission X, and we then apply a limiting principle to those Xs that satisfy the first test. For example, John would not have hit Mary's car if he had never been born. Hence, John's mother and father are causes of the accident according to the first half of the test. Their legal responsibility, however, is limited by the proximate causation requirement: the car accident was not a "harm within the risk" of having a child, or the accident was not foreseeable, or John was an intervening actor.

The first question is a factual one: did the actor actually cause the harm? The second part of the question is one of policy: should we hold the actor responsible for the harm that she factually caused?

If results matter to an actor's blameworthiness, then we need theories of factual and proximate causation that can *actually determine* when an actor has caused a harm. The problem is that we lack such theories.[10]

Factual causation is the less problematic of the two causal tests as a matter of theory, but it is not without its practical and theoretical difficulties. The Satanic Cult and Broken Window hypotheticals illustrate the problem of alternative causation. One person did it, but there are multiple suspects, and no way to determine who the actual cause was. This problem presents itself in the famous torts case of *Summers v. Tice*,[11] in which the plaintiff and the two defendants were quail hunting and both defendants negligently shot in the plaintiff's direction, two

---

[10] For recent forays into this area, *see* Carolina Sartorio, "Causes as Difference-Makers," 123 *Phil. Stud.* 71 (2005); Michael S. Moore, "Patrolling the Consequentialist Borders of Our Obligations" 27 *Law & Phil.* 35 (2008).

[11] 199 P.2d 1 (Cal. 1948) (en banc).

shots of which hit the plaintiff in the eye and lip. Rather than finding that the plaintiff could not satisfy his burden of proof on causation because he could not prove by a preponderance of the evidence which defendant caused his injuries, the California Supreme Court held that both defendants, despite acting independently, could be held jointly liable for the injury unless the defendants could prove which one was responsible.

Similar proof problems also gave rise to market share liability in tort law in *Sindell v. Abbott Laboratories*.[12] There, the California Supreme Court upheld a judgment supporting liability among several manufacturers of diethylstilbestrol (DES) for damages the plaintiff suffered as a result of using that substance. Although it could not be determined which manufacturer actually caused the plaintiff's injury, the court, rather than dismissing the case, apportioned damages among the defendants on the basis of their respective market shares.

Criminal law, however, cannot simply spread money around. If *Sindell* were a criminal case, the question would be whether the defendants deserve punishment, and whether the amount that they deserve is dependent upon the harm they actually caused. In our view, we need not await further scientific advances that would allow us to ascertain which manufacturer's DES actually triggered a particular victim's vaginal cancer, nor would our attitudes be affected by that knowledge. Rather, we know all we need to know to fix desert.[13]

There are also the cases where the actor causes V's death but also prolongs V's life. One of the most famous puzzles is the three prospectors case. A, B, and C are prospecting. C is going out on his own the next day. A secretly wants to kill C, and while B and C are asleep, fills C's canteen with poison. Later, while A and C are asleep, B, who also wants to kill C, but who is unaware of what A has done, pours out the contents of C's canteen (thinking that it's water) and fills the canteen with sand. Later, C dies of thirst. A denies killing C, because C did not die of poison. B also denies killing C, because although C did die of thirst as B

---

[12] 607 P.2d 924 (Cal. 1980).

[13] Suppose that ten actors dump a certain carcinogen in a river recklessly. The victim ingests river water, and twenty years later dies of cancer. Although the victim had particles in his body from each actor's effluent, only one actor's particle lodged in the site where the cancer originated. Would we care to know which actor's particle it was? Would that distinguish the actors in terms of moral desert?

planned, C died later than he otherwise would have had B not poured out the poison. B actually prolonged C's life. We have no problem with such a case. A and B are both equally culpable, and what happened to C is immaterial. Not so for the "results matter" folks.

A similar example is that of D, a doctor, who irradiates V's tongue in order to kill him twenty years hence from cancer that the radiation will induce. Unbeknownst to D, V had a tumor on his tongue that would have killed him in six months but which was destroyed by the radiation. When V dies in twenty years from the cancer D induced, D can plausibly contend that he lengthened rather than shortened V's life. In both of these cases, it is difficult to say that the actor caused the victim's death as opposed to causing his life to be saved. If his desert turns on the former, why does it not also turn on the latter?

Then there is the problem of criminal omissions. (Although the exception rather than the rule, some failures to act *are* criminalized.)[14] If results matter, then we must be able to say that the actor's omission *caused* the material harm. But how can an omission – a not doing – cause anything? Michael Moore, a proponent of the "results matter" position, has wrestled with this problem and concluded that omissions are not "causes" but are "failures to prevent."[15] Moore deems failures to prevent to be similar to causes in that both require the occurrence of harmful results. (One "fails to prevent" only if there is a result that should have been prevented.) Perhaps Moore's approach to result-based crimes of omission is satisfactory. We tender no opinion on the matter, as it is irrelevant to our theory of culpability and desert or to any theory that is unconcerned with results.

Finally, difficulties also arise in cases of causal overdetermination, where either of two causes is individually sufficient. For example, D starts a fire, intending to destroy V's house, and the fire joins with another fire that was itself sufficient to burn down V's house at exactly the same time. Or D_1, a murderous mechanic, tampers with the brakes of the rental car, which is rented by D_2. As D_2 descends the narrow ramp from the garage to the street, he sees his arch-enemy V walking

---

14 *See* Larry Alexander, "Criminal Liability for Omissions: An Inventory of Issues," in *Criminal Law Theory: Doctrines of the General Part* 121 (S. Shute and A. P. Simester, eds., 2002).

15 *See* Moore, *supra* note 2.

past the aperture where the ramp enters the street. D_2 decides not to apply the brakes, but rather coasts into V, killing him. Had D_2 applied the brakes, they would have failed, and V would have died exactly as he did exactly when he did. Neither D_1 nor D_2 was a necessary cause of V's death because both were sufficient for V's dying exactly when and how he did. We have no difficulty with such cases because we would not distinguish D_1 and D_2; they are equally culpable attempted murderers who deserve precisely the same punishment whether or not they are actual – successful – murderers. The "results matter" folks do have difficulty because they have a result – a death – to deal with.

In response to overdetermination questions, commentators have proposed various other tests. The problem is that these tests are either indeterminate and thus easily manipulable or not employed by courts. Michael Moore proposed, but then later rejected, a test whereby we specify the harm – but for the actor's action would the injury *occur as it did* – because the test does not provide any criteria for determining the appropriate description of the harm.[16] The substantial factor test ultimately combines proximate and factual causation, as it asks the jury to consider whether the actor's action was sufficiently "substantial" to count as a cause. Indeed, although the Restatement and Restatement (Second) of Torts had included the substantial factor test as the test of factual causation, it was because of this problem of indeterminacy and manipulability that the drafters of the Restatement (Third) abandoned the test, noting that it had not withstood the test of time.[17] Finally, although the Necessary Element of a Sufficient Set ("NESS") test may be able to give an answer in overdetermination cases, it has never been applied by any court.[18] Thus, even *factual causation* presents problems for the "results matter" position, problems that our position completely avoids.

---

[16] *See* Michael S. Moore, "Thomson's Preliminaries about Causation and Rights," 63 *Chi.-Kent L. Rev.* 497, 508 (1987); Michael S. Moore, "Foreseeing Harm Opaquely," in *Action and Value in Criminal Law* 144 (S. Shute et al., eds., 1993). Moore's current views on cause-in-fact can be found in Moore, *supra* note 2.

[17] Restatement (Third) of Torts: Liab. Physical Harm § 26 cmt. j (Proposed Final Draft No. 1, 2005) ("the substantial-factor test has not, however, withstood the test of time, as it has proved confusing and been misused").

[18] NESS states that "a particular condition was a cause of (condition contributing to) a specific consequence if and only if it was a necessary element of a set of antecedent actual conditions that was sufficient for the occurrence of the consequence." Richard W. Wright,

The most significant doctrinal and theoretical problem for the "results matter" position – aside from its detaching moral desert from what is fully within the actor's control, namely, his decision to risk harm – is that of proximate causation. Every criminal law and tort law casebook is replete with puzzles of proximate causation. Does a wife who leaves poison by her husband's bedside with the intention of killing him "proximately cause" his death if, instead of drinking the poison, he slips on it after it accidentally spills?[19] Or does she "proximately" kill him if she fires a bullet at him that misses but causes a chandelier to fall on his head, or that scares him so much that he runs into traffic and is hit by a car, or that causes him to flee the town on a plane that crashes? Does one who batters and rapes a woman "proximately cause" her death if she commits suicide?[20] Does a trolley operator who exceeds the speed limit "proximately cause" injury to a passenger hit by a falling tree?[21] Does a railroad employee who shoves a passenger carrying fireworks "proximately cause" injury to a woman on whom a scale falls in response to the concussion of exploding fireworks?[22]

Those who adopt the "results matter" position believe that results do *not* matter if the causal linkage between the actor's culpable act and the harmful result that act causes (in fact) is too quirky. But "too quirky" hardly seems like a principled way to determine an actor's blameworthiness. Consider the story of Pierre and Monique (our entry in the "bad fiction writing" contest):

> It was an incredible electrical storm. Lightning was striking every few seconds...and some bolts right outside the house.
>
> Inside, Pierre's hatred of Monique had reached the flashpoint. She had just informed him – matter-of-factly, dismissively, condescendingly – that no, she would not grant him a divorce so that he would be free to take up with his latest conquest, Bridgette. Her tone as much as her verdict enraged him. And as he looked at her, facing him but totally absorbed in a fashion magazine despite his just having informed her that

---

"Causation in Tort Law," 73 *Cal. L. Rev.* 1735, 1790 (1985). For a full critique of the test, see Moore, *supra* note 2.
[19] *See* Sanford H. Kadish and Stephen J. Schulhofer, eds., *Criminal Law and Its Processes: Cases and Materials* 518 (7th ed., 2001).
[20] Stephenson v. State, 179 N.E. 633 (Ind. 1932).
[21] Berry v. Sugar Notch Borough, 43 A. 240 (Pa. 1899).
[22] Palsgraf v. Long Island Railroad Company, 162 N.E. 99 (N.Y. 1928).

he wanted to end their marriage, he realized that everything about her now disgusted him. And those body rings! Not only through her nose, but through her lips, her ears, her navel…everywhere. She was hideous.

But even as he fought to control his emotions, Pierre concocted a plan. He reached in the desk drawer and took out the loaded .38 he kept there, Monique still absorbed in her magazine and oblivious to his movements. He then aimed the gun at precisely 3°NNW and pulled the trigger.

There are two possible endings of this story:

1. The bullet just missed Monique, as Pierre knew it would. And just as Pierre hoped and believed would happen, Monique, believing that Pierre had just tried to kill her, leaped up and desperately ran from the house. Once outside, however, the metal rings on Monique's body did the work that Pierre hoped and believed they would: they attracted a bolt of lightning, which killed Monique on the spot. Pierre's hastily concocted plan had succeeded.

2. The bullet just missed Monique because, although he wanted the bullet to kill Monique, Pierre's aim was off. Monique, alarmed at the realization that Pierre had tried to shoot her, immediately ran from the house. However, as she stepped outside, the metal rings on her body attracted a bolt of lightning, which killed her instantly.

In our view, Pierre deserves the same amount of punishment irrespective of how the story ends. The "results matter" position, however, commits one to the claim that Pierre caused Monique's death in (1), but not in (2), and thus is more blameworthy in (1) than (2). For in (1), surely Pierre "caused" Monique's death in whatever way is required for criminal liability therefore; after all, her death occurred just as he had planned. Whereas in (2), if there was ever a "deviant causal chain" that severed proximate from actual causation, this would be an example. *Yet, (1) and (2) differ only with respect to Pierre's mental states preceding the firing of the gun. And these mental states cannot be said to have caused anything in themselves.* Thus, it is difficult to see how (1) and (2) can be distinguished in terms of proximate causation.[23]

---

[23] Michael Moore, a results-matter defender, agrees with us that whether Pierre proximately caused Monique's death cannot depend on Pierre's mental state. *See* Michael S. Moore, "Causation and Responsibility," 16 *Soc. Phil. & Pol'y.* 1, 19 (1999). In conversation, Moore has recently argued that the Pierre-Monique puzzle is a question about matching the

Besides what some dub "coincidences," there are the intervening human cause cases, which come in many forms – culpable human interventions, nonculpable ones, likely ones and unlikely ones, and so forth. A representative example is *Thabo Meli*,[24] which is usually portrayed as a "concurrence" case, but which is actually a proximate cause case in which the actor's own act is the intervening cause between his initial act and the result. After attempting to kill V, D (nonculpably? mildly culpably?) disposes of what D believes is V's corpse, which actually kills V. The actor culpably attempted to kill the victim, and then nonculpably or less culpably accidentally killed the victim. Does a proper proximate causation analysis yield the result that the actor's own voluntary act broke the causal chain? Or does it yield the opposite result? We argue that there is no principled way to answer that question, nor do we need to.

Doctrinal tests for proximate causation are unsatisfactory. The foreseeability test is problematic, as there is no principled or rationally defensible way to privilege one description of the harm that occurs over another.[25] Moreover, what actors foresee – but not what they "should" foresee[26] – bears on their culpability, not on what they "cause." The Model Penal Code wrestles with the proximate causation limitation and comes up with the unhelpful requirement that the resulting harm not be "too remote or accidental to have just bearing on the actor's liability or the gravity of the offense."[27] The question is, however, whether and why any result caused by the culpable act has a just bearing on the actor's desert-based liability. We cannot know whether results are "too remote or accidental" until we know why results should matter at all.

Finally, even as Michael Moore toils at articulating a metaphysical theory of causation, we doubt the promise of his project.[28] First, we question whether metaphysical causation includes the "breaks" in

content of intentions. *See generally* Moore, *supra* note 10. For an exploration of Moore's view, *see* Kimberly Kessler Ferzan, "Beyond Intention," 29 *Cardozo L. Rev.* 1147 (2008).

[24] *Thabo Meli v. Regina*, (1954) 1 All E.R. 373.

[25] *See* Moore, "Foreseeing Harm Opaquely," *supra* note 16, at 137.

[26] *See* Chapter 3, *supra*, for why we reject the proposition that what actors should foresee affects their culpability.

[27] *See* Model Penal Code § 2.03 (1985).

[28] *See* Morse, *supra* note 1, at 395–397.

the causal chain that our moral and legal theories do. The criminal law distinguishes between actual, usually but-for, causes and proximate causes, but it must be remembered that the original actor who set the chain of causation in motion is a but-for cause, whether or not the causal chain is legally "cut" by a later natural event or human intervention. It is crucial to remember that the legal chain is cut but not the natural one. That is, both the original actor and the later natural event or human action are all part of the complete chain of causation of the ultimate harm. Whether or not we hold an actor responsible for a result in a chain of causation that includes the actor's intentional act, there are no genuine causal gaps. The law indulges the obvious fiction that the causal chain is cut only because its supposed policy considerations seem to create the need for this outcome; but metaphysically, a so-called coincidence or an intentional, wrongful human action is a cause just like any other. Metaphysics does not dictate the legal cut-off points for liability.

Second, even if Moore were correct that metaphysical causation does contain such "breaks," it remains to be seen whether law does, will, or should track metaphysics on this point. Even with such truths of theoretical reason in hand, no particular normative legal policy necessarily follows. If the metaphysics of causation is vastly more complex than the commonsense conception of causation, as we suspect it is, it will command allegiance as a ground for assessing liability only if ordinary people can understand and apply it and if we can be convinced that using that metaphysics will contribute to human flourishing. But there is no a priori reason why this should be so. After all, there is no reason to believe that the physical universe cares about morality or is moral (or immoral). Believing that following the metaphysics of causation will contribute to human welfare will require a moral argument independent of the pure metaphysics of causation. If a convincing moral argument is not forthcoming, and the metaphysics of causation leads to legal results too different from the common sense of causal liability, theoretical reason will rightly be ignored. Finally, if a good theoretical argument to follow the metaphysics is produced, but once again the outcome differs too much from common beliefs about justice, theoretical reason will again be ignored for much the same psychological reasons that the commonsense belief that results matter is also impervious to reason.

No one has come up with a satisfactory test for determining whether an injury caused by the actor's act was "proximately caused" by it. Moreover, no one will. The reason no one will is that the upshot of the proximate cause inquiry – what the actor deserves – is not related to what the actor caused, "proximately" or otherwise. When the causal chain seems too deviant, then the ordinary person's rough sense of justice might be offended by attributing the result to the actor,[29] but this is just a sociological observation and not a rational argument. If this rough sense of justice is too ingrained to be abandoned, then we should recognize that any test is rationally arbitrary. If results were jettisoned as a criterion of criminal liability, then the criminal law could avoid the baroque machinations of legislators, lawyers, and judges as they try to rationalize proximate cause doctrine. In our view, the answer to this problem is clear. Causation and results should not matter to the criminal law.

IV. Free Will and Determinism Reprised

Any discussion of the role of results, often coined "moral luck," raises concerns about free will and determinism. This concern leads to one final objection to our position – why do we eschew the relevance of "moral luck" when "constitutive luck" and "circumstantial luck" cannot be avoided or eradicated? Michael Moore argues that "result luck" is indistinguishable from "constitutive luck" (luck involving the genetic and experiential fortuities that cause one to have the character that produces potentially harmful conduct) and various types of "circumstantial luck," such as "planning luck" (luck involving fortuities that may intervene to prevent one from forming plans to engage in potentially harmful conduct) and "execution luck" (luck involving fortuities that prevent the execution of firmly formed intentions to perform potentially harmful conduct).[30] One may have betrayed a Jewish friend had one lived in Nazi Germany. One may have stolen money had one not inherited it. One may have struck one's enemy had a cop not been standing nearby. And so on.

[29] *See* Robinson and Darley, *supra* note 3, at 188–189.
[30] *See* Michael S. Moore, *Placing Blame: A Theory of Criminal Law* 233–246 (1997).

Moore convincingly argues that in a deterministic world, variables over which the actor had no control exist at every stage, from character to execution. Whether or not one performs a wrongful action is as suffused with luck, and is as beyond our control, as whether results actually occur. If we had a different character, which is largely not up to us, then we would not be the type of person who would have the desire or form the intention to do wrong. If we have the desire to do wrong, then events over which we have no control may distract us from forming the intention to satisfy that desire. Once we form the intention, events over which we have no control, ranging from physical to psychopathological, may prevent us from executing that intention.

The conclusion that in a deterministic universe, luck, understood in this way, "goes all the way down" is correct as a matter of theoretical reason. But, as Moore recognizes, it leads to an unacceptable reductio that those like us who believe results do not matter will be forced to accept. If causal influences over which we have no control undermine responsibility, then no one is responsible for anything, and this conclusion is not limited to results. Genuine desert does not exist. Because this conclusion is morally unacceptable and does not account for the moral and legal world we inhabit, a morally principled line based on luck cannot be drawn. Moore suggests that because we accept the existence of desert for action despite constitutive, planning, and execution luck, we should be willing to accept the existence of desert for results despite result luck.

Moore's suggestion does not follow, however. Luck may not provide a principled basis to draw the line between moral responsibility for action and moral responsibility for results, but perhaps another principle that does not lead to an unacceptable reductio will. Moore's critique of the luck argument depends on that argument's confusion of the distinction between a mechanistic-causal account of behavior and a practical reasoning account. As a good compatibilist, Moore knows that the explanatory causal stories of theoretical reason are not the basis for responsibility and desert. They could not be for just the reasons he gives. Causation is a metaphysically seamless web. In a compatibilist account of the type he endorses – and that two of us also endorse[31] – responsibility and desert are moral concepts implicit in practical

---

[31] *See* Chapter 1.

reason. Compatibilists (and libertarians)[32] believe that human beings are capable of rational deliberation, that our deliberations affect our actions, and that our actions potentially affect the world. For compatibilists, actors do not need contracausal freedom to deserve praise and blame, or punishment and reward, for their actions. It is sufficient if they act intentionally, without compulsion, and with a general capacity for rationality. The only form of control a responsible actor needs is the general capacity to be guided by reason, a capacity most adults possess in ample measure. Thus, compatibilists have good reason to "draw the line" at human action because only action can be guided by reason, and not because action is free of the causal forces of the universe – of "luck." The potential for the law to guide people by reason is a good justification for holding people morally responsible for actions but not for results. For us, as for Moore, there is every reason to distinguish between result "luck," on the one hand, and constitutive and circumstantial "luck," on the other.

Ultimately, our position rests on the assumption that the control we have over our choices – our willings – is immune to luck and is thus qualitatively and morally different from our control or lack thereof over our heredity and environment, the situations in which we find ourselves, and the causal consequences of our choices. No matter our past history, the options we confront, or the causal forces that will combine with those we initiate, what we choose is up to us in a way these other factors are not. It is not just that we have *more* control over our choices than over our constitution, our circumstances, and what we cause. Our control over our choices is different in kind, not different in degree.

---

[32] Libertarians have another argument for distinguishing between result luck on the one hand and circumstantial and constitutive luck on the other. For them, there is no fact of the matter regarding whether someone would have acted wrongly in different circumstances. Nor does the fact that one's character and environment are largely beyond one's control deprive one of the freedom to choose in accordance with good reasons. For an attempt to deal with constitutive, circumstantial, and result luck by arguing for a distinction between *moral worth* and *moral responsibility* and claiming that results matter only for the latter, *see* John Greco, "Virtue, Luck and the Pyrrhonian Problematic," 130 *Phil. Stud.* 9 (2006). For us, who are concerned with culpability rather than worth or responsibility (for outcomes), the line Greco draws occurs at the wrong place. In terms of culpability, one can be constitutively or circumstantially "unlucky" – one can have unfavorable genes or environment, or one can face more or stronger temptations to wrongdoing than others – but one cannot be "unlucky" with respect to results.

Bad luck before choice and bad luck after choice is just bad luck; unlike choice, it cannot affect our culpability.[33]

V. The Immateriality of Results and Ancestral Culpable Acts

The criminal law often charges people with having acted culpably when the conduct in question was clearly not culpable but was the result of prior culpable conduct. Consider Joe, John, and Jake, who all drink themselves into an extreme state of intoxication in a pub. Joe is so drunk he cannot find his car and passes out in the parking lot. John does find his car and drives it quite dangerously, but luckily hits no one. Jake also finds his car, also drives it quite dangerously, and plows into another car, killing its occupants.

The criminal law would charge Jake with reckless homicide despite the fact that Jake was so intoxicated that he did not realize his driving was unduly risky to others. If Jake would have been aware of those risks had he been sober, and if his lack of sobriety was the result of voluntary drinking, then the criminal law attributes recklessness to his driving.[34] John, if apprehended, can also be charged with reckless driving as well as the proxy crime of driving while intoxicated. Again, John is considered reckless, despite his failure to advert to the riskiness of his conduct, because he would have so adverted had he not voluntarily become intoxicated. Joe, on the other hand, because he failed to find his car, is guilty of no crime of recklessness.

What is happening in these cases is that the law is, in effect, holding John and Jake culpable at the level of recklessness for their getting intoxicated, and the law is then attaching that culpability to the fortuitous outcomes of that recklessness. In Jake's case, it is a death. In John's, dangerous conduct. Joe, however, having luckily engaged in no dangerous conduct subsequent to his drinking, escapes criminal liability altogether.

---

[33] *See* Nir Eisikovits, "Moral Luck and the Criminal Law," in *Law and Social Justice* 105, 117 (J. K. Campbell, M. O'Rourke, and D. Shier, eds., 2005).

[34] *See* Model Penal Code § 2.08(2) (1985).

Under our schema, if getting intoxicated in a public place without surrendering one's car keys is unjustifiably risky to others – because one might then drive dangerously – then Joe, John, and Jake have committed the same culpable act in getting intoxicated and are equally culpable. They are not culpable for what they do subsequently if after they become intoxicated they do not perceive their conduct to be risky. John's dangerous driving and Jake's fatal crash are merely fortuitous "results" of their culpable act of excessive drinking and are immaterial to their culpability.

So whether it is drivers voluntarily getting intoxicated, epileptics or psychotics failing to take antiseizure or antipsychotic medications, parents failing to read up on symptoms of childhood diseases, or sailors in a foreign port failing to attend language classes, culpability should attach to those acts of knowingly taking unjustifiable risks – and should be set at the average riskiness the actors believe such conduct entails – and should not turn on the subsequent acts that are the product of that risky conduct but that are not themselves culpable.

VI. The Immateriality of Results and Inchoate Crimes

We have maintained that an actor who acts culpably has his blameworthiness and punishability – his desert – fixed by that culpable act alone, regardless of whether it produces a harmful result. If the actor's act is culpable – whether because he believes it creates an unjustifiable risk of harm to a protected interest, or because, as with "proxy" crimes, he believes it creates an unjustifiable risk that he will engage in forbidden conduct (such as exceeding the speed limit) – his desert is fixed, and results or their absence cannot alter it.

It should be obvious that in maintaining the moral equivalence of culpable acts that cause harms (or cause conduct that is a proxy for undue risks of harm), we are assuming that the actor has taken the last step he believes necessary to unleash the risk and that the relevant level of risk is now beyond his control. If he merely intends to unleash the risk, even as soon as the next moment, his culpability is not as high as that of one who has unleashed the risk. Indeed, whether or not "substantial step" attempts (as opposed to "last act necessary" attempts) or other inchoate forms of criminality (solicitations of crimes, conspiracies to commit crimes, and before-the-fact assistance to criminals) are culpable at all, and if so, on what basis, is a vexing topic and one that we take up in Chapter 6 (and have taken up preliminarily in Chapter 4 in discussing "culpable aggressors"). Even if inchoate forms of criminality are culpable, however, that culpability is less than the culpability of those who believe they have already unleashed the risk. Only the culpability of the latter is equivalent to that of actors who culpably cause harm (or culpably engage in conduct that is a proxy harm).

On the other hand, for those who believe they have already unleashed the risk, their culpability is, as we argued in Chapter 2, an entirely subjective matter. If Ralph is going eighty through a school zone to get home in time to watch his favorite TV program, and he believes that he is creating an extremely high risk of injuring or killing a child, he is culpable – even if there are no children present; even if there are children present but his speedometer is broken and he is actually going only fifteen miles per hour; even if he is not in a car but, unbeknownst to him, is in a car simulator, or has a paralyzed leg and only believes he is, but is not really, depressing the accelerator; and even if he is a brain-in-a-vat who is willing that he depress the accelerator but has no limbs and no vehicle. The same holds if the risk Ralph is unleashing is not the risk of harm to children but is instead the risk of conduct – "exceeding the speed limit" – that amounts to a proxy harm. And the same holds true of Samantha, the voodoo doctor, who, at the moment she sticks a pin in the effigy of Suzy, believes she has irretrievably unleashed the high risk of Suzy's death. And Carla, who puts what she believes is poison in Dan's tea and watches him drink it but has actually mistaken sugar for strychnine. And Mike, who aims at Bob and pulls the trigger, but misses. Or whose gun was, unbeknownst to him, unloaded. Or who tried to squeeze the trigger but discovered it to be stuck. Or whose finger did not respond when he was willing it to squeeze the trigger and thought he had squeezed it. Or who did not realize when he filled him with lead that Bob was already dead. And Lady Eldon, who attempts to smuggle past customs an item she does not realize she is not required to declare. And so on. In every one of these scenarios, the actors commit fully culpable acts that are no less deserving of punishment than had the same acts injured children, exceeded the speed limit, killed Suzy, Dan, and Bob, or resulted in nondeclaration of a dutiable item.

VII. Inculpatory Mistakes and the Puzzle of Legally Impossible Attempts

In all cases in which the actor acts culpably but no harm occurs – cases in which the actual (God's-eye) risk is zero, but the actor estimates it to be sufficiently high to render his act culpable – the actor's causing harm is in some sense "impossible." The criminal law has traditionally referred to a particular category of acts as "impossible attempts," a description that we find unfortunate, given that all attempts that are *attempts* – that is, that fail to bring about harm – are in a very real sense impossible. Given that the gun was unloaded, the trigger jammed, the aim awry, the victim suddenly bent over, and so on, the attempt could not help but fail.

The Model Penal Code brought some helpful order to the topic of impossible attempts by deeming all "impossible" attempts to be criminal with the exception of those in the category of "pure legal impossibility." The latter are those cases in which the actor believes his act violates a particular criminal law that does not in fact exist. If, for example, we mistakenly believe dancing on Sundays is criminally proscribed, and, to protest this absurd law, on Sunday we take to the dance floor, we have attempted to violate a nonexistent law. Although we are in some sense culpable – we are, after all, scofflaws – there is no law in the penal code that we can be charged with attempting to violate. This is a case of pure legal impossibility and not punishable. (The case would be different – and under the Model Penal Code, clearly a punishable attempt – if there were such a law on the books, but we were dancing, not on Sunday, as we believed, but on Saturday.)[35]

In our schema, the equivalent of pure legal impossibility might be the actor who believes that creating perceived risk R of harm H for justifying reason JR is culpable, who nonetheless creates R of H for JR, but creating R of H for JR is *not* culpable. The actor will believe he has acted

---

[35] The line between cases of pure legal impossibility and those cases of impossibility that are punishable is not as neat as the preceding example suggests. For example, what if the law were "One may not dance when there is a red flag over the courthouse, but one may when there is a green flag," and we, being colorblind, mistake a green flag for a red one but dance anyway? For a discussion of inculpatory mistakes of this type, *see* Larry Alexander, "Inculpatory and Exculpatory Mistakes and the Fact/Law Distinction: An Essay in Memory of Myke Bayles," 12 *Law & Phil.* 33 (1993).

wrongly toward others when he has not. And just as the criminal law does not punish the pure legally impossible attempt, so too would we exempt from punishment those who believe themselves to be culpable but who are not. There are, in our schema, no "attempts to be culpable." One either acts culpably or does not, but one cannot culpably try (but fail) to act culpably.

On the other hand, to the extent we make unduly risking proxy conduct criminal, we introduce the following possibility: the actor may believe that he is imposing an unjustifiably high risk of proscribed proxy conduct PC but not an unjustifiably high risk of the harms (H) that PC is meant to avert. The actor thus appears to be culpable with respect to PC but not with respect to H. But what if PC is only a figment of the actor's imagination? (Perhaps PC was proscribed in the past but is not so now.) The actor has displayed insufficient concern for "the law" but not insufficient concern for the harms the law wishes to avert.

Where the law proscribes proxy conduct, do we need a category like pure legal impossibility? Our hypothetical actor displays a sort of culpability – the scofflaw sort – but it is difficult to see what he can be charged with. One possibility, of course, is to say that acting as a scofflaw is a form of culpable conduct and punishable as such. We discuss this possibility again in Chapter 8. That approach would avert the necessity of distinguishing pure legal impossibility from other, clearly culpable, mistakes.

Results do not matter for blameworthiness or punishability. The law seeks to influence the reasons for which a person acts, but it cannot influence the results of these actions. Thus, when an actor risks harm to others for insufficient reasons, the law's influence has failed, and a culpable act has fully revealed the actor's desert. No further information, such as whether the culpable act caused harm (or benefit), is needed for us to determine the degree of her punishment.

Although many people believe that results matter, there is a distinction to be drawn between results mattering (as they must because they affect the world in which we live) and results mattering for the moral blameworthiness of the actor. We can recognize that some results are harmful and, indeed, that we create laws to prevent such harms, without at the same time committing ourselves to the view that results independently affect blameworthiness.

Because the law currently gives independent significance to the role of resulting harm, criminal law doctrine is mired with flaws. Both cause-in-fact and proximate causation present flawed doctrinal accommodations to approximate culpability when causal chains go awry. The better approach is simply to abandon any concern with results completely.

Finally, we can make a principled distinction between moral or result luck and other forms of luck, and that distinction rests on the very choice that is at the root of culpability. No matter what hand we are dealt, moral agents have the capacity to reason and the capacity to choose to violate the law (or not). It is on this choice and this choice alone that responsibility rests and, along with it, culpability and desert.

VI

When Are Inchoate Crimes Culpable and Why?

Having argued that results are neither necessary nor sufficient for blameworthiness or punishability, we must still answer the question of what type of action is necessary for the actor to be said to have acted culpably. Although this problem is traditionally addressed within the doctrinal rubric of the *actus reus* for incomplete attempts, the problem for us applies more generally. We must specify an *actus reus* formulation for all crimes.

There are various potential *actus reus* formulations, drawn along the continuum from the time the actor forms an intention to impose a risk of harm to the time when he believes he is unleashing that risk and it is no longer within his (complete) control. We contend that it is only at the time the actor engages in the act that unleashes a risk of harm that he believes he can no longer control (through exercise of reason and will alone) that he has performed a culpable action.

In this chapter, we begin by setting forth the principles that underlie our adoption of the "last act" formula.[1] We then survey the various points along the inchoate crime continuum, from the formation of the intention to impose the risk, to the Model Penal Code's intention plus "substantial step," to the common law's intention plus "dangerous proximity," to the last act. In our view, it is only the last act – the act through which the actor believes he has relinquished (complete) control over whether he has created an undue risk of harm (or proxy conduct) – that is a culpable act. (In the next chapter, we further refine this view by clarifying that it is the actor's *volition* to move his body in such a way as to engage in the last act necessary for the unleashing of the risk that is the culpable "act.")

I. Our Theory of Culpable Action

A. PRELIMINARY CONSIDERATIONS

Underlying our defense of the last-act test are three separate, but related, claims. First, the criminal law – and the morality that underlies it – aims to influence the actor's reasons for action. Second, an actor can change his mind about imposing a risk of harm to others until he believes he has actually unleashed that risk of harm and can no longer control it through further practical reasoning eventuating in acts of will. Third, an actor should be punished only for what he *has done* and not *what he will do*.

In determining what should count as a culpable act, we should thus first take account of the way that law and morality aim to influence conduct: actors act for reasons, and the criminal law and its underlying morality reflect that there are powerful reasons to abstain from engaging in unduly risky behavior. The law and its underlying morality thus influence (or should influence) the actor's practical reasoning.

Not only do the law and morality seek to influence the actor's reasons for action, but they can also continue to influence these reasons until the point at which the actor engages in some conduct that (he believes) has unleashed a risk over which he no longer has complete control. To

---

[1] This chapter draws from Larry Alexander and Kimberly D. Kessler, "Mens Rea and Inchoate Crimes," 87 *J. Crim. L. & Criminology* 1138 (1997).

illustrate, if the actor is thinking about shooting his victim, he can still change his mind. However, once the actor has fired the gun, unless he is Superman ("faster than a speeding bullet"), he can no longer prevent the result from occurring or reduce the risk thereof.

It may be objected that our theory of control is over- and underinclusive. The actor may not be able to control his reasoning and may be able to control the result. For example, he may not have complete control over whether he will decide to engage in the action – perhaps he will suddenly become distracted – and he may have control over whether the result occurs, as when he can snuff out the fuse that he has lit. But there is an important difference between these cases; this difference lies in the ability for reason alone to affect whether the outcome occurs. In the former case, although the actor may (fortuitously for him) forget his criminal plans, these plans were still subject to revision through practical reasoning; however, in the latter case, although the actor may decide to take another action in order to try to avert the harm, merely changing his mind is not alone sufficient to prevent the harm from occurring.[2]

This brings us to our third point: the law should not punish an actor on the basis of a prediction that the actor will ultimately engage in criminal conduct. When determining whether an *actus reus* formulation is sufficient to demonstrate that the actor has acted culpably, the law cannot focus on what the action reveals about what the actor *might do*; rather, the action itself – what the actor *has done* – must ground blame and punishment. For the reasons discussed here, we believe that only the last-act formulation punishes the actor for what she has done.

B. INTENTIONS

The starting point along the continuum is with the actor's criminal intention. In our view, intentions cannot themselves constitute culpable

---

[2] The actor who lights the fuse in order to burn down another's property or blow up an inhabited building is culpable at the moment he lights it because, even if he changes his mind, he may not be able to snuff out the fuse. He may black out, or be prevented by another, etc. Even Superman commits a culpable act by firing a gun because the sudden appearance of kryptonite may prevent him from stopping the speeding bullet. And, of course, when the lit fuse passes the point that the actor believes puts it completely beyond his power of recall, his culpability is at its zenith.

and hence punishable acts. In the first part of this section, we argue that
the formation of an intention is an act. In the second part of this section, we explain why, despite the fact that the formation of an intention
is an act, it cannot be a culpable act. Specifically, intentions are difficult
to distinguish from fantasies and desires; intentions may involve differ-
ing levels of commitment to the goal; the future conditions in which the
intention will be acted upon are opaque; and intentions are revocable.

1. Are Intentions Acts?

A preliminary question is whether forming intentions is an action at
all – and thus a potentially culpable one – or are intentions merely the
states of mind that accompany other acts? There are, of course, many
kinds of mental acts that are performed intentionally. Mathematical
calculations, silent prayers, and attempts to remember fall into this
category. Are intentions about future conduct like this, so that they can
be criticized, not just for the traits of character they reveal – as would
an involuntary flash of anger at seeing one's spouse acting flirtatiously
around others – but as culpable acts in themselves? Are intentions subject to direct voluntary control in the way that acting on intentions is
subject to direct voluntary control?

The view that an intention might itself be a culpable act rests on two
assumptions. First, this view assumes that forming an intention alters
the world in some way that is material to the criminal law's concerns.
That assumption is surely met, at least under many standard philosophical accounts of intentions. Under those accounts, intentions alter the
balance of reasons for the actor. Before he forms the intention, he has
reasons A, B, and C in support of doing the act and reasons X, Y, and Z
against doing it. After he forms the intention, he has a new reason for
doing the act, namely, the intention itself, a reason that makes the act
more eligible and hence, if the actor is rational, more likely.[3]

Second, this view assumes that forming intentions not only changes
the world in the way indicated but also is something we do intentionally.

---

[3] *See* Michael E. Bratman, *Intentions, Plans, and Practical Reason* 80 (1987); Joseph Raz,
Practical Reasons and Norms 65–71 (1975). For a somewhat different view that holds decisions to act to be actions, but not reason-altering actions, *see* Thomas Pink, *The Psychology
of Freedom* 125–128, 137–165 (1996).

If this assumption is granted, then we can say that forming a culpable intention – an intention to commit a future culpable act – is itself a culpable act.

The argument we are considering here is not that it is the intention itself that is the culpable act but rather the formation of the intention.[4] To illustrate, suppose a person has a certain belief-desire set. Ordinarily, this person will form an intention to act on the basis of his evaluation of his beliefs and desires and a decision regarding what is the best course of action to take in light of them.[5] In pursuance of this decision, the actor forms an intention, a plan to engage in that course of action. Hence, although intending, by itself, is not an act but rather a mental state, the mental act of deciding what to intend is potentially a culpable act.[6]

2. Why Intentions Are Not Culpable Acts

Even if intentions are acts, we must still ask whether they are culpable acts about which the criminal law should be concerned. In one respect, it would make the burden of our argument in Chapter 4 with respect to culpable aggressors (CAs) easier were forming the intent to act culpably itself culpable. (We instead located the culpability of CAs in their unleashing the risk of creating fear.) Nevertheless, despite making defense against CAs easier to justify, we believe that there are a number

---

[4] *See* Bratman, *supra* note 3, at 103 (implicitly acknowledging that forming an intention is an action while discussing the Toxin Puzzle, in which a Genie offers you a million dollars if and when you form the intention to drink a very unpleasant but harmless potion after you have received the money: "[T]he million-dollar reason is a reason for a present action of causing yourself so to intend; this reason is relevant to deliberation about whether so to act now, not to whether to drink the toxin later"). For a different view of the Toxin Puzzle, *see* Pink, *supra* note 3, at 137–165.

[5] *See* Michael S. Moore, *Act and Crime: The Philosophy of Action and Its Implications for Criminal Law* 140 (1993) (noting that "[i]n the face of conflict between prima facie desires, there seems to be a resolution when the actor decides which of the alternative courses of action he is going to pursue").

[6] The triggering of this decision need not be an intentional action itself. Otherwise the objection would be that of regress: one must intend to intend, will to will, decide to decide. *Cf. id.* at 115 (discussing Gilbert Ryle, *The Concept of Mind* 67 [1949]). Our everyday lives present us with many situations where we make choices without deciding that we should first think about choosing. Thus, a belief, a thought, or desire, none of which is controllable, might trigger the deliberations. Nevertheless, the actor does have control over his deliberations and knows right from wrong at the point at which he decides what he plans to do. If John is confronted with his wife sleeping with his best friend, he might suddenly think that he wants to kill her, but he still controls whatever decision he might make in light of that desire.

of reasons to reject the view that forming the intention to impose risks should be sufficient for criminal liability.

a. Distinguishing Intentions from Desires: The first concern is one of line drawing. Gerald Dworkin and David Blumenfeld make the point that the lines between intending, on the one hand, and fantasizing, wishing, desiring, and wanting, on the other, even if philosophically clear, are quite difficult to draw as a practical matter, even for the actor himself:

> This ... objection has two aspects, the difficulty of the authorities distin-
> guishing between fantasying, wishing, etc. and even more importantly
> the difficulties the individual would have in identifying the nature of
> his emotional and mental set. Would we not be constantly worried
> about the nature of our mental life? Am I only wishing my mother-in-
> law were dead? Perhaps I have gone further. The resultant guilt would
> tend to impoverish and stultify the emotional life.[7]

This objection, of course, has no purchase when we are dealing with completed crimes and completed attempts. Nor does it apply to cases where one solicits or encourages another to commit a crime, which we later argue should count as recklessness toward the victim even in the absence of a purpose to harm if the criteria for recklessness are otherwise present. It does apply forcefully, however, to incomplete attempts, where it is the actor's attitude toward his own future conduct that is at issue. The actor may have difficulty distinguishing a mere flight of fantasy from a settled intention.

There are two worries here, one epistemic and one normative. The first is that because forming an intention is an act of will, but wishes, desires, and fantasies are not, an actor may fear being punished for something that is not itself an "act," and most certainly not a culpable act, because he fears the state will not be able to distinguish between the two. The second concern discussed by Dworkin and Blumenfeld is that if actors fear being punished even for these thoughts, they will be constantly policing themselves in a way that diminishes the overall quality of actors' lives. Although this concern is external to retributive justice, it still presents a significant worry. If in our efforts to reach the culpable, we also significantly infringe upon the freedom of the nonculpable

---

[7] Gerald Dworkin and David Blumenfeld, "Punishment for Intentions," 75 *Mind* 396, 401
   (1966).

(those who have only fantasies and never intentions), then the achievement of retributive justice may come at too great a cost.

b. The Conditionality of Intentions and the Opacity of Future Circumstances: In almost every conceivable circumstance, when we form an intention to engage in some future conduct, our intention to do so is conditional. That is, we intend to engage in that conduct only under some conditions and not under others. We intend to drive to the store at three o'clock – but only if the roads are not flooded, the store is open today, we do not find that we already possess the items we intended to purchase, and so forth. Some of the conditions may negate the culpability of the act we intend: we intend to shoot Susan – but only if she is about to blow up a bus full of children. Sometimes the conditions may not negate the culpability of the intended act but make the probability that the intended act will occur and also be culpable extremely unlikely: Roger intends to steal the Mona Lisa, but only if it is in the Met (not the Louvre), and only if it is not heavily guarded. Sometimes the conditions are present in the actor's mind when he forms the intention, so that his conscious intention is to do X on condition Y. Often, however, the conditions are not conscious but nonetheless operative: for example, almost no thief who forms an intent to steal a television set would do so after having inherited a billion dollars, even if that latter possibility never occurred to him.

Now the conditionality of intentions makes assessing their culpability less straightforward than assessing the culpability of the intended acts themselves. As we have argued, the latter are assessed by asking what risks of what harms did the actor believe he was imposing and what reasons did he believe (with what degree of certainty) existed that might justify that risk imposition. But before that act, the actor cannot be certain that he will so act, nor can he be certain about what culpability-enhancing or culpability-mitigating facts will obtain at the time of the act.

So suppose Roger will be culpable at level C if he takes what he believes to be the Mona Lisa from the Met. And suppose that he presently intends to do so, but only if the Mona Lisa is actually in the Met (quite unlikely), only if it is not heavily guarded (quite unlikely), only if he does not inherit a billion dollars tomorrow, and so forth. What is Roger's culpability *now*, the time when he forms that conditional intention to steal the Mona Lisa?

Or suppose Maggie intends to drive to her child's school to pick him up, and she intends to get there in ten minutes. If traffic is moving freely, the road is not icy, and so on, Maggie can get there in ten minutes without recklessly endangering others. And her intention to get there in ten minutes is not unconditional: she would not drive through a Boy Scout parade on the road, mow down pedestrians crossing at crosswalks, and so on. Still, there are some circumstances, quite unlikely but still possible, in which Maggie would drive recklessly to some degree, to which she may or may not be adverting when she forms the intention to get to the school in ten minutes. How should we assess Maggie's culpability for so intending?

Perhaps there is a solution to this problem of the conditionality of intentions. For example, perhaps we should assess the culpability of the actor's intention by asking what probability did he attach to his acting on the intention – or, what is the same thing, what probability did he attach to the conditions obtaining that governed whether he would act? (This, of course, will be difficult and perhaps impossible for those conditions to which the actor did not consciously advert but nonetheless were present dispositionally.) Then we could ask what culpability-enhancing and culpability-mitigating conditions did the actor believe would exist at the time of the intended act, and with what probabilities. The culpability of intending the act would be the average of the culpability of the various scenarios the actor envisioned might obtain at the time of the intended act, weighted by the probabilities he assigned each scenario, and discounted by the probability he attached to his actually engaging in the intended act (the probability that the defeating conditions would not exist).

If this "solution" appears impossibly complex – and it is – the problems of assessing the culpability of intending a (possibly) culpable future act are only beginning. For the actor may assess the probabilities differently at different points in time. Roger may, at the time he forms the intention to steal the Mona Lisa, believe that it is quite unlikely that the Met possesses it. Later, he may assess that likelihood as higher (or lower). Similarly, over time he may alter his assessment of the likelihood of its being heavily guarded. Thus, Roger's estimate of the likelihood that he will ever execute his intention to steal the Mona Lisa will vary over time. Is Roger's culpability dependent on the point in time at which he is arrested? Could he have been more or less culpable if he had been arrested sooner (or later)? And is culpability assessed just at the moment of arrest, or is it the average of his culpability from the moment he formed the intention until the moment of arrest, which, too, will vary with the time of the arrest?

What goes for the actor's estimate of the probability that he will execute the culpable intention also goes for his beliefs about the culpability-relevant facts that will obtain at the time of the intended act. Those beliefs may change during the time in which the intention is held.

For instance, assume that Heidi decides to blow up a football stadium to protest the allocation of funds to the football team instead of a new law school building. At that point in time, she may not have yet considered whether she will blow up the stadium when it is full of people or when it is empty. She may be debating whether to wait until there is a home team present, or whether to ensure that it is a day when no one is in the area. But even if Heidi has resolved to blow up the stadium at a specific time, her beliefs about the attendant risks and possible justifying reasons may change several times between the time she forms the intent and the time she detonates the bomb: she may believe at one time that the stadium will be full of fans, at another that it will be empty, at another that it will be occupied only by a terrorist cell, and so on. If she were to detonate the bomb at any of these times, her culpability for doing so would vary enormously – from extremely culpable to possibly not culpable at all in the case of the terrorist cell. Again, is Heidi's culpability determined by her beliefs at the time she is arrested – in which case it may be high if she is arrested at t_1 but nonexistent if arrested at t_2 – or is it determined by the average culpability of her intention from the time of its formation to the time of her arrest? In either case, because her beliefs about risks and reasons will change over time, her culpability level will depend on when she is arrested. (And how does one "average" a culpable intention, as when Heidi believes the stadium will be full of fans, and a justifiable one, as when she believes the stadium will contain no one but a dangerous terrorist cell?)

Indeed, not only may Heidi's beliefs about risks and reasons change over time, but she simply may have formed no belief whatsoever about the degree of risk that she will ultimately impose, leaving this "detail" to be filled in later. The ultimate risks and reasons for the intended action and therefore its culpability will be indeterminate at the moment of forming the intention.

Or take another case where an intention exists at t_1, but its justifiability, and thus its culpability, fluctuates over time. Leo looks at his seminar roster and discovers that a particularly annoying student from his first-year criminal law class has registered for his upper-level seminar. Leo decides at that point in time to give the student an F. Then, the student performs marvelously in class, meriting a good grade for class participation. Then, the student fails to turn in a rough draft, and then fails to turn in a final paper, warranting the giving of an "F." Given that Leo knew, at the formation of the intention, that he would not actually be assigning a grade until the end of the semester, it is difficult to say that, upon looking at the roster, he formed the intention to assign an F for insufficient reasons. After all, at the time that he looked at the roster, Leo knew that he would have substantial exposure to the student in class that might militate for or against actually assigning the F. And Leo knew that his intention to give the F was, like all intentions, revocable.

Putting the concerns about conditionality of intentions and the opacity of future circumstances into a broader conceptual framework further clarifies these problems. As Michael Bratman has noted, our future intentions – our plans – are partial.[8] In other words, the conditionality of intentions is not simply a matter of there being potential circumstances that might undermine an intention. Rather, intentions are open-ended plans designed to lead to further deliberation about the specifics. Intentions structure our later means-end reasoning, and their conditionality is thus a feature of them that cannot be ignored. Any future plan may or may not lead to a future choice to risk harm to another person for insufficient reasons. An intention to go to the grocery store might lead to a culpable choice if there is heavy traffic and the actor then chooses to drive fast; but the same intention might turn out to be completely benign. How can forming the intention to go to the grocery store itself be a culpable act merely because of the former possibility?

c. The Duration and Renunciation of Intentions: Because intentions can be held for varying lengths of time, and because they can be revoked, we must ask how, if they are to be deemed culpable, their culpability is affected by these features.

First, let us compare Hank and Harry. On January 1, Hank forms the intent to kill Sally next January 1. Later, on July 1, Harry forms the intent

---

[8] Bratman, *supra* note 3, at 29.

to kill Sally next January 1. On July 2, Hank has held the intention to kill Sally for over six months, whereas Harry has done so for only a day. Is Hank more culpable than Harry?

   i. Duration Does Not Affect Culpability: One view would be that the duration of the intention is immaterial to its culpability. On July 2, Hank and Harry are equally culpable. And Hank is as culpable on January 1 as he is on July 2 (barring changes in beliefs about conditions and circumstances that we discussed in the previous subsection).

But suppose that Hank now renounces his intention to kill Sally, whereas Harry does not. What effect does his renouncing it have on his culpability, and does it matter *why* he renounces it? (If he renounces the intended act because he views it as imprudent as opposed to immoral, should that deprive his renunciation of any effect on his culpability?)

If forming an intention to commit a culpable act is itself a culpable act, then it is difficult to understand how the culpability that exists at that time can be expunged by later revoking the intention. The past is fixed and contains the culpable act. It cannot be altered. If Hank was culpable on January 1 for intending to kill Sally, he remains culpable for having so intended on January 1 even if he no longer intends to kill her, whether owing to prudence or conscience. Any view to the contrary would suggest that our concern was not with past culpable acts but only with present character.

If the culpability of intending cannot be expunged by revoking the intent, and if the duration of the intention is immaterial, then Harry is just as culpable as Hank even if Harry revokes his intention after thirty seconds, whereas Hank has held his intention firmly for more than six months. Or if Harry is indecisive and forms the intent to kill Sally, then thirty seconds later revokes it, then forms it again, then again quickly revokes it, Harry has committed several culpable acts of intending to kill whereas Hank has committed only one. But it seems odd to deem indecisive Harry more culpable and deserving of more punishment than steadfast Hank.

   ii. Duration Does Affect Culpability: Alternatively, we might say that Hank's holding the intention to kill Sally for six months makes him more culpable than Harry, who has held the intention for a much

shorter time. The problem is explaining why the duration of the intention should matter. We give an explanation in Chapter 7 for why the
duration of a perceived risky act matters: it matters because duration
affects the degree of risk. (Driving for one minute while intoxicated is
less risky than driving for an hour in that condition.) But the six month's
duration of Hank's intention to kill Sally does not make the risk to Sally
higher on July 2 than the risk from Harry's one day's intention.

d. The Revocability of Intention: There is a final problem with deeming
intentions to be culpable and punishable. As the discussions that both
precede and follow this section reveal, this concern is decisive for us.
This is the problem that intentions are open to reconsideration and thus
revocable. On the one hand, if it is not necessarily rational to reconsider
one's intention,[9] the decision to do wrong may be the point at which the
balance of reasons has shifted for the actor, and he has committed the
culpable – unreasonably dangerous – act. The formation of the intention
might then be analogous to the lighting of a long fuse where, although
the actor may still exert control over whether the harm does materialize,
the risk to the victim has nonetheless increased. One might thus argue
that from the actor's perspective, the risk to the victim has increased
because, even from the actor's perspective, the actor's balance of reasons
has shifted. Thus, if this risk is being imposed for insufficient reasons,
the actor has committed a culpable act in forming the intention itself.

   However, when one is planning to commit a crime, it will always be
rational to reconsider.[10] Indeed, many intentions are formed with the
proviso that there can always be later reconsideration. Although intentions may serve to guide our future decisions, they are not irreversible,
nor may they be carried out without any further effort on our part. The
risk from the actor's point of view – objectively risk is always zero or
one – may have increased, because the actor believes he will act as he
now intends; but the actor still remains in total control of whether this
risk will be unleashed, and he knows this.

---

[9] *Id.* at 64 ("nonreflective (non)reconsideration of a prior intention is the upshot of relevant
general habits and propensities").

[10] *Cf. id.* at 67 ("[I]t seems plausible to suppose that it is in the long-run interests of an agent
occasionally to reconsider what he is up to, given such opportunities for reflection and
given the stakes are high, as long as the resources used in the process of reconsideration
are themselves modest").

Now, it may be said that there is a distinct difference between rationality and culpability. After all, an individual who has lit a fuse will also be under rational pressure to stomp out the fuse, so the pressure to reconsider cannot itself suffice to make the act of forming the intention nonculpable. Even if the actor may be able to change his mind and "revoke" his intention, how does any irrationality in not reconsidering render the initial choice less culpable?

Unlike a lit fuse, however, which the actor may find himself unable to put out even if he now wishes to do so, the actor who only intends to unleash a risk in the future knows that he is still in control of his actions. And, indeed, just as crucially, through the exercise of reason and will alone, he may "stop" the harm from occurring. The common law's focus on *locus penitentiae* is best thought of not as an opportunity to abandon or renounce but as an opportunity to continue deliberating and change one's mind. Just as the criminal law seeks to influence the reasons for which one acts, the criminal law should allow room for deliberation, even including room for the formation and renunciation of an intention. The actor may still deliberate and think the better of his plan.[11]

Moreover, often when actors intend an act that may in some circumstances be culpable, the actor will not have considered whether he will really go through with it in those circumstances. Or he may have considered it, believes that he will, but in fact he will not. He cannot know until he actually commits the act in the culpability-creating circumstances (or fails to commit it).

In our view, even if there is rational pressure to stick with one's intention – pressure that in some way increases the risk of harm – there is also rational pressure to abandon one's criminal plan, pressure that decreases the risk of harm. Hence, rationality cuts in both directions and cannot therefore point to an increase in risk. One may know that forming the intention, or buying the gun, does in some sense make one "more committed" to the crime, but one also knows that one can *and should* think the better of one's plan, and this influence serves as

---

[11] *See also* R. A. Duff, *Answering for Crime: Responsibility and Liability in the Criminal Law* 104 (2007) ("If the state is to treat its citizens as responsible agents who can be guided [who can guide themselves] by reasons, it should be slow to coerce them on the ground that they are likely to commit a wrong if not thus coerced, since that is to treat them as if they will not be guided by the reasons that should dissuade them from such wrongdoing").

an important counterweight. Intentions are guides to future actions that do not prevent our later reconsideration. It follows that an actor has committed a culpable act only at the point where the actor has truly relinquished control, not at the point at which he forms the intention to unleash a risk in the future.

C. SUBSTANTIAL STEPS

For the reasons we reject treating intentions as culpable acts, we likewise reject the Model Penal Code's substantial-step formulation.[12] The Model Penal Code's *actus reus* for an incomplete attempt is quite early in the process from intention to completion. It analyzes not how close to completion the actor is but whether the actor's action corroborates his intention.

The "corroborative" function of the substantial-step test is critical. After all, it does not seem as though the mere looking at the bank floor plans or the buying of a gun is itself risk creating. It seems no more dangerous or culpable than the act of forming the intention itself. Indeed, the requirement of a "substantial step" looks arbitrary from the standpoint of assessing culpability. Consider Dan, who purchases a jackhammer with the intention of causing vibrations that will topple Balanced Rock and kill Victor if Victor walks under it. Arguably, Dan has undertaken a substantial-step attempt when he takes the jackhammer to a spot near Balanced Rock and waits to see if Victor walks under it. But is Dan different from Dana, who is picnicking near Balanced Rock, notices that she is next to a jackhammer, and forms the same intention that Dan has formed? Dana has done nothing other than form an intention. Yet she is in exactly the same position as Dan and just as culpable (or, we would argue, just as *non*culpable). Would it matter that Dana, after forming the intention, moves an inch or two closer to the jackhammer?[13]

The justification for attempt liability for substantial steps must be grounded in the step's ability to alleviate the concerns about punishment for intention formations themselves. In some ways, substantial

---

[12] Model Penal Code § 5.01(1)(c) (1985).

[13] Another consequence of having substantial-step attempts is that to motivate renunciation, one essentially has to deem the attempter guilty of a crime at T_1 that disappears from the history books at T_2, the time of the renunciation.

steps do change the calculus. However, for the reasons we discuss later, we believe that substantial steps are not themselves culpable acts.

Substantial steps do speak to two concerns about punishment for intentions alone. First, the line-drawing concerns articulated by Dworkin and Blumenfeld have no purchase once we are talking about substantial steps. It is one thing for it to be difficult to distinguish the fantasy of killing one's mother-in-law from the intention to do so. But the line between fantasy and purchasing a gun is far easier to draw.

Substantial steps also speak to the firmness of the actor's resolve. We can tell the differences between our mere dreams (to become an accomplished pianist) and our goals (to lose weight) when we see that we sign up for gym membership but not piano lessons. A substantial step is thus evidentiary of the firmness of the actor's resolve.

Still, two significant concerns exist even once the actor has taken a substantial step. The concern about conditional intentions and unforeseen future consequences still exists. First, the law treats, as it must, conditional intentions as intentions. But it does not stipulate any requisite level of probability that the actor must attribute to the condition's obtaining. Thus, if David intends to kill Darlene if and only if she has been unfaithful – and David for that reason always carries a gun when he comes home from work – the law of inchoate criminality presumably deems his intention to kill sufficient *whether he thinks Darlene's infidelity highly likely or highly unlikely.* (If a burglar enters a house intending to steal only diamond jewelry, is he not guilty of burglary if he believes the odds of the owner's possessing diamonds are less than fifty percent? Twenty percent? One percent? If Thelma and Louise agree that they will kill their husbands if their lottery ticket wins the lottery, have they conspired to commit murder if the odds of their winning are one in a million?) Given that the probability of the conditions obtaining may be highly unlikely, the taking of a substantial step may not be very meaningful.

Moreover, it is immaterial whether the actor hopes the conditions on his intention will or will not obtain. David may hope that Darlene has not been unfaithful. But nonetheless, he still has the (conditional) intention to kill her.[14]

---

[14] One last point. Suppose David has a conditional intention, the condition of which negatives the criminal harm. Suppose he intends to have sex with Darlene only if Darlene is

Related to the problem of conditional intentions is that of unknown future circumstances. (Recall Heidi and her plan to blow up the stadium.) Suppose Roger firmly intends to fire his gun at a tree at six o'clock Monday evening. And suppose Roger believes that at that time, several people will be in the vicinity of the tree and that, given the insubstantial weight of Roger's reasons for firing at that time, his act will be reckless. But suppose as well that Roger believes there is some probability P that there will be no people in the vicinity at that time and that, in that event, his shooting will not be reckless. Should we conclude that Roger has an illicit intention *now*? If so, and he takes a substantial step toward acting on that intention – he loads the gun – should he now be guilty of a crime (taking a substantial step toward a culpable risk imposition)? The taking of a substantial step in no way remedies the problem that unforeseen circumstances will alter the culpability with which the actor ultimately acts. One avoids such puzzles if one abandons the idea of substantial-step attempts and uses the last act of unleashing the risk as the touchstone of culpability.

For us, the decisive objection is that actors can still change their minds, even after they have taken substantial steps. If actors have complete control over their future choices, then, no matter how firm their present resolve, they can always change their minds and refrain from

---

over the legal age. It appears that at this time, David's intent is perfectly lawful. (*See* Model Penal Code § 2.02(6) (1985).) But if, "Have sex with Darlene if she is over the legal age" is the major premise of David's practical syllogism, the minor premise might be "Darlene is (thankfully) over the legal age." If so, then the conclusion David reaches is "Have sex with Darlene." For inchoate criminality, which intention should control – the intent in the major premise, which is legal, or the intent in the conclusion, which, if David is in error regarding Darlene's age, is illegal? Because David has not yet done what he intends to do, it is ambiguous whether he intends to have sex with Darlene (because he mistakenly believes she is over the legal age) or not to have sex with her (because he intends to have sex only if she is over the legal age).

(Of course, this problem only arises in connection with crimes that have strict liability elements or elements that require only the *mens rea* of negligence. And because we do not regard negligence as culpable – and strict liability is the antithesis of culpability – we would reject the very underpinnings of this problem.)

The problems of conditional intentions are sufficient to cause a complete rethinking of inchoate criminality – incomplete attempts, solicitation, conspiracy, and complicity. *See generally* Alexander and Kessler, *supra* note 1. Our approach here, which is to handle inchoate criminality under the rubric of recklessness, eliminates the problems of conditional intentions by eliminating the requirement that one intend criminal conduct. *See infra* notes 23–24.

imposing the risk. Often, when in the future they become fully aware of the risks their act will impose, they will cease intending to impose it.

Some have argued that once the actor takes a step that is, for him, solely a means to his intended criminal act (and not a means to alternative ends), the actor is at that point in time "rationally committed" to accomplishing the intended criminal act and is under "rational pressure" to do so.[15] Because it is always rational for one to refrain from acting criminally – at least in the absence of a justification – we fail to see how the notion of rational pressure can be cashed out. The idea that it is somehow incoherent to abandon bad ends that one has taken some step or steps to achieve smacks of recovering sunk costs. Some forms of coherent life narratives are more attractive than others, and there is nothing attractive, much less rational, about persisting in pursuing bad plans. In any event, the actor is always free to reconsider whether he will impose a risk of harm or proxy conduct no matter how many steps he has taken in that direction. Indeed, to the extent that more action creates more rational pressure to engage in the criminal conduct, the closer one comes to harming another, the more rational pressure the law places on the actor to rethink his criminal plan. So long as he has not taken the last step (he believes) necessary, he cannot be deemed culpable: he has not yet imposed *any* risk of harm.[16]

Can one not argue that one who takes a substantial step toward imposing a risk of harm (or proxy conduct) has acted recklessly because, for insufficient reason, he has increased the risk through making it

---

[15] *See, e.g.*, Gideon Yaffe, "Trying, Acting and Attempted Crimes" (unpublished manuscript, on file with the authors). Yaffe does not require the step beyond intending to be a particularly important one for executing the intent. It only has to corroborate the actor's intent. But because determining that it is such a step requires that we know the intent with which it was taken – was the purchase of the gun made for the intended killing or for marksmanship practice? – we must have independent evidence of intent. The step therefore adds nothing to an intent requirement. If one is "rationally committed" to an illicit end by taking a step in that direction, one is "rationally committed" to it by merely intending it.

[16] Daniel Ohana argues that the more costs the actor has sunk into her criminal plan, the more likely she is in fact to carry it out. Daniel Ohana, "Desert and Punishment for Acts Preparatory to the Commission of a Crime," 20 *Canad. J. Law & Jurisp.* 113, 122–123 (2007). He concludes that the actor is culpable and hence deserving of punishment for having formed the plan and made some preparations for carrying it out. *Id.* at 124. Again, we disagree. The actor has still not unleashed an unjustified risk, given that, until she completes the last act necessary to execute her wrongful plan, she remains in complete control and can abandon it at any point, regardless of the costs she has sunk.

more likely that if he does *not* change his mind, he will succeed? In other words, has he not recklessly increased the chance of his own recklessness? Is he not farther along toward recklessness than those whom we forbid to own, say, machine guns, even when they have no present intention to use the machine guns illicitly? After all, our actor *does* have a present illicit purpose. A fortiori, should we not deem him culpable?

The case is not parallel to substantial-step attempts. It is, rather, the case of making otherwise harmless conduct into a proxy crime because it too frequently culminates in culpable acts. Once possessing a machine gun is made into a proxy for ultimate harms, then risking possession for no sufficient reason *is* culpable, or at least it could be so argued. (For our analysis of proxy crimes and culpability, see Chapter 8.) Where possessing a machine gun is not itself illegal, however, it cannot be deemed illegal by virtue of increasing the risk that if its possessor forms the intent to do something risky with it, he is more likely to succeed in imposing such a risk (than if he did not possess it). Nor can possessing it with such an intent be deemed a culpable act without begging the question in issue, namely, whether substantial-step attempts are indeed culpable. (Possessing a machine gun might be culpably reckless if there were sufficient risk of its accidentally firing or perhaps falling into the hands of terrorists.)

In short, our position is that one cannot regard one's own future conduct that will be fully under the control of one's reason and will as a risk that one's present conduct is imposing. For that reason, substantial-step attempts are not culpable acts.

D. DANGEROUS PROXIMITY

Although different jurisdictions have adopted an array of *actus reus* formulations for attempts, here we wish to focus on those tests the gist of which is that the actor is *close* to completing the crime and thus that intervention is necessary and punishment warranted.[17]

Now, unlike more sweeping proposals to detain those whom we predict to be dangerous, here we assume that the actor currently intends to impose a risk harm and has taken an action that appears (to someone) to reveal that the actor is dangerous. Thus, we are using dangerousness

[17] *E.g.*, People v. Rizzo, 158 N.E. 888, 889 (N.Y. 1927); *see generally* Joshua Dressler, *Understanding Criminal Law* § 27.06[B][3]-[4], at 425–427 (4th ed., 2006).

to cull out those actors who not only have an intention to impose an unjustifiable risk but have also committed some act toward that end.

There are two problems with this approach. First, "dangerousness" in itself is not tied exclusively to culpability or intentions. If we really care about those who are dangerous, why should we require an intention at all? For example, if on the basis of our assessments of his character and our knowledge of the world, we can predict that John, who has no present purpose to rape Mary, will in fact likely do so (if we do not intervene), why should we distinguish John from the equally but no more dangerous Joseph, who currently has the purpose to rape Mary? From the standpoint of dangerousness, there is no reason to care about culpability at all. (Recall the discussion of ACAs – anticipated culpable aggressors – in Chapter 4.)

Second, when we speak of "dangerousness," what precisely do we mean? Dangerousness is a prediction that an actor will cause or risk future harm. Do we mean to punish only those actors who are *actually* dangerous or only those who *appear* dangerous? If the latter, from whose point of view are we making the assessment of apparent dangerousness? In terms of the actor's actual dangerousness – the risk that the actor will complete her attempt – that risk is a function of whether, when, and how we choose to intervene. In a very real sense, no actor arrested for an inchoate crime is ever *really* dangerous, for her arrest made the intended crime unlikely or impossible.

If one accepts that inchoate criminality is most plausibly premised either on dangerousness or on general wickedness of character rather than on the commission of culpable acts, then the role of intention looks merely evidentiary. For intentions are neither necessary nor sufficient for dangerousness or bad character. And if inchoate criminality is premised on either dangerousness or wickedness of character, and not on culpable acts, then it is in tension with the presumption that actors freely choose whether they will act dangerously or wickedly. Until the actor completes an attempt, he is just at one end of a continuum with others who harbor culpable intentions and dangerous beliefs. Until he takes what he believes to be the last step necessary to cause the social harm, he can always reconsider. Whether he will or not – which, together with the probability of other harm-negating events, is the determinant of how dangerous he currently is – is, we presume, a matter of his free choice and thus one over which he has complete control.

E. LAST ACTS

For these reasons, we believe it is only when the actor has committed the "last act" that she has committed a culpable act. When an actor forms an intention and engages in other preparatory behavior, she may know that what she intends to do is forbidden by the criminal law, but she also knows that she retains complete control over whether she will actually so act. The law still influences her, and she may decide to reconsider or to stop at any moment. She has the ability to choose not to risk harm to her victim.

It is only when the actor does something that she believes increases the risk of harm to the victim in a way that she no longer can control that she has engaged in a culpable act. This is the point where "what she does" ceases to be guided by her reason and will. This is the point where harm may occur even if she changes her mind. It is at this moment that the law calls upon the actor to refrain from acting, and she acts culpably when she ignores the law's commands.

The strongest counterexample to the last-act test is the case of slow poisoning. What if Mary decides to kill Joe with arsenic, and to do so, she must administer ten doses of poison over ten days? If Joe will not die until the tenth dose, then it seems that our view commits us to the position that Mary has not engaged in a culpable action for the first nine administrations of arsenic.

Of course, the fact that makes the slow poisoning case so compelling is the very fact that undermines it as a counterexample. Certainly Joe has a legally protected interest in not consuming arsenic separate and apart from his legally protected interest in not being killed by arsenic. Every time that Mary gives Joe the arsenic, she is unjustifiably unleashing a risk. It is just that the risk is not death. Moreover, because Mary can still think the better of her course of action and decide not to administer that tenth dose, she has not unleashed a risk of death until she does so. The repetitive nature of the conduct and the fact that it does infringe on Joe's right not to consume arsenic disguise the fact that until dose ten, vis-à-vis *killing* Joe, Mary's administering of the first nine doses is no different from buying a gun, following Joe, and lying in wait. There is nothing special about slow poisoning.

II. Some Qualifications and Further Applications

Even if the criminal law were to endorse our view that "last acts" are the appropriate targets of criminal liability, there are a few clarifications to be made. First, we qualify our position by discussing when the preparation for one crime can also constitute a last act for another. Second, we discuss how our test applies to "lit fuse" cases. Then, we turn to the application of our test to instances of "inherently impossible" attempts. Finally, we discuss the implications of our view for other inchoate crimes.

A. WHEN PREPARATORY ACTS ARE ALSO LAST ACTS

There are two qualifications of our position, both revealing how preparatory acts may themselves be culpable acts. The first refers back to the question we raised in Chapter 2 regarding whether Frankie is reckless in driving (carefully) to Johnny's house for the purpose of shooting him. Her driving might be a substantial-step attempt (compare: lying in wait, "casing" the scene, loading a gun, and so forth), but as such it is not culpable. However, because driving itself creates a risk of harm to others, if she consciously disregards *that risk* by driving, then, given her illegitimate purpose in driving, she is culpably reckless (if only slightly so).

Or, to take a different example, consider Sally, who, with murder in her heart, points a gun at her intended victim. She has not yet committed a completed attempt because she has not yet pulled the trigger and imposed the risk she intends to impose, but she has created an unjustifiable risk that the gun will *accidentally* discharge and wound or kill someone. So, to the extent that she consciously disregards *that* risk by pointing the gun, she is culpable for imposing *that* risk before she pulls the trigger. And Mary, who is slowly poisoning Joe, is also unleashing some risk – both of causing a harm less than death and of causing death through an unplanned overdose.

We see no problem with treating these actors as guilty of some degree of culpable risk creation if they are adverting to those risks beyond their control that they have already unleashed. Moreover, because the risks created by Frankie's driving and by brandishing a weapon are lower than the risks Frankie, the murderous gun brandisher, and Mary intend to impose at a future time, if Frankie, Sally, and Mary renounce their murderous intentions and desist from their plans to kill, they will be less culpable than they would be if they consummated their present plans and shot at or gave the final dose of poison to their intended victims. If that lower culpability entails a lower level of punishment, they will thus have some nonmoral incentive to desist from their murderous plans, even if they will not escape punishment altogether.

The second qualification of the position that incomplete attempts are not culpable is this: when one is about to attempt to impose a severe risk on another, one may be culpable for creating a risk of an apprehension of danger (causing fear) for no sufficient justification. (Because one is intending to commit a culpable act at a future time – that is, because one is intending to impose a risk at a future time for no sufficient reason – the present creation of the risk of causing fear will perforce lack a sufficient justification.) In that way, substantial-step attempts could be culpable, not as attempts, but as the unjustifiable creations of risks of causing fear.

Our analysis bears on the justification for self-defense and defense of others. In discussing defensive (preemptive force) in Chapter 4, we referred to "culpable aggressors." Because such persons will not yet have completed their attempts, they are at most incomplete attempters. And if incomplete attempts are not per se culpable, then what makes a culpable aggressor "culpable"? The answer is in the preceding paragraph. They have culpably created a risk that their intended victim will believe he is in great peril, or that others will believe the intended victim is in great peril. Unlike "innocent aggressors" – lunatics, the young, the mistaken – such aggressors will have created, without excuse, this apprehension for the worst of reasons: their desire to kill, injure, or put at risk of same. This fact may make defensive force against them *socially* and not just *personally* justified. (See Chapter 4.) (If, however, the actor is mistaken in believing he is facing a culpable aggressor, his act of self-defense will be excused – personally justified – not socially justified.) And the culpability of the culpable aggressors may justify arresting them before they have imposed the ultimate risk they intend to impose because they are *presently* imposing a culpable risk of fear creation and perhaps of an accident.

Both of these qualifications may lead to regress concerns. If a substantial-step attempt, which entails doing X with the intent to impose a risk in the future for no good reason (i.e., the intent to be reckless in the future), is itself reckless for either of these two reasons – it itself creates an unjustifiable increase in risk to a legally protected interest, or it itself creates an unjustifiable risk that it will cause fear – then not only is it a culpable act, but acts preceding *it* may be culpable. So suppose doing Y with the intent to do Z in the future is culpable for either of these reasons. What about doing X with the intent to do Y in the future with the intent to do Z in the future? Or doing W with the intent to do X in the future, with the intent to do Y in the future, with the intent to do Z in the future?

What is critical, however, is the actor's conscious disregard of the risk. When the actor engages in early preparation, he may not perceive his actions as creating any additional risk to the victim – after all, he may change his mind. On the other hand, he may very well contemplate that engaging in the preparatory actions increases the risk of harm to the victim through increasing the risk of an accident or through increasing the risk of causing fear. Thus, whether the actor commits a culpable act, and how far back into preparation we might wander in looking for a culpable act, depends upon the actor's decision making and how he perceives his actions and the risks they create.

Anytime that someone acts on an intention to impose a risk at some future time in circumstances that might render his act culpable – and his intention to do so is not conditional on the risk imposition's being nonculpable – then regardless of how unlikely he believes the risk that his present preparatory conduct will cause apprehension in the victim(s) or their protectors, so long as he assigns any risk at all to the creation of fear, he has culpably risked causing that apprehension. For that reason, he can be deemed a culpable aggressor and treated accordingly.[18] How others may respond to him is a matter we have discussed Chapter 4.

---

[18] As we pointed out in Section I.B.2.b, an actor might intend an act that may or may not be culpable depending on the circumstances that obtain at the time he intends to act. However, even if there is a substantial probability that the act will *not* be culpable, intending an act that *might* be culpable, where the intent is not conditional on the act's being nonculpable, should render the actor a CA for purposes of apprehension and defensive response.

What is clear is that although the CA may not objectify the risk that he will actually consummate his intended risk imposition, the victim or a third party may surely assign a risk to that occurring. Because the CA has created the perception of the need for the victim or third party to act to abate the risk, he is liable to the use of defensive force.

B. LIT-FUSE ATTEMPTS

One category of "last act" attempts consists of attempts that are actually incomplete attempts. (In the Model Penal Code, they fall under § 5.01 (1)(b), the section for "last act" result-causing attempts; but unlike other (1)(b) attempts, such as firing a gun or triggering a bomb, they are renounceable under § 5.01 (4).) These are what we call "lit fuse" attempts. Their paradigm is lighting a fuse with the intent to burn down or blow up something, but also with, for at least some time, a perceived chance to eliminate the danger. For a period of time, the arsonist may be able to put out the fire before it causes damage, or snuff out the fuse before it reaches the dynamite or fire propellant.

So let us take, as a paradigmatic case, an actor who lights a dynamite fuse intending to blow up V's building. The fuse is of a length such that it will take one minute from the time it is lit to set off the dynamite. For most of that minute, the actor will have the opportunity, if he changes his mind, to snuff out the fuse.

Let us first consider his lighting of the fuse. Here, the critical question is whether the actor is aware that his actions create a culpable risk. For the most part, such an actor, although believing he retains some control over whether the dynamite will detonate, will also recognize that he may not be able to prevent such detonation. He may slip and fall, may be rendered unconscious by something, and so forth. If the actor truly believes that he is not creating such a risk, he will not be reckless. We believe, however, that such a case will be extremely rare. Rather, the actor lighting the fuse (often with the purpose to cause the harm) will almost always recognize that he now has unleashed a risk over which he no longer has complete control.

Suppose he is in fact able to control the detonation. He can snuff out the fuse. Here, our view is that the actor is under a continuing duty to do so. Lighting the fuse is analogous to pushing someone who cannot swim into a pool – the drowning can still be prevented. The actor now has a duty to avert the peril he has created.

If the actor retains the ability to snuff out the fuse and chooses not to do so, then he is guilty of a culpable omission. In general, the more of the minute that passes without his changing his mind, the higher the risk that, were he to change his mind, he would fail to snuff out the fuse.

In summary, because of the risk that he will fail to snuff it out if he were to change his mind, the actor's merely lighting the fuse with the intent to detonate is culpably risky (reckless). Because of the increasing risk over time even if he were to change his mind, when he has *not* changed his mind, his culpability (recklessness) increases as the minute elapses.

This approach also creates an incentive to renounce. If he does change his mind and tries to snuff out the fuse, his culpability is set at the level it has reached at that point in time, regardless of whether he then succeeds in snuffing out the fuse. Because his culpability increases throughout the minute, if his punishment likewise increases proportionately, he has some nonmoral incentive to change his mind and try to snuff out the fuse.[19]

C. IMPOSSIBLE ATTEMPTS

Our approach also makes sense of the perennially thorny problem of so-called impossible attempts.[20] In all cases of impossibility, the actor has committed the last act. Failure occurs, however, because success was impossible ex ante on that occasion. For example, the actor shoots the potential victim with the intent to kill and the bullet pierces the victim's heart, but the victim is already dead.[21] From the vantage point of practical reason, impossible attempts are indistinguishable from other

---

[19] One should compare and contrast this "lit fuse" scenario with the ordinary case of reckless conduct extended through time – for example, reckless driving. There is a problem that we take up in Chapter 7 regarding how to individuate the crime or crimes committed by virtue of such conduct. But clearly, the longer the actor drives in what he believes is an unduly risky manner – with *his* estimate of the risks and the law's conception of *unduly* as the material ones – the more culpable he is.

[20] In a very real sense, *all* attempts are impossible ones; some fact about the world rendered it incapable of succeeding. The gun was misaimed, or had blanks, or was jammed, etc. The misaimed gun is in principle no different from a failed attempt to kill through voodoo.

[21] *See* People v. Dlugash, 363 N.E.2d 1155, 1162–1163 (N.Y. 1977).

last-act completed attempts because in all of these cases the actor has tried to produce a prohibited harm and has done what would be a sufficient act if the surrounding circumstances were as the actor believed them to be. Whether failure is produced by poor performance, active intervention, or unknown states of affairs is irrelevant to the law's ability to guide the actor's conduct.

In cases of impossible attempts, it may be difficult to determine whether the actor intended to produce the prohibited harm because the actor's manifest conduct may appear innocent to others who do not know what the actor intends and believes. For example, suppose an actor takes and carries away an umbrella he believes belongs to another with the intent permanently to deprive that person of the umbrella, but the umbrella in fact belongs to the actor.[22] In such cases, it might be exceedingly difficult to prove the necessary *mens rea,* but the difficulty is purely epistemic. The actor is morally a last-act attempted umbrella thief, and the actor's desert is indistinguishable from that of those who succeed. The actor is no different from one who speeds through a school zone believing he is creating a high risk to children when, unbeknownst to him, it is a school holiday, and there are no children (or adults, pets, or parked vehicles) anywhere near. That actor has engaged in a reckless act that from a better epistemic vantage point appears safe. Indeed, the impossible attempter is no different from one who fires a gun at someone when everyone but him knows the gun is empty, or is a toy gun, or that he is in a video game simulator.

Our view also provides a sensible approach to cases of so-called inherent impossibility, those in which the actor commits a last-act attempt, but success is impossible because the actor uses means utterly ill-adapted to achieving the prohibited harm. For example, imagine an actor who tries to crack a bank safe using the beam from an ordinary flashlight. Unlike the case of standard impossibility, success in this case was possible only if one suspends the causal laws of the universe. So long

---

[22] *See* Sanford H. Kadish and Stephen J. Schulhofer, eds., *Criminal Law and Its Processes: Cases and Materials* 600 (7th ed., 2001). For a more realistic but still problematic case, *see* United States v. Oviedo, 525 F.2d 881, 882 (5th Cir. 1976) (defendant sold an uncontrolled substance that he said was heroin to an undercover agent and was charged with attempted sale of a controlled substance; defendant claimed that he knew the substance was uncontrolled and intended only to "rip-off" the buyer).

as the actor is capable of being guided by reason and the law, however, the actor is a culpable last-act attempter and should be treated the same as other last-act attempters and as those who successfully complete the crime.[23]

Indeed, because all attempts that fail do so for some reason of which the actor was unaware when he acted – the gun was jammed or unloaded or misaimed, the "poison" was really sugar, the victim was wearing body armor or was already dead – there really is no distinction between mere attempts, impossible attempts, and inherently impossible attempts. Every attempt that fails was inherently impossible given the state of the world.

D. RECONCEPTUALIZING OTHER INCHOATE CRIMES

Once we understand what a culpable action is, there is no need to have separate crimes of solicitation and conspiracy, or the form of criminal liability known as complicity. Instead, the kinds of conduct so criminalized should be brought under the heading of recklessly increasing the risks of others' criminality through unjustifiably risking, encouraging, or aiding others' criminality. We merely ask (1) how much did the actor believe his aid or encouragement increased the risk that others would commit culpable acts over the risk that they would do so that preexisted his aid or encouragement, and (2) what were the actor's reasons for giving and or encouragement.

This reconceptualization has many advantages. For one thing, it does not require that the actor's *purpose* be to facilitate the others' crimes. The actor need only be aware of an unjustifiable risk that he is helping or encouraging future crimes. (Many gang members act without the purpose the law demands – they assist other members' criminal acts out of a desire to help fellow gang members rather than in order that the crimes they assist be committed – and most judges and juries ignore the law and convict, as they should. Dropping the purpose requirement

---

[23] The same goes for the voodoo doctor who sticks the pin in the effigy believing he is killing his victim, or the poisoner who mistakes the packet of sugar for the packet of strychnine. In some cases, however, the mistake may indicate that the actor is not a rational agent and therefore cannot be guided by reason. If so, such an actor should be excused.

eliminates this hypocrisy.) Legitimate merchants can be protected by making a sale at market price conclusively justifiable. And free speech concerns regarding solicitation (e.g., a fiery speech to an angry crowd) can be protected in a similar manner.

A second advantage of this recklessness approach to inchoate crimes comes from the holism of that approach. Instead of having to prove that the actor's purpose in soliciting, agreeing, or aiding was to promote some specific crime – which is often impossible – one need only prove that he adverted to increased risks of various possible crimes.[24]

This form of culpable recklessness is also like lit-fuse attempts. Frequently, there will be a temporal gap between the time of the actor's encouragement or aid and the time that the others whom he has encouraged or aided will impose the risks. During that time, it will frequently be possible for one who has a change of heart to revoke his aid or encouragement. (And, of course, having culpably created a peril, he has an affirmative duty to take steps to eliminate it.)[25] As time passes, the risk

---

[24] The gang member who is told to drive a car to a specific location and does so, who believes that he is aiding some crime, but who does not know whether the crime is a robbery, a bombing, a killing, or something else, does not have the purpose to commit any particular crime. Nonetheless, such persons are routinely convicted as accessories to whichever crime the gang commits. *See, e.g.,* Director of Public Prosecutions for Northern Ireland v. Maxwell, (1978) 3 All E.R. 1140. This not only bends the requirement that the aider intend the crime committed; it also wreaks doctrinal havoc when no crime is committed, as the Model Penal Code, for example, makes an aider into an attempter when the principal commits no crime. *See* Model Penal Code § 5.01(3) (1985). But which of the contemplated crimes did our gang member "attempt" through his aid of driving the car to the location? On our approach, based on the recklessness of giving the aid with respect to all the various possible crimes, and uninterested in the actual results, this doctrinal problem is averted.

As is true under the criminal law generally, one can be guilty through soliciting or aiding conduct that is committed by another who by virtue of excuse or lack of *mens rea* is not himself guilty of a crime so long as one has solicited or aided the *actus reus*. Under our approach, if the one whose conduct the actor encourages or aids is himself imposing risks for his own good reasons, then if the actor is aware of those good reasons, the fact that the *actor's* reasons would not justify the risk imposition does not make the actor's act of encouragement or aid culpable. He is encouraging or aiding what he knows to be justifiable conduct. On the other hand, if the actor believes the risks are higher than the principal believes them to be, or believes that the justifying facts that the principal believes exist do not exist, the actor is culpable even if the principal is not.

[25] Obviously, when the actor has committed a culpable act, and the act has caused harm (or what the actor perceives as harm), but the actor believes the harm, unlike instant death or destruction of property, can still be mitigated by him if he so chooses, the actor has an affirmative duty to take such mitigating action. If he fails to do so, then regardless whether

that, were he to have a change of heart, he would fail to revoke his aid or encouragement increases. So the actor's recklessness in giving aid or encouragement increases over time, just as with lit fuses. Renunciation and withdrawal of the aid or encouragement fixes culpability at the level it has reached as of that time, and it forecloses further increased culpability and increased punishment therefor. So again, there can be a non-moral incentive to renounce and withdraw one's aid or encouragement.

Finally, it is worth noting that the actor's culpability in all of these inchoate crime scenarios is completely unaffected by whether the others, whose wrongful acts the actor has risked bringing about through aid or encouragement, ever commit such acts. (Remember: results do not affect culpability and desert.) Complicity disappears as a concept. Each person is culpable for the risks *he* unjustifiably increases. Nor is the actor's culpability affected by whether his words of encouragement to the principal are actually heard or understood, or his aid actually received. What matters is whether the actor believes that he has acted to impose a risk of harm (or proxy conduct) for no sufficient reason, and whether the actor has subsequently attempted to mitigate or eliminate that risk, thus limiting the degree to which he is culpable.[26]

his mitigating action would have been either necessary or sufficient to prevent further harm, he has acted culpably. He now is on the hook for *two* culpable acts – the initial culpable act that caused (apparent) harm, and the subsequent culpable omission to take (apparently) necessary and sufficient mitigating action. Thus, it follows, perhaps surprisingly but nonetheless correctly, that one assailant who wrongfully shoots and kills his victim is guilty of one culpable act – one wrongful (successful) attempt – whereas another assailant who wrongfully shoots and wounds his victim and then leaves the victim to die from those wounds rather than saves the victim is guilty of two culpable acts. (We return to this issue in the next chapter.)

[26] If, in a case involving the actor's conspiracy, solicitation, or aid regarding some future act of possibly culpable risk imposition, the actor's own further participation is required for that future act to occur, then the actor is at the time of conspiring, soliciting, or aiding no different from an incomplete attempter, that is, one who merely intends a possibly culpable future act. On the other hand, even if the actor understands that he will engage in the future actions, if his agreement, encouragement, or aid increases the chance that someone else will commit the crime (should the actor change his mind, for instance), the actor is culpable for creating this risk. He has, effectively, lit the human fuse.

VII

The Locus of Culpability

At this point, we still need an account of what the unit of action is.[1] Given that we deny that the results of an action increase the actor's blameworthiness, and that we believe instead that the sole locus of culpability is an act that unleashes an unjustifiable risk of harm over which the actor no longer has complete control, we should explicate exactly what "a culpable act" is. Because we view crimes as culpable risk creations, what is it exactly that creates that risk? And are failures to act, which cannot create risks themselves, also culpable?

Moreover, we need an account of how to individuate such culpable acts. Having reduced all criminality to risk creation, we need to explain when one risk creation stops and another begins. There are continuous courses of conduct that can be divided – or not – into multiple acts of

---

[1] This chapter draws from Larry Alexander and Kimberly Kessler Ferzan, "Culpable Acts of Risk Creation," 5 *Ohio State Journal of Criminal Law* 375 (2008).

risk imposition. Take a kidnapping, where the victim is moved over a period of time from A to B, which, as in Achilles and the tortoise, consists of a number of movements approaching infinity over lesser distances.[2] There are also different acts that can occur within one course of conduct. For instance, in a rape case, what determines the number of rapes that have been committed when there are several different forced sexual acts?[3] Then, there are single bodily movements that result in multiple harms. What of an arson during which the actor ignites a building with two people inside?[4] Finally, there are multiple acts in rapid succession. Is an actor who fires six shots in rapid succession less culpable than an actor who fires one shot a week for six weeks?

These crime-counting questions are not just puzzles for us. Rather, because the double jeopardy clause prohibits multiple punishments for the same offense, the criminal law must have an account of when there is but one offense and when there are more.[5] Even within double jeopardy jurisprudence, there has yet to be a satisfactory resolution of these problems. For instance, although some courts hold that one act that affects several people constitutes one crime,[6] still other courts hold that there are as many crimes as there are victims.[7] What is needed is a principled approach to crime counting.

In this chapter, we first discuss the unit of culpable action, arguing that, as a theoretical matter, the appropriate focus is the actor's volition but that, as a practical matter, the willed bodily movement is the more manageable unit of concern. Next, we discuss punishment for

---

[2] *Cf.* Brown v. Indiana, 830 N.E.2d 956 (Ind. Ct. App. 2005) (continuous flight from three police officers held to constitute just one act of resisting arrest).

[3] *See, e.g.,* Sanchez-Rengifo v. United States, 815 A.2d 351 (D.C. Ct. App. 2002).

[4] *See, e.g.,* Illinois v. Myers, 816 N.E.2d 820 (Ill. Ct. App. 2004).

[5] U.S. Const. amend. V.

[6] Ladner v. United States, 358 U.S. 169 (1958) (holding the defendant could be convicted of only one count of assaulting a federal officer where a single pull of shotgun trigger resulted in multiple pellets which injured two federal officers); Smith v. United States, 295 A.2d 60 (D.C. Ct. App. 1972) (one threat uttered to two people constitutes only one crime of threats to do bodily harm).

[7] Arizona v. Henley, 687 P.2d 1220 (Ariz. 1984) (upholding two convictions for aggravated assault where bullet traveled through intended victim into bystander); Wisconsin v. Rabe, 291 N.W.2d 809 (Wis. 1980) (holding defendant was properly charged with four counts of homicide by intoxicated use of a motor vehicle when defendant ran stop sign and killed four people).

omissions. Following that discussion, we add another element to our culpability arsenal: the duration of the risk imposition. Finally, with these elements in hand, we apply our approach to questions of crime counting, ultimately concluding that our approach fully resolves difficult individuation questions.

I. The Unit of Culpable Action

Our theory of the criminal law places all of its emphasis on the actor's choice to release an unjustifiable risk of harm. When we are looking at the risk the actor creates, risks and reasons are assessed holistically. That is, to determine if an actor is culpable, we must weigh all of the reasons for imposing the risk of which the actor is aware – discounted by the actor's estimate of the probabilities of the facts on which those reasons are based – against *all of the risks* that the actor believes that her action imposes. We assess *one* act by reference to the myriad of risks it imposes. But if we are to compare risks to reasons for a discrete action, then we need to know what counts as a discrete action.

A. RETHINKING CULPABLE ACTION

How does an actor increase the risk of harm to others? Typically, it is by *doing something.* Current statutes embody complex action descriptions.[8] That is, it is not a crime to "move your finger." Rather, the crime occurs when moving your finger *results* in the killing of another person. Nor is it a crime to move your arms and legs; and yet, if those movings amount to taking the property of another, you may be committing theft. That is, your willed bodily movement may be qualified by circumstances and results so that your conduct can be redescribed in any number of ways; and some redescriptions render your conduct criminal.

Now, one question within philosophy of action is whether these redescriptions amount to additional actions. That is, if moving your finger is pulling the trigger, which results in the firing of the bullet,

---

[8] *See* Michael S. Moore, *Act and Crime: The Philosophy of Action and Its Implications for Criminal Law* ch. 8 (1993).

which results in the killing of the victim, how many actions have you performed? Donald Davidson famously argues that, after the movement of your finger, "[t]here are no further actions, only further descriptions."[9] In contrast, Alvin Goldman claims that moving your finger and killing the victim are two different actions because the relationship between the two is asymmetric and irreflexive.[10]

Even if there are more actions, not just more descriptions, as we explained in Chapter 5, we believe that only the first action will be a culpable action of concern to the criminal law. Therefore, for our purposes we need not resolve this philosophical debate. Still, we (tentatively) endorse Davidson's account. First, recognizing that the only action that one performs is the willed bodily movement and that other actions are simply redescriptions prevents bizarre metaphysical results. For example, if Alice shoots Betty, placing Betty in a coma, and Alice dies three days before Betty does, when did Alice kill Betty?[11] Before Alice died? But Betty was alive. After Alice died? But how can one *act* after one's death? To us, the answer to the puzzle lies in seeing that Alice acts when she moves her finger and pulls the trigger. After that willed bodily movement, that one action may be redescribed in a multitude of ways to include its results and circumstances. Second, the Goldman view leads to a rather large ontology of actions.[12] Even when we are sitting still, or sleeping, we are still *acting* so long as the results of former willed bodily movements lead to new consequences. Even thinking that we are always acting is itself exhausting!

For us, however, it is not the results of actions that matter but only the risks that the actor is willing to impose. So, if the actor chooses to pull the trigger in order to kill, she is imposing a risk for a terrible reason. She manifests insufficient concern for others, and she should be punished. Redescriptions are thus of little import to us. To us, it is irrelevant

---

[9] Donald Davidson, *Essays on Actions and Events* 61 (2d ed., 2001).

[10] That is, we cannot switch the order – you do not move your finger by killing (indicating an asymmetric causal relationship), and you do not kill the victim by killing the victim (thus irreflexive). Hence, to Goldman, these items cannot be identical and are therefore different actions. Alvin Goldman, *A Theory of Human Action* 5 (1970).

[11] *See* Samuel D. Guttenplan, ed., *A Companion to Philosophy of Mind* 69–75 (1994).

[12] *See also* Moore, *supra* note 8, at 111.

whether the pulling of the trigger *results* in the death. The actor's blame-worthiness is fixed at the point when she pulls the trigger.[13]

Because an actor chooses to take an action that risks harming others, we believe that the volition, wherein the defendant wills the movement of her body, is the appropriate unit of culpable action. It is at this point that the actor unleashes a risk of harm to others. What follows are simply redescriptions (or additional actions that the defendant last exercised complete control over when she willed her bodily movement).

Of course, because our account relies on the notion of a volition, it presupposes that there is some such thing to which the term voli-tion refers.[14] In our view, the most likely account of a volition is that it is a mental state of bare intention that takes a bodily movement as its intentional object.[15] We cannot argue for the existence of volitions here, but we do not doubt that science will ultimately give us a more complete account of volitions and other mental states. When we want to move our fingers, we somehow do it. We all experience this exercise of will, but science has yet to explain just how it is that we do it. However, criminal law cannot wait for scientific conclusions about the brain any-more than we can await the final word (will there be one?) on a myriad of other physical phenomena. We must plug along with the information we have.[16] (Moreover, we make some concessions to current epistemic inadequacies in the next section.)

In summary, actors are culpable because they choose to impose risks on others for insufficient reasons. When an actor chooses to engage in risky conduct, she does so by willing the movement of her body. The point at which she opts to unleash a risk of harm to others is the point at which she exercises her will. It is her volition that moves her finger, that pulls the trigger, that fires the bullet, that wounds (or misses) the

---

[13] She may also be blameworthy for culpably failing to rescue. *See infra* Section III.A.

[14] For the best theoretical defense of the view of volitions that we presuppose here, *see* Moore, *supra* note 8, at ch. 6.

[15] *Id.*

[16] As one of us has argued: "At present and for the foreseeable future, we have no convinc-ing conceptual reason from the philosophy of mind, even when it is completely informed by the most recent neuroscience, to abandon our view of ourselves as creatures with causally efficacious mental states." Stephen J. Morse, "Criminal Responsibility and the Disappearing Person," 28 *Cardozo L. Rev.* 2545, 2555 (2006).

victim. And thus, for us, it is her volition that is the appropriate locus of culpability.

B. FROM VOLITIONS TO WILLED BODILY MOVEMENTS

Now, despite the fact that we believe the appropriate theoretical target of the criminal law to be the volition, for pragmatic reasons we believe it best for the criminal law to focus on what volitions cause – the willed bodily movement. Let us begin with a focus on volitions and other "mental acts." Then, we will explain why we shift our focus from volitions to willed bodily movements.

There can be volitions without actions. Consider David who, because of a car accident, has lost the ability to move his legs. Now, assume that David's mother-in-law comes to visit him, and finding her to be unsympathetic to his plight, David decides to kick her. Indeed, he does everything that he would have done before the car accident to move his leg. Nothing happens. Under our analysis, has David committed a culpable act? It seems to us that the answer is clearly yes. David willed the movement of his body to cause harm to his mother-in-law for no sufficient reason.

There also can be culpable actions without bodily movements. Whether we cast mental acts within our ontology of actions or not, we certainly *do* things in our heads. Certain mental acts that are under the control of the will, were they capable of imposing risks on others, would count as culpable on our account although they would not be willed *bodily* movements. If doing the multiplication tables in your head would somehow detonate a bomb, you could be culpable for doing them, even if your body does not move. Notably, these are not mere *choosings* to impose a risk at a future time; they are mental acts that would themselves unleash a risk over which the actor no longer had complete control.

So, if we assume that volition precedes action, there will be a small class of cases – in addition to deliberate omissions – in which there will be a volition but no bodily movement. We see no problem with admitting that, ultimately, the appropriate basis of criminal liability is the volition itself and not the bodily movement it produces. It is simply the case that, in almost all of our everyday experiences, bodily movements follow from our mysterious ability to exercise our will – our volitions. In other words, we believe that David has committed a culpable act, an act that is ultimately on par with actually kicking his mother-in-law.

But if we place crime completely within the mind, the citizenry may fear being punished for thoughts. In some respects, the concern is unwarranted. One of the primary worries about being punished for thoughts is that one cannot control what one thinks.[17] If thoughts can simply pop into one's head, then thoughts hardly seem like a fair basis for culpability. Just as we want acts to be voluntary so as to ensure that the actor may fairly be said to have had the requisite degree of control, we do not want to punish an actor simply for her thoughts.

But a volition is not merely a thought. One does not suddenly find oneself exercising one's will. Rather, volitions are the outcome of practical reasoning, and we exercise control over our willings by deciding if and when to move our bodies.

There is also another reason to reject the complaint about punishing for thoughts. Our criminal justice system functions quite well by inferring the existence of underlying subjective states from an actor's behavior (including things the actor himself says). Reliance on volitions is no more objectionable than our reliance on other subjective states. It is these subjective states that are determinative of the actor's culpability. Our reliance on folk psychology is fundamental to our understanding and blaming each other.[18]

On the other hand, we do acknowledge that there is at least one legitimate concern about punishment for volitions. If the target of the criminal law lies within the mind, then the criminal law suddenly becomes extremely invasive. The entire object of the criminal law would then be

---

[17] Cf. Douglas Husak, "Rethinking the Act Requirement," 28 Cardozo L. Rev. 2437 (2007) (arguing that the normative work done by the act requirement could be done more effectively through a notion of control).

[18] Consider the following from Jerry Fodor: "[I]f commonsense intentional psychology were really to collapse, that would be, beyond comparison, the greatest intellectual catastrophe in the history of our species; if we're that wrong about the mind, then that's the wrongest we've ever been about anything. The collapse of the supernatural, for example, doesn't compare....Nothing except, perhaps, our commonsense physics...comes as near our cognitive core as intentional explanation does. We'll be in deep, deep trouble if we have to give it up....But be of good cheer; everything is going to be all right." Jerry Fodor, Psychosemantics: The Problem of Meaning in the Philosophy of Mind xii (1987).

mental states and not actions, and there may be legitimate worries about how searches might evolve and how powerful the state might become in monitoring our most intimate of thoughts. Hence, even if crime does occur within the mind, it is a significant worry that we would give up more in terms of security than we would benefit in implementing such a system of crime prevention and retributive justice.

Hence, despite our views that one can control one's volitions in a way that one cannot control one's thoughts, and that a reliance on volitions is as defensible as a reliance on other aspects of folk psychology, we are somewhat inclined to give in on this point. We believe that a willed bodily movement, not a volition, is the more manageable unit of action for the criminal law. In comparison to beliefs, desires, and intentions, volitions themselves are less a part of our ordinary folk psychology, and thus it may be too much to ask that an ordinary citizen apply the concept of a volition. Bodily movements are public; thus, punishment for such movements does not give rise to the same concerns about a police state. Moreover, given that almost all of the time, actions do follow from volitions, we think that the set of unpunishable but criminally culpable acts will be quite small. No one has the ability to prevent an action from flowing from a volition. Rather, it is in the minuscule group of cases where body parts are paralyzed and the like that the body misfires and departs from the actor's will.[19] Given that individuals may fear being punished for thoughts if volitions are the unit of measurement, that we have no way to track volitions themselves, and that action follows from volition in almost every case, we are willing to allow a tiny group of culpable offenders to go unpunished.

Before moving on, let us clarify what we mean by a *willed* bodily movement. That is, one might ask, What do we mean by willed bodily movements if, as we argued in Chapter 4, lack of will is an excuse, not a basis for the act requirement? In our view, there are two senses of

---

[19] We acknowledge that a reliance on the bodily movements that are caused by volitions imports causation into our account. Given that we reject that causing a harm has any independent moral significance, it may seem inconsistent for us to be willing to rely on the volition's causing of a bodily movement. Admittedly, we are swallowing a bit of moral luck here. But we do so out of practical necessity. If we had the ability (epistemically and practically) to punish for volitions irrespective of whether they cause actions, that is what we would do. But just as some criminals are lucky enough never to be caught, some of the culpably deserving may be lucky enough for their volitions to fail to result in actions.

voluntariness, one of which is required for there to be an act, the second
of which is required for the actor to be held responsible. Although
altered states of consciousness sit on the borderline of this distinction,
we are inclined to treat them as excuses.

If an actor's body is moved by reflex or by another person, then it is
not an action. That is, if the bodily movement is not the product of practical reasoning – the product of the actor's reasons and beliefs resulting
in a choice to move her body – then it cannot be said that she has acted
at all. Thus, a bodily movement does not by itself constitute an act.

On the other hand, there are cases in which the actor has clearly
moved her body, but she claims that she lacked free will. The claim
of "no free will," however, is more often a conclusion than part of the
argument. As we discuss in Chapter 4, there are a number of conditions under which the actor will be excused. In these cases, the actor has
exercised her practical reason, but because of some impairment in her
reasoning, she cannot be regarded as culpable.

Dissociative states stand at action's border.[20] In these cases, the
action appears to be goal directed, but the actor lacks fully conscious
control over the action. Is the sleepwalker not *acting,* or is she simply
not *culpable* for her action? As we argue in Chapter 4, we believe that
what the sleepwalker and others in dissociative states do is not culpable.
However, we would reserve the claim of no act for the pure cases and
place dissociative states on the excuse side of the border. Nonetheless,
this is a close question, and nothing of consequence turns on this distinction (unless there were a different burden of proof for excuses).

II. Culpability for Omissions

A. BACKGROUND: THE "NO CRIMINAL LIABILITY FOR OMISSIONS" REGIME AND EXCEPTIONS THERETO

There is a second potential target for the criminal law – an actor's
failure to act. Omissions may seem puzzling for us in two respects.
First, it seems that omissions do not unleash a new risk of harm to

[20] *Compare* Moore, *supra* note 8, *with* Stephen J. Morse, "Culpability and Control," 142 *U. Pa. L. Rev.* 1587, 1641–1652 (1994).

others – omissions do not and cannot *cause* anything and therefore cannot *risk* causing anything. From this perspective, omissions appear ineligible to be culpable acts. On the other hand, the choice not to rescue others often demonstrates that the actor has insufficient concern for them. By failing to act in a particular manner, an actor might fail to reduce the risk of harm that another faces when, by acting, that risk could have been reduced – or so the actor may believe. From this point of view, all omissions have the potential to be culpable.

Anglo-American criminal law generally has not criminalized omissions. Of course, by failing to act in a particular manner, an actor can fail to reduce the risk of harm that another faces when, by acting, that risk could be reduced – or so the actor may believe. Nonetheless, perhaps because of the deontological constraint against appropriating the bodies and labor of some to reduce the risks faced by others, and perhaps as well because of the difficulties in administrability, affirmative acts are rarely mandated by the criminal law.[21] Though we will not argue for the status quo here, we are sympathetic to both of these concerns. Requiring an individual to act is appropriating his labor and talents to reduce harm to others. On our account, then, the actor's omission does not reveal insufficient concern for a victim's *legally protected interests* because the victim has no right that the actor act in the first instance. Moreover, because omissions are failures to act, they raise the same practical and epistemic concerns as does punishment for volitions alone.

There are, of course, standard exceptions to the no affirmative duties regime. They fall into three categories: instances where the actor has caused the victim's peril; affirmative duties to aid predicated on a status relation between actor and victim, such as parent and child or husband and wife; and affirmative duties that are attached to defined roles that are voluntarily undertaken or that are the subject of contractual undertakings. One who becomes a policeman or fireman takes on affirmative duties to aid as part of the voluntarily assumed position. And one may

---

[21] And perhaps they need not be. For a fascinating study detailing that individuals *do* rescue, even in risky situations in which the criminal law would not mandate it, *see* David A. Hyman, "Rescue without Law: An Empirical Perspective on the Duty to Rescue," 84 *Tex. L. Rev.* 653 (2006).

contract to act as a bodyguard or lifeguard and thereby become legally obligated to aid others.[22] (There may be some affirmative duties backed by criminal sanctions that do not fall into these three categories. A military draft places those subject to it involuntarily in roles requiring affirmative acts.)

It is worth mentioning some of the difficult issues connected with these three grounds for affirmative duties under the criminal law. With respect to the causing the peril ground, one issue is whether the actor's causing of the peril must be culpable in order to ground the duty. The scant case law on the subject seems to deny this. For example, actors have been held criminally liable for failing to put out fires that they nonculpably started. Such a result seems intuitively correct. We might say that one's permission to undertake some risky acts, such as lighting a fire, is conditional on undertaking the obligation to take affirmative action if necessary to reduce risks caused thereby. Yet, on the other hand, causal implication potentially casts a very wide net. If, unable to swim, we venture out on a boat only because we believe that other boaters will rescue us if we fall in, then surely in a but for sense their boating has caused our peril, as has the host of the beach party to which we were invited, the Olympic swimmer whom we saw standing by the shore and who we were confident could and would rescue us, and so on, approaching a general Good Samaritan duty to rescue enforced by the criminal law. And limiting the affirmative duties to those who not only were but for causes of the peril but were, in addition, proximate causes throws us back into the indeterminacy of proximate causation that we discussed in Chapter 5.

The status-relationship ground of an affirmative duty to aid appears more manageable – but only if the statuses are defined quite formally. The status of legally married husband and wife fits that description, but common-law spouse does not. Registered domestic partner does so, but not live-in companion. Mother and child, husband-of-mother and

---

[22] Affirmative duties to aid do not cancel duties not to impose risks where the consequentialist balance favors the latter; nor do they override deontological constraints. Thus, in Trolley, if the trolley is heading toward the one worker, someone who has an affirmative duty to aid that person – her husband, for example, or someone who induced her to work on that track – may not rescue her by redirecting the trolley to the track with five workers, or by pushing a fat man into the trolley's path. *See also* Gerhard Overland, "The Right to Do Wrong," 26 *Law & Phil.* 377, 395–401 (2007).

child, certified biological father and child, and adoptive parents and child do; but mother's boyfriend and child does not. And given the variety of adult relationships, and now the variety of procreative methods, the desirability of formality if a status is to trigger an affirmative duty to aid is even more obvious.

With respect to contractual and other voluntary undertakings of affirmative duties, the deep theoretical question is whether they are distinct as grounds from that of causing the peril. That question is presented most starkly when A contracts with B to come to C's aid when necessary, but B does not rely in any way on A's fulfilling his contractual obligation – B would not engage anyone else to do this, even if B were aware that A would breach – and C is unaware of the contract's existence. In such a case, A's agreeing to aid C and then not doing so has not imperiled C; C is no worse off than had A not agreed to aid C. But A *has* contracted to do so.

Most cases of voluntarily undertaking to aid will also be cases where failing to aid will imperil. If B were relying on A to fulfill his contractual obligation – as, for example, a city would be when it hires policemen or lifeguards – so that it is the case that B would have hired someone more reliable in A's place if B were aware that A would breach, then A's breaching will have imperiled those he contracted to aid. But it is still possible for causation of peril and voluntary undertaking to come apart as grounds for the affirmative duties enforced by the criminal law.

B. ELEMENTS OF OMISSIONS LIABILITY

We do not examine further the contours and underlying rationales for the exceptions to the "no affirmative duties" regime. We take it as a given that there are exceptions and that these exceptions are triggered by some conduct or relationship – conduct or relationship that we from here on refer to as "the trigger," or T. Once the trigger exists, the actor may be culpable for not acting. Omissions should be treated as on par with volitions, not as equivalent to mere choosings (or future intentions) to risk. In instances of omission, the risk (as the actor perceives it) already exists, and the actor chooses not to abate it. Omissions, therefore, are not akin to decisions to harm because, from the agent's perspective, decisions to harm do not themselves create risks of harm over which the agent no longer has complete control, whereas omissions do involve perceived present risks. (In other words, the victim will not and cannot drown simply because one intends to throw her in the pool, but the victim can and will drown if one decides not to rescue her when she is already in the pool gasping for air.) So let us focus on the elements of culpability for omissions. In a case where actor (A) fails to engage in rescue conduct (RC) to reduce the apparent peril that victim (V) is in, under what conditions is A culpable?

Let us, as we did with ordinary risk impositions, focus on the various relevant probabilities that A will estimate:

1. The probability that T exists (and thus that A does have an affirmative duty to act)
2. The probabilities that if A does not act, V will suffer various harms (a different probability for each different harm)
3. The probabilities that the various different rescue acts that A might undertake will reduce the various probabilities of harm
4. The probabilities of various harms or costs to A of undertaking the various different acts

With respect to (1), A can never be 100 percent certain that T is present. The person drowning may or may not be someone A accidentally knocked into the swimming pool. He may or may not be A's son. And so on. T may exist, but A may believe the chance is small that it does. Or, conversely, A may believe the chance is high that T exists when it does not. A may be culpable for not acting in the latter case despite T's absence and nonculpable in the former despite T's presence.

With respect to (2), the person in the pool may just be joking. Or he may not be, but in no great peril because the side of the pool is near. Or he may suffer physical injury but not die. Or he may die. A may attach a different probability to each possible outcome if he does not come to V's rescue.

With respect to (3), A may consider various acts he can undertake to rescue V. He may dive in himself, with a given probability of success. He may alert the more distant lifeguard, with perhaps a lower probability of success. He may urge a guest who is a better swimmer to effect the rescue, with a still different probability of success. And so on.

Finally, with respect to (4), A will estimate the risks and costs to himself of the various courses of action considered in (3). What is the chance of his drowning if he goes in? Of ruining his new suit? Of suffering great fatigue or emotional distress? And so on.

A may be culpable either for doing nothing or for choosing one method of rescue rather than another of which he was aware. What will *not* be material to A's culpability is what actually happens to V. Nor will it be material to A's culpability whether T actually exists, whether V was actually in peril, whether the alternative acts would or would not have been successful, or whether they would or would not have harmed or imposed costs of certain magnitudes on A. All that is material to A's culpability is what he chooses to do given the various probabilities he estimates in (1) through (4), and what his reasons are for so choosing. Culpability for omissions mirrors culpability for risk impositions, the only difference being the complexity of the risk analysis. Instead of being concerned merely with the various risks of harm A estimates his *specific act* will *impose* on V, and A's reason for so acting, we now must be concerned not only with the risks to V that *various alternative actions* will *reduce* rather than impose but also with A's reasons for choosing or avoiding the various possible actions and with A's estimate of the probability that he has no duty to act at all. A may estimate that it is 50 percent likely that he has a duty to rescue V – V is, say, 50 percent likely to be A's son, or so A estimates; A may believe that it is 75 percent likely that V will drown if A does nothing, 50 percent likely that V will drown if A hails a lifeguard, but only 25 percent likely that V will drown if A attempts the rescue himself; and A may estimate the risk that he will drown at 5 percent if he attempts to rescue. If A hails the lifeguard because of the 5 percent risk of drowning, then the question will be, given his other estimates, is A culpable for not rescuing V himself? And, again, it will be immaterial whether V in fact drowns, whether V is A's son, or whether A under- or overestimated the risk (relative to others' estimations) that he would drown or that hailing the lifeguard would succeed.

C. THE CRIME OF POSSESSION

Possession of many items – for example, narcotics and various firearms – is criminalized under current criminal codes. Possession crimes almost never represent imposition of undue risk of harm to others or even the actor himself. They must therefore be considered proxy crimes, where being in possession of certain substances is highly correlated with anticipated impositions of undue risks of harm.

We discuss proxy crimes at some length in the next chapter, so we do not discuss this aspect of possession crimes here. Nor do we spend any time on the point that possession typically – almost exclusively – is a crime of omission rather than commission. Although one can possess by the act of physically grasping something, more typically one possesses an item by having it be within one's dominion and control. Because the latter can occur without any voluntary act, the crime of possession usually is predicated on omitting to relinquish dominion and control over the item.

Leaving aside the vagueness of dominion and control (and the vagueness of its correlative of relinquishing such dominion and control), notice that to go from the state of finding oneself in possession to that of having relinquished possession requires some minimum amount of time. If Al notices that someone has left a bag of cocaine on his coffee table, there is some minimum amount of time that it will take Al to cross the room, pick up the cocaine, and dispose of it in whatever way would render him no longer in possession. Until that minimum amount of time has passed, Al cannot be deemed culpable for being in possession of the cocaine, for he has made no culpable choice regarding that possession.

Al might be able to sprint to the cocaine, pick it up, and flush it down the toilet in fifteen seconds. If Al takes twenty seconds to do so, is he culpable for whatever choice left him in possession the extra five seconds? What if he finished his cup of coffee and went to the bathroom before getting rid of the cocaine, costing him an extra five minutes of possession? Would he be culpable for those choices? Because it is not necessary that the extra time of possession increase the risk of harms to others (or to Al), it is not clear how the law should answer these questions. Al's reasons for delay – to finish his coffee and so forth – are not offset by any significant increases in risks of harms and thus appear otherwise justifiable. Perhaps all the law can do here is specify an arbitrary time period – though occasionally an actor who exceeds it will have made no culpable choices en route to doing so.

Beyond the problem of the time period for his possession is the problem of possession's being a continuous omission. Because omissions can range from a second to many years in length, we encounter the same individuation problem we encounter with continuous actions, such as reckless driving, kidnapping, rape, battery, and so on. If Al remains in possession of his cocaine for twenty minutes, but Sue remains in possession of hers for six months, is Sue 13,140 times as culpable as Al? We turn to the duration question in the next section.

III. Acts, Omission, and Duration

To this point, we have argued that one "acts" culpably when an actor wills her body to move in a way that will create what the actor believes is a risk of harm to others that, given its magnitude and the actor's reasons for creating it, is unjustified. We have also argued that some omissions may be an appropriate target of criminal liability, and we have explained when omissions may be culpable. In this section, we seek to show how these two types of culpable "acts" may be related and thus generate more liability under our account than under existing law. We then introduce one additional element that bears on the actor's culpability – the duration of the risk.

A. RISKY ACTS AND FAILURES TO RESCUE

After an actor creates a risk of harm, she will sometimes have the ability to prevent the harm's occurrence. The actor may light a fuse that she can extinguish. Or she may wound the victim but can still call an ambulance to prevent further injury or death. In these situations, her culpably risky conduct now gives rise to a duty to try to prevent a harm's occurrence.[23]

We believe that current law fails to pay sufficient attention to an actor's culpable omissions. The actor did not merely light the fuse or wound the victim. Rather, she performed a second culpable act by omitting to remedy the risk of harm (or further harm) that she created. To

---

[23] *See* Larry Alexander and Kimberly D. Kessler, "Mens Rea and Inchoate Crimes," 87 *J. Crim. L. & Criminology* 1138, 1183–1187 (1997).

illustrate, consider two actors, D_1 and D_2, who impose similar risks on V_1 and V_2. (Assume they try to kill their victims.) D_1's act kills V_1, as D_1 hoped it would. D_2 seriously wounds V_2. Now, however, it is possible for D_2 to save V_2's life by calling an ambulance. Moreover, under the law regarding criminal omissions, D_2 has a duty to do so. If he fails to do so because he still wants V_2 to die, then whether or not V_2 dies, D_2 has committed *two* culpable acts or omissions of risk imposition, as opposed to D_1's *one* culpable act.[24] D_2's circumstantial luck differs from D_1's (and also from D_3's, who shoots and misses) in that D_2 faces a second opportunity to do wrong based solely on luck. (On the other hand, D_2 is no different in terms of circumstantial luck from D_4, who shoots and misses and then shoots again; as we argue later, D_4 has committed two culpable acts, each as culpable as D_1's one-shot killing.)

Many acts of risk imposition may indeed also be followed by failures to rescue. In these cases, the actor has made more than one culpable choice. Again, in our hypothetical, D_2 has committed *two* culpable acts or omissions of risk imposition, as opposed to D_1's *one* culpable act. After firing the first shot, D_2 has the ability to prevent a further harm from occurring, and a duty to do so; and if he decides not to so act, he has made two culpable choices instead of one. Indeed, imagine that D_2 shot his victim, but as he fled the scene, he accidentally pushed a small child into the water. Clearly, even though D_2 had the bad luck of creating this unfortunate situation, he now has a duty to remedy it. We see no reason why the situation should change simply because both the act and the omission involve the same victim.

B. CULPABILITY AND DURATION

To this point, we have argued that culpability is about risks and reasons. We have argued that our "act requirement" consists in a willed bodily movement that creates a risk of harm or in an omission to avert a risk of harm where there exists a legal duty to do so. We have also argued that in cases where the actor has created a risk, her conduct also gives

---

[24] Treating D_2 as having committed two culpable acts or omissions would, of course, give D_2 a nonmoral incentive to rescue V_2; but the question here is, incentive aside, Is D_2 guilty of two culpable acts in shooting to kill and then failing to rescue?

rise to a duty to try to prevent the harm from occurring. In viewing culpable acts through the prism of risk creation, we must now introduce one additional factor for this calculation: duration.

In our view, the anticipated duration of risk of harm also affects the actor's culpability. An actor who sets fire to a building that he expects to burn for three hours unleashes a greater risk than the actor who sets a fire that he expects to terminate in twenty minutes. Choosing to rape a victim for three hours is far more culpable than choosing to rape a victim for fifteen minutes. A fireman who fails to put out a fire for fifteen minutes is more culpable (all other things being equal) than one who fails to do so for five minutes. An actor who imposes a risk for a longer period of time imposes more risk than an actor who imposes a risk for a shorter period of time.[25]

In the next section, we discuss how to individuate these acts of risk creation. That is, we must determine when one act of risk creation ends and the next begins. But even single acts can impose risks over a period of time. Some risk impositions are very short in duration but extremely culpable, as, for example, when an actor fires a gun at her victim's temple to kill her. In other cases, the risk is serious and temporally extended, such as in a typical case of arson. Still other cases, such as speeding, present low levels of risk imposition that may persist over an extended period of time.

Critically, in all of these cases, it is the actor's assessment of the duration of the risk, and not the actual duration, that determines the actor's culpability. If Bob sets fire to a building, believing it will burn for fifty minutes, he is culpable for imposing a risk of that duration, irrespective of whether the fire burns for five hours or five minutes, or is snuffed out by a bystander within seconds.

---

[25] Mitch Berman has suggested to us that the duration of the risk is already built into the risk's magnitude. We do not believe this is a widely shared view. For instance, assume an actor sets her cruise control for ninety miles per hour and drives this way for twenty minutes. To view the magnitude of the risk as including the duration would entail that the risk because of its duration would need a greater justification than imposing this same risk for only five minutes (unless justifications are somehow also understood to include their durations). We think it is far more perspicuous to think of this as an instance in which the risk is unjustified by the reasons, and this degree of unjustifiability extends over the twenty-minute duration. (We add that, even if Berman is correct, our account can be understood as more fully unpacking "risk.")

Of course, adding duration as an element increases the complexity of determining the actor's culpability. And, as we just mentioned, the critical determination will be the actor's assessment of the risks, the reasons the actor believes are available (discounted by the probabilities of their actually obtaining), and the actor's belief regarding the durations of the various risks he is imposing. All of these factors combine with the fact that the actor will often not simply *act* in a way that imposes a risk but will then *omit* to stop the harm from occurring.

To illustrate, assume D_1 lights a bomb fuse that he knows will take twenty minutes to detonate. D_1 immediately boards a plane to Paris. D_2, in contrast, lights a twenty-minute fuse but decides to stay there, figuring he can snuff out the fuse at any time.

D_1's only act is lighting the fuse. His culpability is a product of the risks he believes he is imposing times the duration of that risk in light of his reasons for acting. Holding reasons constant, it seems that D_2's initial act will be less culpable because he will assess the risk to be lower (given that he thinks he may later want to snuff out the fuse). However, D_2 has a duty to snuff out the fuse because he, unlike D_1, retains the ability to do so. Over the course of the twenty minutes, the risk that D_2 realizes he is creating by not snuffing out the fuse increases – he realizes that even if he has a change of heart, he may confront obstacles to snuffing the fuse and have insufficient time to overcome them – so he becomes more culpable over time, with his total culpability approaching that of D_1 as its limit.

IV. Individuating Crimes

Doctrinally, questions of crime counting arise under the double jeopardy clause. The double jeopardy clause has multiple aims: it forbids reprosecution for the same offense after conviction, reprosecution for the same offense after acquittal, and multiple punishments for the same offense.[26] But to prevent reprosecution for the same offense or to prohibit multiple punishments for the same offense, one must know when conduct constitutes the same offense as that for which the

---

[26] *See generally* "Double Jeopardy," 35 *Geo. L. J. Ann. Rev. Crim. Pro.* 422 (2006).

agent has already been prosecuted or punished.[27] To be precise, the double jeopardy clause currently requires both act-type and act-token individuation. That is, we must ask whether one physical act implicates one or many crimes (act type), and we must also be able to discern how many times the actor has committed a crime (act token).[28] Within double jeopardy doctrine, act-type determinations are dubbed "multiple description" problems, whereas act-token determinations are "unit of prosecution" questions.[29]

In this section, we address both questions. We begin by exploring how we would account for types of crimes. We defend our risk creation view against the potential objection that we are losing sight of wrongdoing. We also argue that our approach allows us to distinguish more easily among types of offenses, a continuing dilemma within current double jeopardy doctrine. We then turn to how we would count risk impositions and failures to act. Our purpose here is not to argue that our account passes constitutional muster but rather to use the concerns that animate double jeopardy analysis as a way to explicate how our approach resolves the puzzles that bedevil current law.

A. TYPES OF CRIMES

1. A Brief Normative Defense

We believe that, for purposes of the criminal law, a focus on the willed bodily movement as the unit of action is conceptually and normatively

---

[27] Multiple criminal charges for the same instance of criminal conduct implicate proportionality concerns. Moore, *supra* note 8, at 309. Prima facie, one does not expect that the legislature fixes the punishment for each criminal act with regard to other potential criminal acts with which the defendant might also be charged. That is, when the legislature fixes the penalty for possession of narcotics within 1,000 feet of a school, it likely has not considered whether the defendant will also be charged with possession of narcotics (anywhere). But if the defendant were to be punished for both crimes, this might be disproportionate to his desert, because the punishment for possession near the school is likely to be sufficient. However, where a legislature specifically authorizes cumulative punishments, there is no double jeopardy problem. Missouri v. Hunter, 459 U.S. 359 (1983).

[28] Moore, *supra* note 8, at 320. As Michael Moore explains: "If I practice the violin every morning for a week, there are two very different answers to the question 'How many acts did I do?' For there are two very different questions of identity and individuation that could be asked by such a sentence: 'How many *kinds* of acts did I do?' (Answer: one.) And 'How many *particular* acts did I do?' (Answer: seven.)" *Id.*

[29] Kansas v. Harris, 162 P.3d 28 (Kan. 2007).

superior. Although a full normative defense will have to wait until Chapter 8, let us spend a moment on our approach's normative superiority here. Consider the crime of rape. In our view, conceptualizing a criminal act as "rape," that is, viewing rape as an independent type of wrongdoing, creates more problems than it resolves. Although all rapes involve a violation of sexual autonomy, the degree of physical and emotional injury risked varies from rape to rape. The strategy of considering all rapes to be equal obfuscates the myriad distinct harms that are done or risked to distinct legally protected interests. In other words, we would do away with the legal category of "rape" and focus on bodily movements and the various harms they risk.

Some may argue that stripping crimes down to willed bodily movements removes their moral importance. Moving one's finger is the nub of the crime, not the killing that results. Moving one's foot is speeding. Where, one might ask, is the moral wrongfulness of these supposedly criminal actions?

Of course, crimes such as murder, rape, speeding, and theft are not ultimately about moving one's foot or one's finger. These crimes are about being willing to risk injury to others for insufficient reasons. Certainly, agents understand themselves to be performing murders, rapes, speedings, and thefts. More important, they understand themselves to be risking harm to others. (And the implementation of our theory may lead to citizens' more often thinking in terms of risks rather than in terms of complex-act descriptions.) That the basic act is one of moving one's body does not eliminate the ultimate importance of the context of that bodily movement. After all, we are asking what risks the defendant foresaw from his willed bodily movement and what reasons he was aware of for willing that bodily movement. However, the fact that context ultimately figures into culpability does not entail that context should be included in the notion of the criminal act itself.

2. Disentangling Legally Protected Interests

Our approach also unravels one crime-counting conundrum – determining how many types of crimes are at issue. Counting crime types is easy for us: we have only one crime – manifesting insufficient concern for others' legally protected interests. On the other hand, the current law's focus on complex-act descriptions creates significant difficulties. Consider *Kansas v. Neal*.[30] The victim drove the defendant home from a bar, and upon arrival at the defendant's apartment building, the defendant pretextually requested a "hug." When the victim got out of the car, the defendant carried her to a secluded patch of grass and raped her. In accomplishing this rape, the defendant punched the victim in the face and choked the victim to the point at which she twice lost consciousness. The defendant challenged his convictions for both rape and aggravated assault, claiming that the charges were multiplicitous. According to him, there was just one crime, a rape, accomplished by the use of force.

Despite the state's claim that the defendant went beyond the force necessary to accomplish a rape, the appellate court reversed. Because no distinction was made in the indictment, in the presentation of evidence, or in the jury instructions, the jury may have relied on the very acts of force that constituted the aggravated assault charge to determine that force was used to accomplish the rape. The court went on to say that

> an additional problem with the State's argument that the battery went far beyond the force used to accomplish rape is its imprecision. How much force is necessary to rape someone? By what gauge do we measure violence? Is not each victim unique? This was a horrible crime committed with great continuous violence during its entire course; therefore, the application of single act of violence paradigm is appropriate here.[31]

But why should we assume that all instances of forcible rape are equal? An actor who suffocates his victim risks her life more than an actor who punches his victim and more than an actor who uses force only to hold down his victim. Let us be clear – all of these defendants are exceedingly culpable. But if Neal used excessive amounts of force to accomplish his forcible rape, he should be differentiated from an actor who uses lesser force. He is more culpable and deserving of more punishment.

Under our approach, there are no act types. The question is whether the actor, by way of a willed bodily movement, believed that he risked

---

[30] 120 P.3d 366 (Kan. Ct. App. 2005).
[31] *Id.* at 372.

unjustifiable harm to a legally protected interest.[32] For every willed
bodily movement, we must ask about *all* the reasons the actor was
aware of in support of so acting (discounted by the probabilities of their
being realized) and *all* the risks that the actor believed he was imposing.
Indeed, without an evaluation of all the risks and reasons, the jury cannot assess whether the conduct was justified and, accordingly, whether
the defendant was culpable for imposing the risks. Our approach allows
us to focus on the discrete interests that are risked (sexual autonomy,
bodily injury) and the different magnitudes of the risks imposed. Not
all rapes are created equal.

We believe our approach better distinguishes crimes than does current law. Under the Supreme Court's *Blockburger* test, the question is
whether each crime requires proof of an element that the other does
not.[33] In *Neal*, because the rape charge included the assaults, there was
just one crime. In our view, however, *Neal* reveals that a focus on the
extent to which a defendant risks distinct legally protected interests
should matter in our assessment of his total blameworthiness.

But to see the true clarity that a focus on legally protected interests
brings, consider the Supreme Court's divided opinion in *United States
v. Dixon*.[34] Although *Dixon* involved a pair of appeals, let us focus on
the *Dixon* case itself. Dixon was arrested for second-degree murder and
released on bond, subject to the condition that he not commit any additional criminal offense. Subsequent to his release, Dixon was arrested
for possession of cocaine with intent to distribute. The court held him
guilty of contempt and sentenced him to 180 days in jail. Dixon later
moved to dismiss his indictment for the drug possession on double
jeopardy grounds. The trial court granted the motion, and a majority of
the Supreme Court concurred that the drug prosecution would violate
the double jeopardy clause.

Although the Court was deeply fractured in reaching this decision,
we wish to spend a moment on Justice Scalia's opinion, in which Justice

---

[32] There is probably little practical difference between our view that one looks to risks to
legally protected interests and Michael Moore's claim that one must search for "morally
salient sameness." *See* Moore, *supra* note 8, at ch. 13. But our view deconstructs crimes in
a way that Moore would not.

[33] 284 U.S. 299, 304 (1932).

[34] 509 U.S. 688 (1993).

Kennedy joined, because Scalia rejects the very analysis that we advance here. Scalia reasons that because the contempt order incorporated the drug offense, the underlying substantive drug offense was a species of a lesser-included offense.[35] Scalia explicitly rejects the view that because the interests that the offenses protect are different, the offenses are not the same for double jeopardy purposes.[36] To Scalia, the test turns on legislative definitions – the text of the double jeopardy clause speaks to whether the *offenses* are the same, not whether the *interests* they protect are identical.[37]

But to apply the double jeopardy clause in this manner strikes us as very odd. One of the primary purposes of the double jeopardy clause is to prevent double punishment.[38] If the legislature prohibits burglary, the legislature should not have to consider the possible combinations of crimes with which the defendant could be charged in crafting the punishment for burglary. So, if burglary warrants a maximum of five years in jail, we would not think that the defendant should also be punished for criminal trespass and breaking and entering, if both of these crimes are lesser-included offenses.

Not only does this make sense with respect to how a rational legislature might behave, but it also makes sense with respect to the legally protected interests at stake. A trespass, a breaking and entering, and a burglary all risk harm to the same sorts of legally protected property rights, but they risk that harm to different extents. Thus, the burglary is a greater risk to a property right than a simple trespass, and if one is being punished for the full extent of the risk to the property right, then it would be double punishment to also punish the defendant for the simple trespass.

But once we begin to think of crimes as risks to legally protected interests, we see why it is that the contempt charge did not fully exhaust the punishment that Dixon deserved for the drug offense. Although we find the underlying drug possession charge potentially problematic, the legally protected interests at stake go beyond the interests at stake in the criminal contempt charge. Dixon's violation of his release condition

---

[35] *Id.* at 698 (citations omitted).
[36] *Id.* at 699.
[37] *Id.*
[38] *See supra* note 27.

revealed that he might be either dangerous or a flight risk. *Any* criminal offense would have shown this to be true. By Scalia's reasoning, a rape, a murder, or an arson would also be lesser-included offenses of the contempt charge. Yet it is hard to conceive how these offenses could be fully punished by a conviction for contempt.

In summary, viewing crimes as instances of risk imposition does not obfuscate the underlying blameworthiness of the conduct. To the contrary, a direct focus on risks and reasons allows us to make fine-grained distinctions between criminal defendants who would otherwise be deemed to have committed the same offense. In addition, by tying crime directly to risks to legally protected interests, we avoid the problems of overlapping offenses that present multiple description problems under the double jeopardy clause.

B. TOKENS OF CRIMES

A second crime-counting dilemma remains. How do we determine how many acts of risk imposition a defendant has committed? In this section, we begin by arguing that each willed bodily movement is itself a culpable act of risk imposition. We defend this view against the claim that culpable acts can be reduced to smaller units of movement and against the view that our approach greatly expands criminality. We then turn to the puzzle of "volume discounts" – the defendant who attempts a crime several times in rapid succession. Here, we argue that the defendant has still committed as many acts as there are willed bodily movements, *but* that there may be cases in which multiple attempts over longer periods of time are more culpable because the defendant deliberates better and longer. Finally, we turn to continuous courses of conduct. Here, we argue that continuous crimes are just one crime of long duration.

1. Counting Willed Bodily Movements

As we have argued previously, a culpable "action" to us is a volition, though, conceding to practicalities, we believe the criminal law should focus on willed bodily movements. The token counting problem, then, is, in some respects, quite simple – there are as many criminal acts as there are willed bodily movements, and there are as few criminal acts as there are willed bodily movements.

So, consider *People v. Myers*, where the defendant, after being picked up while hitchhiking, violently opposed being dropped off prior to his destination.[39] Myers threatened one of the passengers in the car by holding a machete to the passenger's neck. Myers then sought to prevent the driver from turning on the interior car light by cutting the driver's hand, after which he returned the machete to the passenger's neck and severed the passenger's windpipe. The defendant was charged with two crimes – armed violence for the first attack on the passenger and attempted murder for the second, and the Supreme Court of Illinois had to determine whether there was just one criminal act, or whether there were two distinct assaults, ultimately holding that there were two crimes because there were two distinct physical acts.

We believe this case was correctly decided. The defendant chose to impose a risk of death on the victim in the first attack. After some time elapsed, the defendant ceased to impose that risk. The defendant then made another culpable choice to risk harm to the victim and acted in a way that imposed a greater risk of harm (moving the machete so as to sever the windpipe). The defendant then had committed two distinct culpable acts.

Even moving from volition to willed bodily movement may seem too quick for some. Despite our claim that a bodily movement is a discrete and measurable unit of action, one might wonder whether bodily movements can be reduced further still. Cannot moving one's finger be reduced into even smaller (perhaps infinite) units of movement? And is that movement the movement of a body, an arm, a finger, or just the surface of the actor's finger?[40]

This question requires us to join the movement of one's body (which may be divided into infinite parts) with the volition that causes it. Even if our fingers move over a distance that may be broken into an infinite number of smaller segments, we typically do not will these microparts. Rather, we decide to move my finger. So even if the bodily movement may be broken up, the volition is not.

Moreover, recognizing that the object of a volition is likely to be a larger bodily movement serves the function of our act requirement. We

---

[39] 426 N.E.2d 535 (Ill. 1981).
[40] Moore, *supra* note 8, at 375.

are concerned with an actor's choosing to risk harm to others for insufficient reasons. When an actor chooses to move her body in a way that creates unjustifiable risks, she is culpable. The ultimate unit of action must,
therefore, be one by which risks and reasons can be assessed. An actor
does not choose to move his body in microparts and millimeters, but to
move my finger.[41] Of course, to the extent that an actor with expertise in
throwing a ball, playing the piano, or firing a trigger can will more discrete movements, he has willed more actions. Because this is the unit by
which the actor makes his culpable choice, the criminal law, too, can use
it as the unit by which to evaluate his choice. Our approach is, after all,
an approach that looks to *culpable acts* as the unit of criminality.

The opposite objection might also be made against our view: we
seem to be creating too many units of prosecution. In any case of risk
creation, the defendant may commit many acts. An act of rape includes
many thrusts; an illegal boxing match includes lots of bobbing and
weaving; speeding may require multiple pressings of the gas pedal.

Admittedly, our view increases the number of units of prosecution.
However, each unit may entail smaller risks and risks of lesser duration.
More important, we are introducing a principled approach to an area
full of confusion. Current law is inconsistent in how it breaks up crimes
that require multiple actions. Consider the facts in *Brown v. Indiana*:[42]

> [T]he record shows that Officer Zigler spotted Brown, identified himself
> as a police officer, and verbally ordered Brown to stop. Notwithstanding
> these demands, Brown continued to run. After Brown entered the barn
> that was on the Richardson property, he started the snowmobile, accel-
> erated it out of the building, and struck Officer Simmons in the right
> leg. During this chase, Deputy Smith grabbed Brown's arm and was
> dragged a short distance before he lost his grip and fell.[43]

According to the Indiana court, this conduct – running from Zigler,
striking Simmons, and dragging Brown – was just one act of resisting

[41] *Cf. id.* at 380 (discussing the "smallest choosable [sic] bits"). The description "move my
finger" may exist on the preconscious level, whereas the actor may consciously avert to
the description "kill John." Nevertheless, the actor does choose to act under the former
description, as we discuss in Chapter 2 in the context of opaque recklessness.
[42] Brown, *supra* note 2.
[43] *Id.* at 965–966 (citations to trial record omitted).

THE LOCUS OF CULPABILITY

arrest. In contrast, an Illinois court found multiple acts of resisting arrest for the following interchange:

> When asked to produce his driver's license and proof of insurance by Officer Harrison, the defendant refused and began to walk away from the vehicle. Officer Harrison then grabbed the defendant by the right arm and instructed him to stop. The defendant responded by placing his hands in his pockets and pulling away from Officer Harrison. After Officer Harrison told the defendant he was being placed under arrest for obstructing an officer, the defendant started to pull away to walk away. At this point, Officer Dietz came over from the other side of the vehicle and grabbed the defendant's left arm. Both officers unsuccessfully attempted to pull the defendant's hands out of his pockets. The defendant began to struggle with the officers, culminating in Officer Harrison spraying the defendant with pepper spray and hitting the defendant twice in the face. A further struggle ensued in which the officers wrestled the defendant to the ground and eventually placed the defendant in handcuffs.[44]

Here, conduct that consisted of simply walking away and refusing to pull one's hands out of one's pockets amounted to as many crimes as there were officers. Both Brown and Wicks engaged in multiple actions in their efforts to prevent law enforcement from arresting them. There is no principled reason for one of these defendants to be guilty of one crime and the other to be guilty of multiple crimes. Rather, each action should be evaluated independently for the risk of harm that it created.

Although some courts have attempted to parse crimes into conduct crimes (which are committed once no matter how many victims) and result crimes (where there are as many crimes as there are victims or injuries), this sort of approach leaves too many questions unanswered. Arson is a result crime because it results in the destruction of property, but it also risks other injuries. So, if an actor sets one building on fire, which fire almost ignites a second building and almost kills two people, there is typically but one arson charged; but if the fire actually spreads to the second building, are there now two arsons? And if the arson kills the people, should we assume that there cannot be additional arson charges because arson only *indirectly* protects people but does not

---

[44] Illinois v. Wicks, 823 N.E.2d 1153, 1157 (Ill. Ct. App. 2005).

actually criminalize setting them on fire? Should it be that a defendant is guilty of two counts of carjacking for stealing *one car* because he takes possession from both the driver and the passenger?[45]

Moreover, even when courts know *what* they are counting, it is unclear *how* they are counting. In *Washington v. Soonalole*, the defendant fondled the victim's breasts while he was driving; then, he stopped and parked the car; then, he resumed fondling her.[46] The statute barred sexual contact with a minor, defining sexual contact as [any] touching. The court thus reasoned that there were two acts of third-degree child molestation.

By this reasoning, however, the prosecutor could have charged each contact as a different instance of child molestation. And it strikes us that this would have been the more principled approach. If we look to how many contacts there were and for how long the unconsented-to touchings lasted, we know everything we need to know about the actor's culpability (and, for that matter, the extent of harm to the victim).

Our approach is superior to current token identity approaches. It gives us an identifiable unit of action from which to assess risks, reasons, and duration. Moreover, this approach allows us to focus on what matters about crime – how it reflects the actor's culpability.

2. *Volume Discounts*

We should consider a second issue that arises when we join the question of multiple acts with an assessment of culpability. Here is the problem: what should we say about the relative culpability of A, who fires one shot at V with the purpose of killing him every day for six days; B, who fires six shots at V for the same purpose at the rate of one shot per hour; and C, who fires all six shots at V for the same purpose in a thirty-second period?

If each shot is a separate and discrete reckless risk imposition, then A, B, and C are equally culpable. And yet, one might think that A is more culpable than B, who is more culpable than C. But how can this be so? Each actor has performed the same risky act with the same mental state the same number of times.

---

[45] California v. Hamilton, 47 Cal. Rptr. 2d 343 (Cal. Ct. App. 1995).
[46] 992 P.2d 541 (Wash. Ct. App. 2000).

Let us first put one solution to the side. We are not subscribers to the theory of volume discounts. It simply cannot and should not be the case that C is less culpable than A simply because C's actions took place over a shorter period of time. C did not perform one action – he performed six.[47] A condensed time frame does not change the number of actions that one performs, just how quickly one performs them.

But perhaps there is a hidden criterion that distinguishes these cases from one another. Although the hypothetical case does not specify this fact, we may believe that A's intention to kill V persisted over the course of six days, whereas C's intention to kill V lasted for only thirty seconds. Thus, the difference between A and C lies in the length of time over which they deliberated whether to kill.

The critical question, then, is whether premeditation aggravates an actor's culpability. There is significant skepticism surrounding premeditation. The first concern is conceptual. Given that, as interpreted, premeditation can occur an instant before or simultaneous with an act, we may doubt that we understand what it means to premeditate.[48] Even when the actor has time between his decision to act and the act itself, how precisely do we quantify premeditation? If A decides to kill V, fires a shot, misses, decides to wait another week, goes about eating, sleeping, and watching television, and returns to fire a shot a week later, for how long did A premeditate?

Moreover, even if we can surmount the conceptual objection, there remains a normative one. Is the person who deliberates over a period of time more culpable than someone who does not? The argument against premeditation is simply this: premeditation is over- and underinclusive. Mercy killings are used to illustrate why it is overinclusive; mercy killers, who may deliberate for significant periods of time, are arguably not nearly as culpable as many killers who do not deliberate at all.[49] The

---

[47] Leo Katz argues that when two actions occur in quick succession, we view them to be one action. *See* Leo Katz, "Before and After: Temporal Anomalies in Legal Doctrine," 151 *U. Pa. L. Rev.* 863, 878, 883 (2003).

[48] *See* Benjamin Cardozo, *What Medicine Can Do For Law* 26–27 (1930; 2005). "I think the distinction is much too vague to be continued in our law. There can be no intent unless there is a choice, yet by the hypothesis, the choice without more is enough to justify the inference that the intent was deliberate and premeditated.... [D]ecisions are to the effect that seconds may be enough. If intent is deliberate and premeditated whenever there is choice, then in truth it is always deliberate and premeditated, since choice is involved in the hypothesis of intent." *Id.*

[49] *See, e.g.,* Samuel Pillsbury, *Judging Evil: Rethinking the Law of Murder and Manslaughter* 105 (1998).

case used to illustrate underinclusiveness is *People v. Anderson*, where
the defendant, in an intoxicated state, stabbed his live-in girlfriend's
ten-year-old daughter more than sixty times. The California Supreme
Court held that Anderson was not guilty of first-degree murder because
the killing was not premeditated.[50]

Although both of these cases seem to indicate the failure of premeditation as a normative benchmark, we believe there is much more to be
said. First, mercy killings are, quite frankly, red herrings. The problem
is that all of the intuitive work is being done by the belief that mercy
killings are perhaps justified or nearly so. Thus, the ban on mercy killings, which punishes those whom we do not believe to be very culpable
or culpable *at all*, does not illustrate the problem with premeditation.

Anderson, on the other hand, is a more challenging counterexample,
but the importance of *Anderson* has yet to be appreciated. The argument
from *Anderson* is that those individuals who are indifferent to others
may be just as culpable, if not more culpable, than premeditated killers.
Thus, to the extent that premeditation is used as a proxy for the actor's
reasons for action,[51] it is being wrongly employed. As we have argued,
culpability depends upon one's reason for acting, and premeditation
itself does not bear on the actor's reasons.

This, however, is not the end of premeditation. That is, even if we
believe that reasons for action matter and that intended harms are not
necessarily more culpable than those that are foreseen, that does not
resolve the question of whether there is any room for premeditation. In
our view, culpability includes the *quality* of the actor's decision making.
We contend that when an actor's decision making is degraded, the actor
is less culpable.[52] Conversely, in some instances, enhanced decision-
making quality can aggravate culpability. We cannot and will not fully
sketch out a new version of premeditation here, but, preliminarily, a
premeditation assessment is best viewed as an assessment of the quality
of the actor's deliberation, given the time period in which the decision
had to be made.

---

[50] 447 P.2d 942 (1968).
[51] *See* Pillsbury, *supra* note 49, at 110–120.
[52] *See* Kimberly Kessler Ferzan, "Holistic Culpability," 28 *Cardozo L. Rev.* 2523, 2534 (2007);
      see generally Stephen J. Morse, "Diminished Rationality, Diminished Responsibility," 1
      Ohio St. J. Crim. L. 289 (2003).

We believe that a focus on the quality of deliberation best accounts for any difference among A, B, and C. If C fires in rapid succession, he may not have deliberated about the shots after the first one to the same extent as A, who fires one bullet a day at V for six days. (However, it is at least possible that C deliberated more than A did.) We believe that quality of deliberation is the only thing that can and should distinguish these actors. The time interval between culpable acts cannot itself change the number (or quality) of the culpable actions.

3. Analyzing Continuous Courses of Conduct

Let us consider one final puzzle. Sometimes an actor imposes one risk for a long period of time. An actor may speed for twenty minutes, or steal a car for twenty days, or fail to rescue for three hours. How many crimes has the actor committed?

Many cases involving a continuous course of conduct involve multiple willed bodily movements. In such instances, we should simply count the willed bodily movements (and the duration of each bodily movement expected by the actor). So, if an actor has pummeled a victim with fists for twenty minutes, the actor has committed a number of culpable acts, each of a very short duration.

However, there are other crimes where one willed bodily movement is followed by an omission. An actor pushes down on the accelerator once and then fails to remove his foot. Or, as in *Myers*, he keeps the machete at his victim's throat. Of course, because we believe that an omission, following an act of risk creation, is itself a locus of culpability, we can have extended periods of culpably doing nothing.

To ask how long and how many continuous acts the actor has performed is already to answer the question. For a continuous act, the actor has performed one act, which is as long as its duration. Or, as Michael Moore says, we know when a continuous act ends by asking when the conduct stopped.[53] Our account thus has no problem counting continuous courses of conduct and no problem accounting for the defendant's culpability, which turns not on the number of actions but on the perceived duration of the risk imposed.

---

[53] Moore, *supra* note 8, at 388.

Duration, it turns out, is a critical factor in allowing us to fully account for the actor's culpability. The element of duration fully accounts for the actor's culpability in ways that simply counting crimes cannot. The number of crimes does not tell us about the perceived degree of risk imposed, the reasons for which the risk is imposed, the quality of the actor's deliberation, and the length of time the actor thought he was imposing the risks. The arsonist's blameworthiness does not depend upon whether the fire he ignited counts as one arson or two – what matters is the degree of risk imposed and the perceived duration of that risk.

By contrast, the criminal law currently creates artificial breaks in continuous courses of conduct. To illustrate, consider *Village of Sugar Grove v. Rich*.[54] The defendant, the owner of J.R.'s Retreat, violated a noise ordinance. On one day, he was cited at 8:39, 9:00, 10:10, and 10:16 p.m. The court held that the defendant could not be punished for violating the same noise ordinance four times because the statute specified each day such violation is committed or permitted constitutes a separate offense.

The ordinance's selection of one day as the unit for determining how many tickets the actor deserves to receive – a decision that will ultimately turn on pragmatics and not morals – will serve only as a rough proxy for the full amount of risk imposed and the actor's culpability for imposing it.[55] By contrast, our approach – which directly takes duration into account – yields the conclusion that the defendant deserves punishment for the exact amount of time that he violated the noise ordinance. He did not commit four crimes; nor did he commit only one merely because all violations occurred during one day. Rather, he committed a continuous offense that lasted as long as the defendant perceived it to last.

With duration as an additional element, we can fully account for the culpability inherent in both risky acts and culpable omissions. Consider the lit-fuse cases. Here, suppose the actor lights the fuse and it is instantly out of his control. His culpability when he lights it is the product of his

---

54   808 N.E.2d 525 (Ill. Ct. App. 2004).
55   *Cf.* Achille C. Varzi and Giuliano Torrengo, "Crimes and Punishments," 34 *Philosophia* 395, 403 (2006) ("In practice, when it comes to temporally extended actions, it is contextual and pragmatic considerations that determine what counts as a relevant "unit" the performance of which deserves to be punished").

reasons (again, discounted by his estimate of the probabilities of their obtaining) and the risks of harms of various types he believes he has imposed (including his assessment of the probability that the fuse will go out before igniting, or be snuffed out by someone else, and so forth). Call the risk of harms R and the resultant level of culpability C.

Now, compare this case with the actor who lights a fuse for the same reasons and who believes in the same risks of harms, except that this actor retains (he believes) the ability for a while to snuff out the fuse. At first, he believes his chance of snuffing it out to be very high – not 100 percent, as he might faint, be hit by a meteorite, and so forth, but close to 100 percent. At this point, he does not yet believe he has imposed R or close to R. His culpability is greater than zero but less than C. As time goes by, and he gets nearer the point in time at which the fuse will be beyond recall, his chances of snuffing it out, though still high, are less than they were when he lit the fuse. (Then, if he were to have a change of heart but slip and fall, he would still have time to recover and snuff out the fuse. But as the point of no return approaches, a slip and fall might prevent snuffing the fuse out were there a change of heart.) Once the actor passes the point of no return, his culpability, like that of the first actor, is C. If, however, he does have a change of heart, or if he is arrested before the point of no return, his culpability will be assessed as would the culpability of someone engaged in a continuous course of conduct: average risk times duration. In no case will this ever exceed C, however, as the average risk with a long-burning fuse will be very low (unlikely the actor will not be able to snuff it out if he wants to), even though the duration is great.

Our approach thus allows us to account for the different perceptions of the risk created, how abandonment can factor into culpability, how actors are culpable for failing to terminate the risks they have created, and how the duration of the risk can affect the actor's ultimate culpability. Thus, we do not just have a theory about how to *count* crimes. Rather, we have a theory about how to *account* (fully) for the actor's blameworthiness.

Actors are culpable for choosing to unleash an unjustified risk of harm to others' legally protected interests. The locus of this culpable act is the actor's volition wherein he wills the movement of his body so as to unleash this risk. Nevertheless, for pragmatic reasons, the willed bodily movement is better suited to serve as the *actus reus* for the criminal law.

Omissions may also be culpable. Although we do not advocate the creation of particular legal duties to act, when such duties exist, an actor may be culpable for refraining from acting. Most possession offenses fall within the omission paradigm. Most clearly, when an individual has imposed a culpable risk but still has the ability to prevent the harm from occurring, the actor is under a legal duty to act.

In this chapter, we have added two additional factors to our culpability assessment arsenal. First, the quality of an actor's deliberations may affect his culpability. Second, the perceived duration of the risk imposed affects the actor's culpability: the longer the perceived risk exists, the more culpable the actor.

With these additional factors in hand, we are able to fully account for the culpability inherent in any unjustified risk creation. Our focus on legally protected interests better accounts for individuating crime types than does the Supreme Court's *Blockburger* test. Our focus on duration provides a more principled way to account for an actor's culpability and overall blameworthiness than any attempt to count how many times the actor committed any particular crime.

PART FOUR

A Proposed Code

VIII

What a Culpability-Based Criminal Code Might Look Like

To us, there is really only one injunction that is relevant to criminal culpability: choose only those acts for which the risks to others' interests – as you estimate those risks – are sufficiently low to be outweighed by the interests, to yourself and others, that you are attempting to advance (discounted by the probability of advancing those interests). In Model Penal Code parlance, we have done away with the special part of the criminal code. We have a general rule that applies to all crimes, not specific rules of conduct.

Our view of culpability is not the end of the matter, however. Even our idealized code has a significant amount of work to do. The criminal law must identify those interests that it will protect. In addition, the criminal law must have a system for adjudicating the actor's culpability, which must determine not just what harms the actor is aware he is risking but also his estimate of the probability of those harms obtaining. Moreover, in adjudicating culpability, the criminal law must balance this estimate against the actor's reasons for acting, which must also be discounted by the actor's estimate that those reasons will obtain. And if the determination of that balance reveals that the actor's action is unjustifiable, the assessment of the actor's culpability is still not complete. For, as we have noted, the criminal law must also assess the quality of the actor's deliberation – a factor that can either mitigate or aggravate the actor's culpability. Finally, the criminal law must determine the duration of the risk imposed.

The first part of this chapter discusses the mechanics of our idealized criminal code. We begin by normatively defending our "unpacking" of crimes. We then survey the types of interests that the law could potentially protect. We then describe how we believe a criminal code could function under our regime.

In the second part of the chapter, we turn to practical considerations and discuss how our ideal criminal code could be implemented, including how it could be modified for application in the real world. We begin by describing the significant problems with the status quo, arguing that our radical departure from current law should be viewed in the context of the currently problematic system. Next, we argue that the basic difficulties with implementing our code are just instantiations of the rules-standards problem. We ultimately defend a standards-based approach, and we note ways in which the law may be able to give guidance without resorting to "proxy crimes." Finally, we defend our view against claims that our criminal code encounters problems of legality and enforceability.

I. An Idealized Culpability-Based Criminal Code

A. LEGALLY PROTECTED INTERESTS

Our criminal code must enumerate those interests that it seeks to protect. This requirement raises a number of questions. The first question is whether, as a normative matter, we should "unpack" criminal wrongs into these building blocks. Although in Chapter 7 we defended such unpacking on conceptual grounds, in the first part of this section we defend this approach on normative grounds. In the second part of this section, we turn to the question of which interests should be protected by the criminal law. Although we cannot defend a theory of criminalization here, we raise some of the critical questions concerning punishing risks of harm to self and others, risks of offense, and risks of harmless wrongs. We also briefly discuss the role of consent.

1. A Normative Defense of Unpacking Crimes

In the previous chapter, we argued that it is conceptually preferable to understand a crime as a volition to move one's body in a way that the agent believes will create a risk (which is unjustifiable) to a legally protected interest. This approach is conceptually superior because it resolves a host of thorny problems ranging from how to treat continuous courses of conduct to how to approach the double jeopardy clause.

Still, one might object that something is missing from a criminal code that does not list *wrongs* – those specific act types that harm specific legally protected interests. We speak of rape, murder, and robbery, not of unjustifiable risks. Is there not something missing from an account of the criminal law that does not mirror our ordinary understanding of wrongful conduct?

In our view, our approach brings precision, clarity, and deeper understanding to the criminal law. One significant problem with an act-type system is that too much hangs on the ability to place any specific act of risk creation within any given act-type category. As we noted in the previous chapter, rape is a clear example of this. Long ago, Susan Estrich bemoaned the disparate treatment between "date rapes" and "real rapes."[1] Her claim was that they are all *rapes*.

We disagree. We do not doubt that date rapes are serious wrongs, and we will assume that the criminal justice system still underpunishes these (and other) serious wrongs. What we question is whether the effort to place the myriad of different unconsented-to acts of sexual intercourse within the rubric of "rape" is a worthwhile effort. Why, for example, should we understand rape, at its core, to be simply about the use of another human being?[2] Should not the criminal law take into account whether the victim found the rape pleasurable (as might

---

[1] *See* Susan Estrich, *Real Rape* 3–4 (1987).
[2] *See* J. Gardner and S. Shute, "The Wrongness of Rape," in *Oxford Essays on Jurisprudence* (J. Horder, ed., 2000).

happen in a case of deception); or whether the victim was sleeping; or whether the victim did not communicate consent but also did not resist; or whether the victim was brutally beaten during the act? Let us be clear – society can accept that all of these acts are criminal. But they present different risks to different legally protected interests. Which interests of those affected are more important? Which acts risk more harm? These are important issues, and they are obscured by the effort to place all of these acts into one criminal act type. We can more readily identify and rank these interests when we look at each one individually. To summarize, one reason to abandon labels of particular types of wrongdoing is because such labels tend to obscure rather than to clarify the underlying normative justifications for punishing these different types of culpable riskings.

A second significant problem with the act-type approach is that the current system will often declare an act criminal and hence punishable without any thought to the interest that is being protected. Although, theoretically, a statute may be subject to a constitutional challenge if it lacks a rational basis, the number of statutes that are currently rationally but remotely linked to actual harms is staggering. Drug offenses, particularly possession offenses, are a classic example of this phenomenon. Although we may be able to articulate the *crime* of drug possession, one will be hard-pressed to articulate its underlying rationale. What precisely are the harms that are risked by an actor possessing one ounce of marijuana?[3] By contrast, our approach equates the crime with its underlying justification by equating crime with culpable acts, and culpable acts with risks imposed for inadequate reasons. Thus, if one cannot articulate an interest excessively put at risk, one cannot articulate a crime.

A third reason to reject act-type categorization is that it creates false distinctions between types of offenses, potentially allowing similarly culpable actors to receive significantly different penalties. Consider murder and manslaughter. Currently, an actor may be guilty of murder on the basis of several different culpability types. He may act

---

[3] *See* Douglas Husak, *Overcriminalization: The Limits of the Criminal Law* 166–167 (2008). Husak calls this unidentified harm, "harm X." *See also* Douglas Husak, *Legalize This! The Case for Decriminalizing Drugs* (2002).

purposefully, knowingly, or recklessly if such recklessness manifests a depraved heart. On the other hand, an actor is guilty of only manslaughter if he kills recklessly or negligently. The distinction, then, between murder and manslaughter is a fine one – a jury decision along a continuum. At some point, a homicide becomes so reckless that the jury thinks it warrants more punishment (murder) than does another, slightly less reckless, homicide (manslaughter). The bottom line is that there is no definitive line between murder and manslaughter – they are different in degree but not in kind. Thus, even though it appears that we have clear conceptual categories of homicide – murder and manslaughter – the reality is somewhat different. Both protect the same interest, and the culpability that supposedly distinguishes them is an arbitrary line (and a different one in different jurisdictions with different juries) on a culpability continuum.

Finally, we should discuss the concern that our approach cannot capture a certain type of wrongdoing, and that is the group of intention-drenched wrongs. One cannot lie without the intention to lie. One cannot torture without the intention to cause pain. These crimes are unraveled by our approach not only because we focus on risks to interests and not act types, but because we deny the significance of intention as its own separate culpable mental state.

We believe that nothing is lost by our approach, however. These offenses can and should be analyzed by their discrete elements. Indeed, one of the paradigmatic examples of an intention-drenched crime is the crime of attempt, a crime we have no problem unraveling.[4]

Moreover, although these crimes entail intention, there is no reason we need to rely on these particular crimes as currently understood. First, as we have argued, conceptually, intention (or purpose) is but a particular species of recklessness so there is no conceptual reason why we cannot speak of recklessness instead of intentions. Even if consciously imposing a high risk that another will be misled is not "lying," it still may be – or may not be, depending upon the actor's reasons – a culpable, reckless act with respect to the interest in not being misled.

---

[4] This is a case where even those theorists who believe that crimes can be understood without mental elements, like Paul Robinson, create an exception. *See* Paul H. Robinson, *Structure and Function in Criminal Law* 133 (1997).

Indeed, recognizing the relationship between recklessness and intention may resolve current confusions. For example, New York courts have struggled with the question of whether a depraved indifference murder conviction is appropriate where an actor shoots his victim at point-blank range but the jury acquits on an intentional murder charge. Current New York cases maintain that depraved indifference is inappropriate because intentional killings cannot be depraved heart killings.[5] But this conclusion is certainly incorrect. A person who shoots at point-blank range with no good reason has surely manifested extreme indifference to human life. Intentional killings are just one (typical) species of such indifference.

Normatively, there is no reason to restrict punishment to instances of risking with the intent to bring about the harm risked. If the actor consciously disregards an unjustifiable risk of harm, her action is culpable even if she does not want that harm to occur. Indeed, given an actor's reasons for acting, her "reckless attempt" may be more culpable than another actor's "intentional attempt."

Or, consider complicity. When Iago taunts Othello, he may not wish for Desdemona to die. Instead, Iago may believe it sufficient to mentally torture Othello. But when Othello kills Desdemona, Iago is to blame for this action. His conduct – lying about Desdemona's infidelity – created an unjustifiable risk that Othello would kill his wife. We see no reason why Iago should escape liability because Desdemona's death was not within the scope of his intention.[6]

Indeed, although ordinary language and lay intuitions may be useful, they cannot be the last word on drafting criminal codes. Even if, as a matter of semantics, an actor cannot "attempt" a reckless homicide because one cannot intentionally commit an unintentional act, we may alternatively label the reckless actor's conduct "endangerment";[7] but, labels aside, the only distinction then between the "attempt" and the "endangerment" is the actor's reason for imposing the risk. We see

---

[5] *See, e.g.,* People v. Payne, 819 N.E.2d 634 (N.Y. 2004); People v. Suarez, 844 N.E.2d 721 (N.Y. 2005).

[6] *See* Larry Alexander and Kimberly D. Kessler, "Mens Rea and Inchoate Crimes," 87 *J. Crim. L. & Criminology* 1138 (1997); Sanford H. Kadish, "Reckless Complicity," 87 *J. Crim. L & Criminology* 369 (1997).

[7] *See generally* R. A. Duff, "Criminalizing Endangerment," 65 *La. L. Rev.* 941, 960–961 (2005).

no reason not to focus on the interest risked and the actor's culpability regarding that risk rather than on the actor's intention.

2. Which Interests?

The starting point for drafting our criminal code is determining which interests the law should protect against culpable risk impositions. Outside of our brief discussion in Chapter 1, we have had nothing to say about which risks the law should protect us from. Some risks are relatively straightforward. The law should protect us from inordinate risks of being killed, maimed, or even punched in the face. Beyond these obvious "harms to others," however, lie a host of thorny questions about what interests the criminal law ought to protect. Although we do not have time to resolve these questions here, we do flag some of these issues.

a. Harm to Others and Beyond: Following Mill and Feinberg, one might catalog the various justifications for criminalization as harm to others, harm to self (paternalism), offense to others, and legal moralism.[8] We discuss criminalization questions within each of these categories.

i. Harm to Others: Although preventing harm to others is the clearest justification for state interference, there are difficult issues even here. First, there are some potential harms that may be difficult to specify. That is, it is easier to criminalize the conduct than to articulate the precise harm. Of course, when one sees a crime like this, one immediately suspects that the crime stands on normatively shaky ground. But this is not always true.

Take public corruption crimes. Under section 1346 of the United States Code, it is a violation of the federal mail and wire fraud statutes to deprive another of your "honest services."[9] This honest services statute certainly should apply to a public official who takes a bribe. But does this apply to criminalize the conduct of the Internal Revenue Service

---

[8] *See generally* John Stuart Mill, *On Liberty* (1859); Joel Feinberg, *Harm to Others* (1984); Joel Feinberg, *Offense to Others* (1985); Joel Feinberg, *Harm to Self* (1986); Joel Feinberg, *Harmless Wrongdoing* (1988).

[9] 18 U.S.C. § 1346 (2000).

employee who improperly reads others' tax returns?[10] Must a state employee's action violate state law to fall within the statute?[11] Although the latter question raises federalism concerns, the underlying issues are the type of duty of "honest services" owed and to whom that duty is owed – two extremely difficult questions to answer.[12] For our criminal code, it will no longer be sufficient to criminalize first and analyze later. Rather, an understanding of the precise interests threatened will be necessary in order to criminalize the conduct in the first instance.

A second difficult category of harms involves fear and other emotional injuries. Although the criminal law prohibits some actions that cause fear, it typically does not prohibit them *because* they cause fear but because that fear is incidental to some other harm. For example, having a gun pointed at you may cause fear, but it causes fear because it risks harm, and it is the risk of harm that the criminal law is actually targeting. Even tort law, which is often far more expansive than the criminal law, is unwilling to recognize all sorts of emotional distress as compensable harms. Although some theorists distinguish between public and private wrongs, we need more than this labeling in order to justify, say, not criminalizing cruelly breaking someone's heart while simultaneously criminalizing the stealing of five dollars. Although there is room to argue that we are entitled to more liberty within self-defining spheres, the leeway to which any individual is entitled is relevant to the actor's justifying reasons, not to whether the victim's interest should be protected in the first instance.

Finally, we do not doubt that there will be particularly contested cases – such as whether fetuses should be protected by the law. Here, we only caution once more that the question of whether an interest is protected is not the question of whether risking harm to that interest may be justified.

---

10 United States v. Czubinski, 106 F.3d 1069 (1st Cir. 1997).
11 *Cf.* United States v. Sawyer, 239 F.3d 31, 42 (1st Cir. 2001) (no need to prove lobbyist's giving of gratuities and gifts to state official violated state law) *with* United States v. Brumley, 116 F.3d 728, 734 (5th Cir. 1997) ("the official must act or fail to act contrary to the requirements of his job under state law").
12 For a recent attempt, *see* Joshua A. Kobrin, Note, "Betraying Honest Services: Theories of Trust and Betrayal Applied to the Mail Fraud Statute and § 1346," 61 *N.Y.U. Ann. Surv. Am. L.* 779 (2006). For an analysis of white collar offenses generally, *see* Stuart Green, *Lying, Cheating, and Stealing: A Moral Theory of White-Collar Crime* (2006).

ii. Paternalism: A second question is whether our code should protect individuals from themselves.[13] Indeed, one might wonder how one shows insufficient concern for others when the only person the actor seeks to harm is himself. We find this objection to be significant.

Moreover, even if we could say that someone can be culpable for risking harm to herself, there is the question of whether the law should intervene to prevent such harms. Many theorists draw a distinction between hard and soft paternalism and would permit the law to step in when failures of information or rationality prevent an agent from choosing according to her own theory of the good. However, it may be doubted whether the distinction between hard and soft paternalism can be drawn. Let us explain.

One tenet of liberalism is that normal adults should not be prevented from acting as they choose merely because would-be preventers believe those choices will be harmful to the choosers. Yet liberals make an exception for cases labeled "soft" paternalism. Thus, if Joy does not realize that the bridge of San Luis Rey is dangerously weak, and if she has no desire to end her life, it is supposedly permissible to restrain her from crossing the bridge. Although Joy believes she wishes to cross the bridge at the time her choice is interfered with, her false belief about the bridge's condition and her desire to live – a desire that trumps any desire she might have to cross this bridge at this time – justify the interference with her choice. Without undergoing any change in her stable values and commitments, Joy can be expected to welcome others' interference with her choice to cross the bridge once she is made aware of the bridge's condition.

As we said, the kind of paternalism exemplified in preventing Joy from crossing the bridge of San Luis Rey is termed "soft paternalism." The soft paternalist argues that choices such as Joy's can be interfered with on grounds of *her* good only when she lacks information that, given her values, *she* would deem material to those choices, or when she is too young or too defective in rationality to process that information correctly. The soft paternalist contrasts her position with that of the hard paternalist, who believes in overriding choices whenever they

[13] This section draws from Larry Alexander, "Scalar Properties, Binary Judgments," 25 *J. Applied Phil.* 85 (2008).

are contrary to the chooser's good and irrespective of why those choices were made. Most liberals endorse the position of the soft paternalist but for obvious reasons reject that of the hard paternalist.

The relationship between hard and soft paternalism is, however, a matter of degree rather than a difference in kind. People are more or less rational and more or less informed. They are on a smooth continuum in these respects, and there is no obvious threshold point marking a morally relevant difference.[14]

Consider Joy2, who wants to cross the bridge. The defect that makes the bridge unsafe not only is not apparent to her but requires years of study of structural engineering to discern. Perhaps in twenty years Joy will finally come to understand that the bridge really was unsafe. Perhaps she will never come to understand it and thus never thank – but always resent – those who in fact prevented her from falling to her death. Would the difficulty in getting Joy2 to understand the bridge's condition cast doubt on the propriety of stopping her from crossing the bridge?

Or consider Joy3, who understands that crossing the bridge is unsafe but is in a suicidal frame of mind. She believes, erroneously, that her life is no longer worth living. If she is prevented, she may in several years come to see that she was wrong and be grateful to those who prevented her death. Or she may never come to see that she was wrong – though she was – perhaps because her capacity for understanding her good is impaired. Would these facts about Joy3 impugn the interference with her choice?

These examples are sufficient, we believe, to illustrate the problem of identifying a threshold point that distinguishes hard from soft paternalism. The hard paternalist can always maintain that if an agent is choosing contrary to her own good, she must have either an informational or a rationality deficit. And those deficits can be different only in degree and not in kind from the deficits that the soft paternalist relies on.[15]

---

[14] This is not the only area of law with such problems. *See generally id.* For the view that the law must adopt sharp distinctions, *see* Leo Katz, "Why the Law Is Either/Or" (working paper, on file with authors).

[15] The line-drawing problems in justifying paternalistic interferences with acts have a direct parallel in the free speech area, where governments are frequently motivated to suppress speech because it will mislead, factually or evaluatively, some of the audience to its or to others' detriment.

iii. Legal Moralism: Among the potential justifications for criminalization is legal moralism.[16] Here, the critical question is whether a legislator should criminalize actions that are harmless but morally wrong – so-called harmless wrongdoings.[17]

Michael Moore is a contemporary defender of legal moralism. Moore argues that the point of criminal law is to see that wrongdoing (and culpable attempts and risks of wrongdoing) is punished.[18] Moore does not believe that the criminal law should be limited to acts that cause or risk harm or offense. For Moore, if an act is morally wrong, there is always a reason to prosecute and punish it through the criminal law.

What is perhaps most striking about Moore's brand of legal moralism is that to make it palatable, it must come with a variety of constraints. Indeed, Moore's views would probably lead him to reach conclusions largely in line with those who would restrict the legitimate reach of the criminal law to acts that risk harm to others. For

On the scalar nature of autonomy, *see, e.g.*, Lawrence Haworth, *Autonomy: An Essay in Philosophical Psychology and Ethics* (1986). For an optimistic view of our ability to non-arbitrarily set thresholds for autonomous action on smooth continua, but one that offers no theory for doing so, *see* Tom L. Beauchamp, "Who Deserves Autonomy, and Whose Autonomy Deserves Respect?" in *Personal Autonomy: New Essays in Personal Autonomy and Its Role in Contemporary Moral Philosophy* 310–329, 316–317 (J. S. Taylor, ed., 2004).

The first of these three conditions of autonomy – intentionality – is not a matter of degree: acts are either intentional or nonintentional. However, acts can satisfy both the conditions of understanding and absence of controlling influences to a greater or lesser extent. For example, threats can be more or less severe, and understanding more or less complete. Actions are autonomous by degrees, as a function of satisfying these conditions to different degrees. For both conditions, a continuum runs from fully present to wholly absent. For example, children exhibit different degrees of understanding at various ages, as well as different capacities of independence and resistance to influence attempts. This claim that actions are autonomous by degrees is an inescapable consequence of a commitment to the view that at least one of the conditions that define autonomy is satisfied by degrees.

For an action to be classified as either autonomous or nonautonomous, cutoff points on these continua are required. To fix these points, only a *substantial* satisfaction of the conditions of autonomy is needed, not a full or categorical satisfaction of the conditions. The line between what is substantial and what is insubstantial may seem arbitrary, but thresholds marking substantially autonomous decisions can be carefully fixed in light of specific objectives of decision making, such as deciding about surgery, buying a house, choosing a university to attend, making a contribution to charity, driving a car, or hiring a new employee.

[16] For the leading legal moralist defense, *see* Michael S. Moore, *Placing Blame: A General Theory of Criminal Law* ch. 16 (1997).

[17] This section draws from Larry Alexander, "The Philosophy of Criminal Law," in *The Oxford Handbook of Jurisprudence and Legal Philosophy* (Jules Coleman and Scott Shapiro, eds., 2002).

[18] Moore, *supra* note 16, at 70.

Moore holds that although the immorality of conduct is always a reason for its prescription, the legitimate reach of the criminal law is tempered by three countervailing moral concerns. First, Moore refuses to equate what is immoral with what a legislative majority, or a majority of the populace, believes to be immoral. A criminal statute is legitimate for Moore only if the conduct it forbids is truly immoral; and whether conduct is truly immoral is a matter of moral reality, not moral belief.[19]

Second, Moore believes that the costs of criminalizing conduct – costs in terms of resources, erroneous convictions, loss of privacy, corruption, and disrespect for law – are reasons that weigh against criminalization and that in many cases dictate that immorality go unpunished.[20] Additionally, there is what Moore deems the "presumption of liberty," which treats the criminal law's reduction of autonomy and acting from virtue as a moral bad that weighs against criminalization.[21]

Third, Moore endorses a right to liberty, a right that immunizes from punishment many types of immoral conduct.[22] The right to liberty strongly protects "self-defining choices," including choices that are immoral and otherwise legitimately subject to criminal proscription and punishment. In other words, Moore endorses a right to do wrong.[23]

One significant question for a legal moralist is why *the state*, as opposed to any other actor, should punish the moral wrong.[24] For instance, Doug Husak argues that a state must have a substantial state interest that it seeks to advance.[25] To Husak, the act of criminalization is itself a consequentialist – forward-looking – enterprise.[26]

We, on the other hand, believe that an actor's negative moral desert *is* a valid reason for state punishment. That desert is, in turn, a function of the actor's culpability. The question we would pose to the legal moralist would be whether an actor who imposes no risk of harm or

---

[19] *Id.* at 662–663.
[20] *Id.* at 103.
[21] *Id.* at 76–78, 747–748.
[22] *Id.* at 763–777.
[23] *Id.* at 765–767.
[24] *See* Husak, *Overcriminalization, supra* note 3, at 265.
[25] *Id.*
[26] *Id.*

offense is truly *culpable* merely because his act violates a nonharm-, nonoffense-based moral norm – assuming there are such moral norms.

iv. Offense to Others: One final question is whether the criminal law should protect us not only from harm but also from offense.[27] The case for criminalizing at least some offensive conduct is vividly set forth by Joel Feinberg when he takes his readers on "a ride on the bus."[28] In just over three pages, Feinberg describes thirty-one cases of conduct that might – and in most cases surely would – cause offense. His examples include a loud boom box, the public eating of vomit and feces, public acts of fellatio and cunnilingus (including with an animal), and a variety of religious, racial, and gender insults. We suspect that hardly anyone will fail to be convinced that at least some of these acts are justifiably punishable.

What is more difficult for liberals (such as us) is to justify punishment for these offenses. In our view, most of the conduct that offends us does so because it flouts moral norms. People are offended by public nudity because it violates a norm about how one should appear in public. People are offended by the desecration of a corpse because it violates a norm about how to treat the dead. Because it is the underlying immorality that justifies criminalizing offensive conduct, a liberal is required to give an account of liberalism that is consistent with punishing some truly sordid and degrading (but not harmful) conduct.

b. The Role of Consent: A final criminalization question that we cannot fully address here is the role of consent. For some crimes, it is indisputable that the absence of consent is required for there to be a legally protected interest. That is, the criminal law has no reason to protect individuals from acts of sexual intercourse; it has reason to protect individuals only from unconsented-to acts of sexual intercourse.

On the other hand, some theorists argue that other actions are prima facie wrongful and that consent serves only as an affirmative defense.[29] That is, one might think that a boxing match, where each boxer suffers

[27] For further discussion of the issues set forth in this section, *see* Larry Alexander, "Harm, Offense and Morality," 7 *Canad. J. L. & Jurisp.* 199 (1994).
[28] *See* Feinberg, *Offense to Others, supra* note 8, at 10–22.
[29] *See* Vera Bergelson, "The Right To Be Hurt: Testing the Boundaries of Consent," 75 *Geo. Wash. L. Rev.* 165 (2007); *see also* George P. Fletcher, *Rethinking Criminal Law* § 9.2.2

(consented-to) harm, differs in some significant conceptual way from consensual sexual intercourse (where there is no harm or injury at all). Yet, as we note in Chapter 4, our approach eviscerates the distinction between a prima facie norm violation and an affirmative defense. To us, this distinction is a bit of form over substance. If the victim has consented to the harm or the act risking the harm, the actor has not risked harming a legally protected interest. Once the victim consents, there is no interest to protect; the victim has in effect conveyed his right to legal protection from the actor, at least for some duration. At the end of the day, the actor's culpability – with which the criminal law should be concerned – does not hinge upon whether we understand the criminal "act" as entailing the lack of consent.

Now, one might ask whether there are any limits on the types of acts to which one may consent. Can one give legally effective consent to sadomasochistic conduct, maiming, torture, killing, being eaten? One argument for prohibiting some of this conduct is that it is degrading to the actor and his "victim," and this degradation is socially contagious and will therefore ultimately harm others. (Such a "harm to others" rationale may be thought to come close to effacing any otherwise clear line between harm to others and legal moralism.) Another argument is premised straightforwardly on paternalism.[30] On the other hand, it seems that this sort of behavior is difficult to distinguish from the behavior we criminalize because it is offensive. Is there really any difference between the reasons why we criminalize consensual homosexual sodomy performed in public and consensual heterosexual sadomasochism behind closed doors? Both behaviors violate societal norms and thereby upset us. Naturally, where to draw the line between criminal and noncriminal offense will be exceedingly difficult. Moreover, if the true reason that we criminalize some consensual behaviors is because they cause offense, then the punishment should be proportionate to that offense and not to the nonexistent harm the "victim" suffers.

Our code needs a definition of consent, and it should, of course, be formulated so as to adjudicate when consent is rational and voluntary.

(1978) (discussing whether consent to sexual intercourse functions as an element of the definition or a justification for the conduct).

[30] *See* Bergelson, *supra* note 29.

Two of us have offered somewhat competing conceptions of such a formulation.[31] We do not attempt to reconcile them here.

B. CALCULATING CULPABILITY

1. Some Preliminaries

The first task in drafting a criminal code is to identify the types of harms that the criminal law wishes to avert through its prohibitions and to construct a hierarchy (or hierarchy range) of these interests. Although initially one might suspect that there will be widespread disagreement over the ordinal rankings, empirical studies do not bear this out. Rather, in Paul Robinson and Robert Kurzban's recent empirical study, they found widespread agreement as to the rank order of twenty-four short scenarios that encompassed 94.9 percent of the crimes committed in the United States.[32] In contrast, there was less agreement (although still some considerable concordance) regarding the "offenses of drunk driving, prostitution, marijuana purchase, purchase of alcohol for use by teenagers, bestiality, late-term abortion, cocaine purchase, date rape, third felony offense (jewelry grab), large-scale cocaine selling, and very large-scale cocaine importation and distribution."[33] We note that in many of these latter, more controversial, cases, the difficulty arises precisely because the offense is not tied directly to, and clearly articulated as threatening, an interest worthy of legal protection.

Our code also requires a decision regarding how many categories the code should contain. Harms, reasons, capacity – all of these can be placed on continua from more to less serious, more evil to less evil to praiseworthy, greater to lesser – with the result that the culpability level

---

[31] Larry Alexander, "The Moral Magic of Consent (II)," 2 *Legal Theory* 165 (1996); Kimberly Kessler Ferzan, "Clarifying Consent: Peter Westen's *The Logic of Consent*," 25 *Law & Phil.* 193 (2006).

[32] Paul H. Robinson and Robert Kurzban, "Concordance and Conflict in Intuitions of Justice," 91 *Minn. L. Rev.* 1829 (2007). "The scenarios included such offenses as theft by taking, theft by fraud, property destruction, assault, burglary, robbery, kidnapping, rape, negligent homicide, manslaughter, murder, and torture, in a variety of situations, including self-defense, provocation, duress, mistake and mental illness."

[33] *Id.* at 45.

that they determine will also be on a continuum. And even if, from a God's-eye perspective, they could be perfectly placed on their continua, any criminal code will have to yield to epistemic considerations. Although we deal with most of the real world practicalities later in this chapter, we must address here the question of how individualized culpability should be.

For instance, in looking at legally protected interests, we could have a scalar system that allows juries to distinguish between even two ever-so-slightly different types of serious mayhem, or we could group all types of mayhem into one category of "risking substantial harm."[34] The arguments for more and fewer categories are well known. If we have fewer categories, we will make fewer mistakes in assigning conduct to a category;[35] but if we have more categories, we will make more mistakes, but the consequences of each mistake will be smaller.

Several different factors determine overall culpability, but for each factor we make only a handful of distinctions here. We are not opposed to the addition of more distinctions or to allowing juries to make finer gradations than the distinctions we make. We also provide for a sentencing "safety valve" determination by the judge.

2. A First Attempt

Our criminal code is quite complex and requires a calculation based upon a series of decisions by the jury. There seems to be something cold and impartial about this calculation, and we do not mean the kind of impartiality with which we want juries to act. Rather, there seems to be something amiss with reducing crime to numbers.

For this reason, we advocate a two-part system. The jury will first be asked to render a general verdict that the defendant was culpable. (Even

---

34 As one of us has argued, "Suppose a defendant charged with aggravated battery or mayhem permanently disfigured his victim by inflicting a facial wound with a knife with the intent to cause a permanently disfiguring injury. The wound might require an extremely broad range of number of stitches to close. The lengthier the wound, the more disfigurement will result. Should a punishment be inflicted proportionate to wound length or number of stitches? . . . I suggest that a principled, consistently applicable fine-grained retributive response in such cases would be impossible. We lack the moral and epistemic resources to use more than a few rough categories to individuate." Stephen J. Morse, "Equality and Individuation in Punishment," *Law & Phil* (forthcoming).

35 *Id.*

this determination requires a series of instructions, a sample of which we have set forth in the Appendix.) Only after this threshold standard is satisfied would a jury be asked to make the fine-grained calculations set forth here. Moreover, if the jury, after calculating, determined that the actor was not culpable, the actor would then be acquitted. A guilty verdict would thus require both an abstract moral decision and a more nuanced accounting of the actor's culpability.

In making this second determination, we need a more complex code. The primary function of this latter part of our code, with all the intricacies we now explore, is to guide a jury's determination regarding the amount of punishment the actor deserves.

A useful starting point for developing our framework is the United States Sentencing Guidelines Manual (USSG). Here is a brief summary of how the USSG works. The actor's sentence is determined by a matrix – on one axis is the actor's offense level and on the other axis is the actor's criminal history. The point at which the actor's offense level and criminal history intersect locates the sentencing range.

The calculation begins with the offense level. For any given federal offense, the USSG provides a base offense level. For instance, for attempted murder, the base offense level is 33 if the object of the offense would have constituted first-degree murder, and otherwise, it is 27.[36] From here, the USSG may provide for specific offense characteristics to increase the offense level. Under the attempted murder provision, if the victim sustains permanent or life-threatening injury, the offense level is increased by four; if the victim sustains serious bodily injury, the level is increased by two; and if the injury lies between the two types, there is a three-level increase.[37] If the actor was paid to commit the offense, there is a four-level increase.[38]

More additions and subtractions may be made. For instance, if the actor was the organizer of the criminal activity, his offense level may be increased by four.[39] If the actor accepted responsibility for his offense, he may be entitled to a two- or three-level decrease.[40] The USSG then

---

[36] *See* U.S. Sentencing Guidelines Manual § 2A2.1 (2005).
[37] *Id.*
[38] *Id.*
[39] *Id.* at § 3B1.1.
[40] *Id.* at §3E1.1.

has a series of provisions that determine the actor's criminal history level, and his punishment may be increased based upon the number and type of prior convictions.[41]

We use the USSG only as a starting point. We recognize that some of the criminal acts it includes may impose risks of several different harms that need to be separately articulated.[42] For instance, the crime of arson is both a crime of property damage – the severity of which turns on the value of the property – and a crime that also often risks serious bodily injury or death to other people. "Relevant factors" under the USSG may also need to be translated into facts that we believe are material in order to be incorporated into our code. For instance, the USSG often provide for an increase for the use of certain dangerous weapons. In our view, however, the particular weapon used is irrelevant except to the extent that it increases the risk or increases the risk's duration.

Our code also needs illustrations and definitions. Although we later turn to how a definition or commentary section will often be a better guide for the judge and the jury than the alternative of a proxy crime, here we simply note that we recognize that terms that we employ such as "serious" and "less serious" are seriously in need of more precise definition.

We are also well aware of the multitude of problems with the USSG. For instance, the USSG allows a variety of (sometimes competing) factors to determine the offender's ultimate sentence. It also allows factors that we would consider irrelevant – for example, the amount of harm actually caused – to determine the offender's sentence.

a. Valuing Legally Protected Interests: The jury will have to determine which harms the actor's conduct risked. The criminal code should pre-determine the relative value of these legally protected interests. That is, we do not believe that each individual jury should determine the value of an individual life (although it will do so implicitly by determining whether the actor acted culpably in risking such a life). Rather, questions

---

[41] *Id.* at ch. 4.

[42] This is no easy task. For an attempt to peel away the layers of different property offenses, *see* A. P. Simester and G. R . Sullivan, "On the Nature and Rationale of Property Offenses," in *Defining Crimes: Essays on the Special Part of the Criminal Law* (R. A. Duff and Stuart Green, eds., 2005).

about how serious unconsented-to intercourse is, or the killing of a fetus, or littering on a public highway, are all decisions that should be made ex ante.

Applying the USSG model to our theory of culpability, we might start with base offense levels like those set forth by the USSG:

Death	43
Unlawful restraint, autonomy deprivation	32
Unconsented-to sexual intercourse	30
Harm to government functions (currently bribery and perjury)	14
Serious bodily injury	14
Minor bodily injury	4

Interestingly, threats to property can become quite serious under the USSG – surpassing even rape – when the amount of the theft is very substantial. That is, while theft's base offense level is only a six, the loss table provides:

$5,000 or less	No increase
More than $5,000	Add 2
More than $10,000	Add 4
....	
More than $100,000,000	Add 26
More than $200,000,000	Add 28
More than $400,000,000	Add 30

We should note that in our view, these levels are better understood as negative numbers (corresponding to negative desert) – the greater the harm, the more negative the number should be.

These numbers are for illustrative purposes only. We recognize that even the numeric rankings provided by the USSG are not the product of any sort of reliable methodology or analysis.[43] Although our code would

---

[43] *See* "Dissenting View of Commissioner Paul H. Robinson to the Promulgation of Sentencing Guidelines by the United States Sentencing Commission," 52 Fed. Reg. 18121–18132 (1987).

require a normative theory for the relative weights of various legally protected interests, the USSG provides a useful illustration of how our code would work.

b. *Discounting the Harms:* After a jury determines which legally protected interests the actor believed himself to be risking, the jury will need to discount these interests by the actor's belief as to the magnitudes of the various risks he was imposing. These magnitudes might range from virtual certainty (95 percent or above), to high risk (95–60 percent), to risk (40–60 percent), to low risk (20–40 percent), to very low risk (5–20 percent), to virtually no risk (less than 5 percent). Once again, we must ask how many categories there should be. Should the jury discount all "low risks" by 30 percent, the midpoint of the range, or should it attempt to estimate the exact probability?

Here, some empirical work would be useful. We need to know the extent to which people actually think in numeric probabilities. We (from our arm-chair perspective) think it rather unlikely. Thus, we would tend to err on the side of using set discounts for each level of certainty: if "virtually certain," discount by 5 percent; if "high risk," discount by 25 percent; if "risk," discount by 50 percent; if "low risk," discount by 75 percent; if "virtually no risk," discount by 95 percent.

Let us work through this calculation with a case of arson. The jury might find that the actor set fire to a building, believing it virtually certain the building would burn down, and believing there to be some risk of death. Calculating the actor's culpability would require taking a base level for risking harm to property, say −15, and discounting it 5 percent to arrive at a culpability level of −14.25.

The risk of death to others might be a bit trickier. Any given actor may aggregate or disaggregate the risk across multiple persons. An actor might believe that his act imposes a high risk on one (particular) person. On the other hand, he may believe that his action imposes a less significant risk but to more than one person. So, for example, our arsonist may believe that his incendiary device will certainly work and that therefore he will certainly kill the one person inside. Or our arsonist may believe that there is only a 50 percent chance that his incendiary device will work but also believe that if it does work he will certainly kill the *two* people inside. As a matter of mathematics, the risk of net one death is the same in both cases. Moreover, as a matter of culpability, we likewise believe that these cases are morally the same. In either arson example, then, whether the actor believes one death is virtually certain or two deaths are each risked 50 percent, we would take the base level for death (–43), and discount it by 5 percent (the discount for belief to a virtual certainty that the harm would occur), with a resulting total of –40.85.

c. Duration: We must next take into account the duration of the risk *as the actor perceived it.* Our code will need to break duration into workable increments. Our recommendation is that the increment be rather small – two minutes – but if one considers how many voluntary acts one can commit in two minutes, two minutes seems quite generous to defendants. We propose that for every additional two minutes, the offense level be multiplied by the number of two-minute increments for which the risk continued. Thus, if an episode of reckless driving or battery is twenty minutes long, its base culpability level will be multiplied by a factor of ten.

Here, however, we will need a provision to avoid overpunishing someone who is imposing multiple risks, all of which are accomplished within two minutes. This approach does create a "volume discount" for someone who fires at his victim five times within a two-minute period. Unfortunately, in the real world of rough categories, this result may be unavoidable. (On the other hand, one who fires more often – say, with an automatic weapon – may believe the risk he is imposing *is* higher than one who fires once.)

To illustrate, assume that Alex commits rape by using (extraordinarily and unimaginable) long thrusts, each of which takes two minutes. He commits 3 willed bodily movements in a six-minute rape. On the other hand, Bob's six-minute rape includes 200 thrusts, each of which occurs for less than two seconds. Then, although Alex and Bob both committed rape, and both did so for six minutes, Alex's willed bodily movements will count only for 3 (with no multiplier because each thrust took no more than two minutes), whereas Bob's same risk imposition will be multiplied by 200 because each bodily movement is calculated separately. Thus, we will need some sort of grouping mechanism, so that if the actor imposes multiple risks for unjustifiable reasons, through several separate willed bodily movements, these risk impositions can be grouped together to count as only one risk imposition if they all "occur within" the two-minute interval.[44] In other words, although our approach may be a bit underinclusive in allowing for some volume discounts, it will not, at the very least, be overinclusive in grossly overestimating the actor's culpability.

Now back to the arson example. For our purposes, we will assume that the risks to life and property were of equivalent duration and that the risk lasted for twenty minutes. Multiplying the discounted risk of each by nine, and then adding them yields a total of −551.

d. *Quality of Contemplation:* Another factor to be considered is the quality of the actor's deliberation. As we argued earlier, an actor with diminished rationality is less culpable than an otherwise equivalent actor with normal ability. And an actor who plans his culpable actions long and well may be more culpable than the average actor.

There are different methods for accounting for this aggravating or mitigating factor. Once again, we might select some gross categories: substantial impairment (reduce by 75 percent); moderate impairment (reduce by 25 percent); no impairment (no change); better than average deliberation (increase by 25 percent); and excellent deliberation (increase by 50 percent). Of course, in our view, the underlying morality is a continuum; however, blunter categories may be practically necessary.

Unlike the USSG, which allows for only slight reductions for calculations such as "more than minimal planning," we give this qualitative component a substantial role in aggravating or mitigating the actor's culpability. If the choice made by the actor is the critical component of the actor's manifestation of insufficient concern, then we must look at the quality of the actor's decision making. To be sure, sometimes a rash decision will reflect indifference – but this indifference will be fully accounted for by weighing the risks and reasons. We believe, though, that if we hold risks and reasons constant, an actor who has more time to reflect and still chooses to risk harming another manifests insufficient concern to a greater extent than someone who acts without that opportunity. On the other hand, someone whose rationality is impaired – for

[44] *Cf.* U.S. Sentencing Guidelines Manual § 3D1.2 (groups of closely related counts). Unlike the USSG, we are not discounting crimes because different criminal acts are "closely related"; our grouping is simply temporal and thus requires no normative or conceptual judgments.

whatever reason – is not making a choice that reveals the same degree of indifference.

Taking into account this last factor, all of these calculations would yield an "offense level" or, more aptly, a "risk level." This level takes into account the risks the actor perceived himself to be creating, his estimate of their probabilities, his degree of contemplation, and the duration that he believed each risk would last. This would yield a series of numbers on one axis of our matrix. If we assume that our arsonist engaged in no more than typical thought, his risk level would remain –495.9.

e. Weighing the Reasons: The other axis of our matrix will be based upon the actor's reasons for action. For instance, the jury should consider whether the actor's reasons were evil, substantially enhancing the actor's culpability; antisocial, enhancing the actor's culpability; trivial, leaving the actor's culpability unaffected; decent, reducing the culpability substantially, but insufficient to justify the act; or weighty enough to justify or require the act socially (justification) or personally (excuse).

Here, too, these reasons will have to be spelled out more elaborately. We are not able here to list all of the reasons that would fall into each category. We leave that for future theorists. However, as one illustration, consider the suggestion by Samuel Pillsbury that premeditation be replaced by aggravated murder where the motives to kill are particularly egregious. Listing these motives from, what is in his view, least to most controversial, Pillsbury enumerates killings (1) for profit, (2) to further a criminal endeavor, (3) to affect public policy or legal processes, (4) out of group animus, and (5) to assert cruel power over another.[45] We do not evaluate Pillsbury's enterprise here. We believe it is sufficient to show that thoughtful theorists (and hopefully thoughtful legislators) will be able to further articulate the types of reasons that fall within each category.

f. Determining the Sentence: Finally, the actor's sentencing range would be set forth in the matrix. One axis would specify the "risk level," and the other axis would specify the reasons level. The points at which a risk

---

[45] Samuel H. Pillsbury, *Judging Evil: Rethinking the Law of Murder and Manslaughter* 113–117 (1998).

level meets a reasons level would contain a sentencing range. For many matches, the matrix would provide for no liability because the reasons would outweigh the risks. There would also be a gray area (providing for limited incarceration, if any) in which a jury could determine whether the actor's behavior represented a *gross* deviation from that of a reasonable person and thus merited punishment.

A judge would ultimately impose a sentence within the range the matrix provides. Here, we think it would be appropriate to allow the judge to also consider whether there are any desert criteria (the factors discussed previously) that were not adequately taken into account in the jury's calculation. Although a judge would be permitted only to depart downward,[46] she could do so whenever she believed that the metrics provided failed adequately to account for the actor's culpability. (Such decisions would then be subject to an abuse of discretion review.) Our code would also allow a judge to decrease the sentence based upon appropriate nondesert considerations, such as cooperation with the government. (The extent to which our code will have to deal with such practicalities of the real world is something we address later in the chapter.)

g. Two Complications: First, does the culpability of one whose purpose is to cause harm vary with the perceived risk? We raised this issue in Chapter 2 in our discussion of how the *mens rea* of "purpose" could be subsumed by recklessness. One objection to our position was that no matter how small the perceived risk of harm, the actor who imposes that risk for the purpose of causing the harm risked is always more culpable than the actor who consciously imposes a much greater risk of the same harm but who does so for some reason other than to produce that harm. We rejected that position. We believe that the culpability of the second actor can equal or exceed that of the first. If we are wrong, however, then, if the actor imposes a risk in order to bring about the harm risked, his culpability will be equivalent to that of one who believes to a certainty that he will bring about the harm and whose purpose is to do so – no matter what risk of harm he actually believes he is imposing.

---

[46] The structure of our code combined with current Supreme Court precedent would prevent a judge from constitutionally departing upward. *See* Apprendi v. New Jersey, 530 U.S. 466 (2000); Blakely v. Washington, 542 U.S. 296 (2004); United States v. Booker, 543 U.S. 220 (2005).

Second, how should the culpability of one who violates a deonto-logical constraint be determined? A more serious problem, and one to which we also alluded in Chapter 2, is calculating the culpability of one who imposes a risk that is consequentially justifiable but that violates a deontological constraint. We said, for example, that in Trolley, one who switches the trolley to save five but who will kill one acts justifiably; however, one who pushes someone into the trolley's path to save five does not do so because, in saving net four lives, he violates a deontologi-cal constraint against using people as means.

But just how culpable is this second actor? He acts for a noble end (saving lives). He is surely less culpable than an actor who pushes some-one into the path of the trolley out of hatred or avarice and unaware that he is saving five lives.

There are two fairly well-known problems associated with deontolog-ical constraints. One is the so-called paradox of deontological rights: one cannot violate deontological constraints even to minimize the number of violations of those constraints.[47] The other is the problem of "thresh-old deontology," a problem faced by anyone who believes that deonto-logical constraints give way if the consequences of abiding by them are bad enough (or the consequences of violating them are good enough).[48]

The problem of culpability that we are pointing to here is a third distinct problem, though it has a structure much like the problem of threshold deontology. If the culpability of a violator of deontological constraints declines as the expected gains from the violation increase, then the problem is to identify and explain the threshold at which he ceases to be culpable and starts being admirable. If the culpability of the violation is invariant, on the other hand, then the culpability of one who pinches another (without consent) to save a million lives is identical to that of one who pinches another just for the heck of it – a quite coun-terintuitive result. We offer no solution to this puzzle for those, like us, who believe in deontological constraints. Clearly, however, it is a puzzle that must be resolved in a retributive system.

---

[47] This paradox is discussed in Larry Alexander and Michael S. Moore, "Deontological Ethics," *Stan. Encyc. Phil.* (November 21, 2007), available at http://plato.stanford.edu/entries/ethics-deontological/.

[48] For a discussion of the theoretical problems faced by threshold deontology, *see* Larry Alexander, "Deontology at the Threshold," 37 *San Diego L. Rev.* 893 (2000).

II. From an Idealized Code to a Practical One: Implementing Our Theory in "the Real World"

No doubt, our idealized code will seem bizarre to many people. Gone are references to rape, murder, and intention. In their place are risk impositions and legally protected interests. One might object that although our "Golden Rule culpability formulation" works in theory, it can never work practically.

This section looks at how one might implement our idealized code in the current legal system. Before turning to the practicalities of implementing our code – a process that will not be without its difficulties – we discuss the current state of the criminal law. We argue that the status quo is far from acceptable, and it should not be entitled to deference simply because it is the status quo. We also argue that our current criminal codes, although they appear to be rule based, ultimately rely on standards. Thus, it is no argument in favor of the status quo and against our code that ours is standards based.

After surveying the current state of criminal law, we turn to the question of whether a rule- or standards-based system is preferable. Here, we discuss the value of having rules, and how values that law is meant to serve are better served by rules than by standards. However, we then discuss a significant problem with rules – the existence of an ineliminable gap between the reasons for promulgating a rule and the reasons that a citizen has to obey it. For a retributivist, this problem is particularly worrisome because any actor who falls within this gap is an innocent (nonculpable) actor who does not deserve punishment – even if he has violated the rule.

Because this gap exists and cannot be eliminated, we argue that in almost all cases, the criminal law should opt for standards. However, we note that in some cases, the pressure for rules may be overwhelming. We thus discuss the form in which these rules should be enacted and how violations should be punished.

We then turn to a range of other considerations. We argue that our standards-based system is consistent with the principle of legality. We address enforcement concerns, particularly as related to plea bargaining and to our simultaneously wide and narrow conception of a criminal act. And we conclude with a brief discussion of procedural, evidentiary, plea-bargaining, and sentencing considerations.

A. WHAT WE ARE SEEKING TO REPLACE

Our position radically recasts the criminal law landscape. It challenges the status quo. What burden of persuasion do we have when we seek to replace the current system?

The weight to be accorded to the current system depends on how well the current system works. Do we currently punish the guilty and acquit the innocent? Are our statutes narrowly tailored to prohibit only conduct that is culpable? Do our statutes speak with one voice regarding the justification for criminal punishment? Do they give sufficient notice regarding what conduct is prohibited?

Anyone even somewhat familiar with our criminal justice system will quickly realize that the answer to these questions is no. Our criminal law system is defective, in several different respects. We discuss three significant problems here: overcriminalization, conflicting codes, and vagueness.

1. Three Significant Problems with the Current State of Criminal Law

a. Overcriminalization: One of the greatest problems with the current criminal law is overcriminalization. We currently punish conduct that does not risk harm to any interest the criminal law might wish to protect. There are two principal types of overcriminalization problems.

The first is where the type of conduct prohibited bears only a quite attenuated connection to legally protected interests. As an example, the criminalization of possession of marijuana is arguably unjustifiable because an individual who possesses or uses marijuana is unlikely to harm other people merely by virtue of that possession or use. Indeed, even when the harm principle is invoked,[49] there may be little empirical support for how the conduct risks the harm.[50]

---

[49] *See generally* Bernard E. Harcourt, "The Collapse of the Harm Principle," 90 *J. Crim. L. & Criminology* 109 (1999) (discussing how the regulation of morality has evolved from legal moralism to the co-option of the harm principle).

[50] Where a fundamental right is threatened, the Supreme Court does require a more stringent relationship between the act and the potential harm. Thus, in Ashcroft v. Free Speech Coalition, 535 U.S. 234 (2002), the Court invalidated a statute banning virtual child pornography on First Amendment grounds. The court noted that "[t]he Government has shown no more than a remote connection between speech that might encourage thoughts or impulses and any resulting child abuse. Without a significantly stronger, more direct connection, the Government may not prohibit speech on the ground that

The second type of problem is overinclusiveness. Even if we can identify some group of people who will harm others, the criminal statutes routinely sweep within their prohibitions conduct that is harmless.[51] It is possible that some people who drive while talking on cell phones cannot do so safely but that others can. To bar *everyone* from driving while talking on cell phones is to restrict the liberty of even those people whose use of cell phones does not significantly increase the risk of harm to other people.

Both legislatures and courts may be faulted for the overcriminalization problem. The political incentives are such that legislatures have every reason to criminalize and no reason not to criminalize. One might hope that courts would step in, but the Supreme Court has had little to say about substantive criminal law.[52] Criminal statutes, unless burdening a fundamental right, are subject only to rational basis review.[53] Thus, as one commentator has noted, a state could constitutionally criminalize eating sausage to prevent obesity.[54] The ultimate result of such rampant criminalization is that police and prosecutors – not legislatures, judges, or citizens – have the ultimate power in determining when to prosecute and what punishment individuals deserve.[55] The problem is obvious – unchecked and unguided discretionary power is incompatible with the rule of law.[56]

b. Haphazard and Conflicting Codes: Beyond the enactment of crimes that punish harmless conduct, the manner in which the criminal laws are

---

it may encourage pedophiles to engage in illegal conduct." *Id.* at 253–254. The Court's solicitude for an actor's First Amendment right to view virtual child pornography does not carry over to its solicitude, or lack thereof, for the right to be free from criminal punishment.

[51] This is, of course, quite similar to the last problem. But with the prior problem, it may be that no instance of the criminalized conduct will actually result in harm, whereas, here, some instances of the criminal conduct will.

[52] Marcus Dirk Dubber, "Toward a Constitutional Law of Crime and Punishment," 55 *Hastings L.J.* 509, 509 (2004) ("It has become a commonplace that there are no meaningful constitutional constraints on substantive criminal law").

[53] Douglas N. Husak, "Guns and Drugs: Case Studies on the Principles Limits of the Criminal Sanction," 23 *Law & Phil.* 437, 465–466 (2004).

[54] *Id.* at 476.

[55] William J. Stuntz, "The Pathological Politics of Criminal Law," 100 *Mich. L. Rev.* 505 (2001); Husak, *Overcriminalization, supra* note 3, at 21.

[56] *See* Husak, *Overcriminalization, supra* note 3, at 27.

enacted is also highly problematic.[57] Because of special-interest-group lobbying, many criminal statutes that are duplicative of already existing ones are enacted. For example, as Paul Robinson and Michael Cahill report, the Illinois criminal code, which already contained a prohibition on theft, also contains a special offense for theft of delivery containers.[58] Often, in response to some sort of public outcry over a dramatic crime, legislators view it as politically expedient immediately to criminalize the precise behavior involved. At these times, no thought is given as to how this ad hoc addition to the criminal code will affect the code as a whole.[59] Thus, the new enactment may use different terms or provide a sentence that is disproportionate to the otherwise similar crimes within the code.

c. *Lack of Guidance:* If a citizen wishes to know whether he may permissibly engage in conduct, the criminal law should provide him with guidance. It should tell him what he may and may not do. For the criminal law to give such guidance, the criminal law's rules should be accessible to those regulated. But that is hardly the case with current criminal codes.

First, many criminal statutes contain vague terms, the meanings of which are determined by courts. However, the decisions of courts are hardly easily available to the average person who seeks to know for any given activity whether it is prohibited and punishable. To the extent that the criminal law requires a juris doctor (or more) to understand its full contours, it gives woefully little guidance to the citizenry.[60] Adding insult to injury is the failure of the current criminal law to provide a mistake of law defense.[61] Even when a citizen makes a good faith effort to learn the law, if she gets it wrong – even if her mistake is reasonable and in good faith – she will not be entitled to any defense.[62]

---

[57] *See generally* Paul H. Robinson and Michael T. Cahill, "Can a Model Penal Code Second Save the States from Themselves?" 1 *Ohio St. J. Crim. L.* 169 (2003); Husak, *Overcriminalization, supra* note 3, at 36–39.

[58] Robinson and Cahill, *supra* note 57, at 170.

[59] *Id.* at 170–171; *see also* Paul H. Robinson, Michael T. Cahill, and Usman Mohammad, "The Five Worst (and Five Best) American Criminal Codes," 95 *NW. L. Rev.* 1, 2 (2000).

[60] *See* John Calvin Jeffries Jr., "Legality, Vagueness, and the Construction of Penal Statutes," 71 *Va. L. Rev.* 189, 207–208 (1985).

[61] *Id.* at 208–209.

[62] *But see* Peter Westen, "Two Rules of Legality in Criminal Law," 26 *Law & Phil.* 229 (2007) (arguing that, in most cases, current criminal law mistake-of-law rules accurately track the actor's culpability).

Even when criminal law statutes are not so vague as to be unintelligible, they can be too specific and detailed to be comprehended. As Paul Robinson and John Darley have pointed out, the Model Penal Code's formulation of self-defense is riddled with exceptions to exceptions.[63] Not only is it unreasonable to expect a citizen to know the details of such a code, but also it is ridiculous to assume that any citizen in such a situation would have time to consult it. The citizenry needs simple rules that it can understand and obey. Notice has no value when understanding cannot be achieved.

In summary, current criminal codes suffer from an overcriminalization of conduct, haphazard and conflicting statutes, and both overly vague and overly detailed norms. If it manages to achieve retributive justice, that would be miraculous and accidental.

2. Do Our Current Criminal Codes Contain Rules?

Beyond the question of whether our current law serves rule-of-law values is the question of whether it contains rules at all. In our view, the criminal law embeds standards within its statutes, thus resulting in a standards-based system, not a rule-based system.

We should note at the outset that we are not making a normative claim here as to whether rules or standards are preferable. We address that question shortly when discussing how to implement our theory. For now, the question is an empirical one – what sort of criminal code do we have?

Although our criminal code may have many specific criminal statutes, ultimately the criminal law is standards based. Indeed, it is standards based in every criminal statute that requires a *mens rea* of either recklessness or negligence.

Consider first the number of standards embedded within the Model Penal Code. Attempts require the actor take a "substantial step."[64] Some attempts are entitled to mitigation (or even dismissal) if they are "so inherently unlikely to result...in the commission of a crime."[65]

---

[63] Paul H. Robinson and John M. Darley, "Does Criminal Law Deter? A Behavioural Science Investigation," 24 *Oxford J. Legal Stud.* 173, 181 (2004).

[64] Model Penal Code § 5.01(1)(c) (1985).

[65] *Id.* at § 5.05(2).

An actor is guilty of gross sexual imposition if he compels his victim by "any threat that would prevent resistance by a woman of ordinary resolution."[66] One may commit a crime by "loitering" or "prowling."[67] Mistake of law is a defense if the actor "acts in reasonable reliance upon an official statement of law."[68] An actor has a duress defense if he succumbs to a threat "which a person of reasonable firmness would have been unable to resist."[69] An actor is held to consent to "reasonable foreseeable hazards of joint participation in an athletic contest."[70] An actor is justified if, among other things, "the harm or evil sought to be avoided is greater than that sought to be prevented by the law defining the offense charged."[71] Law enforcement may not use deadly force if it creates a "substantial risk of injury to innocent persons."[72] Parents may not use force on their children if such force is "known to create a substantial risk" of death, serious bodily harm, or "extreme pain" or "gross degradation."[73]

State statutes likewise embed standards. One can be guilty of murder if one commits a crime recklessly under circumstances manifesting *extreme indifference* to human life[74] or guilty of manslaughter for acting recklessly as to death.[75] Recklessness is also a sufficient *mens rea* for offenses that range from the mundane to the bizarre: aggravated unpermitted use of indoor pyrotechnics,[76] arson,[77] assault,[78] bigamy,[79] child abuse,[80] computer crimes,[81] criminal mischief,[82] criminal nuisance,[83]

---

[66] *Id.* at § 213.1(2)(a).

[67] *Id.* at § 250.6.

[68] *Id.* at § 2.04(3)(b).

[69] *Id.* at § 2.09(1).

[70] *Id.* at § 2.11(2)(b).

[71] *Id.* at § 3.02(1)(a).

[72] *Id.* at § 3.07(2)(b)(iii).

[73] *Id.* at § 3.08(1)(b).

[74] Ala. Code § 13A-6-2 (West 1975).

[75] *Id.* at § 13A-6-3; Conn. Gen. Stat. Ann. § 53a-56 (2007).

[76] N.Y. Penal Law § 405.18 (2003).

[77] Ala. Code § 13A-7-43 (West 1975) (arson in the third degree).

[78] Conn. Gen. Stat. Ann. § 53a-59 (2007); 18 Pa. Cons. Stat. Ann. § 2701 (West 2003).

[79] Mo. Rev. Stat. § 568.010 (2007).

[80] N.Y. Education Law § 1125 (2001) (child abuse in an educational setting).

[81] Conn. Gen. Stat. Ann. § 53a-251 (2007).

[82] *Id.* at § 53a-117.

[83] N.Y. Penal Law § 120.20 (2007).

deceptive business practices,[84] defacing traffic signs and signals,[85] false advertising,[86] hazing,[87] interference with police service animals,[88] mixing, coloring, staining, or other alterations of drugs or medicines,[89] obstructing highways,[90] public lewdness,[91] riot,[92] and simulating legal process.[93] Moreover, many states have also followed the Model Penal Code's lead and enacted a blanket misdemeanor for reckless endangerment.[94]

These examples are just the tip of the iceberg. Juries determine when an act goes beyond "mere preparation" to "dangerous proximity" such that the actor has committed an attempt.[95] A jurisdiction that extends complicity to crimes that "naturally and probably" follow from the encouraged act also requires a jury determination about that linkage.[96] The insanity determination is not rule bound, even though it may appear to be. Empirical evidence shows that juries reach the same conclusions about legal insanity irrespective of the legal tests.[97] And even when the culpability term has a clear legal meaning to law professors, a jury may infuse the term with its own interpretation.[98]

In the next section, we turn to the question of whether rules or standards are preferable. At this point, we hope to have established at least a prima facie case that (1) the current criminal system should not be

---

[84] Haw. Rev. Stat. § 708–870 (2006).

[85] N.J. Stat. Ann. § 2C:17–3.1 (2007).

[86] Haw. Rev. Stat. § 708–871 (2006).

[87] Md. Code Ann., Crim. Law § 3–607 (2007).

[88] Tex. Penal Code Ann. § 38.151 (2007).

[89] Mich. Comp. Laws Ann. § 750.18 (2007).

[90] Ga. Code Ann. § 16–11–43 (2007).

[91] Tex. Penal Code Ann. § 21.07 (2007).

[92] Conn. Gen. Stat. Ann. § 53a-175 (2007).

[93] Tex. Penal Code Ann. § 32.48 (2007).

[94] *See, e.g.,* Ala. Code § 13A-6-24 (West 1975); Conn. Gen. Stat. Ann. § 53a-63 (2007); Md. Code Ann., Crim. Law § 3–204 (2007); N.Y. Penal Law § 120.20 (2007); 18 Pa. Cons. Stat. Ann. § 2705 (West 2007).

[95] *See* Michael T. Cahill, "Punishment Decisions at Conviction: Recognizing the Jury as Fault-Finder," 2005 *U. Chi. Legal F.* 91, 101 (2005).

[96] *E.g.,* People v. Luparello, 231 Cal. Rptr. 832 (Cal. Ct. App. 1986). Of course, this view is antithetical to ours.

[97] *See* Rita J. Simon and David E. Aaronson, *The Insanity Defense: A Critical Assessment of the Law and Policy in the Post Hinckley Era* 126–135 (1988); Henry J. Steadman et al., *Before and After Hinckley: Evaluating Insanity Defense Reform* 8 (1993).

[98] *See* Darryl K. Brown, "Plain Meaning, Practical Reason, and Culpability: Toward a Theory of Jury Interpretation of Criminal Statutes," 96 *Mich. L. Rev.* 1199 (1998).

entitled to great deference, and (2) the current criminal system, although appearing to be rule based, relies largely on standards.

B. IMPLEMENTING A PRACTICAL CODE

1. Rules versus Standards: In General

Our view as articulated thus far is a standards-based view. Indeed, to this point, we have argued for only one standard: take only those risks to legally protected interests that, as you perceive those risks, are justified by your reasons for acting. One might wonder, however, whether the criminal law should be structured in this way. Should the criminal law be standards based, or should it contain discrete determinate rules?

Of course, the debate between rules and standards is not a new one.[99] But the question for us is quite specific: Should the criminal law simply use one (or many) standards? Or should criminal law rules be criminal law *rules?*

In this section, we argue that, with a few exceptions, criminal law serves its function best by being standards based. Importantly, most of the values that underlie having *rules* are consequentialist. As we have mentioned, there is an ineliminable gap between when a legislator should create rules and when a citizen should follow them. A citizen can thus violate a justified rule justifiably. Such a citizen should not be punished because he is not culpable and therefore does not deserve punishment. A criminal law that truly cares about an actor's culpability cannot punish a nonculpable actor simply to preserve the (consequentialist) value of rules.

2. The Argument for Rules over Standards

The value of rules is that they authoritatively settle moral disagreements.[100] That is, even when individuals are ethically well-disposed

---

[99] The problem is perhaps most famously embodied in the debate between Oliver Wendell Holmes and Benjamin Cardozo. Holmes sought to establish per se rules of conduct, believing that the "featureless generality" of negligence would ultimately give way to specific rules. *See* Baltimore & O.R.R. v. Goodman, 275 U.S. 66, 70 (1927); Oliver Wendell Holmes, *The Common Law* 111 (1881). In response, Cardozo noted that such rules could not take into account all the circumstances so as to adjudicate negligence correctly in future cases. *See also* Pokora v. Wabash Ry. Co., 292 U.S. 98, 104 (1934).

[100] For further discussion of this argument, *see* Larry Alexander and Emily Sherwin, *The Rule of Rules: Morality, Rules, and the Dilemmas of Law* ch. 1 (2001).

actors, they need the assistance of posited, determinate rules. Authoritative settlement by determinate rules resolves problems of coordination, expertise, and efficiency.

Rules solve coordination problems.[101] In some cases, there are several incompatible ways to act and no reason to prefer one solution to another.[102] Which side of the street to drive on is one example. In other instances, rules solve social coordination problems: in a world of imperfect information, and in which the morally right thing to do turns at least in part on what others are likely to do, rules provide actors with a basis for such a prediction.[103]

In other instances, the rules reflect the expertise of their promulgators. We may believe that a particular authoritative decision maker has greater moral and factual expertise than the typical rule subject. Although there may be reason to doubt this superior expertise in any given case, in general, legal rules can resolve questions about how to act that most individuals on their own may not be capable of resolving as well because they lack the rule promulgator's information or expertise.[104] Rules also avert errors. When, owing to complexity, actors must look at a multitude of factors in order to determine what to do, they may simply get the calculations wrong.[105]

Finally, rules reduce decision-making costs. It is simply more efficient for us to have a traffic law that tells us how fast to go than for us to calculate a safe speed each moment that we are driving.[106] A rule that dispenses with the necessity of complex calculations can also be said to promote predictability because everyone will arrive at the same result – what the rule prescribes – rather than different results through different calculations.[107]

All of these benefits of rules stem from both rule addressees and rule enforcers having the same understanding of the rule.[108] In other words,

---

[101] *Id.* at 56; Frederick Schauer, *Playing by the Rules: A Philosophical Examination of Rule-Based Decision-Making in Law and in Life* § 7.7 (1991).

[102] Alexander and Sherwin, *supra* note 100, at 56.

[103] *Id.* at 57–58.

[104] *Id.* at 55.

[105] Schauer, *supra* note 101, at 150.

[106] *Id.* at § 7.3.

[107] *Id.* at 137.

[108] *Id.* at 138.

it is rules' determinacy that produces these consequential and hence moral benefits.

All of these reasons for having legal rules are thus reasons for having legal *rules*, not standards. Enacting a legal rule settles normative disputes. In this respect, standards are unhelpful. For example, laws that tell individuals to "drive safely" – a standard – leave (ethically well-disposed) individuals with no better idea about what to do than if there were no laws at all.[109]

As one of us has argued:

> The quality that identifies a rule and distinguishes it from a standard is the quality of determinateness. A norm becomes a rule when most people understand it in a similar way. When this is so, the rule will give the same answer to unsettled moral questions to every affected individual and so bring about coordination. Although a standard is transparent to background moral principles and requires particularistic decision-making, rules can be applied without regard to questions of background morality. They are opaque to the moral principles they are supposed to effectuate. Thus, a rule is a posited norm that fulfills the function of posited norms, that is, that settles the question of what ought to be done.[110]

3. Problems with Rules

Despite the benefits of having legal rules, there are also problems with having them. Rules may be overinclusive.[111] Because rules rely on act-type generalizations, and not on particulars, there is always a possibility that a particular instance of the act type would not be prohibited if one relied solely upon the underlying justification for the rule.[112] Fred Schauer enumerates three possible ways that a rule might be ill-fitting: the probabilistic generalization may be incorrect on this occasion; the universal generalization turns out not to be universal; or a property suppressed by the rule is germane.[113]

---

[109] Alexander and Sherwin, *supra* note 100, at 29.
[110] *Id.* at 30.
[111] Rules may also be underinclusive. That is, the reason that justifies prohibiting conduct *a* may also extend to conduct type *b*, but the rule may apply only to conduct type *a*. Schauer, *supra* note 101, at 32–33.
[112] *Id.* at 32; Alexander and Sherwin, *supra* note 100, at 35.
[113] Schauer, *supra* note 101, at 39.

Given that rules can be overinclusive, it is a bit surprising that rules are followed as often as they are. In our view, the reason why rules generally work is through a form of (benign) deception.[114] People believe that rules dictate the morally preferable course of action in all cases that they cover, and because of that belief they blindly comply. The use of a rules-based law ultimately entails deceiving the citizenry, leading it to believe that rules dictate correct results when they do not.

Although the overinclusive nature of rules – the fact that they apply even when their underlying justifications do not – is generally troubling, it is far more troubling in the context of the criminal law. In the criminal law context, an overinclusive rule is a rule that creates the potential for punishing an innocent actor. There will be cases where it is rational for a lawmaker to create a specific rule, and at the same time, there will be cases where it is irrational for a citizen to obey it. For it is neither rational nor morally preferable for a citizen to obey a rule the underlying justification for which does not apply in the case at hand.

This gap – between what a legislator should proscribe and what a citizen should do – cannot be closed.[115] There are different approaches to confronting this gap, but none of these approaches will eliminate it. Thus, a retributivist will have to face the reality that a rule that promotes authoritative settlement may do so at the expense of punishing an "innocent" person.

One of us has written extensively on this problem, so we briefly recapitulate the arguments for why the gap cannot be eliminated.[116] One attempt at eliminating the gap is simply to calculate the value of having a rule and add that to the other reasons for following a rule, an approach dubbed "rule-sensitive particularism" by Fred Schauer.[117] But there are problems with rule-sensitive particularism in many cases. First, when a rule is based on the supposed expertise of the lawmaker, an individual actor will have reason to violate the rule any time that she does not believe that the lawmaker is reliable source of advice. The rule may give guidance to the actor that this is the type of question about which

---

[114] *See generally* Larry Alexander and Emily Sherwin, "The Deceptive Nature of Rules," 142 *U. Pa. L. Rev.* 1191 (1994).

[115] Alexander and Sherwin, *supra* note 100, at 54.

[116] *See generally id.* at ch. 4.

[117] *Id.* at 61–68; Schauer, *supra* note 101, at 94–100.

individuals often err, but the rule then ultimately functions as simply an advisory rule of thumb – cautionary guidance that the individual may have the facts wrong. In those cases where the actor does not believe she has the facts wrong, however, she has no reason to follow the rule. There is no value of the rule to be put into the calculation. Second, with regard to coordination problems, if everyone is a rule-sensitive particularist, and thus every actor will look behind the rule (and many will err), then the individual rule-sensitive particularist will once again be caught in a coordination dilemma. Coordination problems can be solved only if most of the community members believe that rules are serious rules and do not engage in rule-sensitive particularism. Thus, rule-sensitive particularism leads to giving rules zero weight, with the result that there is no "rule value" for the rule-sensitive particularist to weigh against the reasons for violation.

A second approach – presumptive positivism – is also problematic. This view, endorsed by Fred Schauer, holds that rules are entitled to presumptive weight. It is difficult, however, to understand exactly how this presumption functions. Are all rules entitled to the same weight? Or does the amount of weight vary depending upon the rule? It may be that as a descriptive matter citizens do presumptively follow (deceptive) rules, but this does not eliminate the gap or the deception. At times, an actor will obey a rule (presumptively) that she should not. Conversely, a lawmaker may have reasons to enact a serious rule (because of problems with error) that a given individual will not have reason to obey.

A third approach is to view rules as "exclusionary" reason for action. In Joseph Raz's view, a rule provides a "second-order" reason that excludes moral consideration of "first-order" reasons.[118] However, if rules are necessary to solve coordination problems or to provide epistemic guidance, it is not clear how they have this exclusionary power. Moreover, if this exclusionary power is supposed to be derived from some sort of consent or precommitment, to follow the rules, it is difficult to see the moral value in obeying a morally suboptimal rule or application of a rule simply because one has consented or promised to do so. One cannot convey by promise or consent a moral right to demand

---

[118] Joseph Raz, *The Authority of Law: Essays on Law and Morality* 16–19, 22–23, 30–33 (1979). *But see* Heidi M. Hurd, "Challenging Authority," 100 *Yale L.J.* 1611 (1991).

a performance that one does not possess a moral right to perform prior to such conveyance.

A final approach is to endorse Meir Dan-Cohen's "acoustic separation."[119] Under this approach, the serious rule is widely publicized, but a more lenient decision rule is actually employed by judges and juries. This approach provides the benefits of serious rules by reinforcing the view that rules are meant to be followed, but it also allows for justice in individual cases. The problem, in our view, is that it does so at too great a cost – it sacrifices the integrity of our government. It involves double deception. Not only are the rules deceptive in claiming (implicitly) that there are dispositive reasons to follow them (when there are not), but they are also deceptive with respect to the consequences of disobeying them.

Because the gap cannot be eliminated, the retributivist faces a dilemma. She must decide whether to announce broad standards – standards that ultimately rely on the preexisting moral knowledge of citizens – or narrow rules that may ultimately mandate the punishment of nonculpable actors.[120]

One puzzle that the retributivist-deontologist must resolve is how this overinclusiveness bears on the potential to punish the innocent. Recall that the moderate retributivist takes two positions about punishing people according to desert. First, the moderate retributivist holds that there is a deontological constraint against knowingly punishing the innocent. Second, the moderate retributivist believes that giving people what they deserve is intrinsically good. With respect to this second

---

119 Meir Dan-Cohen, "Decision Rules and Conduct Rules: On Acoustic Separation in Criminal Law," 97 *Harv. L. Rev.* 625 (1984).

120 Doug Husak argues that overinclusive legislation is permissible so long as it is no more extensive than necessary. Husak, *Overcriminalization, supra* note 3, at 155–156. In justifying a blanket rule prohibiting crossing a median line on a curved highway, Husak argues that, although some actors will be epistemically privileged (and know that crossing is safe), others will be epistemically arrogant (and therefore culpable). According to Husak, because there is no reliable method to distinguish these two types of actors, we may justly punish them both.

The problem, however, is that even if we cannot distinguish these two actors ex ante, there may be ways to distinguish them ex post. We must justify not only a rule that may be overinclusive but also *punishing* an actor for violating the rule in situations in which, had we perfect information (or simply the information available ex post), we never would have criminalized his conduct to begin with.

element, a retributivist can and will trade off the good of punishing the guilty against the evil of mistakenly punishing the innocent. And because we may believe that the latter is a worse evil than the former is a good, we set our burden of proof to favor false negatives over false positives.

However, with respect to the overinclusiveness of rules, although ex ante they, too, may appear to present a trade-off of risks, they do not do so ex post, at the time of the imposition of punishment. So we must ask, what should the law do when it is clear that an actor is, in fact, morally innocent but has been caught within the web of an overinclusive rule? When the judge sees before her the person who falls within the overinclusive gap, the judge – and thus our criminal justice system – does not *risk* punishing the innocent. If it punishes the morally innocent person, it does so knowingly.

The result is that the retributivist must now confront the question of what the deontological constraint against punishing the innocent means. If, as we argued in Chapter 4, the deontological constraint is only against *appropriating* people, then although we may not use the innocent as scapegoats, it could nonetheless be the case that we may permissibly punish a person whom we know to be morally innocent (nonculpable). The argument would be that although the overinclusive rules are overinclusive for consequentialist reasons, they are not appropriating the moral innocents who fall within the rules' overinclusive scope to produce those beneficial consequences. If so, then this overinclusiveness gap is not so problematic; rather, our notions of retributivism must be readjusted to allow for the punishment of the nonculpable.

For those who believe this case to be a strong counterargument to the position we take in Chapter 4 with respect to deontological constraints, we note that the intending versus foreseeing position is no better off. First, it seems to us that when one punishes a nonculpable actor caught within an overinclusive rule, under the common understanding of intention, one is not purposefully punishing the innocent but is doing so only knowingly. Under some formulations of the deontological constraint, knowing punishment of the innocent would itself violate it. Moreover, we think the case can be made that this is a case of intending to punish the innocent. If one intends to punish an actor and knows that actor is morally innocent, then it seems to us that one has intentionally punished an innocent. That is so, we believe, because one cannot understand whom one is punishing without recognizing that one is punishing *this innocent actor*. Accordingly, if one intends to punish a person whom one knows to be innocent, one is violating the deontological constraint even if it is formulated as a constraint on what one does intentionally.

Although we do not resolve this problem here for the retributivist-deontologist, erring on the side of caution, we do endorse a standards-based view here. As we have said, whether recognized or not, our criminal law is currently chock full of standards. Every recklessness calculation entails an unguided balancing of the actor's reasons and the risks she has created. Of all the problems that currently exist within the criminal law, implementing and understanding recklessness would not make it into the top one hundred.

4. An Empirical Experiment

One likely objection to our proposal is that it is not practically workable. We will not be able to sell it. Converting criminal law rules into mushy standards will cause widespread public outrage. It is, some might claim, the end of the world as we know it.

Well, we feel fine. At the outset, we doubt that this change is as monumental as it first appears. As noted previously, many, many, many criminal law "rules" contain standards.

However, there are cases in which a switch from rules to standards might seem more profound. One might imagine speed limits to be such a case. In this section, we explore the "real" possibility of a standards-based speed limit.

Now, initially, we should note that we find driving to be a particularly tricky question. After all, if Heidi decides to attend a conference on "Intention" in Death Valley, California, that requires her to drive two hours, does her increase in knowledge justify the life and limb that she endangers on the road? If she had to internalize that activity cost, would she even drive?[121] It seems that driving has become part of the American identity, and no campaign for public transportation seems likely to change that. Our decision to drive, our choice of cars, and so forth has become as self-defining as our choice of sexual partners or whether to

---

[121] *Cf.* Steven Shavell, "Strict Liability versus Negligence," 9 *J. Legal. Stud.* 1 (1986).

procreate.[122] Thus, it seems that driving, even for trivial or slightly important reasons, may be more "justifiable" than would otherwise appear.

But back to the empirical question. What would happen if we deleted speed limits and just required actors not to take unjustifiable risks? Well, for a few years, Montana did just that. In 1999, Robert King and Cass Sunstein investigated the effect of this law.[123] From 1955 to 1974, Montana had a law that required citizens to drive in a "careful and prudent manner," at a reasonable rate of speed, taking into account the traffic, condition of the vehicle, condition of the roadway, and visibility conditions.[124] In 1974 Congress imposed a mandatory speed limit of 55 m.p.h.[125] Montanans implemented the requirement in name only, ticketing violators only five dollars.[126] With the enactment of the National Highway System Designation Act, Montana once again had control over the regulation of its highways.[127] And, on December 9, 1995, Montana's standard of reasonable and prudent driving once again became law.[128]

According to King and Sunstein, the effects of Montana's action varied. First, the change from rules to a standard *did not significantly alter* driving behavior.[129] The authors attribute this lack of change to the treacherous road conditions in Montana – drivers ultimately had to do what was safe because that was in their own self-interest. The authors did find, however, that Montana became a destination for "speed tourists," those who came to Montana just so they could drive fast.[130] According to King and Sunstein, this led to some coordination problems because in-state and out-of-state drivers had different norms.[131] In our view, however, this gap is better viewed as one between Montanans, who understood that the standard was still *law*, and out-of-state drivers who thought that no speed limit was equivalent to *no regulation*. The fatality figures were inconclusive, suggesting a possible increase in unsafe driving by

[122] *Cf.* Lawrence v. Texas, 539 U.S. 558 (2003); Griswold v. Connecticut, 381 U.S. 579 (1965).
[123] *See* Robert E. King and Cass R. Sunstein, Essay, "Doing without Speed Limits," 79 *B.U. L. Rev.* 155 (1999).
[124] *Id.* at 158.
[125] *Id.* at 158–159.
[126] *Id.* at 159.
[127] *Id.* at 161.
[128] *Id.* at 162.
[129] *Id.* at 161–162.
[130] *Id.* at 164.
[131] *Id.* at 167.

1997, but, according to the authors, it is hard to draw this conclusion, given that fatality figures typically fluctuate year-to-year.[132]

The most significant problem with the law was its effect on law enforcement. There were administrative costs. Police officers had to debate with motorists whether the motorists deserved their tickets.[133] More motorists went to trial.[134]

Additionally, there was doubt as to what type of driving the standard required. The requirement seemed "subjective,"[135] as different police officers believed different speeds were dangerous. Moreover, judges did not always agree with police officer's ticketing practices, causing officers to feel that dangerous drivers were being set loose onto the streets.[136] King and Sunstein concluded:

> The cause of the "standards" problem emanates not only from the law's vagueness, but also from patrolmen's and judges' variable interpretations of the Basic Rule's expressed "reasonable and prudent" standards. Those officers and judges who establish their own, perhaps idiosyncratic, numerical limits and uniformly stop or convict defendants under fixed guidelines might be thought to endanger both the spirit and the letter of the Basic Rule, in turn creating an uncertain patchwork of rule-free and rule-bound law enforcement.[137]

The experiment in standards-based speed limits ended in 1998, when the Montana Supreme Court held that the standard was unconstitutionally vague.[138] During oral argument, the Montana Supreme Court was particularly troubled that the attorney general could not articulate *any* speed at which it was permissible to drive.[139] The court claimed the result was not just the allowance but the requirement that law enforcement act arbitrarily and discriminatorily.[140]

---

[132] *Id.* at 170–171.
[133] *Id.* at 179.
[134] *Id.* at 180.
[135] *Id.* at 181.
[136] *Id.* at 182.
[137] *Id.* at 184.
[138] *Id.* at 188; State v. Stanko, 974 P.2d 1132 (Mont. 1998).
[139] Stanko, 974 P.2d at 1137.
[140] *Id.*

Interestingly, the court claimed that there were just too many factors for any individual to calculate and no guidance as to how much each factor should be weighted.[141] But the conclusion that follows is quite limited – Montanans cannot be punished for "speed alone" without notifying them about the appropriate speed.[142] We doubt, however, that the court would have reached the same view if the driver who had the prudent driving standard declared unconstitutional had killed another person and had been prosecuted for manslaughter. Indeed, we need not guess about this: the Montana Supreme Court upheld the constitutionality of punishing Stanko for reckless driving.[143]

What conclusions should we draw from this experiment? Well, let us note its limitation. What works for Montanans might not work for Californians, and certainly not for New Yorkers. Montana is a thinly populated state, with vast stretches of highway, and a particularly libertarian population.[144]

Still, it seems to us that the sense that speed limits are the paradigm of a necessary rule is completely unfounded. Montanans were not driving any faster with the standard than with specific speed limits. Indeed, the difference in discretion – between Montana's standard and the typical rule – may be illusory.[145] After all, speed limits are rarely enforced exactly. Rather, every driver knows that going some indeterminate amount above the speed limit may be permissible, and this amount varies from highway to highway, officer to officer. The critical question is whether actors and enforcers need *guidance*, but, as we address in the next section, there may be ways to give guidance without enacting rules.

We do not wish to deny the problems with standards. Their failure to provide the guidance of rules and to settle determinately what ought to be done creates problems ex ante and ex post. Ex ante, actors may be chilled from taking justifiable risks. Alternatively, they may take risks that they believe are justifiable but that are not, or risks that they know

---

[141] *Id.* at 1138.
[142] *Id.*
[143] *Id.* at 1139.
[144] King and Sunstein, *supra* note 123, at 157 and 177.
[145] Husak, *Overcriminalization, supra* note 3, at 27 (making the point that discretion of this sort is incompatible with the rule of law).

are unjustified but that, given the inevitable vagueness of standards, they believe they can convince prosecutors or juries were justified. Ex post, prosecutors and juries will have more difficulty applying standards than applying rules, leading to the possibility of either too many prosecutions and convictions or too few.

Despite these considerations, we stand by the preference for standards. Although we believe that there may be times that rules ("proxy crimes") are in fact necessary, we believe those cases are few and far between. Criminal law as it stands is a standards-based world. And even those situations that appear to require rules, such as speed limits, may not in fact require them.

C. INEVITABLE PROXY CRIMES

Despite our defense of standards over rules, we recognize that there may be cases in which a legislature chooses to reject our arguments. Indeed, according to Carol Rose, the fluctuation between "crystals" (rules) and "mud" (standards) is simply inevitable.[146] Rather than dismissing these enactments of proxy crimes as possibly immoral, we believe that it may be better to "get real" and give some guidance to legislatures about how and when proxy crimes should be enacted.

1. Recognizing the Alternatives

The first question is whether there is some sort of halfway house between a broad standard and an overinclusive rule. We wish to introduce four methods for getting the benefits of rules in a standards-based system.

The first method for achieving rulelike precision in a standards-based world is to move beyond the criminal law. The government has a tremendous array of resources that stop short of the criminal sanction. To the extent the war against drunk driving has been successful, it has not been so solely because of enforcement; it has also achieved success by changing the social norms. It is simply no longer acceptable to the degree that it once was to drink and to drive. Indeed, the government's ability to create and to reinforce social norms will also indirectly achieve

---

[146] *See* Carol M. Rose, "Crystals and Mud in Property Law," 40 *Stan. L. Rev.* 577 (1988).

the benefits sought by the criminal law. If public service announcements make clear the risks inherent in any given activity, any given actor will be (1) less likely to minimize the risk and (2) less able to justify the risk he recognizes.

A second method is to allow a legislature to place "commentaries" within the criminal code.[147] This would allow the legislature to elaborate on when a harm is "serious," or to specify when a particular reason for acting is "evil" as opposed to "antisocial." The commentaries could also inform citizens that certain "personal considerations" may be valued, such as the liberty interests we all enjoy by driving instead of using public transportation, biking, or walking. These commentaries, when applicable, could also be read to juries. A significant benefit of these commentaries is that they can serve to counteract the possibility of overdeterrence. The commentaries can inform both actors and juries that certain conduct is presumptively acceptable, thus giving actors guidance that, for example, driving at fifty-five miles an hour is generally safe driving in the absence of extenuating conditions.

Another key advantage of the use of commentaries is that they require the legislature to "fit" their commentaries within our framework. This prevents any given legislature from disrupting an entire statutory scheme by introducing new terminology or providing too harsh a punishment for one type of conduct relative to the rest of the statutory scheme. It allows legislatures to achieve some degree of specificity without creating the gap inherent in rules – the norm is still a standard, not a rule – but the commentary provides *guidance* and *structure* for decision making.

A third method also seeks to strike a balance between providing the determinacy of clear rules and providing the justice of standards. Legislatures could specify legally protected interests but insist upon a mental state of recklessness as to those interests. A crime that specifies a legally protected interest and requires the mental state of recklessness (as we have refined it) will simply be an instance of insufficient concern.

---

[147] *See* Paul H. Robinson and Michael T. Cahill, "The Accelerating Degradation of Criminal Codes," 56 *Hastings L.J.* 633, 654–655 (2005) (proposing this alternative to criminal legislation and reporting that during the authors' work revising the Kentucky criminal code such a proposal was met with considerable support).

It will not be an imperfect approximation. That is, if the law states that it is criminal to "recklessly create a risk of death," this crime is merely a specific instance of the more global prohibition on risking harm, an instance where the type of legally protected interest is specified.

The enactment of these types of crimes, which are delineated simply by the type of legally protected interest, are not overinclusive. However, they are problematic to the extent that they raise the question of when multiple crimes may be charged for the same conduct. That is, they have the potential to resurrect the problems inherent in our current system of individuating offenses. What these "proxies" do not do, though, is create overinclusive crimes.

Finally, the legislature could consider using presumptions. For instance, in defining murder as "extreme indifference to human life," the Model Penal Code further clarifies that this indifference is presumed when the actor is taking part in one of several enumerated felonies.[148] Likewise, it could be "presumed" that one is driving recklessly if one's blood alcohol level is above a certain percentage, in contrast to making such driving per se criminal. If the use of a presumption is only permissive – for example, one that allows the jury to infer extreme indifference from participation in what is now a discrete felony – then such a presumption would function in the same way that code commentaries would.

Could a jurisdiction go beyond permissive presumptions and employ a mandatory rebuttable presumption, and would such a presumption be constitutional? A mandatory rebuttable presumption would state a *rule*, but would permit the actor to show, by some burden of proof, that the underlying justification for the rule did not apply. Given that an actor who then violates the rule would have to have good reason – that is, show that she was epistemically privileged or the like – there is some merit in such a rebuttable rule. Such an approach is also better than just enacting an irrebuttable rule, one that would completely bar the actor from showing that she does not fall within the rule's justification.[149]

---

[148] Model Penal Code § 210.2 (1985).

[149] *See* Paul H. Robinson and Michael T. Cahill, *Law without Justice: Why Criminal Law Doesn't Give People What They Deserve* 205–209 (2006) (advocating burden shifting approaches).

One substantial hurdle to such a burden-shifting approach is the current state of constitutional law. Because the presumption would undoubtedly apply to an element of our offense (we have no defenses per se), such a presumption violates the requirement that the government prove every element beyond a reasonable doubt.[150] Ironically, although such an approach would create greater fairness, it is unconstitutional. In contrast, a rule that is simply overinclusive – without any ability to rebut its applicability – would undoubtedly pass constitutional muster.[151]

2. Enacting Proxy Crimes

In translating our idealized code into a practical one, we recognize that a legislature might wish to enact "proxy crimes." A proxy crime is a particular instance of conduct, commission of which risks harming a legally protected interest. But because there is only a risk of harming a legally protected interest, proxy crimes may be overinclusive. That is, they may sweep in the nonculpable actors along with the culpable.

Not all proxy crimes are alike. Although some may be (potentially) justifiable, others may not be. We begin with the latter first.

Unlike proxy crimes that are created because of the inability to craft a standard so as to give sufficient guidance to individual actors, some proxy crimes are created for the benefit of law enforcement. For example, we argued in Chapter 6 that an actor has not committed a culpable act until she has unleashed a risk of harm over which she no longer has control. So, a would-be house thief has not committed attempted theft at the point at which she cases the house or purchases tools for the upcoming act. However, to stop some crimes early, while simultaneously claiming to distinguish between "mere preparation" and "dangerous proximity," the criminal law has created proxy crimes, such as possession of burglar's tools. The possession of such tools, however, does not risk harm in and of itself. Rather, it is an early act in the chain of acts leading ultimately to the entry and commission of some fully consummated crime, if, that is, we assume that committing a crime is the reason for possessing the tools.[152]

---

[150] See Sandstrom v. Montana, 442 U.S. 510 (1979).
[151] See Robinson and Cahill, supra note 149, at 208–209 (noting this difficulty).
[152] See Moore, supra note 16, at 784 ("The problem with...'wrongs by proxy' is that [they] give liberty a strong kick in the teeth right at the start. Such an argument does not even

We do not believe that these acts should be criminalized, unless, of course, they are committed for the purpose of a later risk imposition and culpably risk causing fear of that future act. It is true that, given such a law, and assuming that our would-be burglar knows the law and chooses to possess the tools, then we are not punishing her on the basis of a prediction of what she might do but for something that she has done. However, the underlying moral justifiability of this law hinges on the creation of a risk to a legally protected interest over which the defendant no longer has control. The act of possessing burglar tools does not in itself create such a risk because the would-be burglar still controls whether the risk will be imposed – that is, whether she will burgle. Therefore, the legislature should not criminalize such conduct.

The same analysis also applies to any crime created because of practical enforcement concerns. Strict liability generally and felony murder specifically have been justified because of the need to "ease the prosecutorial burden." We see no reason to ease the burden such that an actor who creates no unjustified risk of harm to any legally protected interest may be criminally punished despite having done nothing culpable.[153]

We believe the proxy crimes that a legislature is justified in enacting are precisely those crimes that give actors significant epistemic guidance. In particular, these rules may be justified in circumstances where agents are particularly prone to rationality errors.[154]

One area in which we may find "proxies" to be necessary is where there are questions of maturity and capacity. For instance, at some point, a teenage girl becomes sufficiently rational to consent to sexual intercourse. But this point varies from girl to girl. Here, miscalculations may occur on both sides of the equation – some fifteen-year-olds are sufficiently mature that they should be able to determine for themselves whether to consent to intercourse, but many may not be. The putative defendant, who has every incentive to *want* to believe that his future partner is competent, may not adequately take opposing information

pretend that there is any culpability or wrongdoing for which it would urge punishment; rather, punishment of a non-wrongful, non-culpable action is used for purely preventive ends").

[153] *Id.* at 784 (noting this is just an evasion of the requirement that the government must prove every element beyond a reasonable doubt).

[154] Husak, *Overcriminalization, supra* note 3, at 38–39.

into account. Because we know that these mistakes are bound to happen, a nice clear cut-off point – a set age restriction – gives epistemic guidance to actors who may greatly need it.

Clearly, under these conditions, the criminal law should require recklessness as to this new material element. Indeed, because age is a mere proxy for consent, and we wish to punish only those actors who risk having unconsented-to intercourse, it would make no sense whatsoever to punish the actor who honestly believes the victim was at the appropriate age (and also consenting).

Of course, allowing for any proxy crimes returns us to where we began. What should we do with a person who does not culpably risk the harm but who does violate the proxy crime?[155] We advocate a modified rule-sensitive particularist view. If the actor does not risk harm to a legally protected interest, the question is whether he has still shown sufficient respect for the "rule of law." Here, the jury could be asked whether the actor, knowing that he was violating the law (the proxy crime), (1) gave sufficient weight in his justifying reasons to the chance that he might be wrong about the girl's capacity to consent, and thus, enough weight to the risk of epistemic error, and (2) gave sufficient weight to the value of having rules decide these cases for all citizens (i.e., to the risk that he is undermining the moral message of the law). If taking these values into account, his action was still justified – for example, in this particular case, he had excellent reasons to believe the girl had the capacity to consent – then he is not culpable for violating the proxy crime. On the other hand, if he is epistemically arrogant without good reason – she was very mature and gave valid consent, but he had no good reason to believe this – then he may be punished for his failure to show sufficient respect to rule-of-law values.

Of course, this does not completely resolve the problem. The actor may honestly believe that the woman (girl?) with whom he is about to

---

[155] Antony Duff favors punishing these individuals because they manifest "civic arrogance." One might also say "epistemic arrogance." R. A. Duff, "Crime, Prohibition, and Punishment," 19 *J. Applied Phil.* 97 (2002). But Duff's view – that we should punish actors because they do not *know* the rule does not apply – simply ignores the fact that in some cases actors know exactly this fact. Moreover, Duff cannot explain why this arrogance leads to punishment for the underlying offense instead of the arrogance itself. *See also* Husak, *Overcriminalization, supra* note 3, at 107–112 (critiquing Duff's approach).

have intercourse is sufficiently mature to consent, no matter what the statutory required age. And the actor may be wrong. He may be wrong because he is weak-willed, foolish, or simply aroused and not thinking straight. Whatever the case may be, these errors that cause him to miscalculate may not be culpable in themselves, and he may not then be culpable for taking the risk of miscalculation. The actor may not be culpable for the underlying rape – his estimate of the risk of nonconsent was sufficiently low – and he may not be culpable for disrespecting the law. He may simply be a fool. But it is not the criminal law's purpose to punish rationality errors or character flaws per se.

Because we advocate "undermining the rule of law" as its own legally protected interest, there are two related questions we should address here. These are the questions of how to deal with exculpatory and inculpatory mistakes of law.

First, let us consider the type of exculpatory mistake of law that we briefly addressed in Chapter 4. Imagine that Alex intends to have sexual intercourse with Betty, and he accurately assesses that she is sufficiently mature to consent. As it turns out, a proxy crime has been enacted that prohibits females under seventeen from consenting to intercourse. Betty is sixteen. Alex, however, does not know about the existence of the proxy crime.

In our view, if the actor does not know about the proxy crime's existence, then he should be entitled to a mistake-of-law excuse. Indeed, this "excuse" is built into the nature of the legally protected interest. Because Alex does not culpably risk undermining "the rule of law," he *should* not be punished for refusing to follow the guidance of a proxy crime of which he was unaware.

On the other side of the coin, allowing the value of the rule of law itself to be a legally protected interest may allow us to punish actors who until this point have been beyond the law's reach – those who commit legally impossible attempts. A legally impossible attempt is an action that the actor believes violates the law but does not do so because there is no law of the sort that he believes he is violating. Under our idealized regime, a legally impossible attempter would be someone who believes that he is risking harm to a legally protected interest, but the interest is not protected (dancing on Sundays, perhaps?). With the addition of proxy crimes, one can imagine an actor who believes that it is an offense to have intercourse with a sixteen-year-old, only to find that (1) she is sufficiently mature to consent and (2) the proxy age is set at fifteen. If the actor chooses – indeed, perhaps desires – to break the law (but to have consensual sexual intercourse), should anything be done with such an actor?

We believe that once we deem "undermining the rule of law" to be a legally recognized harm, then such an actor is culpable. Moreover, because the seriousness of the offense is not tied to the imagined harm but to the specific value of the rule of law, the same weight will apply to all potential scofflaws. Likewise, our "epistemically arrogant" actor, who ignores the proxy crime's bright line of sixteen because he believes he can ascertain valid consent in a fifteen-year-old girl, if he is not reckless as to nonconsent, will be guilty, not at the level of one who is so reckless, but at the uniform level set for all scofflaws.

D. LEGALITY QUESTIONS

Our preference for standards over rules may be seen as raising legality concerns. Indeed, Justice Scalia has argued for the "rule of law" as a "law of *rules*."[156] The rule-of-law values said to be served by rules are the "appearance of equal treatment" and "predictability."[157] Indeed, where a statute fails to provide fair notice or allows for too much discretion, the Supreme Court may declare the statute void for vagueness.[158] The Montana Supreme Court voiced the same concerns in invalidating the standards-based speed limit.

Recently, Peter Westen has argued that these two reasons for finding statutes void for vagueness are unpersuasive.[159] In his view, lack of notice is not the problem. After all, a vague term is potentially quite broad, so an actor can hardly claim that he did not have *notice* that the term applied. Rather, the concern is the concern that underlies the "rule of lenity" – the concern that actors not be punished unless "it can confidently be said the political community believes [the actor] is deserving

---

[156] Antonin Scalia, "The Rule of Law as a Law of Rules," 56 *U. Chi. L. Rev.* 1175 (1989).

[157] *Id.* at 1178–1179.

[158] *See* Westen, *supra* note 62, at 292; City of Chicago v. Morales, 527 U.S. 41 (1999); Kolender v. Lawson, 461 U.S. 352 (1982).

[159] Westen, *supra* note 62, at 293–302.

of it."[160] According to Westen, arbitrary and discriminatory enforcement raises equal protection or liberty concerns – not due process (fair notice) ones.[161] We find Westen's reasoning persuasive on these matters, and we add our voice to his in the discussion here.

1. Notice

One critical question is whether our culpability standard actually fails to give notice. We doubt it. A brief example should make our point clear. One of us (and you can likely guess which one) was visiting a pre-K to fifth-grade school to decide whether her son should attend. In the fourth-grade classroom, she saw a poster board that listed the rules of the classroom. There was no rule forbidding hitting; there was no rule forbidding kicking; there was no rule forbidding biting. There was, in fact, only one rule – the Golden Rule. It was clear, concise, and easy to memorize.

Indeed, the Golden Rule is arguably more understandable than the indefinitely many narrow conduct rules that it potentially instantiates. For even if it were possible to write down every potential risk and every potential justifying reason, such a set of classroom rules would be so expansive that no student could hope to have notice of what the school requires. Moreover, any attempt to narrow the coverage to fewer rules creates gaps. The set of articulated rules would then be woefully underinclusive.

Standards can give as much notice as rules in cases such as this. It seems to us that there is little doubt that these nine-year-olds understand that the Golden Rule applies to hitting, kicking, and biting.[162] And, as Westen notes, the only question will be how to treat conduct that lies at the boundaries of the Golden Rule – a point at which the principle of lenity should be applied. This principle of lenity is built into our code, as no jury can convict unless it finds that what the actor did is a "gross deviation" from what the ordinary citizen, with ordinary concern for the interests of others, would do.

---

[160] *Id.* at 293.

[161] *Id.*

[162] *Cf.* United States v. Ragen, 314 U.S. 513, 523 (1942) ("The mere fact that a penal statute is so framed as to require a jury upon occasion to determine a question of reasonableness is not sufficient to make it too vague to afford a practical guide to permissible conduct").

2. Constraining Power

Rules are also believed to curb abuse – not only those abuses caused by whim or caprice but also, and more importantly, those abuses that stem from bias and prejudice.[163] Such abuses may result from decisions by jurors, who, consciously or unconsciously, are biased, but they may also result from decisions by police officers and prosecutors.

Although we believe that police and prosecutors may be tempted to employ discriminatory practices, we are unpersuaded that rules are the answer to the problem. For one thing, although there has been little scholarly attention to this matter,[164] laws may be underenforced in a discriminatory manner. But a nonenforcement decision – not to devote resources to investigating or prosecuting a particular crime – has nothing to do with whether the conduct at issue violated a rule or a standard. Rather, the problem is a lack of transparency in determining when police and prosecutors choose not to investigate or prosecute. Where a law is being enforced discriminatorily, the correct remedy is not to invalidate the law but to invalidate the discriminatory prosecution.[165]

Moreover, a second check on unfettered discretion is the requirement that the actor's culpable choice must constitute a gross deviation from that of a law-abiding citizen. Not just any slip-up will do. Criminal conduct will not be the sort of behavior about which reasonable minds will likely disagree. Instead, to be criminal, the actor's discounting or dismissal of the interests of others must differ sharply from how the rest of the community believes those interests should be treated. Although this test may not prevent discriminatory selection for prosecution, it does provide some check on the ability of jurors to apply different standards to different actors.

Jurors are the appropriate parties for determining the punishment the actor deserves.[166] Since *Apprendi*, there has been a renewed interest in the jury's role in sentencing. Although some commentators argue

[163] Jeffries, *supra* note 60, at 212–213.
[164] *But see* Alexandra Natapoff, "Underenforcement," 75 *Fordham L. Rev.* 1715 (2006).
[165] *See* Westen, *supra* note 62, at 300. *See also* Larry Alexander, "Equal Protection and the Prosecution and Conviction of Crime," 2002 *U. Chi. Legal F.* 155.
[166] *See generally* Morse, *supra* note 34.

that the jury should, at the very least, be apprised of the sentencing consequences of its decisions,[167] others seek to give the jury even greater sentencing power.

Those who argue for increased jury power point to the Framers' view that the jury should serve as an important check on the power of the state – be it the executive, the legislature, or the judiciary.[168] Indeed, the jury's unreviewable power is the one significant safety valve for combating the overinclusive nature of criminal law rules.[169] According to Rachel Barkow,

> Even if the people's representatives agreed that certain behavior should be criminalized, the Framing generation wanted the people themselves to have a final say in each case. In criminal trials – trials that, at their core are trials of the human condition and morality – the jury would allow the morality of the community and its notions of fundamental law to inform the interpretation of the facts and, in some cases, to overcome the rigidity of a general criminal law. That the jurors have no expertise in questions of legal interpretation was not a cause for concern. The purpose of the jury was to inject the common-sense views of the community into a criminal proceeding to ensure that an individual would not lose her liberty if it would be contrary to the community's sense of fundamental law and equity.[170]

Of course, one might argue that there is a difference between giving the jury the power to nullify a law and giving the jury the power to "make" law. However, our jurors' decision making will be constrained by the code and its guidelines for determining the actor's culpability. Moreover, we believe that the threshold question – did the actor manifest insufficient concern for others – is a question about community expectations and our societal understanding of what citizens owe each other. These are precisely the questions the jury should be answering.

[167] *See, e.g.,* Cahill, *supra* note 95.
[168] *Id.* at 103–104. Rachel E. Barkow, "Recharging the Jury: The Criminal Jury's Constitutional Role in an Era of Mandatory Sentencing," 152 *U. Pa. L. Rev.* 33, 49–51 and 60–61 (2003).
[169] Barkow, *supra* note 168, at 36, 39.
[170] *Id.* at 58–59.

E. ENFORCEMENT PROBLEMS

1. Do We Unjustly Empower Prosecutors?

In the first part of this chapter, we introduced a new format for criminal codes and sentencing. Our perspective places significant responsibility on *jurors* to ascertain the risks the actor foresaw, to determine the actor's reasons for his action, to assess the justifiability of imposing the foreseen risk in light of those reasons, and ultimately to determine whether the actor deserves blame. The jury is the linchpin of our proposed system.

What jury? The vast majority of criminal cases do not involve a jury. Plea bargains resolve as many as 90 percent of criminal cases.[171] What is it to which our criminal defendants plead guilty? Exhibiting insufficient concern? If the shoplifter, the thief, the rapist, and the murderer are all in theory guilty of the very same crime, we have greatly increased the power of prosecutors.

Our first response is that, of course, there is more to the calculation than "insufficient concern." One must look at the harm risked, the actor's belief in its probability, the actor's reasons, and the like. But, still, the concern is very real. Do not prosecutors (and defendants) have considerable power to stipulate what those perceived risks and reasons were?

Perhaps. But in our view, the question is not whether there is room to bargain, but whether the bargain is fair. Our approach promotes fair bargains by not allowing for overinclusive laws that punish innocent actors. The prosecutor does not start out from an unfair position – that is, with the ability to threaten the defendant with more punishment than he deserves. Right now, the law does little to determine who shall be punished because overinclusive laws create a prosecutorial feast, at which a prosecutor may simply choose which of the many choices on the menu to select.

Our system could also employ mechanisms to provide guidance as to how previous similar cases have been treated, so that like cases will more likely be treated alike. Jury determinations in previous cases

---

[171] *See* Russell L. Christopher, "The Prosecutor's Dilemma: Bargains and Punishments," 72 *Fordham L. Rev.* 93, 97 and n.11 (2003).

could be published in a manner that allows prosecutors, defendants, and judges to determine how similar cases have been decided, and a judge could refuse to accept a plea that unjustifiably departed from those previous reports. Then, perhaps bargaining would take place within the law's shadow.

We also believe that there should be other restrictions on prosecutors. It is a fact about our world that prosecutors simply lack the resources to pursue all cases. The critical question is how to distribute desert among the deserving in a world of limited resources. One problem, to which we alluded to in Chapter 1, is the question about comparative versus noncomparative desert. Should we worry if some people get what they deserve and others do not? Because we believe retributive desert is ultimately noncomparative, those who are punished to the full extent they deserve are not treated unjustly vis-à-vis those culpable actors who escape any or full punishment. But choosing whom among the culpable to prosecute may still be unfair because the criteria of selection are improper. In other words, we do not doubt that even under our system, "plea bargains [will] take place in the shadow of prosecutors' preferences, voters' preferences, budget constraints, and other forces,"[172] but we have faith that there are moral principles to guide which exercises of discretion are permissible and which ones are not.

2. Reconciling Our Act Requirement with Concerns about Law Enforcement

There are related questions about our culpability-based code that do not stem from our endorsement of standards, but rather from our view of the criminal law's act requirement. These concerns point in both directions. Theorists may argue that, in some ways, we improperly grant too much discretion, whereas in other ways, we tie the hands of law enforcement.

a. Concerns about Policing Thoughts: The objection that we are creating too strong a police state might best be understood as a concern about "thought police." This concern is not new, but, one might argue, the

---

[172] *See* William J. Stuntz, "Plea Bargaining and Criminal Law's Disappearing Shadow," 117 *Harv. L. Rev.* 2548, 2550 (2004).

worrisome effects are more significant under our system. The objection arises in the case of factual impossibility, where the conduct itself is objectively neutral.[173] So, if a hunter decides to kill his hunting buddy, but upon seeing movement in the trees he shoots at what he believes to be his buddy but is actually a deer, the hunter's conduct from all objective appearances seems innocuous. Should we not want the conduct itself to corroborate the actor's culpability? If not, could the police arrest perfectly legitimate acts of deer killing on the grounds that these are in fact attempts to kill human beings?

Now, of course, this objection is nothing new, but our view widens its potential applications. Because we premise liability on risking and not on harming, all sorts of seemingly innocuous conduct may actually be criminal. Perhaps more important, even truly innocent conduct could be prosecuted (mistakenly) for being criminal.

We believe this concern is unfounded. First, with any criminal case, we depend on a meaningful burden of proof. The jury must find that the actor consciously disregarded what he believed to be an unjustifiable risk. Obviously, hitting a deer is not sufficient to prove that one intended to kill (and thus consciously disregarded the risk of killing) another human being. Second, the requirement that an action unequivocally manifest criminality strikes us as wrongheaded. It has long been recognized that additional evidence that shows intent will often give meaning to an otherwise ambiguous action.[174] It is this additional evidence that the jury will need to hear in order to convict; but when this evidence is available, there is no reason to require that the act speak for itself. Indeed, we find the idea that acts "objectively manifest criminality" to be incoherent; all attempts that (by hypothesis) fail will appear innocuous to an observer if she assumes no culpable mental state but "criminal" if she assumes the opposite.

In summary, our code does not require the criminal act to "manifest criminality." Indeed, given that we believe that the heart of criminal liability is culpability, which is itself subjective, there is no way for a criminal act to perform this function. Nevertheless, we believe

---

[173] *See* Sanford H. Kadish and Stephen J. Schulhofer, eds., *Criminal Law and Its Processes: Cases and Materials* 600 (7th ed., 2001) (raising this issue in a comment in a hypothetical law review).

[174] *See* Glanville Williams, *Criminal Law: The General Part* 630 (2d ed., 1961).

that a meaningful burden of proof is sufficient to combat the fear of false convictions.

b. Concerns about Crippling Law Enforcement: Although many may believe that our code gives too much power to law enforcement, others might complain that our approach ties the hands of law enforcement. This objection likewise stems from our act requirement. Specifically, our view that an actor has not committed a culpable act until he has unleashed a risk of harm over which he no longer has control may prevent law enforcement from preventing crime.

To take the strongest case against our position, consider sexual predators. A current law enforcement technique is to have a police officer pose as a young child in an Internet chat room. An email exchange might ultimately result in the discussion of sexual activity, and "the minor" will set up a meeting. The "sexual predator" will then appear at the designated place in the hope of engaging in illegal sexual conduct. Under current law, these are attempts to engage in the unlawful sexual conduct.[175] Under our approach, however, they appear not to be punishable, as their risks have yet to be unleashed and beyond the predators' control.

Let us begin by admitting that these cases would not be crimes under our framework. A sexual predator who only gets near his victim retains complete control over whether or not he will ultimately engage in the sexual conduct. Although at some point, a sexual predator (or even a common rapist) may get close enough to consummation that he will cause fear of a nonconsensual attack – a fear that will in fact give rise to the victim's right to use defensive force – he still will not have unleashed the risk of violating the victim's sexual autonomy and causing the victim physical harm. Indeed, in cases involving what, but for the victim's age, would be consensual sexual activity, it appears that the culpable act will be the act of penetration (or a similar act).

If, however, we are to remain a liberal society committed to the idea that individuals possess free will and moral responsibility, we cannot say that the actor *deserves* criminal punishment until he has committed this culpable act. We may fear that such an actor will eventually succeed

---

[175] For a discussion of the issues presented by such cases, *see* Audrey Rogers, "New Technology, Old Defenses: Internet Sting Operations and Attempt Liability," 38 *U. Rich. L. Rev.* 477 (2004).

in his quest to have sex with a minor. We may wish to stop such an actor. Nevertheless, we cannot punish such an actor.

Our view may present a new obstacle for law enforcement, but we believe that this obstacle can be overcome. Police will be able to intervene at the point at which the actor causes fear, as consciously risking causing fear for the purpose of risking harm is itself a culpable act. In addition, law enforcement may stop and detain an individual before the point that justifies arresting the actor.[176]

There is also the question of preventive detention. When we may permissibly detain someone who has not committed a culpable act is a difficult question.[177] After all, these detentions, or "quarantines," are not based on what people have done but rather on what these individuals *might do* or *likely will do*. For this reason, we must have extremely good predictive abilities before we can even begin to justify detaining them, given that they are neither culpable nor nonresponsible. How good must we be at such prediction? This is a troublesome question, but at least it is the right question. As Paul Robinson aptly describes the problem, at the moment the criminal law "cloaks" preventive detention as criminal justice.[178] But the criminal code we advocate does not allow for such deception. If we wish to restrict people's liberty – not because they *deserve it* – but because we predict they will harm others, then we need to analyze when and if we may do so. We believe that a virtue of our code is that it unmasks this issue and refuses to conceal preventive detention within the rubric of the criminal law.

F. PROCEDURAL, EVIDENTIARY, AND SENTENCING CONSIDERATIONS

The practical implementation of the criminal law will inevitably involve some trade-offs. Burdens of proof affect the allocation between false positives (punishing the innocent) and false negatives (freeing the guilty).[179]

---

[176] *See* Terry v. Ohio, 393 U.S. 1 (1968).
[177] *See* Stephen J. Morse, "Neither Desert nor Disease," 5 *Legal Theory* 265 (1999).
[178] *See* Paul H. Robinson, "Punishing Dangerousness: Cloaking Preventive Detention as Criminal Justice," 114 *Harv. L. Rev.* 1429 (2001).
[179] Some argue that the trade-off is broader still, as one may trade off innocents against innocents – the innocent victim versus the innocent accused. *See, e.g.,* Cass R. Sunstein and Adrian Vermeule, "Is Capital Punishment Morally Required? The Relevance of Life-Life Tradeoffs," 58 *Stan. L. Rev.* 703 (2005). We disagree with Sunstein and Vermeule because they fail to see that not punishing the innocent and not punishing the less culpable as if

Evidentiary rules affect the admissibility of evidence in determinations of guilt and innocence. Plea bargains sacrifice punishing the guilty to the full extent of their retributive desert under situations of epistemic uncertainty and limited resources. Sentencing departures allow the government to reward cooperation and plea bargaining and allow the court to take account of specific defendant characteristics, such as extraordinary family circumstances.

No real-world code can fail to take account of these practicalities. Of course, having defended a comprehensive view of criminal culpability, we believe that, at this point, it would be far too ambitious an endeavor to undertake solving all these real-world concerns. Moreover, as we noted in Chapter 1, some of these questions are deeper questions about retributivism, questions that we do not undertake to answer here. Nevertheless, we conclude with some passing thoughts about these final implementation questions.

1. Burdens of Proof and Evidentiary Rules

The "beyond a reasonable doubt" standard for conviction prevents false positives at the expense of false negatives. However, according to some theorists, retributivism as a theory is agnostic about this allocation.[180] We doubt, however, that a criminal law theorist can also be agnostic. That is, one question – and this is not a question we answer here – is whether this trade-off is a question for a *retributivist*.[181] However, it is certainly clear that a criminal law theorist who adopts retributive principles will ultimately need an account of rights and an account of political theory that determines how the right against being unjustly punished – punished more than one deserves – is to be weighed against the goal of seeing the guilty receive their just deserts. We doubt these two are of equal weight. As Peter Westen states, "Of all the injustices that can be wrongly inflicted in the name of the people, there is scarcely any as

they were more culpable are deontological constraints that apply to the government in the same way that they apply to individuals.

[180] *See* Richard A. Bierschbach and Alex Stein, "Mediating Rules in Criminal Law," 93 *Va. L. Rev.* 1197, 1208 (2007) ("retributive theory expresses no strong preference for whether such rules skew more toward the side of false positives or more toward false negatives").

[181] According to Michael Moore, the question is whether one is a deontological retributivist or a consequentialist one. *See* Moore, *supra* note 16, at 156–158.

great as punishing a person – and, thus, holding him out to deserve to suffer hard treatment by virtue of having engaged in prohibited conduct – when he did *not* engage in the conduct the statute prohibits."[182] Nevertheless, one needs richer theory than we have developed here to account for how this trade-off can be made and thus to assess whether the reasonable doubt standard strikes the correct balance.

2. *Plea Bargaining*

Like allocations of the burden of proof, the propriety of plea bargaining depends on the extent to which one believes that giving people their just deserts is a duty or whether it is simply an intrinsic good.[183] We do believe, though, that a retributivist who denies the permissibility of plea bargaining loses any power to influence the application of her theories to the real world in which resource limitations require trade-offs.[184] Moreover, as we discussed earlier in this section, we also believe that there are more and less principled ways to go about exercising such prosecutorial discretion.

3. *Sentencing Considerations*

Along with the other consequentialist trade-offs we have mentioned, there may be occasions when it is appropriate for a sentencing judge to take factors into account that do not pertain to the desert of the offender. We recognize that retributive desert may be trumped, overridden, or outweighed by some consequentialist concerns. When the need to decrease punishment is sufficiently costly to other worthwhile goals (a test we do not even attempt to quantify here), the actor's punishment may be decreased.

There are myriad reasons to reduce punishment. Plea bargaining and witness immunity are typical examples.[185] Moreover, sometimes

---

[182] See Westen, *supra* note 62, at 283 (arguing that the presumption of innocence and the principle of legality both "derive their content from the shared belief that unwittingly convicting the innocent is a far more frightful harm than unwittingly acquitting the guilty").

[183] See Moore, *supra* note 16, at 156–158.

[184] See generally Michael T. Cahill, "Retributive Justice in the Real World" (Legal Studies Paper No. 77, Brooklyn Law School, 2007), available at http://ssrn.com/abstract=996140.

[185] See generally Robinson and Cahill, *supra* note 149, at ch. 4.

the consequences of punishment for those other than the defendant may simply be too severe to countenance. Downward departures under the USSG for extraordinary family circumstances are based not on a lack of desert but on the significance of the consequences for others. As the Second Circuit noted in one case, "The rationale for a downward departure here is not that Johnson's family circumstances decrease her culpability, but that we are reluctant to wreak extraordinary destruction on dependents who rely solely on the defendant for their upbringing."[186] For such reasons, a judge may depart *downward* from a sentencing range. Although an actor should not receive more punishment than he deserves, there may be times when our justice system will have to sacrifice giving the individual what she deserves for some other important end. Because the sentence reduction does not deal with the actor's blameworthiness, but rather some other societal goal, we believe that these sorts of reductions are best administered by a judge, not a jury.

This chapter is simply a rough sketch of how one might try to implement our theory in the real world. Because our idealized theory must deal with real-world practicalities, there is little doubt that sometimes the criminal law will be forced to opt for second-best solutions. Errors and inadequacies in other parts of our criminal justice system are occasionally "fixed" through the distortions of criminal law doctrine. Nevertheless, when we make these allowances, we move away from punishing only those who deserve punishment and only as much as they deserve. To be clear about the nature and extent of these sacrifices, we should first think through how an idealized code would work and only then decide which sacrifices we are willing to make. We should also think clearly about whether matters are best resolved through changes to substantive criminal law doctrine as opposed to through criminal procedure, evidentiary rules, or even better oversight of law enforcement officials. Though we cannot solve these problems, we hope that this chapter has provided a sufficient framework to elucidate the structure and substance of the debate.

[186] United States v. Johnson, 964 F.2d 124 (1992).

Epilogue

Our entire book has been devoted to the implications of having criminal
liability turn on the pivots of the risks the actor perceives and the reasons for which he chooses to impose those risks. In many respects,
our analysis and prescriptions are clear departures from criminal law
orthodoxy, both doctrinal and theoretical. Although we believe that
our approach is perhaps not as radical as it might appear to be – after all,
many critics are uncomfortable with making inadvertent negligence a
basis for criminal liability; many (theorists, at least) are persuaded that
results should not matter to criminal liability; recklessness, with its axes
of risks and reasons, is already a fundamental component of criminal
law; and inchoate criminal liability is a controversial and confusing
domain – we concede that all our proposals taken together will be sufficiently dramatic that the burden of persuasion we carry is properly a
heavy one. Nonetheless, we believe we have met it. At the very least, we
believe we have presented and justified an internally coherent version of
a criminal law based on meting out retributive justice.

Appendix

Sample Initial Instructions (Prior to Calculation by Guidelines)

General instructions:

It is criminal for an actor to take an unjustified risk of causing harm to a legally protected interest or to take an unjustified risk that his conduct constitutes prohibited behavior.

The following are harms to legally protected interests [list those applicable]:

Death

Fear of death

Serious bodily injury

Less serious bodily injury

Etc.

The law does not protect an individual from a risk of harm to which she consents. If the person subjected to the risk of harm knowingly and voluntarily consented to that risk, then the defendant cannot be liable for risking that harm. (An exception to this principle exists when the law specifically denies the capacity of the person to give legally effective consent to the particular risk in question.)

For behavior to be justified, the reasons that the actor has for engaging in his behavior should be weighed against the risk that the actor perceives that his conduct will cause a prohibited result or results.

An actor may never justify "appropriating" or "using" another human being (unless the appropriation is minor and the harm to be averted serious?).

The actor's reasons for action include not only the reason or reasons that motivate his conduct but also any other reason that might justify his conduct of which he is aware. These reasons should be accorded weight by (1) their positive or negative force and (2) the actor's perception of the likelihood that the facts underlying the reasons do or will obtain.

When acting to prevent great harm, the actor need not take the action that causes the least evil; she must simply engage in conduct that is a lesser evil than the harm that she believes would have otherwise occurred.

Defense of self and others:

An actor is justified in using the force he believes necessary to stop a culpable attacker. By "culpable" is meant an attacker who is aware that her conduct imposes an unjustifiable risk on another.

If an actor is uncertain whether her attacker is culpable, she is entitled to discount the value of that attacker's interests in proportion to her belief that the attacker is culpable. So, if an actor believes to a 50 percent certainty that her attacker is culpable, she is entitled to value her attacker's interests at half of what it would otherwise be worth.

You must also determine whether this defendant's decision was a gross deviation from that of a reasonable person. In making this evaluation, you should consider, given the gravity of the risk the defendant otherwise faced, discounted by its likelihood, and taking into account the feasibility, costs, and risks of any alternatives, whether defendant had sufficient personal reason so to act.

In making this determination, I advise you that:

A reasonable person may weigh the lives of loved ones more than the lives of strangers. A reasonable person may react to both natural threats (e.g., a boulder) and human threats. A reasonable person may harm or even kill another human being, if faced with a significant threat.

You need not conclude that what defendant did was the "right thing to do," but rather, that taking into account a realistic sense of faults and failings of the ordinary human being, we could not have expected a reasonable person, one who shows proper regard for the interests of others, to have acted otherwise than defendant acted.

After looking at this choice, you should also evaluate how defendant made this choice. You should find him to be less culpable if his rationality was impaired. You should find him more culpable if he engaged in substantial deliberation and planning – that is, more planning than simply deciding to take the risk.

If, having considered all of these factors, you believe that the risk defendant took was not justified by the reasons of which he was aware, and that given the difference between risks and reasons, he grossly deviated from what an ordinary, reasonable, law-abiding actor would do, you should find defendant guilty.

If you find defendant guilty, you will be asked to calculate the risks and reasons precisely and determine whether and the extent to which defendant was culpable.

Bibliography

Primary Materials

Annotated Code of Maryland, Criminal Law (2007).

Apprendi v. New Jersey, 530 U.S. 466 (2000).

Arizona Revised Statutes Annotated (West 1998).

Arizona v. Henley, 687 P.2d 1220 (Ariz. 1984).

Ashcroft v. Free Speech Coalition, 535 U.S. 234 (2002).

Atkins v. Virginia, 536 U.S. 304 (2002).

Baltimore & O.R.R. v. Goodman, 275 U.S. 66 (1927).

Berry v. Sugar Notch Borough, 43 A. 240 (Pa. 1899).

Blakely v. Washington, 542 U.S. 296 (2004).

Blockburger v. United States, 284 U.S. 299 (1932).

Brown v. Indiana, 830 N.E.2d 956 (Ind. Ct. App. 2005).

California v. Hamilton, 47 Cal. Rptr. 2d 343 (Cal. Ct. App. 1995).

Code of Alabama (West 1975).

Code of Georgia Annotated (2007).

Connecticut General Statutes Annotated (2007).

California Penal Code (West 1999).

City of Chicago v. Morales, 527 U.S. 41 (1999).

Director of Public Prosecutions for Northern Ireland v. Maxwell, (1978) 3 All E.R. 1140.

Griswold v. Connecticut, 381 U.S. 579 (1965).

Hawaii Revised Statutes (2006).

Illinois v. Wicks, 823 N.E.2d 1153 (Ill. Ct. App. 2005).

In re Steven S., 31 Cal. Rptr. 644 (1994).

Kansas v. Harris, 162 P.3d 28 (Kan. 2007).

Kansas v. Neal, 120 P.3d 366 (Kan. Ct. App. 2005).

Kolender v. Lawson, 461 U.S. 352 (1982).

Ladner v. United States, 358 U.S. 169 (1958).

Lawrence v. Texas, 539 U.S. 558 (2003).

Martin v. Ohio, 480 U.S. 228 (1987).

Maryland Code Annotated (2007).

Mattingly v. United States, 924 F.2d 785 (8th Cir. 1991).

Michigan Compiled Laws Annotated (2007).

Missouri Revised Statutes (2007).

Missouri v. Hunter, 459 U.S. 359 (1983).

Model Penal Code (Official Draft and Revised Comments) (1985).

New Jersey Statutes Annotated (West 2007).

New York Education Law (2001)

New York Penal Law (McKinney1999).

New York Penal Law (2003).

New York Penal Law (2007).

Palsgraf v. Long Island Railroad Company, 162 N.E. 99 (N.Y. 1928).

Pennsylvania Consolidated Statutes Annotated (West 2003).

People v. Anderson, 447 P.2d 942 (1968).

People v. Decina, 138 N.E.2d 799 (N.Y. 1956).

People v. Dlugash, 363 N.E.2d 1155 (N.Y. 1977).

People v. Luparello, 231 Cal. Rptr. 832 (Cal. Ct. App. 1986).

People v. Myers, 426 N.E.2d 535 (Ill. 1981).

People v. Myers, 816 N.E.2d 820 (Ill. Ct. App. 2004).

People v. Payne, 819 N.E.2d 634 (N.Y. 2004);

People v. Rizzo, 158 N.E. 888, 889 (N.Y. 1927).

People v. Suarez, 844 N.E.2d 721 (N.Y. 2005).

Pokora v. Wabash Ry. Co., 292 U.S. 98 (1934).

Regina v. Smith (David), (1974) 2 Q.B. 354.

Restatement (Third) of Torts: Liability for Physical Harm (Proposed Final Draft No. 1, 2005).

Sanchez-Rengifo v. United States, 815 A.2d 351 (D.C. Ct. App. 2002).

Sandstrom v. Montana, 442 U.S. 510 (1979).

Sindell v. Abbott Laboratories, 607 P.2d 924 (Cal. 1980).

Smith v. United States, 295 A.2d 60 (D.C. Ct. App. 1972).

State v. LaFreniere, 481 N.W.2d 412 (Neb. 1992).

State v. Stanko, 974 P.2d 1132 (Mont. 1998).

State v. Williams, 484 P.2d 1167 (Wash. Ct. App. 1971).

Stephenson v. State, 179 N.E. 633 (Ind. 1932).

Summers v. Tice, 199 P.2d 1 (Cal. 1948) (en banc).

Terry v. Ohio, 393 U.S. 1 (1968).

Texas Penal Code Annotated (2007).

Thabo Meli v. Regina, (1954) 1 All E.R. 373.

United States Code, title 18, § 1346 (2000).

United States Constitution, Amendment V.

United States Sentencing Guidelines Manual (2005).

United States v. Bergman, 416 F. Supp. 496 (S.D.N.Y. 1976).

United States v. Booker, 543 U.S. 220 (2005).

United States v. Brumley, 116 F.3d 728 (5th Cir. 1997).

United States v. Carroll Towing Co., 159 F.2d. 169 (2d Cir. 1947).

United States v. Czubinski, 106 F.3d 1069 (1st Cir. 1997).

United States v. Dixon, 509 U.S. 688 (1993).

United States v. Incorporated Village of Island Park, 888 F. Supp. 419 (E.D.N.Y. 1995).

United States v. Jewell, 532 F.2d 697 (9th Cir. 1976).

United States v. Johnson, 964 F.2d 124 (1992).

United States v. Mancuso, 42 F.3d 836 (4th Cir. 1994).

United States v. Oviedo, 525 F.2d 881 (5th Cir. 1976).

United States v. Ragen, 314 U.S. 513 (1942).

United States v. Sawyer, 239 F.3d 31 (1st Cir. 2001).

United States v. Whittington, 26 F.3d 456 (4th Cir. 1994).

Village of Sugar Grove v. Rich, 808 N.E.2d 525 (Ill. Ct. App. 2004).

Washington v. Soonalole, 992 P.2d 541 (Wash. Ct. App. 2000).

Wisconsin v. Rabe, 291 N.W.2d 809 (Wis. 1980).

Secondary Materials

Alexander, Larry. "A Unified Excuse of Preemptive Self-Protection," *Notre Dame Law Review* 74 (1999), 1475–1506.

"Consent, Punishment, and Proportionality," *Philosophy & Public Affairs* 15 (1986), 178–182.

"Crime and Culpability," *Journal of Contemporary Legal Issues* 5 (1994), 1–30.

"Criminal Liability for Omissions: An Inventory of Issues," in *Criminal Law Theory: Doctrines of the General Part* (S. Shute and A. P. Simester, eds., Oxford: Oxford University Press, 2002), 121–142.

"Deontology at the Threshold," *San Diego Law Review* 37 (2000), 893–912.

"The Doomsday Machine: Proportionality, Prevention, and Punishment," *Monist* 63 (1980), 199–227.

"Equal Protection and the Prosecution and Conviction of Crime," *University of Chicago Legal Forum* (2002), 155–162.

"Foreword: Coleman and Corrective Justice," *Harvard Journal of Law & Public Policy* 15 (1992), 621–636.

"Harm, Offense and Morality," 7 *Canadian Journal of Law & Jurisprudence* 199 (1994).

"Inculpatory and Exculpatory Mistakes and the Fact/Law Distinction: An Essay in Memory of Myke Bayles," *Law & Philosophy* 12 (1993), 33–70.

"Insufficient Concern: A Unified Conception of Criminal Culpability," *California Law Review* 88 (2000), 931–954.

"Lesser Evils: A Closer Look at the Paradigmatic Justification," *Law & Philosophy* 24 (2005), 611–644.

"The Moral Magic of Consent (II)," *Legal Theory* 2 (1996), 165–174.

"The Philosophy of Criminal Law," in *The Oxford Handbook of Jurisprudence and Legal Philosophy* (Jules Coleman and Scott Shapiro, eds., Oxford: Oxford University Press, 2002), 815–867.

"Reconsidering the Relationship among Voluntary Acts, Strict Liability, and Negligence in Criminal Law," *Social Philosophy & Policy* 7 (1990), 84–104.

"Scalar Properties, Binary Judgments," *Journal of Applied Philosophy* 25 (2008), 85–104.

"Unknowingly Justified Actors and the Attempt/Success Distinction," *Tulsa Law Review* 39 (2004), 851–860.

Alexander, Larry, and Kimberly Kessler Ferzan. "Culpable Acts of Risk Creation," *Ohio State Journal of Criminal Law* 5 (2008), 375–405.

Alexander, Larry, and Kimberly D. Kessler. "Mens Rea and Inchoate Crimes," *Journal of Criminal Law & Criminology* 87 (1997), 1138–1193.

Alexander, Larry, and Michael S. Moore. "Deontological Ethics," *Stanford Encyclopedia of Philosophy* (November 21, 2007), available at http://plato.stanford.edu/entries/ethics-deontological/.

Alexander, Larry, and Emily Sherwin. "The Deceptive Nature of Rules," *University of Pennsylvania Law Review* 142 (1994), 1191–1227.

The Rule of Rules: Morality, Rules and the Dilemmas of Law (Durham: Duke University Press, 2001).

Arenella, Peter. "Convicting the Morally Blameless: Reassessing the Relationship between Legal and Moral Accountability," *UCLA Law Review* 39 (1992), 1511–1623.

Arneson, Richard J. "Just Warfare Theory and Noncombatant Immunity," *Cornell International Law Journal* 39 (2006), 663–688.

Ashworth, Andrew. "The Doctrine of Provocation," *Cambridge Law Journal* 35 (1976), 292–320.

Baker, Brenda M. "Mens Rea, Negligence, and Criminal Law Reform," *Law & Philosophy* 6 (1987), 53–88.

Barkow, Rachel E. "Recharging the Jury: The Criminal Jury's Constitutional Role in an Era of Mandatory Sentencing," *University of Pennsylvania Law Review* 152 (2003), 33–128.

Bayles, Michael D. *Principles of Law: A Normative Analysis* (Dordrecht: D. Reidel; Norwell: sold and distributed in the U.S.A. and Canada by Kluwer Academic Publishers, 1987).

Beauchamp, Tom L. "Who Deserves Autonomy, and Whose Autonomy Deserves Respect?" in *Personal Autonomy: New Essays in Personal Autonomy and Its Role in Contemporary Moral Philosophy* (J. S. Taylor ed., Cambridge: Cambridge University Press, 2004), 310–329.

Benbaji, Yitzhak. "Culpable Bystanders, Innocent Threats and the Ethics of Self-Defense," *Canadian Journal of Philosophy* 35 (2005), 585–622.

Bentham, Jeremy. *Introduction to the Principles of Morals and Legislation* (1781; Buffalo: Prometheus Books, 1988).

Bergelson, Vera. "The Right to Be Hurt: Testing the Boundaries of Consent," *George Washington Law Review* 75 (2007), 165–236.

"Victims and Perpetrators: An Argument for Comparative Liability in Criminal Law," *Buffalo Criminal Law Review* 8 (2005), 385–488.

Berman, Mitchell N. "Justification and Excuse, Law and Morality," *Duke Law Journal* 53 (2003), 1–78.

"Lesser Evils and Justification: A Less Close Look," *Law and Philosophy* 24 (2005), 681–709.

"Punishment and Justification," working paper (December 15, 2006), available at SSRN: http://ssrn.com/abstract=956610.

Bierschbach, Richard A., and Alex Stein. "Mediating Rules in Criminal Law," *Virginia Law Review* 93 (2007), 1197–1258.

Bok, Hilary. *Freedom and Responsibility* (Princeton: Princeton University Press, 1998).

Brady, James. "Punishment for Negligence: A Reply to Professor Hall," *Buffalo Law Review* 22 (1972), 107–122.

Bratman, Michael. *Intentions, Plans, and Practical Reason* (Cambridge, Mass.: Harvard University Press, 1987).

Brown, Darryl K. "Plain Meaning, Practical Reason, and Culpability: Toward a Theory of Jury Interpretation of Criminal Statutes," *Michigan Law Review* 96 (1998), 1199–1268.

Byrd, B. Sharon. "Wrongdoing and Attribution: Implications beyond the Justification-Excuse Distinction," *Wayne Law Review* 33 (1987), 1289–1342.

Cahill, Michael T. "Punishment Decisions at Conviction: Recognizing the Jury as Fault-Finder," *University of Chicago Legal Forum* (2005), 91–148.

"Retributive Justice in the Real World," Legal Studies Paper No. 77, Brooklyn Law School (2007), available at http://ssrn.com/abstract=996140.

Calabresi, Guido, and Phillip Bobbitt. *Tragic Choices* (New York: Norton, 1978).

Cardozo, Benjamin. *What Medicine Can Do for Law* (1930; Clark: Lawbook Exchange, 2005).

Cavanaugh, T. A. *Double-Effect Reasoning: Doing Good and Avoiding Evil* (Oxford: Clarendon Press, 2006).

Christopher, Russell L. "The Prosecutor's Dilemma: Bargains and Punishments," *Fordham Law Review* 72 (2003), 93–168.

Conlisk, John. "Why Bounded Rationality," *Journal of Economic Literature* 34 (1996), 669–700.

Dan-Cohen, Meir. "Decision Rules and Conduct Rules: On Acoustic Separation in Criminal Law," *Harvard Law Review* 97 (1984), 625–677.

Davidson, Donald. *Essays on Actions and Events* (2d ed., Oxford: Clarendon, 2001).

Delaney, Neil Francis. "A Note on Intention and the Doctrine of Double Effect," *Philosophical Studies* 134 (2007), 103–110.

"Two Cheers for 'Closeness': Terror, Targeting and Double Effect," *Philosophical Studies* 137 (2008), 335–367.

Dennett, Daniel Clement. *Content and Consciousness* (London: Routledge & Kegan Paul; New York, Humanities Press, 1969).

Freedom Evolves (New York: Viking, 2003).

Domsky, Darren. "There Is No Door: Finally Solving the Problem of Moral Luck," *Journal of Philosophy* 101 (2004), 445–464.

"Double Jeopardy," *Georgetown Law Journal Annual Review of Criminal Procedure* 35 (2006), 422–464.

Dressler, Joshua. "Battered Women Who Kill Their Sleeping Tormenters: Reflections on Maintaining Respect for Human Life While Killing Moral Monsters," in *Criminal Law Theory: Doctrines of the General Part* (Stephen Shute and A. P. Simester, eds., Oxford: Oxford University Press, 2002), 259–282.

"Does One Size Fit All? Thoughts on Alexander's Unified Conception of Criminal Culpability," *California Law Review* 88 (2000), 955–964.

"Justifications and Excuses: A Brief Review of the Concepts and the Literature," *Wayne Law Review* 33 (1987), 1155–1176.

Understanding Criminal Law (4th ed., New York: Lexis, 2006).

"Why Keep the Provocation Defense?: Some Reflections on a Difficult Subject," *Minnesota Law Review* 86 (2002), 959–1002.

Dubber, Marcus Dirk. "Toward a Constitutional Law of Crime and Punishment," *Hastings Law Journal* 55 (2004), 509–572.

Duff, R. A. *Answering for Crime: Responsibility and Liability in Criminal Law* (Oxford and Portland, Oregon: Hart, (2007).

"Crime, Prohibition, and Punishment," *Journal of Applied Philosophy* 19 (2002), 97–108.

"Criminalizing Endangerment," *Louisiana Law Review* 65 (2005), 941–967.

"'I Might Be Guilty, But You Can't Try Me': Estoppel and Other Bars to Trial," *Ohio State Journal of Criminal Law* 1 (2003), 245–260.

Intention, Agency, and Criminal Liability: Philosophy of Action and the Criminal Law (Oxford: Blackwell, 1990).

"Rethinking Justifications," *Tulsa Law Review* 39 (2004), 829–850.

Dworkin, Gerald, and David Blumenfeld. "Punishment for Intentions," *Mind* 75 (1966), 396–404.

Edmundson, William. "Morality without Responsibility," manuscript on submission (2007), on file with author, University of San Diego School of Law.

Eisikovits, Nir. "Moral Luck and the Criminal Law," in *Law and Social Justice* (J. K. Campbell, M. O'Rourke, and D. Shier, eds., Cambridge, Mass.: MIT Press, 2005), 105–124.

Enoch, David. "Ends, Means, Side-Effects, and Beyond: A Comment on the Justification of the Use of Force," *Theoretical Inquiries in Law* 7 (2005), 43–59.

Estrich, Susan. *Real Rape* (Cambridge, Mass.: Harvard University Press, 1987).

Ezorsky, Gertrude. "The Ethics of Punishment," in *Philosophical Perspectives on Punishment* (G. Ezorsky, ed., Albany: State University of New York Press, 1972), xi–xxvi.

Fabre, Cecile. *Whose Body Is It Anyway?: Justice and the Integrity of the Person* (Oxford: Oxford University Press, 2006).

Feinberg, Joel. *Doing and Deserving: Essays in the Theory of Responsibility* (Princeton: Princeton University Press, 1970).

Harm to Others (New York: Oxford University Press, 1984).

Harm to Self (New York: Oxford University Press, 1986).

Harmless Wrongdoing (New York: Oxford University Press, 1988).

Offense to Others (New York: Oxford University Press, 1985).

Ferzan, Kimberly Kessler. "Act, Agency, and Indifference: The Foundations of Criminal Responsibility," *New Criminal Law Review* 10 (2007), 441- 457.

"Beyond Intention," *Cardozo Law Review* 29 (2008), 1147–1167.

"Clarifying Consent: Peter Westen's *The Logic of Consent*," *Law & Philosophy* 25 (2006), 193–217.

"Defending Imminence: From Battered Women to Iraq," *Arizona Law Review* 46 (2004), 213–262.

"Don't Abandon the Model Penal Code Yet! Thinking Through Simons's *Rethinking*," *Buffalo Criminal Law Review* 6 (2002), 185–218.

"Holistic Culpability," *Cardozo Law Review* 28 (2007), 2523–2544.

"Justifying Self-Defense," *Law & Philosophy* 24 (2005), 711–749.

"Opaque Recklessness," *Journal of Criminal Law & Criminology* 91 (2001), 597–652.

Finkelstein, Claire O. "Excuses and Dispositions in Criminal Law," *Buffalo Criminal Law Review* 6 (2002), 317–360.

"Self-Defense as Rational Excuse," *University of Pittsburgh Law Review* 57 (1996), 621–650.

Fischer, John Martin. "'Punishment and Desert: A Reply to Dolinko," *Ethics* 117 (2006), 109–118.

"Recent Work on Moral Responsibility," *Ethics* 110 (1999), 93–139.

Fitzpatrick, William J. "The Intend/Foresee Distinction and the Problem of 'Closeness,'" *Philosophical Studies* 128 (2006), 585–617.

Fletcher, George P. *The Grammar of Criminal Law: American, Comparative, and International*, vol. 1: *Foundations* (Oxford: Oxford University Press, 2007).

"The Nature of Justification," in *Action and Value in Criminal Law* (Stephen Shute et al., eds., Oxford: Oxford University Press, 1993), 175–186.

Rethinking Criminal Law (Boston: Little, Brown, 1978).

"The Right Deed for the Wrong Reason: A Reply to Mr. Robinson," *UCLA Law Review* 23 (1975), 293–322.

"Should Intolerable Prison Conditions Generate a Justification or an Excuse for Escape?" *UCLA Law Review* 26 (1979), 1355–1369.

Structure and Function in Criminal Law (Oxford: Clarendon Press, 1997).

"The Theory of Criminal Negligence: A Comparative Analysis," *University of Pennsylvania Law Review* 119 (1971), 401–438.

Fodor, Jerry. *Psychosemantics: The Problem of Meaning in the Philosophy of Mind* (Cambridge, Mass.: MIT Press, 1987).

Fuller, Lon L. "The Case of the Speluncean Explorers," *Harvard Law Review* 62 (1949), 616–645.

Gardner, J. "The Gist of Excuses," *Buffalo Criminal Law Review* 1 (1998), 575–598.

Gardner, J., and S. Shute. "The Wrongness of Rape," in *Oxford Essays on Jurisprudence* (4th ser., J. Horder, ed., Oxford: Oxford University Press, 2000), 193–218.

Garvey, Stephen P. "Passion's Puzzle," *Iowa Law Review* 90 (2005), 1677–1746.

"Self-Defense and the Mistaken Racist," *New Criminal Law Review* 11 (2008), 119–171.

"What's Wrong with Involuntary Manslaughter?" *Texas Law Review* 85 (2006), 333–384.

Goldman, Alvin I. *A Theory of Human Action* (Englewood Cliffs, N.J.: Prentice-Hall, 1970).

Goodin, Robert E., and Frank Jackson. "Freedom from Fear," *Philosophy & Public Affairs* 35 (2007), 249–265.

Greco, John. "Virtue, Luck and the Pyrrhonian Problematic," *Philosophical Studies* 130 (2006), 9–34.

Green, Stuart. *Lying, Cheating, and Stealing: A Moral Theory of White-Collar Crime* (Oxford: Oxford University Press, 2006).

Guttenplan, Samuel D. *A Companion to Philosophy of Mind* (Oxford: Blackwell, 1994).

Haji, Ishtiyaque. "An Epistemic Dimension of Blameworthiness," *Philosophical and Phenomenological Research* 57 (1997), 523–544.

Hall, Jerome. "Negligent Behavior Should Be Excluded from Penal Liability," *Columbia Law Review* 63 (1963), 632–644.

Halpin, Andrew. *Definition in the Criminal Law* (Oxford: Hart, 2004).

Harcourt, Bernard E. "The Collapse of the Harm Principle," *Journal of Criminal Law & Criminology* 90 (1999), 109–194.

Hart, H. L. A. *Punishment and Responsibility: Essays in the Philosophy of Law* (New York: Oxford University Press, 1968).

Haworth, Lawrence. *Autonomy: An Essay in Philosophical Psychology and Ethics* (New Haven: Yale University Press, 1986).

Hieronymi, Pamela. "Responsibility for Believing," *Synthese* 16 (2008), 357–373.

Hodgson, David. "Responsibility and Good Reasons," *Ohio State Journal of Criminal Law* 2 (2005), 471–484.

Holmes, Oliver Wendell. *The Common Law* (London: Macmillan, 1881).

Horn, Mike. Note, "A Rude Awakening: What to Do with the Sleepwalking Defense?" *Boston College Law Review* 46 (2004), 149–182.

Huigens, Kyron. "Is Strict Liability Rape Defensible?" in *Defining Crimes: Essays on the Special Part of the Criminal Law* (R. A. Duff and Stuart P. Green, eds., Oxford: Oxford University Press, 2005), 196–217.

Hurd, Heidi M. "Challenging Authority," *Yale Law Journal* 100 (1991), 1611–1678.

    "Justification and Excuse, Wrongdoing and Culpability," *Notre Dame Law Review* 74 (1999), 1551–1574.

Hurley, Paul E. "Does Consequentialism Make Too Many Demands, or None at All?" *Ethics* 116 (2006), 680–706.

Husak, Douglas N. "Already Punished Enough," *Philosophical Topics* 19 (1990), 79–99.

    "Crimes outside the Core," *Tulsa Law Review* 39 (2004), 755–780.

    "Guns and Drugs: Case Studies on the Principles Limits of the Criminal Sanction," *Law & Philosophy* 23 (2004), 437–493.

    "Justifications and the Criminal Liability of Accessories," *Journal of Criminal Law & Criminology* 80 (1989), 491–520.

    Legalize This! The Case for Decriminalizing Drugs (London: Verso, 2002).

    Overcriminalization: The Limits of the Criminal Law (New York: Oxford University Press, 2008).

    "Rethinking the Act Requirement," *Cardozo Law Review* 28 (2007), 2437–2460.

    "The Sequential Principle of Relative Culpability," *Legal Theory* 1 (1995), 493–518.

Husak, Douglas N., and Craig A. Callender. "Willful Ignorance, Knowledge, and the 'Equal Culpability' Thesis: A Study of the Deeper Significance of the Principle of Legality," *Wisconsin Law Review* (1994), 29–70.

Hyman, David A. "Rescue without Law: An Empirical Perspective on the Duty to Rescue," *Texas Law Review* 84 (2006), 653–738.

Jeffries, John Calvin, Jr. "Legality, Vagueness, and the Construction of Penal Statutes," *Virginia Law Review* 71 (1985), 189–246.

Kadish, Sanford H. "Reckless Complicity," *Journal of Criminal Law & Criminology* 87 (1997), 369–394.

"Respect for Life and Regard for Rights in the Criminal Law," *California Law Review* 64 (1976), 871–901.

Kadish, Sanford H., and Stephen J. Schulhofer, eds. *Criminal Law and Its Processes: Cases and Materials* (7th ed., Boston: Little, Brown, 2001).

Kahan, Dan, and Martha C. Nussbaum. "Two Conceptions of Emotion in Criminal Law," *Columbia Law Review* 96 (1996), 269–374.

Kamm, F. M. "The Doctrine of Triple Effect," *Aristotelian Society* 74 (2000), 21–39.

"Failures of Just War Theory: Terror, Harm, and Justice," *Ethics* 114 (2004), 650–692.

"Terror and Collateral Damage," *Journal of Ethics* 9 (2005), 381–401.

"Terrorism and Several Moral Distinctions," *Legal Theory* 12 (2006), 19–69.

Kane, Robert. *The Significance of Free Will* (New York: Oxford University Press, 2002).

Katz, Leo. *Bad Acts and Guilty Minds: Conundrums of the Criminal Law* (Chicago: University of Chicago Press, 1987).

"Before and After: Temporal Anomalies in Legal Doctrine," *University of Pennsylvania Law Review* 151 (2003), 863–886.

"Choice, Consent, and Cycling: The Hidden Limitations of Consent," *Michigan Law Review* 104 (2006), 627–670.

"Why the Law Is Either/Or," working paper, on file with authors.

Kessler, Kimberly D. Comment, "The Role of Luck in the Criminal Law," *University of Pennsylvania Law Review* 142 (1994), 2183–2237.

King, Robert E., and Cass R. Sunstein. Essay, "Doing without Speed Limits," *Boston University Law Review* 79 (1999), 155–194.

Knobe, Joshua, and John M. Doris. "Strawsonian Variations: Folk Morality and the Search for a Unified Theory," in *The Oxford Handbook of Moral Psychology* (J. M. Doris et al., eds., Oxford: Oxford University Press, forthcoming).

Kobrin, Joshua A. Note, "Betraying Honest Services: Theories of Trust and Betrayal Applied to the Mail Fraud Statute and § 1346," *New York University Annual Survey of American Law* 61 (2006), 779–822.

Kugler, Itzhak. *Direct and Oblique Intention in the Criminal Law: An Inquiry into Degrees of Blameworthiness* (Aldershot: Ashgate, 2002).

Lenman, James. "Compatibilism and Contractualism: The Possibility of Moral Responsibility," *Ethics* 117 (2006), 7–31.

Levy, Ken. "The Solution to the Problem of Outcome Luck: Why Harm Is Just as Punishable as the Wrongful Action That Causes It," *Law & Philosophy* 24 (2005), 263–303.

Lippke, Richard L. "No Easy Way Out: Dangerous Offenders and Preventive Detention," *Law & Philosophy* 27 (2008), 383–414.

Luban, David. "Contrived Ignorance," *Georgetown Law Journal* 87 (1999), 957–980.

Luntley, Michael. *Contemporary Philosophy of Thought: Truth, World, Content* (Oxford: Blackwell, 1999).

McAdams, Richard H. *"A Tempting State: The Political Economy of Entrapment,"* Working Paper No. 33, Illinois Law and Economics (2005).

McMahan, Jeff. "The Basis of Moral Liability to Defensive Killing," *Philosophical Issues* 15 (2005), 386–405.

"The Ethics of Killing in War," *Ethics* 114 (2004), 693–733.

The Ethics of Killing in War: The Oxford Uehiro Lectures, forthcoming, manuscript on file with authors.

"Self-Defense and Culpability," *Law & Philosophy* 24 (2005), 751–774.

"Self-Defense and the Problem of the Innocent Attacker," *Ethics* 104 (1994) , 252–290.

Mellow, David. "Iraq: A Morally Justified Resort to War," *Journal of Applied Philosophy* 23 (2006), 293–310.

Mikhail, John. "Aspects of the Theory of Moral Cognition: Investigating Intuitive Knowledge of the Prohibition of Intentional Battery and the Principle of Double Effect," Georgetown Law and Economics Research Paper, Paper No. 762385 (2002), available at http://ssrn.com/abstract=762385.

Michaels, Alan. "Acceptance: The Missing Mental State," *Southern California Law Review* 71 (1998), 953–1036.

Mill, John Stuart. *On Liberty* (London: John W. Parker and Son, West Strand, 1859).

Mongin, Philippe. "Does Optimization Imply Rationality," *Synthese* 124 (2000), 73–111.

Montague, Phillip. "The Morality of Self-Defense: A Reply to Wasserman," *Philosophy & Public Affairs* 18 (1989), 81–89.

Montmarquet, J. "Zimmerman on Culpable Ignorance," *Ethics* 109 (1999), 842–845.

Monty Python and the Holy Grail (EMI Films, 1975).

Moore, Michael S. *Act and Crime: The Philosophy of Action and Its Implications for Criminal Law* (Oxford: Oxford University Press, 1993).

Causation and Responsibility, forthcoming, manuscript on file with authors.

"Causation and Responsibility," *Social Philosophy and Policy* 16 (1999), 1–51.

"Foreseeing Harm Opaquely," in *Action and Value in Criminal Law* (S. Shute et al., eds., Oxford: Oxford University Press, 1993), 125–155.

Law and Psychiatry: Rethinking the Relationship (Cambridge: Cambridge University Press, 1984).

"Patrolling the Consequentialist Borders of Our Obligations," *Law & Philosophy* 27 (2008), 35–96.

Placing Blame: A General Theory of Criminal Law (Oxford: Oxford University Press, 1997).

"Responsibility and the Unconscious," *Southern California Law Review* 53 (1980), 1563–1678.

"Thomson's Preliminaries about Causation and Rights," *Chicago-Kent Law Review* 63 (1987), 497–522.

Moriarty, Jeffrey. "Ross on Desert and Punishment," *Pacific Philosophical Quarterly* 87 (2006), 231–244.

Morse, Stephen J. "Criminal Responsibility and the Disappearing Person," *Cardozo Law Review* 28 (2006), 2545–2576.

"Culpability and Control," *University of Pennsylvania Law Review* 142 (1994), 1587–1660.

"Diminished Rationality, Diminished Responsibility," *Ohio State Journal of Criminal Law* 1 (2003), 289–308.

"Equality and Individuation in Punishment," *Law & Philosophy,* forthcoming.

"Neither Desert nor Disease," *Legal Theory* 5 (1999), 265–309.

"Rationality and Responsibility," *Southern California Law Review* 74 (2000), 251–268.

"Reasons, Results, and Criminal Responsibility," *University of Illinois Law Review* 2004), 363–444.

"Uncontrollable Urges and Irrational People," *Virginia Law Review* 88 (2002), 1025–1078.

Murphy, Mark. *Natural Law in Jurisprudence and Politics* (Cambridge: Cambridge University Press, 2006).

Natapoff, Alexandra. "Underenforcement," *Fordham Law Review* 75 (2006), 1715–1776.

Norcross, Alastair. "Contractualism and Aggregation," *Social Theory & Practice* 28 (2002), 303–314.

"Harming in Context," *Philosophical Studies* 123 (2005), 149–173.

Ohana, Daniel. "Desert and Punishment for Acts Preparatory to the Commission of a Crime," *Canadian Journal of Law and Jurisprudence* 20 (2007), 113–142.

Overland, Gerhard. "The Right to Do Wrong," *Law & Philosophy* 26 (2007), 377–404.

Pendleton, Hibi. "A Critique of Rational Excuse Defense: A Reply to Finkelstein," *University of Pittsburgh Law Review* 57 (1996), 651–676.

Pereboom, Derek. *Living without Free Will* (Cambridge: Cambridge University Press, 2001).

Perry, Stephen R. "Risk, Harm, and Responsibility," in *Philosophical Foundations of Tort Law* (David G. Owen, ed., Oxford: Clarendon Press, 1995), 321–346.

Pillsbury, Samuel H. "Crimes of Indifference," *Rutgers Law Review* 49 (1996), 105–218.

Judging Evil: Rethinking the Law of Murder and Manslaughter (New York: New York University Press, 1998).

Pink, Thomas. *The Psychology of Freedom* (Cambridge: Cambridge University Press, 1996).

Pollard, Bill. "Explaining Actions with Habits," *American Philosophical Quarterly* 43 (2006), 57–70.

Porat, Ariel. "Offsetting Risks," Olin Working Paper No.316, University of Chicago Law and Economics (2007), available at SSRN: http://ssrn.com/abstract_id=946764.

Portmore, Douglas. "Are Moral Reasons Morally Overriding?" *Ethical Theory and Moral Practice* 11 (2008), 369–388.

Quinn, Warren. "Actions, Intentions, and Consequences: The Doctrine of Double Effect," in *Morality and Action* (W. Quinn and P. Foot, eds., Cambridge: Cambridge University Press, 1994), 175–193.

Radcliffe-Richards, Janet. *Human Nature after Darwin: A Philosophical Introduction* (London: Routledge, 2000).

Raz, Joseph. *The Authority of Law: Essays on Law and Morality* (Oxford: Clarendon Press, 1979).

Practical Reasons and Norms (London: Hutchinson, 1975).

Robinson, Paul H. "The Bomb Thief and the Theory of Justification Defenses," *Criminal Law Forum* 8 (1997), 387–409.

Criminal Law Defenses, vol. 2 (St. Paul: West, 1984).

"Dissenting View of Commissioner Paul H. Robinson to the Promulgation of Sentencing Guidelines by the United States Sentencing Commission," *Federal Register* 52 (1987), 18121–18132.

"Prohibited Risks and Culpable Disregard or Inattentiveness: Challenge and Confusion in the Formulation of Risk-Creation Offenses," *Theoretical Inquiries in Law* 4 (2002), 367–396.

"Punishing Dangerousness: Cloaking Preventive Detention as Criminal Justice," *Harvard Law Review* 114 (2001), 1429–1456.

Structure and Function in Criminal Law (Oxford: Oxford University Press, 1997).

"A Theory of Justification: Societal Harm as a Prerequisite for Criminal Liability," *UCLA Law Review* 23 (1975), 266–292.

Robinson, Paul H., and Michael T. Cahill. "The Accelerating Degradation of Criminal Codes," *Hastings Law Journal* 56 (2005), 633–656.

"Can a Model Penal Code Second Save the States from Themselves?" *Ohio State Journal of Criminal Law* 1 (2003), 169–178.

Law without Justice: Why Criminal Law Doesn't Give People What They Deserve (Oxford: Oxford University Press, 2006).

Robinson, Paul H., Michael T. Cahill, and Usman Mohammad. "The Five Worst (and Five Best) American Criminal Codes," *Northwestern University Law Review* 95 (2000), 1–90.

Robinson, Paul H., and John M. Darley. "Does Criminal Law Deter? A Behavioural Science Investigation," *Oxford Journal of Legal Studies* 24 (2004), 173–205.

Justice, Liability and Blame: Community Views and the Criminal Law (Boulder: Westview Press, 1995).

Robinson, Paul H., and Robert Kurzban. "Concordance and Conflict in Intuitions of Justice," *Minnesota Law Review* 91 (2007), 1829–1907.

Rodin, David. *War and Self-Defense* (Oxford: Oxford University Press, 2002).

Rogers, Audrey. "New Technology, Old Defenses: Internet Sting Operations and Attempt Liability," *University of Richmond Law Review* 38 (2004), 477–524.

Rose, Carol M. "Crystals and Mud in Property Law," *Stanford Law Review* 40 (1988), 577–610.

Rosen, Gideon. "Skepticism about Moral Responsibility," *Philosophical Perspectives* 18 *(Ethics)* (2004), 295–313.

Royzman, Edward, and Rahul Kumar. "Is Consequential Luck Morally Inconsequential? Empirical Psychology and the Reassessment of Moral Luck," *Ratio* 17 (2004), 329–344.

Ryle, Gilbert. *The Concept of Mind* (Chicago: University of Chicago Press, 1949).

Sartorio, Carolina. "Causes as Difference-Makers," *Philosophical Studies* 123 (2005), 71–96.

"Moral Inertia," *Philosophical Studies* 140 (2008), 117–133.

Scalia, Antonin. "The Rule of Law as a Law of Rules," *University of Chicago Law Review* 56 (1989), 1175–1188.

Scanlon, Thomas. "Replies," *Social Theory and Practice* 28 (2002), 337–358.

Schafer-Landau, Russ. "Retributivism and Desert," *Pacific Philosophical Quarterly* 81 (2000), 189–214.

Schauer, Frederick. *Playing by the Rules: A Philosophical Examination of Rule-Based Decision-Making in Law and in Life* (Oxford: Clarendon Press, 1991).

Schauer, Frederick, and Richard Zeckhauser. "Regulation by Generalization," Working Paper No. 05–16, AEI-Brookings Joint Center for Regulatory Studies (2005), available at http://ksgnotes1.harvard.edu/Research/wpaper.nsf/rwp/RWP05-048.

Schopp, Robert F. *Automatism, Insanity, and the Psychology of Criminal Responsibility: A Philosophical Inquiry* (Cambridge: Cambridge University Press 1991).

Schulhofer, Stephen J. "The Gender Question in Criminal Law," *Social Philosophy & Policy* 7 (1990), 105–137.

Shavell, Steven. "Strict Liability versus Negligence," *Journal of Legal Studies* 9 (1986), 1–26.

Shaw, Joseph. "Intention in Ethics," *Canadian Journal of Philosophy* 36 (2006), 187–223.

"Intentions and Trolleys," *Philosophical Quarterly* 56 (2006), 63–83.

Sher, George. "Out of Control," *Ethics* 116 (2006), 285–301.

Shoemaker David. "Moral Address, Moral Responsibility, and the Boundaries of the Moral Community," *Ethics* 118 (2007), 70–108.

Simester, A. P., and G. R. Sullivan. "On the Nature and Rationale of Property Offenses," in *Defining Crimes: Essays on the Special Part of the Criminal Law* (R. A. Duff and Stuart Green, eds., Oxford: Oxford University Press, 2005), 168–195.

Simon, Rita J., and David E. Aaronson. *The Insanity Defense: A Critical Assessment of the Law and Policy in the Post Hinckley Era* (New York: Praeger, 1988).

Simons, Kenneth W. "Culpability and Retributive Theory: The Problem of Criminal Negligence," *Journal of Contemporary Legal Issues* 5 (1994), 365–398.

"Does Punishment for 'Culpable Indifference' Simply Punish for 'Bad Character'? Examining the Requisite Connection between Mens Rea and Actus Reus," *Buffalo Criminal Law Review* 6 (2002), 219–316.

"Rethinking Mental States," *Boston University Law Review* 72 (1992), 463–554.

"Tort Negligence, Cost-Benefit Analysis and Tradeoffs: A Closer Look at the Controversy," *Loyola of Los Angeles Law Review*, forthcoming.

Slobogin, Christopher. *Minding Justice: Laws That Deprive People with Mental Disability of Life and Liberty* (Cambridge, Mass.: Harvard University Press, 2006).

Smilansky, Saul. *Free Will and Illusion* (Oxford: Clarendon Press, 2000).

Smith, Angela M. "Responsibility for Attitudes: Activity and Passivity in Mental Life," *Ethics* 115 (2005), 236–271.

Smith, J. C. *Justification and Excuse in the Criminal Law* (London: Stevens, 1989).

Steadman, Henry J., et al. *Before and After Hinckley: Evaluating Insanity Defense Reform* (New York: Guilford Press, 1993).

Steinhoff, Uwe. "Torture – The Case for Dirty Harry and against Alan Dershowitz," *Journal of Applied Philosophy* 23 (2006), 337–353.

"Yet Another Revised DDE? A Note on David K. Chan's DDED," *Ethical Theory & Moral Practice* 9 (2006), 231–236.

Stevenson, Jim, and Robert Goodman. "Association between Behavior at Age 3 Years and Adult Criminality," *British Journal of Psychiatry* 179 (2001), 197–202.

Strawson, Galen. "The Impossibility of Moral Responsibility," *Philosophical Studies* 75 (1994), 5–24.

Strawson, Peter. "Freedom and Resentment," in *Free Will* (Gary Watson, ed., Oxford: Oxford University Press, 1982), 72–93.

Stuntz, William J. "The Pathological Politics of Criminal Law," *Michigan Law Review* 100 (2001), 505–600.

"Plea Bargaining and Criminal Law's Disappearing Shadow," *Harvard Law Review* 117 (2004), 2548–2569.

Sunstein, Cass R., and Adrian Vermeule. "Is Capital Punishment Morally Required? The Relevance of Life-Life Tradeoffs," *Stanford Law Review* 58 (2005), 703–750.

Tadros, Victor. *Criminal Responsibility* (Oxford: Oxford University Press, 2005).

Tasioulas, John. "Punishment and Repentance," *Philosophy* 81 (2006), 279–322.

Thomson, Judith Jarvis. "Self-Defense and Rights," Lindley Lecture at the University of Kansas (April 5, 1976), reprinted in Judith Jarvis Thomson, *Rights, Restitution, and Risk: Essays in Moral Theory* (William Parent, ed., Cambridge, Mass.: Harvard University Press, 1986), 33–48.

"Some Ruminations on Rights," 19 *Arizona Law Review* 45 (1977).

Varzi, Achille C., and Giuliano Torrengo. "Crimes and Punishments," *Philosophia* 34 (2006), 395–404.

Vierkant, Tillman. "Owning Intentions and Moral Responsibility," *Ethical Theory & Moral Practice* 8 (2005), 507–534.

Vranas, Peter B. M. "I Ought, Therefore I Can," *Philosophical Studies* 136 (2007), 167–216.

Walen, Alec. "The Doctrine of Illicit Intentions," *Philosophy & Public Affairs* 34 (2006), 39–67.

"Permissibly Encouraging the Impermissible," *Journal of Value Inquiry* 38 (2004), 341–354.

Wallace, R. Jay. *Responsibility and the Moral Sentiments* (Cambridge, Mass.: Harvard University Press, 1994).

Wasserstrom, Richard A. "H. L. A. Hart and the Doctrines of Mens Rea and Criminal Responsibility," *University of Chicago Law Review* 35 (1967), 92–126.

Westen, Peter. "An Attitudinal Theory of Excuse," *Law & Philosophy* 25 (2006), 289–375.

"Individualizing the Reasonable Person in Criminal Law," *Criminal Law & Philosophy* 2 (2008), 137–162.

"Two Rules of Legality in Criminal Law," *Law & Philosophy* 26 (2007), 229–305.

"Why Criminal Harm Matters: Plato's Abiding Insight in the Laws," *Criminal Law & Philosophy* 1 (2007), 307–326.

Williams, Glanville Llewelyn. *Criminal Law: The General Part* (2d ed., London: Stevens, 1961).

Wright, Richard W. "Causation in Tort Law," *California Law Review* 73 (1985), 1735–1828.

Yaffe, Gideon. "Trying, Acting and Attempted Crimes," unpublished manuscript, on file with the authors.

Zaibert, Leo. *Punishment and Retribution* (Aldershot: Ashgate, 2006).

Zimmerman, Michael J. "Moral Luck: A Partial Map," *Canadian Journal of Philosophy* 36 (2006), 585–608.

"Moral Responsibility and Ignorance," *Ethics* 107 (1997), 410–426.

Zohar, Noam J. "Innocence and Complex Threats: Upholding the War Effort and the Condemnation of Terrorism," *Ethics* 114 (2004), 734–751.

Index

349